The Joy of Eternal Life

A Thorough Description of the Glory of Eternal Life in All Its Aspects, Rightly and Intelligibly Drawn from God's Word; and Furthermore, a Well-Founded Account and Explanation of the Beautiful and Glorious Existence Already Enjoyed by the Souls of the Elect in the Heavenly Paradise Even before the Last Day; Written for the Blessed and Living Comfort of All Afflicted Christians, Who in Various Ways Are Made to Dwell As Exiles in This Vale of Tears,

By Philipp Nicolai,
Doctor of Holy Scripture
and Minister of the Word of God in Hamburg.

Translated from the German
by Matthew Carver

CONCORDIA PUBLISHING HOUSE · SAINT LOUIS

Published by Concordia Publishing House
3558 S. Jefferson Avenue, St. Louis, MO 63118-3968
1-800-325-3040 • cph.org

Unless otherwise indicated, all quotations from Scripture and other texts are translated from the original work.

Manufactured in the United States of America

Library of Congress Cataloging-in-Publication Data

Names: Nicolai, Philipp, 1556-1608, author. | Carver, Matthew, translator.

Title: The joy of eternal life / Philip Nicolai ; translated by Matthew Carver.

Other titles: Frewden Spiegel desz ewigen Lebens. English

Description: Saint Louis, MO : Concordia Publishing House, [2021].

Identifiers: LCCN 2021018347 (print) | LCCN 2021018348 (ebook) | ISBN 9780758669674 (paperback) | ISBN 9780758669681 (ebook)

Subjects: LCSH: Future life--Biblical teaching--Miscellanea. | Future life--Christianity--Miscellanea.

Classification: LCC BS680.F83 N5313 2021 (print) | LCC BS680.F83 (ebook) | DDC 236/.2--dc23

LC record available at https://lccn.loc.gov/2021018347

LC ebook record available at https://lccn.loc.gov/2021018348

---

4 5 6 7 8 9 10 11 12 31 30 29 28 27 26 25 24 23

Contents

Translator's Preface

THIS TRANSLATION, presenting for the first time in English the entirety of Dr. Philipp Nicolai's important work on eternal life, is designed to be accessible to the layperson without compromising accuracy. It has been made chiefly from the second edition (1607), an edition significant in the history of the work because of its appearance after a terrible recurrence of the plague that originally occasioned the first edition. The Latin and Greek phrases here and there, which might have been intelligible to an average reader of the sixteenth century, have been silently replaced with English, except in a few places where clarifications of technical terms are provided with the nearest English equivalents. The abundant marginal notes and glosses have been converted into headings. Scriptural quotations have been translated directly from the German with some modification to agree with familiar biblical English idiom. Concerning the numerous Scripture references under those headings, it should be noted that all verse indications have been supplied by the translator, and none were given by Nicolai or the authors quoted by him, nor should any errors or doubtful readings be ascribed to Nicolai here. Often the verse intended is clear; occasionally, it is unclear whether a verse is meant, or the whole chapter, or perhaps whether the indicated chapter is a typographical error. Because the Scriptures are often quoted only in part, or rhetorically adapted, or merely alluded to, and to avoid impediments to reading, the references have been left in the headings and not inserted in their respective places in the paragraph. Hymn translations conform with those found in the most familiar hymnals. For the hymns appended by Nicolai at the end of the book, a literal translation in prose has been provided in addition to the rhymed translation.

By way of introducing the author to the unacquainted reader, it seems helpful here to include a brief biographical note on Nicolai found in *Der Lutheraner*, vol. 14, no. 25, p. 197, in a column by Rev. Eduard Koch focusing especially on the great hymnwriters of the Lutheran Church:

> Philipp Nicolai was born August 10, 1556, in Mengeringhausen, in the county of Waldeck, where his father was a pastor and the inspector of the Waldeck clergy. Philipp, then, spent time under various fateful preachers in a number of places: first in 1576 in the city of his birth, along with his father; then in 1583 in the Hardeck Cloister, from which he was expelled by the Roman Catholics that same year. He then showed very great zeal and spiritual boldness in the defense of the evangelical faith against both the Catholics and the Calvinists, and for this reason came to author a number of disputations. In 1586 he then came to the Lutheran congregation under the cross at Cologne, then in 1587 to Wildungen, and then in 1596 to Unna in Westphalia. Here in the year 1597 a plague raged across

all of Westphalia, so that in a brief time more than 1,400 people in Unna died. From his window Nicolai looked on as one after another was buried. He himself, however, was untouched by the plague, although many of his closest relatives died and his own household was struck. In these days of tragedy he spent his time in daily contemplations of death, turned his thoughts away from the world, and immersed himself in the question of eternal life. This had the effect of lifting his spirit tremendously, and so it was that the work he was then committing his contemplations to was given the title "Joyful mirror of eternal life." In 1601 he eventually left Unna for Hamburg as pastor of St. Catherine's church. Here on October 26, 1608, at the age of 52, he himself was inducted into the joy of eternal life. Of the four hymns he composed, the most renowned are "Wachet auf ruft uns die Stimme [Wake, Awake, the Night Is Flying]" and "Wie schön leucht uns der Morgenstern [How Lovely Shines the Morning Star]." The first is the more famous of the two hymns, based on Matthew 25:1–13, and is a precious pearl in the hymnodic wreath of the Lutheran church. It made its way into every hymnal and was even translated into Malabar, Portuguese, and Danish. The melody, rightly dubbed the king of chorales, was probably devised by Nicolai himself along with the hymn text. The second hymn, "How Lovely Shines the Morning Star," was likewise composed by Nicolai in the year 1597, when the plague was raging so fearsomely in Unna. One morning, being in great distress, he seated himself in his quiet workroom, and from the distress and death that surrounded him he soared in spirit up to the Redeemer and Savior, and in these hours this precious hymn appeared. Here he fell so completely into a blessed reverie that he forgot to eat dinner (around midday), nor did he let anything distract him in his poetic labor until he had finished the hymn. When this finally happened around three o'clock in the afternoon, he is supposed to have come to his family uncommonly overjoyed and in utter rapture. He gave the hymn the title "A spiritual wedding hymn of the believing soul concerning Christ Jesus, its heavenly Bridegroom, based on the forty-fifth Psalm of the prophet David." Through good times and bad, this hymn was the favorite hymn of our old evangelical congregation. They would sing it both at weddings and the Lord's Supper, but most of all it was heard resounding by the deathbeds of those believing Christians who had a constant love for their Savior and, now being called to the wedding of the Lamb, were departing this world. This hymn even resounded in the place of executions and helped to bring a sweet comfort of dying to those condemned to death. There is hardly a more blessedly perfect hymn or hymn stanza than this one, so often mentioned in the descriptions of people's lives and the announcements of their death.

How fitting, then, that the hymn "O Morning Star, How Fair and Bright," resounding in a church one Sunday during Epiphanytide in the year 2020, should have so moved our dear departed brother in the faith Rev. Paul T. McCain with greatest urgency to initiate the present translation! Who (but the Lord God) knew that the same year would see the translator surrounded by tidings of contagion as he committed to English Nicolai's words of comfort, themselves first penned in the midst of a terrible plague (see Nicolai's dedicatory epistle), or that the Lord would call Rev. McCain home on November 25 of that year? With the reader's permission, therefore, the translator ventures to offer here the following verses in that man's memory.

In Memoriam Paul Timothy McCain

Premature it seems that Paul should be
Asked to go before this task for me,
  Urged by his good heart, was yet complete—
  Lord, yet wise You are! It was not meet
That Your friend should go on endless days
In these plagues and peril-studded ways:
  More than mortal now his life abides,
  On the Word he feeds, in You resides!
Things here hinted—Very Love—he knows.
Here we grope in darkness, there he glows.
  Your Paul, brethren, in God's house is found—
  My Paul too! By grace my heart is bound
Co-heir with him in our fellow Lord.
Cherish then his zeal for that pure Word
  As these lines (in number fit, though few)
  I subjoin, moved by his fervor true—
  Now God grant this book His work may do!

Matthew Carver
Nativity of St. John the Baptist
AD 2021

Abbreviations

LSB The Commission on Worship of The Lutheran Church—Missouri Synod. *Lutheran Service Book*. St. Louis: Concordia, 2006.

PG *Patrologiae cursus completus: Series Graeca*. Edited by J.-P. Migne. 161 vols. in 167. Petit-Montrouge: Apud J. P. Migne, 1857–66.

PL *Patrologiae cursus completus: Series Latina*. Edited by J.-P. Migne. 221 vols. in 223. Paris: Garnier Fratres, 1844–64.

StL Johann Georg Walch, ed. *Dr. Martin Luthers sämmtliche Schriften: Neue revidirte Stereotypausgabe*. 23 vols. in 25. St. Louis: Concordia, 1880–1910.

WA *D. Martin Luthers Werke: Kritische Gesamtausgabe*. 73 vols. in 85. Weimar: H. Böhlau, 1883–.

WA Br *D. Martin Luthers Werke: Briefwechsel*. 18 vols. Weimar: H. Böhlau, 1930–.

WA TR *D. Martin Luthers Werke: Tischreden*. 6 vols. Weimar: H. Böhlau, 1912–21.

Wackernagel Philipp Wackernagel, ed. *Das deutsche Kirchenlied von der ältesten Zeit bis zu Anfang des 17. Jahrhunderts*. 5 vols. Leipzig: Teubner, 1864–77.

Walch *D. Martin Luthers sowol in Deutscher als Lateinischer Sprache verfertigte und aus der letztern in die erstere übersetzte Sämmtliche Schriften*. Edited by Johann G. Walch. 24 vols. Halle: Gebauer, 1740–53.

Walch *D. Martin Luthers sowol in Deutscher als Lateinischer Sprache verfertigte und aus der letztern in die erstere übersetzte Sämmtliche Schriften*. Edited by Johann G. Walch. 24 vols. Halle: Gebauer, 1740–53.

Zahn *Die Melodien der deutschen evangelischen Kirchenlieder*. Edited by Johannes Zahn. 6 vols. Gütersloh: Bertelsmann, 1889–1893.

Dedicatory Epistle

To the Honorable, Most Estimable, Most Learned, Judicious, and Most Wise Lord Burgomaster, Councilor, and Duodecimvirate of the Worthy City of Soest, My Very Favorable, Dear Lord and Friend: Grace and Comfort from God the Father of All Grace and All Comfort through Our Lord Jesus Christ, in the Holy Spirit, Together with My Prayer and Willing Service.

HONORABLE, highly esteemed, highly learned, judicious, and very wise, very favorable lords, and friends: The final article of our Christian Creed, which is to say, "I believe in the life everlasting," is the true helmet of our salvation and the end of our hope, in which the dear martyrs and all God-loving hearts took comfort in the midst of their troubles, cross, frailty of the body, as well as in the midst of death, and valiantly passed through death into life. "No eye has seen," says Scripture, "no ear has heard, and into no man's heart has entered what God has prepared for those who love Him" (Isa. 64:4; 1 Cor. 2:9). "Blessed are those who dwell in Your house; they will ever be praising You. . . . For a day in Your courts is better than a thousand elsewhere. I would rather keep the door in the house of my God than dwell long in the tents of the ungodly" (Ps. 84:4, 10).

Then we will (to quote St. Augustine in his conclusion of his book *The City of God*[1]) have wisdom without error, light without darkness, love without satiety, righteousness without sin, life without death, rest or refreshment without toil and labor, joy without sorrow, worthiness without fear and trembling, life without temporality, health without illness—the fullness or full abundance of all goods. Then God will be all things in all people, and we will behold Him without ceasing, love Him without weariness, worship Him without feeling of burden or toil.

Let us rightly consider and take to heart the end of all the benefits of God that He shows to His elect on earth, namely, that He has created us for eternal life, and, when we were condemned and lost because of our sins, He, in His fervent love and unfathomable mercy, through His only-begotten Son, Jesus Christ, redeemed us from death, devil, and hell unto eternal life and gave us His Holy Spirit and in His salvific Word calls us to eternal life. Everything—the creation, the work of redemption, sanctification, the institution of the preaching office and of the holy, most worthy Sacraments, likewise, the kindling in us of faith, hope, love, new obedience, and patience—is intended and directed by Him to the end that we may be new creatures, plants of His glory, and children of light, who live with Him forever.

But because we little and seldom consider this, and all have by nature world-seeking and earth-loving hearts which long more for the temporal than the eternal, and are more attentive to perishable goods than to the imperishable,

1 Augustine, *De Civitate Dei* 30.1 (PL 41:801–2).

our dear God, according to His most wise, fatherly council, has prepared and ordained the dear, holy cross (which He lays on His children) as a salutary means by which to turn them away from the world and worldly cares and incline them to Himself for their own good and eternal salvation.

"O Lord," says Isaiah, "when there is distress, You are sought; when You discipline, they call anxiously upon You. As a pregnant woman, when she is about to give birth, has anguish, and cries in her pain, so is it with us, O Lord, before Your presence. Then we, too, are pregnant, and we are afraid so that we can scarcely breathe" (Isa. 26:16–18). Likewise, David says, "It is good to me that You have humbled me, that I might learn Your statutes. . . . My soul longs for Your salvation. I hope in Your Word. My eyes yearn for Your Word, and say, when will You comfort me?" (Ps. 119:71, 81–82). "As the hart pants for fresh water, so my soul pants for You, O God. My soul thirsts for God, for the living God. When will I come thither, that I may see the face of God?" (Ps. 42:1–2). "Deliver my soul from the ungodly by Your sword, from the people by Your hand, O Lord, from the people of this world, which have their portion in their life, whose belly You fill with Your treasure, who have children to the full, and leave their abundance to their young. But I will behold Your face in righteousness, I will be satisfied when I awake after Your likeness" (Ps. 17:13–15).

But included among the many fatherly blows of the cross by which our dear God gives His children in this world cause to die each day to the temporal and perishable world and to seek without pause the eternal good which produces steadfast boldness is the heavy epidemic and plague of the raging pestilence of recent time. The Hebrews call it in their language "*deber*," which is as much as "word" or "sermon," since by it God openly preaches to us concerning His righteous wrath and His ignited and burning anger and zeal at the world's wickedness, and admonishes us to repentance, that we may depart from sin, believe in Christ, and acquire a thirsty longing for the everlasting goods of heaven.

Such a *deber* He also preached zealously to this city of Unna last year in 1597, when He attacked her with "the pestilence that walks in darkness and with the sickness that destroys at noonday" [Ps. 91:6], so that in a short time more than 1,400 went on their bed to the Last Day. And thus it was really His intention to begin by disciplining this city in Westphalia, since death followed in the other neighboring districts and is still demonstrating its fierce slaughter in cities, towns, and villages here and there.

In this tragedy and misery (it was said here in Unna in all the streets, and often for several days in a row, more than twenty—twenty-four, twenty-seven, -eight, or -nine, and up to thirty—dead bodies were laid to rest in the cemetery not far from my dwelling), I have always had to strike myself with thoughts of death, and more than once I felt as King Hezekiah, when he said, "Now I shall no longer see the Lord, even the Lord in the land of the living. . . . My age is departed and is removed from me as a shepherd's tent, and I have torn off my life like a weaver" (Isa. 38:11–12).

The plague with its fury and rage fell upon the city like an unforeseen thunderstorm and tempest, and soon left no house unharmed, and lastly broke into my own dwelling, and the people for the most part went about with shattered spirit and terrified heart as if they were blind and half-dead, so that someone could have applied to our situation what Moses writes in Deuteronomy 28[:65–67] with the following words. "The Lord will give you a trembling heart and failing eyes and a parched soul so that your life will hang before you. Night and day will you be afraid and unsure of your life. In the morning you will say, 'Oh, that I might live until the evening!' In the evening you will say, 'Oh, that I might live until the morning!'—for the fear of your heart, which shall terrify you, and for that which you will see with your eyes."

Neither is it absent from Lübeck, Hamburg, Lunenburg, Hildesheim, Göttingen, etc., nor from Lower Hessia and the County of Waldeck, my dear homeland, Corbach, Wildungen, and Mengeringhausen. Neither does a man hear at all concerning those familiar friends which he had in such places here and there except that they fall sick and depart from this life. So also for myself, nothing but sad news and sad messages came to my ears concerning some of my sisters, kinsmen, and in-laws killed and taken away by the plague, which increased my grief and gave me all the more cause to turn all my confidence and heart and thoughts away from the world.

During that time, nothing was sweeter, fonder, or more pleasant to me than contemplating the precious lofty article of eternal life procured by Christ's blood. I let this fill my heart day and night, and I searched the Scriptures to see what they testified concerning it, and also read the ancient doctor St. Augustine's sweet treatise on that subject, where he bites into this high mystery like a nut and pulls out its wondrously sweet kernel. Following this, I recorded my meditations day by day with pen and ink and found that I (God be praised) had success in the enterprise, being well cheered at heart, joyful in spirit, and completely at peace. I gave my manuscript the name and title *Joyful Mirror of Eternal Life* and undertook to leave behind this *Joyful Mirror*, which I composed as a testimony of my peaceful, joyful, and blessed Christian departure, whenever God should summon me from this world; or, if He should spare my health, then out of due Christian love to use it to serve other troubled Christians to whose homes also He sent the plague, and in this way to visit them with tangible comfort.

But our gracious, faithful God, in the midst of the dying, most graciously preserved me from the terrible plague and wondrously delivered my life beyond all my hope and imagining so that I am able to say to Him with the prophet David:

"How great is Your goodness which You have concealed from those who fear You! O Lord, You have brought my soul out of hell, You have kept me alive, when they went into hell. O saints, sing praise to the Lord, thank and bless His glory. For His wrath endures for a moment, and He delights in life. For the evening the weeping lasts, but in the morning is joy. You have turned my lamentation into rejoicing, You have taken off my sackcloth and girded me with gladness" (Ps. 31:19; 30:3–5, 11).

Further, I say, "How shall I repay the Lord for all His benefits which He does for me? I will take the cup of salvation and preach the name of the Lord. I will pay my vows to the Lord in the presence of all His people. O Lord, I am Your servant. I am Your servant, the son of Your maidservant. You have broken my bonds asunder. I will offer a sacrifice of thanksgiving to You and preach the name of the Lord. I will preach Your name to My brethren. I will extol You in the congregation. Extol the Lord, you who fear Him. Let all the seed of Jacob honor Him, and all the seed of Israel draw back before Him. For He has not despised nor contemned the misery of the poor, nor concealed His countenance from Him. And when He cries to Him, He hears it. I will glorify You in the great congregation" (Ps. 116:12–19[; 22:22–25]).

Therefore, that I may pay this vow to the Lord, I now direct and address this, my preface, to your honorable, highly esteemed, very wise, and very favorable lordships, that the consolations of eternal life from God's Word may sound in your ears, and the sorrowful heart may even find joy amid this epidemic. For because the almighty Lord of Sabaoth, who kills and makes alive, brings into hell and out again, has sent the poisonous, contagious pestilence also to the same, your honorable, highly esteemed, very wise, and very favorable lordships, and thereby caused great loss by the death of many important leaders of the council and other prestigious persons—therefore, I, as one of the least, feel sincere Christian sympathy at these things on account of the dear Gospel and because of our spiritual condemnation, and I beseech the Father of my Lord and Savior Jesus Christ that, even as He has graciously had mercy on Unna at last and turned away the fierce plague, so He will also have pity at the evil sent upon your honorable, highly esteemed, very wise, and very favorable lordships and over the whole congregation, and say to the destroyer as in the time of David, "It is enough" (1 Chron. 21:15), that he may sheathe the sword of execution and desist.

We ministers of the Gospel of Christ in the church of Unna have one unanimous mind and opinion with the worthy ministerium in your honorable, highly esteemed, very wise, very favorable lordships' widely renowned city—in every parish church of which (God be praised and thanked) His salvific Word is taught and preached purely, clearly, and unadulterated by any Calvinist or sectarian corruptions, and the pastors perform their office faithfully with Christian attentiveness, with chastisement and warning, where the necessity of case demands, no less than with comforting instruction and strengthening of the spiritually downcast and humbled hearts, in the time of the predominant pestilence, as is attested by the three profitable and learned sermons of the worthy, estimable, and highly learned lord John Schwartz, pastor of St. Thomas's church, my dear, favorable brother in Christ—in which sermons he has thoroughly shown from God's Word where the plague originates, what means may be used against it, and how a Christian should comfort himself against fear, fright, and terror, and, if he should be assailed, how he should prepare and ready himself for a blessed departure.

Likewise, I am not unmindful of the honor and friendship shown me by your honorable, highly esteemed, very wise, and very favorable lordships, when, upon my first visit from the County of Waldeck two years ago, at the neighborly pleasure of an honorable councilman of this city of Unna, the same your lordships gave me favorable advancement by having my little council conducted and brought over into their own city, or Brilon, that your lordships might cause your sincere inclination toward my humble person to be detected and discerned.

Therefore, second to my prayer to God Almighty, I would again at the present time be greatly pleased and comforted to repay your honorable, highly esteemed, very wise, very favorable lordships in these present troubles with my own service, nor can I do so in any more fitting or better way than by setting forth the wondrously sweet and pleasant article of eternal life—namely, how, after the toilsome pilgrimage of this fleeting life, our dear God revives His people above in heaven, wipes away the tears from the eyes of His elect who have wept here on earth, lets neither heat nor frost disturb them, leads them to the spring of living waters, feeds them with the hidden, heavenly manna of eternal life, is Himself their shield, their great reward, and their highest good, and gives them to drink of the rich bounties of His house so that in perfect love, consummate joy, and glorious honor they agree together with one accord, shout for joy, rejoice, and know no more of any anguish, sorrows, sickness, or care.

It is with this precious article that we must comfort, strengthen, and revive ourselves in every necessity that befalls us and, in the tribulations of body and soul, cling to the certain assurance and infallible hope that our heavenly Father will, after a little while, summon and take us (who believe in the name of the only-begotten Son of God) from this wretched valley of sorrow to Himself in heaven.

Thus with this mirror of comfort and joy I would be honored to dedicate and devote these meditations of mine to your honorable, highly esteemed, very wise, and very favorable lordships and to the whole worthy congregation, that you and they and all godly townspeople who in this world have been robbed of their close relatives during the epidemic by temporal death may be refreshed therein, discover from it the blessed and happy condition of all elect persons with our dear

God in His kingdom of sight, take comfort in it, and turn all their thoughts from the world to God in heaven and to the eternal fatherland.

Moreover, I am of good hope and confidence in doing so, seeing as your honorable, highly esteemed, very wise, and very favorable lordships and the Christian congregation have for many years now publicly and unhesitatingly confessed your adherence to the pure and holy teaching of God's Word compassed in the prophetic and apostolic Scriptures and are also well aware (and in this time of mortality have learned by experience) that, when the heart is sad and all temporal joy, glory, and hope dissolves in the face of mortal anguish, fear, and terror, the Word of God alone is the best rod and staff broken from the tree of life to comfort us. As David says, "Let Your Word quicken me, let Your grace be my comfort. If Your Law were not my comfort, I would have perished in my misery. Sustain me, O Lord, by Your Word, and let me not be ashamed because of my hope" (Ps. 23:4; 119:92, 116). Wherefore, in contemplation of these reasons, may you be pleased to accept with good will this my labor drawn from God's Word and composed with diligent consideration.

The eternal, almighty God and Father of our Lord and Savior Jesus Christ with all fatherly tenderness preserve your honorable, highly esteemed, very wise, and very favorable lordships and the whole Christian congregation from the noxious plague, as many of you as are still left, and after your great sorrow give you joy again, graciously open the eyes of His fathomless goodness and mercy upon the churches, political government, schools, and domestic estates, visit you with rich blessings for the hallowing of His name and the propagation of His kingdom, graciously preserve you from every evil of body and soul, possessions and reputation, and grant us all that we may cultivate Christian behavior in this temporal life, grow and increase in repentance, in faith, in the knowledge of God, in the blessed hope, in love, in new obedience, patience, and good works, and, finally, when the hour of death comes, fall blessedly asleep in Christ, pass through death to life, and on the Last Day arise at the final heavenly trumpet to eternal joy and the glad communion of the entire Holy Trinity and the heavenly fellowship of the dear angels and all the elect, and be and remain eternal citizens of the new heavenly city of Jerusalem. Amen.

The city of Unna, August 10, AD 1598.

Your honorable, highly esteemed,
very wise, and very favorable lordships'
willing servant,
Philipp Nicolai, D. Eccl. in that city.

INTRODUCTION TO *THE JOY OF ETERNAL LIFE*

The article of eternal life produces comfort and joy in believing Christians.

John 16:20–24; Ps. 17:15; 1 John 3:2; Matt. 8:11; 2 Sam. 12:23; 1 Sam. 25:29; Jer. 31:16–17; Rev. 14:12–13; 7:17; Ps. 30:11; Isa. 65:13–14, 19; John 16:22

I EXULT heartily in the Lord, and my soul rejoices in God my Savior, whenever I recall the comforting article of eternal life and the glorious fatherland, where we believing Christians will see with joyful eyes the almighty King of glory and invincible Serpent-crusher, our only Redeemer and Savior, Jesus Christ, and be gathered to the holy patriarchs, prophets, and apostles and with great rejoicing will again behold our dear kinsmen, such as father, mother, brothers, sisters, husband, wife, children, and all acquaintances who fell blessedly asleep in the Lord and in true faith departed before us. And God will wipe away all tears from our eyes and turn our complaint into a song of joy. He will gird us with gladness so that our heart will rejoice forever, and this joy no man shall take from us.

The location and glory of eternal life.

Heb. 12:22–23; Isa. 65:14; 1 Cor. 3:21; Gen. 15:1; Rev. 21:22; Ps. 27:1; 1 Cor. 15:28; Luke 15:7, 10

We will enter into the heavenly Jerusalem, into the city of the living God, to the multitude of many thousand angels and to the congregation of the firstborn who are written in heaven. And there we will shout for joy with a glad heart at the noble, precious treasure: that heaven and all imperishable heavenly goods which Christ has are to be ours. God Himself will be our very great reward, our temple, our light, and all in all, which we will not trade for all the pomp, glory, gladness, and majesty of the perishing world. The holy angels will look at us kindly and smile upon us, and the whole heavenly host will call us blessed to have believed in Jesus Christ and trusted in His truthful Word even till death.

Admonition to spiritual joy in all godly Christians who pass through the valley of sorrow in this world.

Heb. 11:33–40; Matt. 5:10–12; Luke 6:20–23; Ps. 84:4–5; Matt. 10:16–32; Luke 21:12–19; John 15:18–21; Lam. 3:29; Hab. 1:13–14; 1 Cor. 4:10, 13, 9

"My heart and mind are comforted, calm and quiet,"[2] whenever I remember this, and I am not disturbed by the fact that we wretched worms and the sheep of Christ's pasture in this world, "in the midst of life, are by death surrounded"[3] and that, because of our faith and our hope, we must always pass through the fires of the devil and his accursed horde. The children of God are not to despair but to wait for eternal life in the sure hope that, although they pass through the valley of sorrow with tribulation, want, mockery, scorn, and inequality, and live in exile, and are comfortless widows and orphans, reviled preachers, afflicted creatures, a poor, sick, captive, and grief-ridden band which everyone wishes to destroy, who put their mouth in the dust and let themselves be smitten on the cheek, accept perverse judgment, cry out over evildoing and receive no help, are made out to be fools for Christ's sake, the purge offering of all men, and a spectacle to angels and men.

Our redemption draws near, and eternal life will soon begin.

Luke 18:7–8; Jer. 31:13; Rom. 8:18; 2 Cor. 4:17; Isa. 64:4; 2 Cor. 2:9

The Lord will come soon and has already mercifully heard the sighing and crying of His elect (who call upon Him night and day). He will deliver us shortly, and His Church will rejoice after her sorrow. And what we now suffer a little while in this world is not worthy to be compared with the unspeakable, magnificent glory that will be revealed in us. For our tribulation, which is temporal and easy, produces an eternal and immeasurably weighty glory, the likes of which no eye has seen and no ear has heard, neither has it ever entered into the heart of any man.

Great glory, joy, and bliss of the heavenly paradise.

Rev. 12:11; Luke 23:43; Heb. 12:22–24; Exod. 3:8; Ps. 68:5; 1 Cor. 15:28; Acts 7; Ps. 36:8; 16:6; 17:15; 1 John 5:20; Matt. 18:10; Isa. 6:2–3; John 16:13–15; 17:5; 1 Cor. 13:12; Ps. 103:21; Matt. 8:11; 22:31–32; Gen. 25:8, 17; Wisdom 3:1–9; Isa. 56:7; Rev. 14:13; 2 Sam. 12:23

Oh, the unspeakable glory, the great joy, the blessed good, and the eternal majesty that we will live to see there and that causes every part of the heavenly hall of gladness to shine as a blessed comfort and blessed refreshment of all children of light, who have overcome the devil, the world, and all tribulation by the blood of Christ! Oh, the precious, wondrously beautiful paradise, the glorious city of God, and the heavenly land of Canaan, where there is nothing but hills of gladness and mountains of comfort flowing with sheer milk of consolation and honey of joy, and where God is all in all! What a wondrously beautiful world it must be—a delightful place, a pleasant habitation, a splendid garden of gladness,

2 From the hymn "Mit Fried und Freud ich fahr dahin" (Luther, 1524), st. 1; see *LSB* 938.

3 From the hymn "Mitten wir im Leben sind" (Luther, 1524), st. 1; see *LSB* 755.

and a kingdom full of all comfort, where God the Father reveals His sweetest and kindest face to His elect children, angels, and men with all clarity and wondrous comfort and where Jesus Christ shows His glory, which He had with the Father before the foundation of the world was laid. Likewise, also, with wondrous sweetness and kindness the Holy Spirit will be seen in the Father and in the Son. Oh, the beautiful, noble life, where the holy angels praise God with joy, where the dear patriarchs, prophets, and apostles dwell, where all godly Christians are gathered out of this vile and treacherous world to their people, where our godly parents, father, mother, husband, wife, children, brothers, sisters, and other familiar friends, in faith trusting in Christ's blood, have been taken before us and await our arrival with great joy and delight!

Augustine, Meditations, ch. 22;[4] *likewise, Manual, chs. 7–8*[5]

"O blessed life," says Augustine, "that God has prepared for those who love Him! What a truly lively life you are! You are a blessed life, you are a constant, secure life, you are a quiet, peaceful life, you are a pure, chaste life, you are a holy life, you are an eternal, joyful life, where no death or sorrow or sadness is heard of. You are a life without blot, without anguish or trouble, without corruption or change, without fear, fright, or terror. You are a life in which all things are exceedingly lovely, beautiful, graceful, and delightful, where there is no adversary who assails us, where there is no incitement to sin, where there is perfect love, one heart, mind, and sense, and a constant unity, where there is an eternal, bright, shining day, where God is seen face-to-face, and where with this food of life man is so satisfied that he hungers no more!

Christians should desire nothing higher nor ponder anything more than eternal life.

"O eternal, blessed life! It is my heart's desire and joy that I may think on you. How splendid life is in you! I am heartily delighted by your excellent bounties, for which I have a deep longing. And the more I think of you and embrace your loveliness and sweetness, the more love, desire, and longing for you grows and increases within me. And whenever I think of you, my heart smiles for joy within my body. Therefore, I take pleasure in turning my heart, mind, and sense toward you and considering and contemplating your loveliness.

We should always desire to speak and sing of eternal life during our toilsome pilgrimage.

"It is my delight daily to speak of you, to hear of you, to write of you, to talk of you, and to read of your eternal blessedness and heavenly glory, and to close in my heart what I have read and to ponder it constantly that I may thus tear and turn myself away from the present care, danger, toil, and labor of this mortal and transitory life and take refreshment like a pilgrim and wanderer with the sweet,

4 Author uncertain, *Meditationes* 22 (PL 40:917).

5 Author uncertain, *Manuale* 7–8 (PL 40:955). The theme and language bear marked similarities to *Meditationes* 22.

cool air of your lively goodness, that whenever I go to sleep, I may lay my weary head in your bosom and find my rest in you, O eternal life!

Eternal life cannot be sought or found on this earth except in Scripture.

"Therefore, I find my delight and refreshment in the pleasant, beautiful pasture of Holy Scripture, and there by diligent gathering I pluck many green, comforting herbs of passages, and I read these gathered passages as if I were eating and tasting plucked herbs, and just as a man digests things inwardly, so I ponder them diligently, and when I have contemplated, weighed, and compared them well, I put them down and close them in my heart, that by such savor of your sweetness I may feel all the less the bitterness of this most miserable life.

Joy and glory of an elect Christian in eternal life.

"O most blessed life! You are indeed a blessed kingdom and know of no death and have no end. In you there is eternity and no change of time. In you there is one day and it permits no night to come, but endures and abides eternally. There a Christian soldier who has overcome the world, the devil, death, and all calamity is a fellow, brother, and companion of the angelic thrones and dominions that continually praise God with a jubilant voice, and he sings to our God without pause the joyful hymn of joy of the glory of Zion and wears on his brow the crown of life everlasting."

Christians desire that the doctrine of eternal life might be expounded fruitfully.

Luke 24:32; John 5:39; 2 Pet. 1:3; Deut. 32:2; Isa. 64:1–4

Oh, if only there were a man somewhere on earth who could speak, sing, preach, and write of this so sweetly, splendidly, comfortingly, and encouragingly that among the afflicted, troubled children of God many hearts might thereby be roused to blessed gladness and richly comforted! How is it, O dear God, that we are so lazy to believe Your Holy Word, which testifies of eternal life and has been made known to us in the prophetic and apostolic Scriptures? Oh, that it might, by the power and working of the Holy Spirit, burn like a light in our hearts and flow like a fruitful rain which drips upon the grass and falls like the dew that moistens the tender herb! Oh, that it might cut to our heart like piercing spears and nails and bear utterly rich comfort and living joy for the alleviation and dispelling of the great sadness, heaviness, and tribulations with which Your poor Christians are ceaselessly troubled, tormented, and afflicted in this valley of sorrow!

The joy of eternal life can never be grasped or described in this world.

1 Cor. 2:7, 9; 13:11–12; Isa. 64:4

It is true, dear Lord God, and we must confess it: This sweet, precious mystery is far too deeply hidden, the joy too great, and the glory too weighty for our reason; while our heart is too narrow, our eyes too sleepy, and our mind far too weak and far too inept to fathom the precious mystery, the great and lofty joy, and the weighty glory. And even if Your enlightened children in this world get a part of it right and understand it somewhat, so that they speak, sing, and write of it, yet all their knowledge and prophecy is in part, incomplete, and a child's beginning. Therefore, I am cast down within me and think: How shall I speak and write perfectly of the gladness of eternal life when I cannot understand it perfectly nor attain to it perfectly in my thoughts? And whatever does not enter into my heart, how shall I bring it to my tongue or give the pen free course? Surely Pericles, Demosthenes, Cicero, Isocrates, and similar widely famed orators, even if they understood this subject rightly, would be far too weak and lowly in eloquence and rhetorical skill to reflect it rightly and to give it sufficient description.

We should and must begin in this world like young children, to lisp and babble about eternal life, until we arrive in the perfection of yonder world.

Ps. 89:15–16; 36:8–9; 16:11; 108:1; 57:8; 96:11–12

And yet, dear God, in Your Word You will and command us to make a beginning in this world where we know in part and to speak, preach, sing, and talk of eternal life as much as Holy Scripture reveals of it. "Oh, blessed is the people," says David, "that can shout for joy! O Lord, they will walk in the light of Your countenance. They will rejoice at Your name daily and be glorious in Your righteousness. They will be drunk with the rich bounties of Your house, and You give them to drink of pleasure as with a flood. For with You is the fountain of life, and in Your light do we see light. In Your presence there is fullness of joy, and at Your right hand is pleasure forevermore. Therefore, O God, it is my earnest desire: I will sing and rejoice, even with my glory. Arise, psaltery and harp, I will rise in the morning. Let heaven rejoice and the earth be glad, the sea rumble, and what is therein. Let the field rejoice, and all that is upon it, and let all the trees of the forest exult."

Prayer to God.

Ps. 89:16; 100:4; 43:3; 31:19; 36:10

Oh, let us likewise rejoice and be glad in Your name daily, dear God, and be glorious in Your righteousness, according to this exhortation from Your prophet David. Oh, let us sing of Your heavenly grace, as much of it as has been revealed to us, and extol Your truth with our mouth forever and ever! Oh, let us enter Your gates with thanksgiving and Your courts with praise, glory, and the honor of Your name! Bring us to Your holy hill and to Your habitation, O Lord, our joy and rejoicing, that we may see and acknowledge Your great goodness which You have laid up for those who fear You and which You spread upon all who know You.

Division of *The Joy of Eternal Life* in Two Parts

Part I: What Eternal Life Is. Part II: How God Readies Us for It.

WITH heartfelt joy I eagerly desire to help to make such a beginning and to indicate pleasantly and sweetly from the prophetic and apostolic Scriptures of the Old and New Testament, first, what kind of precious and joy-filled life the eternal life of the elect children of God is above in heavenly paradise; and, second, from whom this salutary good comes and how the Holy Trinity, God the Father, God the Son, and God the Holy Spirit, out of sweet, unspeakable love and kindness, prepares us poor children of Adam for eternal life and causes us to reach it.

Invocation of God for His help and grace for the explanation of this article.

Ps. 25:14; 71:15–17; 8:2; 51:15

O great King of glory and Captain of eternal life, my dearest Savior and Redeemer, Lord Jesus Christ, who out of great, sincere love for men has earned and obtained eternal life for us poor sinners with Your precious crimson blood; who reveals this secret wisdom to those who fear You and causes them to know Your covenant; who also prepares Your own praise from the mouths of children and babes so that they gloriously honor, proclaim, and spread abroad Your wonders and benefits: I beseech You to make me also one of those babes! Open my lips, that by the power and working of Your Holy Spirit I may expound fruitfully the precious article of eternal life to the glory of Your great majesty and as a blessed consolation to all sorely aggrieved and despondent hearts who weep and wail here on earth while the world rejoices and for the sake of Your name must be subjected to all manner of threats, distress, mockery, and danger. Grant to them, O God of all comfort, that this article may be their cup of consolation, from which they may draw the true living water and salutary draft of refreshment, a comfort to gladden and revive their thirsty, weary soul.

Part One
What Eternal Life Is

The first article concerning eternal life provides all godly Christians with instruction for gladness and rejoicing.

Matt. 25:21, 23; Rom. 8:18; John 16:20–22; 1 John 3:2; Rev. 3; John 5:24

CAREFUL contemplation of this precious and lofty article of eternal life in our Christian Creed produces and works in us a living comfort, constant joy, and sincere delight. Rejoice and celebrate, all you Christians who heartily long for eternal life! Let us sing, leap, shout for joy, and be glad at heart in the Lord our God and Savior because of the blessed good of heavenly glory, gladness, and majesty, which out of sweet, unspeakable love He has prepared for us, His sorrowful children, from the beginning of the world and will bring to a glorious revelation so that we will see it in front of us with our very own eyes as soon as we have faithfully finished the contest and fight of our faith on earth and by the power of the Holy Spirit have passed from this toilsome valley of sorrow through the final throes of death into the heavenly fatherland.

CHAPTER I

IS THERE AN ETERNAL LIFE?

Proof from our Lord Christ's testimony that there is assuredly an eternal life.

John 14:27; 10:28; 5:24; 12:26; 17:24; Luke 23:43

THIS IS my heart's highest comfort, my joy, and my delight, and a lovely refreshment in all cross and adversity. Here say to your soul: Why are you cast down, O my soul, and so disquieted within me? You will not abide forever in this afflicted valley of sorrow. An eternal life has been prepared for you after this misery. And why do you doubt this? "Let not your heart be troubled," says the Son of God. "You believe in God, believe also in Me. In My Father's house are many mansions: if it were not so, I would tell you. I go to prepare a place for you. And if I go to prepare a place for you, I will also come again and receive you to Myself, that you may be where I am. I give My sheep eternal life. He who believes in Me has eternal life and shall not enter into judgment, but has passed from death into life. For where I am, there shall My servants also be, and he who shall serve Me, him will My Father honor. O Father, I will that they whom You have given Me may be with Me where I am, that they may behold My glory, which You have given Me." And what kind of glory may this be? "Truly, truly," He says to the dying thief on the cross, "I say to you, today you will be with Me in paradise."

From God's Word we are given full assurance of the doctrine of eternal life so that we need not doubt that God's Word is the pure truth.

Rev. 3:14; 2 Cor. 1:20; John 14:6; [1 Pet. 2:22]; Isa. 53:9; 14:27; Ps. 33:4; Ezek. 12:24–25

Here we hear not a mere man's utterance but God's Word, God's promise, and God's testimony concerning eternal life. Who would not trust this divine testimony? Meanwhile, the pagans also write about it and make fables—especially the poets—about the Elysian Fields, that is, a new world and beautiful, pleasant place where the souls of upright and virtuous men are supposed to go after they die in this world. But who would trust their fables? They are the dreams of men and poetic works in which no one can trust. To us, however, this precious, lofty mystery is proclaimed and made known by the great Amen of God, Jesus Christ, who is the way, the truth, and the life and in whose mouth no deceit was found. "The Lord has decided," says Scripture, "and who will change it?" "The Word of the Lord is true, and what He promises, that He keeps with certainty." "You shall remember," God Himself says, "that no prophecy shall lie. For I am the Lord; what I speak shall be performed."

All the works of God—creation, redemption, rebirth, as well as God's Word, the Gospel, Baptism, the Supper, and our whole Divine Service—testify that there is an eternal life.

Indeed, what do all the works of the great love and kindness of God do but preach to us of eternal life? For to what end were we created? To what end did Christ redeem us from death, the devil, and hell? To what end are we born again by the Holy Spirit through the Word and Holy Sacraments? Surely the Holy Trinity did not intend it chiefly for this brief period of our perishable life in this world. Neither are we baptized for this temporal life, nor do we go to church and the Supper and hear God's Word to learn how to farm, sow, build, plant, raise animals, sell merchandise, and make use of this world. For non-Christians, Jews, Turks, and pagans also do these things, and they require no Baptism, no Sacrament, no Gospel, and no Absolution. Rather, our dear God intended it all for our heavenly salvation and eternal life. We were created for eternal life, we were redeemed for eternal life, we are born again for eternal life, we are baptized for eternal life, we are called by the Gospel for eternal life. And what is the end of our faith and of our blessed hope other than eternal life? And for what does a Christian die in the Lord but that he may rest and go from this world into eternal life?

In contemplation of eternal life Christians are to rejoice, not to grieve like the heathen.

1 Thess. 4:13

O my soul, why are you afflicted and cast down with such heaviness and anxious thoughts? If it is true that all the chief works of God, such as creation, redemption, and sanctification, and also God's Word, Baptism, Absolution, the Supper, as well as our faith, hope, and Christians' final departure from this valley of sorrow, all bear strong witness to the article of eternal life and are all properly intended and directed toward eternal life—why, then, should we not heartily rejoice and be glad? Why should we Christians, for anguish and impatience, pluck out our hair, fret and worry ourselves to death, and grieve like the heathen, who have no hope?

Holy Scripture gives eternal life many glorious names.

Luke 23:43; Rev. 19:9; Luke 12:31; Matt. 25:34; John 14:2; Rev. 21:3; Ps. 16:6; 17:15; 36:8–9; Luke 19; 1 Pet. 1:4; Rom. 8:23; Col. 1:12; 2 Cor. 4:17; Ps. 16:11; Heb. 11:16; 12:22

And what is the purpose of the splendid and comforting names with which eternal life is crowned here and there in Scripture? Why is it called a paradise? Why does the Lord Christ call it a wedding feast? For what cause does it receive so lovely a name as to be called the kingdom of God, the eternal Father's house, an everlasting tabernacle, and the holy hill of the Lord, the river of pleasures, the fountain of life, the holy temple, fullness of joy, an eternal marriage bond with God, the joy of the Lord, the imperishable, undefiled, and unfading inheritance, the inheritance of the saints in light, the great and immeasurably weighty glory, pleasant existence, the heavenly country, the land of the living, the holy city of the living God, the new Jerusalem?

The reason why the Holy Spirit gives so many precious, lovely, and comforting names to eternal life.

To what end do these words serve us, and why does the Holy Spirit exalt eternal life with so many comforting names, except that in our faith and in our hope we might be encouraged and exhorted to heartfelt joy and gladness? For what is more delightful than a beautiful paradise and garden of pleasure? What is more pleasing to young people, to young men and women, than nuptial joy, nuptial love, and marital union? What is more splendid than the assembly of great lords and their majestic glory, joy, and delight? What enriches children more than their great inheritance and large estates? What is more prestigious than a powerful and beautiful city? What is more renowned in the whole world than Jerusalem? What sounds statelier than a great kingdom? What lifts the spirit more than one's own country? Who is not eager to see pleasant tabernacles of wildflowers and fruitful, beautiful hills? What is lovelier than pleasures? What revives and refreshes thirsty souls on earth better than a sweet and pleasant drink? What has a more glorious appearance than heartfelt gladness, weighty glory, and pleasant existence.

The world is corrupt and inclined toward nothing but perishable good, pleasure, honor, splendor, and prosperity.

Eccles. 1–2

I see great vanity under the sun in the way the world strives and seeks after perishable good, splendor, honor, glory, and pleasure. Kings, princes, and great lords build stately palaces, delight in beautiful parks and pleasure gardens, and plant all manner of fruitful trees in them. Young men and women occupy themselves with love, and their desire is for marital life. Others delight in seeing the world, that they may know of the widely renowned and distant kingdoms and to write and tell of India, America, Tartary, China, of Prester John's lands,[6] etc. I see how,

6 A legendary Christian territory variously placed in Ethiopia, the Middle East, or the Orient.

when there is a great estate and riches to be inherited, the closest kinsmen strive and quarrel passionately for it. I see how earthly kings and potentates and great lords with hostility snap up cities, villages, lands, and peoples and wage great wars. Likewise, we also see that, among the common man, there is to be found no end or limit of seeking and striving for temporal happiness, riches, and pleasure, lofty rank and reputation.

Majestic names of temporal goods and glories are lent to eternal life that Christians may thereby be drawn to heavenly joy.

Here awake, my soul, and consider with joy the reason why Scripture borrows so many words and names from the goods, splendor, glory, and pleasures of this world and applies them to eternal life. O dear soul, Holy Scripture does this to attract and turn our heart and mind to the eternal, heavenly, and imperishable good. Indeed, by this it teaches us that no wedding feast, no marital love, no nuptial bond in this world can be so pleasant, so glorious, so desirable as eternal life in heaven. It teaches that no princely or royal pleasure garden is to be compared to the most delightful paradise of God. It also teaches that eternal life is such a treasure, such a kingdom, such a city, such a country, such a joy, such a glory, such a pleasure, and such a good that it spreads its wings on high and soars far above all the perishing treasures, above all the kingdoms, above all the lands, above all the fair cities, and above all the splendor, riches, pleasure, joy, and glory of this world.

The contemplation of eternal life is to awaken heartfelt joy in us.

Ps. 89:15; 103:1–2

Blessed, therefore, are the people who can shout for joy! Blessed are the children of light who with heartfelt rejoicing consider this wondrously cheering mystery! Bless the Lord, O my soul, and all that is within me, bless His holy name. Bless the Lord, O my soul, and forget not all His benefits. For who would not rejoice in this precious, lofty good and with all diligence eagerly strive and seek after it? We ought to cry from our heart with St. Augustine's mother, Monica:[7] What are we doing still in the world, and why do we not fly up to heaven? Why do we not forsake all that we have and follow after Christ, that we may possess this salutary good here in faith and hereafter in sight? We who believe in Christ should always be leaping for pure joy and walking in heaven with our thoughts.

7 St. Monica is described in legends as having cried, "Let us fly to heaven!"

CHAPTER II
WHAT KIND OF LIFE IS ETERNAL LIFE?

Ps. 77:6

BUT WHAT kind of life, precisely, is eternal life, that I should so highly rejoice in it and seek it so fervently? "I speak with my heart," says David, "and my spirit must search" what precisely is the nature of its joy, delight, and glory.

Answer and description of eternal life.

Luke 12:36; Hosea 2:19–20; Ps. 45:14–15; 1 John 1:2–3; Col. 2:2–3; Rev. 19:1, 7; Zech. 2:5; Isa. 65; 66; Rev. 7:15–17; John 14:2–3; 1 Cor. 3:16–17; 6:15–17; 2 Cor. 6:16–18; Rev. 21:3–7; 1 Cor. 13:8–10; Jer. 31:33–34; Isa. 55; 56:4–7; 1 John 3:2, 24; 1 Cor. 15:28; 2 Pet. 1:3–4; Isa. 61; 1 John 4:16; Dan. 12:3, 10; Matt. 13:43; Wisdom 3; Deut. 6:2; Matt. 22:30–32; Lev. 19:2; 2 Tim. 1:16–17; Col. 3:4; 1 Cor. 13:12–13; Rom. 12:4–5; Eph. 5:30; Isa. 59:21; John 17:3, 11; 1 Cor. 6:15, 19–20

Answer: O dear soul, it is a life of pure, burning love, a life of true marriage, a life of sweet, heavenly pleasure, and a life of indissoluble communion which the elect enjoy with God the Father, God the Son, and God the Holy Spirit forever, full of all comfort, full of all joy, and full of all glory. It is also a life composed entirely of holy love, bound up with holy love, and founded upon a strong holy love such that the entire Holy Trinity, true God, encircles, encloses, and enfolds all the elect angels and men with His unspeakable love as with a fiery wall and causes them to enjoy wondrously sweet rest and gladness in Him, their wondrously beautiful temple. And as He loves them, He is also loved by them with perfect counter-love[8] so that by this bond and medium of fervent love and counter-love He, with His great goodness, power, joy, glory, wisdom, and righteousness, resides, dwells, and rests happily in them as in His noble pleasure-houses and palaces and is all in all and makes them partakers of His divine nature. Thus from this inhabitation and indwelling of the living God, they are all wondrously beautiful, wondrously strong, and, according to the measure given them, perfectly wise, perfectly righteous, perfectly holy, friendly, joyful, and filled with all

8 *Gegenliebe*; i.e., requited, reflected love.

virtues. They love their indwelling Lord God with all their heart, all their soul, and all their strength, and one another also as themselves. By this love they cling together in unity as members in one body, are thoroughly and sweetly filled with and occupied by the Holy Spirit, the Breath of God, and God is one with them, and all of them with one another—God, angels, and men, as one body, one Spirit, one mass full of all heavenly joys, full of heavenly pleasure, and full of everlasting glory.

Eternal life is a life of pure love. Every part of heaven shines and burns with sheer holy love and the glory of love.

Behold, dear soul, such is the form and nature of eternal life. Thus is it a paradise, a hall of joy, a city of God, a land of the living, and a marriage supper, where God lives, reigns, and governs with His holy angels, patriarchs, prophets, apostles, and all the elect who have departed yonder from this valley of sorrow, in utter burning love, in love's power, in love's joy, in love's glory, and in love's brightness. It burns, shines, and storms in every part with holy, fiery love, and in holy, pure, fiery love they are all—namely, the angels and men—with God and in God as one cake so that they do nothing, say nothing, and think nothing else, but all things flow from pure, burning love. Their glorious joy in one another is a joy and rejoicing of love. Their unity and knitting together is the bond of love. Their light and brightness are a radiance and glow of love. Their psalms and hymns of joy are glad declarations and proclamations of holy love. Their eternal conversation is an eternal praise of eternal love. Their beauty, power, and honor are a splendid glory of love, and their gracious communion is utter comfort, utter quickening, utter loveliness, and a pure, holy pleasure of pure, holy love. So entirely has love usurped everything, possessed everything, and knit everything strongly together that neither death nor hell, neither authority nor power, neither height nor depth, neither things present nor things to come, can tear us apart from one another.

All godly Christians go from this valley of sorrow into the blessed paradise and fatherland of eternal life.

Luke 23:43; 16:22; Acts 7:56, 59; Heb. 11

Into that wondrously beautiful kingdom went the converted thief on the cross to whom the Son of God declared the comforting promise: "Truly, I say to you, today you will be with Me in paradise." There went the poor godly Lazarus when, having overcome death in faith, he was carried by the holy angels with joy into Abraham's bosom. There went St. Stephen when, at his final end, he saw heaven opened and commended his soul to the Lord Jesus. And there, with all the citizens of the heavenly kingdom, our loved ones—father, mother, husband, wife, children, brothers, sisters, relatives, and acquaintances—who have died a blessed death in God have been gathered and now rest joyfully in God, who with all holy angels smiles, comforts, and quickens them in a wondrously loving manner so that they desire no further glimpse of this world. Oh, that noblest life of all which they live there without death or tribulation! Rightly and in all truth may that be called eternal life.

CHAPTER III

OBJECTION FROM THE VERSE "NO EYE HAS SEEN" &C.

1 Cor. 2:9

"BUT," YOU say, "where do we get this description of eternal life? And what foundation and testimony does it have? After all, Scripture says, 'No eye has seen and no ear has heard, neither has it entered into the heart of any man.' How, then, can you speak so boldly about it?"

St. Paul shows how to understand the saying of Isaiah.

Isa. 64:4; 1 Cor. 2:10–13

Answer: It is true that St. Paul, quoting the prophet Isaiah, writes, "No eye has seen and no ear has heard, neither has it entered into the heart of any man, what God has prepared for those who love Him." Yet he goes on to add these words: "But to us God has revealed it by His Spirit. For the Spirit searches all things, even the depth of the Godhead. For what man knows what is in man save the spirit of the man which is in him? Even so, no man knows what is in God save the Spirit of God. But we have not received the spirit of the world, but the Spirit from God, that we might know how richly we have been graced by God; which things we speak not with words which the wisdom of man can teach, but with words which the Holy Spirit teaches."

The sense and meaning of St. Paul's words. While the mystery of eternal life is hidden to reason, nevertheless it is revealed to Christians in God's Word.

1 Cor. 2:9; Matt. 13:15; Luke 24:25; 18:27; John 1:5; 3:19

With this addition, the apostle clearly intimates that although eternal life is not to be searched out or fathomed in this world by human senses and investigation of nature, nevertheless to Christians it is not hidden but revealed by the Holy Spirit, and so richly laid bare that from this revelation in the prophetic and apostolic Scriptures it is certainly possible to detect and learn how richly we have been graced by God and what blessings He has prepared for those who love Him. We are missing nothing in this revealed Word of God; we have it in sufficient shape, and whoever wishes can read, examine, listen, and consider it. Rather, what we are missing is in ourselves, in that our flesh and blood, the natural man, cannot comprehend it, but is earthly-minded and has dull eyes, deaf ears, and a cold, sluggish heart toward the Word of Life so that it does not seek the kingdom of God. "The Light," says Scripture, "shines in the darkness, and the darkness did not comprehend it," for "men loved darkness rather than the Light."

Our blindness, ignorance, and sluggishness in divine matters ought to be mourned. Parable: How we are to search the Scriptures for eternal life.

Matt. 13:44–46; Eph. 5:14; John 5:39; 2 Pet. 1:19

Therefore, we might well bewail our great blindness, darkness of mind, and dullness of heart, sitting as it were across the table and sleeping through the royal banquet and the majestic meal. We have the description of eternal life close before us in the Word of God, but we little regard it. We let our thoughts venture elsewhere and then imagine it is completely concealed from Christians on earth. Not so, my soul! Awake, you who sleep, and consider the Word, and Christ will shine on you! If you found pearls of great price in a field, would you not be so glad that you would go and sell all that you have and acquire the field, that you might dig for that secret treasure and pearls? Is it not so that whatever is pleasing, that is what we think about, and where we hope to find good, that is where we look? Now, Holy Scripture is a heavenly field sown with the Word of God, beneath which the treasure of eternal life lies hidden. Why, then, do we not seek and search therein? Why are we so sluggish, so cold, and so weary? "Search," says the Son of God. "Search, search the Scriptures. For you think that in them you have eternal life." If we will follow this counsel and pay close attention to the Scriptures as to a lamp shining in a dark place, then the day will dawn with loveliness, and the article of eternal life will arise like the morning star in our hearts with all brightness and comfort.

The summary teaching of Holy Scripture on the glory and whole nature of eternal life. The wondrously comforting glory, pleasure, and properties of eternal life.

Ps. 87:1; Rev. 19:9; John 3:2; 1 John 3:2; Ps. 45:9–17; Eph. 5:23; 1 Cor. 3:16; Col. 3:14; Isa. 54:5–6; Song 5:1; 1 John 4:16; 3:1–2; 1 Cor. 13:8; Matt. 19:17; 22:37; 1 Cor. 8:3; Rom. 8:38–39; John 17:22–26

And what does Scripture say about eternal life? What does it reveal of its glory, its pleasure, and its entire nature? O dear soul, glorious things are preached therein concerning the city of God, how it is founded in the holy mountains, and how the Lord loves it more than all dwellings. It calls the elect the citizens of heaven, the joyful wedding guests, the children of God, the Bride of God, the friends of God, and the temple and dwelling of the Holy Spirit perfected in love and perfectly one in God through pure, fervent love, which is the bond of perfection. It preaches glorious things of utterly pure love, the joy of love, and the glory of love: "God is love," it says. "And he who abides in love abides in God, and God in him." "Behold, what love the Father shows us, that we should be called children of God." "Beloved, we are children of God, and it has not yet appeared what we shall be. But we know that when He shall appear, we shall be like Him." "Prophecies shall cease, and tongues shall cease, even so faith and hope: but love will never cease." "If you wish to enter into life, keep the commandments." "You shall love the Lord your God with all your heart, with all your soul, and with all your mind, and you shall love your neighbor as yourself." "He who loves God, the same is known by Him." "Neither death nor life, nor angels nor principalities nor powers, nor things present nor things to come, nor height nor depth, nor any other created thing shall separate us from the love of God which is in Christ Jesus our Lord." "Father," says Christ, "I have given them the glory which You gave Me, that they may be one, as We are one: I in them, and You in Me, that they may perfectly be in one, and the world may know that You have sent Me, and love them even as You love Me. Father, I will that they also whom You have given Me may be with Me where I am, that they may see My glory that You have given Me because You loved Me before the world was founded. I made known to them Your name, and will make it known to them, that the love with which You love Me may be in them, and I in them"; and so on.

Scripture, in describing eternal life, speaks of pure perfect love and love's glory. Love is the fulfilling of the Law.

Rom. 13:10; Song 8:6

But is this not to preach of pure heavenly love and to include everything under love so that eternal life is essentially nothing but a life of joyful, fervent love between God and His elect children? What else does the Law fundamentally require than such a life of perfect love? And where will it be fulfilled more mightily and meetly than in the third heaven? And for what has Christ redeemed us from the devil, death, and hell and quenched the wrath of His Father with His blood, but that we might once more stand with God in heartfelt love and live with Him forever in eternal love? What is sweeter, what is nobler, what is lovelier, and what invites more joy and more pleasure than love? And what is stronger than love? And what binds God, angels, and men more closely and firmly together than perfect love? "Love," says Solomon, "is strong as death, and its coal is fiery and a flame of the Lord."

How to understand Christ's calling eternal life a knowledge of the true God.

John 17:3; Gen. 4:1; Amos 3:2; John 10:14

Now, it is from this fiery coal and flame of pure perfect love that heaven above with all its inhabitants burns and gives forth light. The Lord Christ describes it briefly as knowledge of God. "This," He says, "is eternal life: that they know You, the only true God, and Him whom You have sent, even Jesus Christ." It is well to note this and keep it diligently. For wherever in Scripture true love, such as marital love and other tender love, is described, along with its joy, pleasure, and pleasant works, it uses the word *know*. "Adam," it says, "knew his wife Eve." Here we are well aware what Scripture means and how both things—namely, marital love and the sharing of the marriage bed—are, for the sake of decency, indicated and implied by the word *know*. Likewise, God says to the people of Israel, "You only have I known of all the families on earth." Likewise: "I know My own and am known of Mine. As My Father knows Me, so I know the Father." These and similar sayings speak of pure loving knowledge and testify to God's fervent love for us which He has demonstrated in deed and in truth. And in the same way, eternal life also consists of true knowledge of God and of His only-begotten Son, that is, of pure heavenly love, and for the loving enjoyment of the wondrously sweet love of God, that the rich goods of His house might be tasted and that a man might live in eternal love with Him as one cake, additionally participating in the divine nature and a dwelling of God the Father, the Son, and the Holy Spirit.

Eternal life is portrayed to a certain degree in a well-appointed marriage and household.

Gen. 29:20

This heavenly life is portrayed to us to a certain degree in a loving and prosperous marriage and beautiful household. For when in a household all manner of fitting love truly flourishes and holds sway among husband, wife, children, brothers, sisters, and the whole domestic staff in its order, so that they love and esteem one another sincerely, then their love is a pattern of heavenly life, and it is not unjust to say that this is a slice of heaven, and God and His dear angels are dwelling in this house. Likewise, where bride and groom love each other with heartfelt love, their life also is like the life of paradise, and they can spend a long time in such a way that they take no notice of length. So Scripture testifies of Jacob the arch-patriarch that he served seven years for his bride Rachel, and it seemed to him as though it had been a few days, on account of the great love which he bore for Rachel.

The glorious pleasure and sweetness of eternal life.

2 Pet. 3:8

But what is this love, pleasure, and joy compared to the perfect love, joy, and glory of eternal life, where everything shines and burns with unspeakable heavenly love? If Jacob and Rachel could live a life of such chaste love that seven years seemed to them merely seven days, what a life of sweet, fervent love must eternal life then be, where all elect angels and men so heartily love the Lord their God and Savior and are in turn surrounded by such great love from Him, and together are so sweetly kindled and lighted in true love, one for another, that next to this sweet life, joy, and pleasure of heavenly love, a thousand years seems to them scarcely a single day? For St. Peter the apostle refers to this mystery of heavenly joy when he writes, "Beloved, do not be ignorant of this one thing: that one day is to the Lord as a thousand years, and a thousand years as one day."

CHAPTER IV

THE SIX PROPERTIES OF ETERNAL LIFE

Holy Scripture ascribes six properties to eternal life.

WHO, THEN, would not heartily long for such a life? Who would not desire to hear of it? The portal to this mystery is unlocked by defining or describing eternal life. Who would not ponder further? I will go on to greater explanation of the noble, comforting article and indicate six properties which the Holy Spirit applies and ascribes to eternal life. (1) The first is known as the love and counter-love between God and His elect. (2) The second is the honor and glory of this love. (3) The third is God's loving inhabitation or indwelling in His elect. (4) The fourth is known as God being all in all. (5) The fifth appears in the love of neighbor. (6) The sixth consists of perfect unity and union through the bond of love.

The First Property: Love and Counter-Love between God and His Elect

Deut. 32:46; 2 Cor. 13:11; Deut. 6:5; Matt. 22:37; 1 Cor. 13:8, 13; Rom. 8:38–39

Love and counter-love in God and His elect is the substance of the first property and first good of eternal life, and it is full of living joy, living comfort, and living refreshment. O precious joy, O precious comfort, O precious refreshment where God and man live together in sweet, holy love! For God loves with a surpassing love and is a God of love and is holy Love itself. And as He loves man heartily, He also desires heartily to be loved in turn and makes counter-love the chief of all commandments so that His covenant established with us and revealed in the Law consists of nothing but love and counter-love. Now there is no doubt that this contract and covenant of love, with which the Law is concerned, is kept nowhere so perfectly, firmly, and indissolubly as in eternal life. For there, as St. Paul says, hope and faith cease, but love never ceases. Rather, it is so strong and powerful that no authority, nor things present nor things to come, nor height nor depth can abolish or destroy it.

What God and all His saints do in heaven.

Therefore, if you wish to know what God and all the saints do in heaven, I can answer safely and say in truth that they celebrate an eternal, joyful wedding feast and live in altogether perfect love. God loves the angels and men, and the blessed angels and men love their God in turn with all their heart and with all their soul and with all their mind.

The love and counter-love of God and His elect in that world is a great mystery.

Augustine, Manual, ch. 20[9]

Now, this love with which God is loved by His elect in that world is a great mystery, for the thoughts and words of the elect there, as Augustine says, taste of heavenly love and smell of heavenly love, so entirely has God's love claimed and possessed them.[10] God loves them and with His love kindles a counter-love in them—in those who turn wholly to Him. He loves that He may be loved, and in His loving asks nothing but that He may be loved in turn, so that God, angels, and men may all rejoice and glory with one another in love. Therefore, also the blessed angels and men are concerned with no other affects or thoughts but attend only to love: that they may love their God and may requite His love with their love.

God and His elect in that life spring and flow with pure, holy love and counter-love.

Isa. 55:2

There the elect soul pours itself out and springs like a flowing fountain with eternal love toward God. And as the soul is a spring and fountain of eternal love toward God there, what sort of inexhaustible fountain and everlasting spring do you think that God must be in turn to the precious soul, His beloved lover and chosen bride? There in truth the soul swims, moves, and flows in unmixed love and feels only heavenly pleasure. Indeed, out of fervent and heartfelt love it speaks of this deep mystery of love with its God, and in the midst of this conversation it tastes of the sweetness of His love, and from this taste of the sweetness of God it continually grows and increases in love and, as Isaiah has put it, grows fat in delight so that it desires nothing more dearly and thinks of nothing more dearly than its dear God.

True love and counter-love encompass seven virtues which will be explained in order.

Surely it is apparent among men on earth how, where there is firm friendship and two persons have sincere love for each other, their love burns like a fire and binds

9 Author uncertain, *Manuale* 20 (PL 40:960).

10 Author uncertain, *Manuale* 20 (PL 40:960).

their hearts and minds as if they were welded together with a fiery coal. First, they are like-minded; second, they know each other; third, they have the same will; fourth, they trust each other; fifth, they are heartily glad to see each other; sixth, they talk together in friendly manner; and seventh and last of all, they cannot rest unless they are always together.

(1) In God and His children there is a likeness of mind.

Ps. 17:15; 1 Cor. 15:49; 1 John 3:2; 4:16

How glorious, then, do you think it is in that world, in the eternal life of eternal, perfect love and counter-love between God and His elect? Oh, what noble likeness of sense there must be there, where the soul has no other nature and disposition than that which it sees that God has according to His being! For there it bears perfectly the exact image of God and is like Him. As St. John writes, "It has not yet appeared what we shall be. But we know that when He shall appear, we shall be like Him." But what is the image of God, and what kind of being does He have, that the children of light are able to be like this image and this being? St. John answers this, saying, "God is love Himself, and he who abides in love abides in God, and God in him."

St. John's statement, "God is love," gloriously expounded by Dr. Luther, tom. 1, Witt. Germ., fol. 54B[11]

"What use to say much more about it?" writes Dr. Luther on these words. "When people talk at length, saying that love is a noble, lofty quality in the soul, and the most admirable and most perfect virtue, as the philosophers and teachers of works say of it, all this is still nothing compared to what he here pours out from his full mouth, saying, 'God is Love, and His being is utter, unadulterated Love,' so that if anyone wished to depict and rightly capture the likeness of God, he would have to capture an image of utter love, as though the divine nature were nothing but a furnace and conflagration of this love that fills heaven and earth. And, conversely, if love could be painted and depicted, you would have to make the image in such a way that it was not artificial or human, indeed, not angelic or heavenly, but God Himself. Behold, the apostle here is able to paint in such a way that he makes God and love one and the same thing to attract and entice us all the more to ponder this noble, admirable, and lovely image that we, too, may love one another and guard ourselves against envy, hate, and division. For love is the image of God—not a dead image nor one drawn on paper, but a living being in divine nature, which burns full of every good," etc.

By diligent study of the Holy Trinity it is possible to deduce that God must be Love itself.

In addition, the contemplation of the Holy Trinity also shows that God must be nothing other than pure love and Love itself. For I ask you, from what source do these works, such as begetting, being begotten, and dwelling lovingly in the

11 From *Several Beautiful Sermons on 1 John, On Love* (1532): cf. AE 78:369–70) (= sermon for Trinity 1 on 1 John 4:16–21 [1532], WA 36:423–24).

bosom, originally come other than from pure, great love and from a good which springs from goodness and is apportioned through begetting so that it is held in common? As the Father begets, He must do so out of eternal love. As the Son is eternally begotten and yet abides eternally in the bosom of the Father, He, too, must be eternal Love with the Father. And as both the Father and the Son have one Spirit, whom they breathe out simultaneously from eternity, this Spirit must in the same way be eternal Love with the Father and the Son. But all three persons, the Father, the Son, and the Holy Spirit, must be the essence of Love itself, especially because the Son does not receive His own separate substance or being through His begetting, nor the Holy Spirit through His procession, but they are and remain of one substance with the Father.

God the Father, God the Son, and God the Holy Spirit are Love itself.

Thus the Holy Trinity is entirely and utterly Love, and all the internal works of the Holy Trinity, such as eternally begetting, eternally being begotten, eternally dwelling in the bosom, and eternally proceeding, are works of internal, eternal Love, and this eternal Love is no quality or created virtue, but is a being which is called God.

Proof from the works of creation, redemption, and sanctification that God must be Love itself.

Deut. 33:3

Next, that God is Love itself is also attested by the outward works of the Holy Trinity, namely, the work of creation, the work of redemption, and the work of holy rebirth. See what the Holy Trinity does, that we might live eternally. Out of great love God the Father created angels and men for eternal love. And when man fell, the Son of God, out of great love, was made man and died and thereby redeemed us from death for eternal life. Likewise, out of sincere and fervent love the Holy Spirit sanctifies, gathers, and enlightens us for eternal life. And the entire Holy Trinity treats our salvation and blessedness as so important that one might well cry out with Moses in amazement: "How dearly He loves the people!" And with St. Augustine: "God eagerly desires our salvation."[12] And what are all these works but strong testimonies that God is Love itself?

How people in heaven are like God.

Now, if God is Love itself and if the blessed people in heaven are like and conformed to this image and being of God, it follows that they, too, must be filled with pure, holy love, and that just as they are loved heartily by God, they also love Him with all their heart, all their soul, and all their mind.

12 Augustine, *Enarratio in ps.* 99, no. 10 (PL 37:1276).

All the attraction of natural love in this world is to be counted as nothing compared to the glory of the love of God in that life.

Ps. 77:6

Yet I am amazed and ponder with astonishment what a coal of fiery love with which God, who is Love itself, must embrace His elect children in heaven! I speak with my heart, as David says, and my spirit must search: What kind of love is this? What nature does it possess? And to what shall I liken it? O my soul, it is in truth no earthly love, nor like any transitory love of man and wife, fathers, mothers, siblings, or even of angels, nor like any other common love. Rather, it is an unspeakable, unfathomable love above that of fathers, mothers, angels, and men—a supernatural, heavenly love many hundred thousand times, and again a thousand thousand times, lovelier, sweeter, more sincere, and more attractive than all temporal and terrestrial love can be.

The great love and kindness of God in heaven, with its power and working, surpasses all angelic and human love.

Listen, beloved soul: if all manner of friendship or all manner of love and varieties of love enjoined and commanded by God in the Second Table of the Law were to be combined, and if you had such a great friend and great lover on earth who at the same time was able to love you like a father, mother, brother, sister, bride, and bridegroom—indeed, an angel—and was able to prove this love with works, nevertheless all this love and these varieties of love combined into one love would scarcely be worth a spark—no, would be worth nothing—compared to the great love of God with which He loves His children in heaven. And if all human and all angelic love in heaven and on earth merged into one love for one man, nevertheless this mingled love could not give the least loveliness, power, virtue, or glory as springs from God's great kindness and love for men, with which He lovingly and comfortingly refreshes His heavenly housemates in that life so that by it they are eternally strengthened, eternally young, eternally encouraged, eternally healed, eternally rejoicing in it with unspeakable joy.

God loves His elect in heaven and is in turn loved by them with perfect love.

O blessed joy that flows from this kindness of God and has thoroughly possessed and claimed the blessed children of light! Oh, how this love of God kindles the hearts of His elect with a sincere counter-love so that they love God, their highest Friend and kindest Lover, with entirely holy love according to the degree given them! Oh, how with what affection and gladness they glorify, honor, and exalt Him there high above all natural friends, above father, mother, brother, sister, bride, and bridegroom—indeed, above every creature! Oh, how they love Him there, truly with all their heart, with all their soul, and with all their strength, passing the eternal ages with sweet eternal love, of which they never weary, never tire, and never grow sick, but always receive new strength, new power, new comfort, and pure heavenly pleasure from it so that in this way their whole life is pure love, the joy of love, the sweetness of love, the comfort of love, the power of love, and the glory, honor, praise, and majesty of pure heavenly love!

(2) God and His elect know one another in eternal life.

1 Cor. 13:12; [1] Cor. 8:3

Second, this love and counter-love in God and His elect above are also full of heavenly light and full of blessed knowledge. No blind love is known there, no blind joy nor blind pleasure, as among the deranged youth and unchaste Venusians on earth, who rush along blindly in carnal lust, looking only at the outward shape and outward beauty. In heaven, God knows the children of His kingdom within and without and is sincerely known by them in turn. To this perfect knowledge St. Paul testifies openly, saying, "Now I know in part, but then shall I know even as I am known." And again: "If any man loves God, the same is known by Him."

The knowledge with which God knows His own in heaven is wonderful.

My mind is filled with wonder, and I cannot marvel enough at this mystery that I hear—that whoever loves God is known by Him. What is the nature of this knowledge in heaven? Where there is marital love, there is also marital knowledge between man and wife. Where there is natural love, such as between parents and children or brothers and sisters, natural knowledge also holds sway. Yet the love of God with which He loves us is a supernatural, superhuman, and superangelic love, which with its power and sweetness transcends all love of men and angels. How many thousand times higher, how many thousand times nobler, how many thousand times lovelier must that knowledge then be with which He knows all those who love Him?

How God knows His own in heaven.

Ps. 45:10

"Hearken, O daughter," says David, "consider, and incline your ear." So I say also to my soul: Take note, O my soul, and incline your ear. The elect of that world and in that hall of gladness of eternal life are known by God with unspeakable love and kindness, and this knowledge produces nothing but heavenly pleasure, heavenly refreshment, and heavenly joy since it transcends all natural knowledge and is a thousand times sweeter, more comforting, and lovelier than that with which bride and groom, man and wife, parents and children, and brother and sister know one another in this world.

Proof of God's knowledge.

1 Tim. 2:4; Joel 2:28; Isa. 44:3; Ps. 36:8; Isa. 49:16; Ps. 139:5; Isa. 62:5; 46; John 10:14, 28

God knows His own in that world so dearly and so tenderly that He fills them with His Spirit and gives them to drink of pleasure as with a river. He has engraved them in His hands and furnishes all that they do before and after. And as a bridegroom rejoices over the bride, so does He rejoice over them. He is much less able to forget them than a mother her child. He loves and knows them as though He bore them in His womb, as though they lay in His matrix. He keeps His hand over them and fulfills especially what Christ says, "I know My own, and am known of My own; and I give them eternal life, and they will never perish, and no man shall pluck them out of My hand."

Blessed Christians in that world know their God in turn, as well as His mystery.

John 15:15

Now therefore, as He knows them, so they know Him in turn, and His heart's desire and joy is that they may see and understand the deep mystery of His blessings and His glory, because they are His friends and His elect Bride. "A servant," says the Lord Christ, "does not know what his master is doing. But to you I have said that you are friends. For all that I have heard from My Father I have made known to you."

How the blessed children of light know our dear God in heaven.

1 Cor. 13:10–12; 2:10–13; Ps. 25:14; 51:6; John 6:45; Jer. 31:34; Isa. 54:13; John 17:3

Therefore, their intellect—their reason, heart, and understanding—are kindled with a miraculous light of the perfect knowledge of God by the Holy Spirit dwelling in them fully according to the measure given, that they may know how richly they have been graced by God, understand His secret wisdom, and have no need of any other instructor. Rather, they are all taught by God. "This is eternal life," says God's Son, "that they may know You, that You alone are God, and Him whom You have sent, even Jesus Christ." This life and this knowledge are realized in full joy when they see the heart of our dear God, behold His great goodness, wisdom, grace, righteousness, and mercy, taste and enjoy in their hearts the heavenly sweetness of His love, and find in actuality that the Lord is very good and His mercy endures forever.

(3) Uniformity of the will of men in heaven with the will of God.

In the third place, their will also agrees with the will of God, and whereas God wills that, since He is essential Love and has created angels and men according to this image of His, they also should love Him with all their heart and with all their soul and with all their mind, and one another as themselves—therefore, they do so without loathing, without murmuring, without dispute from the heartfelt love kindled in them, and they love their heavenly Father and their eternal Bridegroom and their heavenly Comforter with all their heart and with all their soul and with all their strength, and one another as themselves. Thus whatever God wills, they also will, and what they will, God wills in turn, and their will is so like and conformed to God's will that the will of either springs forth from heartfelt love, and the elect citizens of heaven, male and female, have their perfect desire and eternal joy in God's will.

Parable: The glory of the heavenly life, where God, in His great kindness and love of men, asks and desires nothing from men but that they love Him in turn.

If on earth a mighty king took a poor maiden to wife, had her crowned, and put her in possession of all his goods, and asked nothing of her in return except that she should love him heartily, would she not do so with joy? But how many thousand times more glorious must it be in the city of the living God above, where God, essential Love itself, so highly exalts His children with heavenly goods above all the royal splendor of Europe, Asia, Africa, and the whole wide world—far surpassing even all the earthly love of spouses, parents, and children, and all natural love, and loves His own with unspeakable love—in return for which He asks and seeks and desires nothing else than that He be loved in turn? Oh, with what gladness of heart they will do this—the dear angels and the blessed men—and follow the will of God with great joy, with all their power, and with all their heart, look at the heart of their dear God, and understand all that He desires of them, and do it willingly, happily, and with all gladness of heart, without tiring and with one accord, so that He takes fatherly joy, royal delight, and eternal pleasure in this childlike obedience of theirs.

God's will is done so cheerfully in heaven that we therefore pray that it would also be done as cheerfully on earth.

Ps. 103:20–21

Therefore, we pray in the Lord's Prayer: "Thy will be done on earth as it is in heaven." That is: Grant, O merciful God, that the obedient fulfilling of Your will may be as cheerful, glorious, and tireless among Christians on earth as it is in heaven, where the angels and archangels together with all holy patriarchs, prophets, apostles, and other elect attend to Your will with great joy and eternal rejoicing and do all that is pleasing to You. O dear God, so let it be on earth as well. "Bless the Lord," says David, "you His angels, you mighty champions who fulfill His command, that the voice of His Word may be heard. Bless the Lord, all His hosts, you His ministers who do His will."

God commands and rules in heaven out of great love, and His will is accomplished out of great love.

Job 38

What God commands them flows from unspeakable love, and what they do according to His will is all done from perfect counter-love with all their heart and all their soul and all their strength. Thus all the children of God together praise Him, the beautiful Morning Star. And as St. Ambrose and Augustine testify in their symbol,[13] "all angels, the heavens, and all the powers, cherubim and seraphim sing to Him unceasingly with a loud voice, 'Holy, Holy, Holy Lord God of Sabaoth.' The glorious company of the apostles, the worthy fellowship of the prophets, the

13 I.e., the *Te Deum*.

spotless army of martyrs together with the whole Church Triumphant praise Him, the Father of an infinite majesty, His true and only Son, and also the Holy Spirit."

(4) God and men in heaven trust one another.

In the fourth place, this love and counter-love in the heavenly paradise is strengthened and confirmed with eternal faithfulness and eternal truth, in that God trusts His elect as a holy people and true children, and they in turn heartily confide in Him.

How God trusts His elect in heaven.

Matt. 25:23; Luke 19:12–27; 2 Tim. 4:7; 1 Cor. 4:2; Heb. 11:36–38; Matt. 10:13–22; John 15:19; 16:2; Ps. 66:10–12

"O good and faithful servants," He says to them. "In the world I entrusted to you My gifts as if they were hundredweights and talents—to one less, to another more. You managed them as faithful stewards over My mysteries. You fought the good fight and kept faith to Me. You were made to suffer contempt, mockery, and scorn, and moreover bonds and imprisonment, on earth for My sake. You were stoned, beaten, pierced, and slain with the sword. You wandered about in sheepskins and goatskins, being destitute, afflicted, and tormented. The world was not worthy of you that it should hate you, and it rejoiced at your sorrow. You wandered in exile, in deserts and in mountains and in the dens and caves of the earth. I tested you in the world and tried you as silver is tried. I caused you to be cast into the prison and laid a burden upon your loins. I caused men to ride over your heads, and you went through fire and through water.

God extols the faithfulness of His elect in heaven.

Sirach 2:4; Ps. 119:139, 28, 46; Rev. 3:8; 2:10; Matt. 25:23

"But you held firm and did not waver. You took cheerfully whatsoever was put upon you and were patient in all tribulation. Zeal consumed you for My Word, and your heart melted for affliction. You spoke of My testimonies before kings and were not ashamed. You kept My Word and did not deny My name. You were faithful unto death. Therefore, I now set you over many goods and give you the crown of eternal life."

What God entrusts to the children of light in heaven.

Ps. 36:8; Rev. 3:4–5; Luke 12:8; 1 Cor. 12; Rom. 12:6; Ps. 25:8–13; Prov. 8

These are the words of Holy Scripture with which our dear God beyond all doubt extols the faithfulness of His elect in eternal life and entrusts to them all the rich goods of His house. The Son of God causes them to walk with Him in white raiment and confesses their names before His Father and His angels; and the Holy Spirit entrusts to them not only the firstfruits but also the fullness of His great gifts, and they learn the depth of the manifold mysteries of God and abide forever in His bond.

How the children of light trust our dear God in heaven in turn.

Ps. 92:15; Deut. 32:4; Ps. 89:14; Num. 23:19; 2 Cor. 1:20; Isa. 53:9; 1 Pet. 2:22; Ps. 33:4–5; 84:11–12; 89:33–34; John 16:22; Ps. 92:12

So also the elect, by the full power and working of the Holy Spirit, trust their God in turn and say, "God is faithful, and there is no wickedness in Him. Righteous and upright is He. Judgment and righteousness are the foundation of His throne; grace and truth are before Him. He is not a man, that He should lie, nor a son of man, that He should change His mind. All His promises are *Yes* in Him and are *Amen* in Him, and there is no deceit in His mouth. O Lord, Your Word is true, and what You promise You certainly keep. You love righteousness and justice. You are a sun and shield; You give grace and glory. You will not withhold any good thing from the upright. Therefore, we trust You, and our heart confides in Your Word. You will never take Your loving-kindness away from us nor let Your faithfulness fail us. You will not violate Your covenant established with us nor alter the thing that has gone forth from Your mouth. According to Your Word we will therefore live forever and flourish like the palm trees and grow like the cedars of Lebanon."

(5) In heaven, God and His children look at one another in friendship; there God reveals Himself visibly

John 17:24; 1 John 3:2; John 14:19; 16:22; Matt. 18:10; Job 19:27; Ps. 42:2; 17:15; 36:9

In the fifth place, heavenly love and counter-love are also noticeably strengthened by the eternal contemplation of the divine Being. "We shall see Him," says John, "as He is." Likewise, Christ prays, "Father, I will that they also whom You have given Me may be with Me where I am." Likewise: "You shall see Me; for I live, and you also shall live, and I will see you again, and your heart shall rejoice, and your joy shall no man take from you." In addition, He says of the angels, "Your angels in heaven always see the face of My Father in heaven." Likewise, Job and David rejoice to see the face of God. Job says, "I shall see God in my flesh, and my eyes shall behold Him." Likewise, David: "When shall I come and behold the face of God? I will behold Your face in righteousness. For with You is the living fountain, and in Your light do we see light."

How God reveals and displays His will and being in heaven.

Now, because God is Love itself and reveals His being visibly in heaven so that angels and men behold His face, I ask you, what do they then behold and see in God with their spotless eyes but pure Love? And what is the majestic glory of the divine Being but pure flames of Love and glory of Love, shining and flashing with great joy upon all the citizens of heaven? And what could gladden and refresh the children of God more than the sweet contemplation of that most beloved Being?

Illustration of marital love and marital contemplation.

Ezek. 24:25

For it is indeed pure love and pure joy when godly parents and children, gracious groom and bride, and harmonious brothers and sisters look at one another with kindness and are united one with another. And a loving wife is called the desire of her husband's eye, or *Euphrasia*, the comfort of her husband's eye, because (as Mathesius writes in his twelfth marriage sermon)[14] when an honest man sees his dear wife, he takes pure delight and joy in her, she gladdens the heart of his body and puts him in good spirits so that he dismisses all sorrow from his heart and forgets all toil and labor which he suffered in his business or duty.

Loveliness and beauty of human faces.

Gen. 46:30

Many a man also glories in the idea that there seems to be no more pleasant image on earth than a man's face. The queen Dido sees the Trojan prince Aeneas and cannot grow weary of him, as Virgil writes, "She cannot appease her heart, and she is inflamed with gazing."[15] The patriarch Jacob is happy to die after seeing his son Joseph again. The poet Catulus praises very highly the handsome form of the young man Roscius, and as a blind pagan dares to prefer it to the beautiful face of God.[16] Concerning the daughter of Cleisthenes named Agaristë and her attractive appearance, Herodotus writes that many a young man from Greece came in swarms to this virgin's wedding day in order to see her face and to live with her in joy.[17]

The beauty and lovely form of God surpasses the beauty of all creatures.

Now, the adornment and beauty of all mankind is utter child's play and poor botched work compared to the wondrously comforting and supremely beautiful form of the all-holy Trinity, who reveals Himself in that life and shows Himself glorious with great joy. Indeed, I consider this mystery and say thus: If there is any beautiful human face on earth which can draw the eyes of many people to itself as a magnet attracts iron, and if the contemplation of trusted friends in parents and children, man and wife, bridegroom and bride is so pleasant and comforting that it gladdens the heart, even though men are not love itself but only possess loving feelings and inclination for their friends—how many hundred thousand times friendlier and more loving must the beautiful being of God be, who is Love itself, and the bright, uncovered countenance of our heavenly

14 Johann Mathesius, *Vom Ehestandt und Haußwesen Fünfftzehen Hochzeytpredigten* . . . (Nürnberg: Vom Berg & Neuber, 1563), fol. Pp[a–b].

15 Virgil, *Aeneid* 1.713.

16 Not to be confused with the more famous Roman poet Catullus. Quintus Lutatius Catulus's famous epigram describing the actor Roscius's face as "more beautiful than a god" is preserved in Cicero, *De natura deorum*, 1.79.

17 Herodotus, *Histories* 6.127.

Father and of His only-begotten Son, our most beautiful and supremely gracious Bridegroom, Jesus Christ, and of the Holy Spirit in eternal life?

The power and loveliness of the revealed divine Being.

Oh, how lovely it must be there where the majestic eyes of God shine and burn with pure flames and brightness of love! Oh, how strongly He must draw to Himself the eyes of all angels and men with His kind and fervent gaze so that they are not eager to see anything in heaven or earth so much as Him nor to find satisfaction in any activity so much as in the contemplation of God!

The elect in heaven see in God pure love, and in this seeing their heart is always glad.

Here in God the Father they see such fatherly love and loveliness as no fatherly or motherly face on earth can give. The Son of God makes Himself to be seen as a dear Brother and heavenly Bridegroom, more beautiful and splendid than any bridegroom on earth. They also see in the Holy Spirit such a comforting sight that nothing can appear more comforting in heaven or earth. And since the Holy Trinity, God the Father, Son, and Holy Spirit, looks and smiles at them with His bright and most beautiful face more lovingly than a father, more comfortingly than a mother, more kindly than a brother, and more joyfully than a splendid bridegroom, they are healed by this contemplation and their heart is glad and is far more wonderfully quickened and gladdened by this than a young child may be quickened and gladdened by the kind look of his gracious mother, or a bride by the voice and presence of her gracious bridegroom.

Men's eyes in that world are able to endure the bright face of God without harm to their sight.

Ps. 17:15

Here, however, let no one think that, since no human eye in this world can endure the bright, shining appearance of the sun without harm to its sight, it must be much less possible to view with human eyes the radiance of the divine Being in that world. For here on earth we still carry with us our sinful flesh and blood, but in that world the children of God are without fault, without blemish, without transgression, without sin, and without sinful passion and enjoy forever their wonderful exchange, that is, their blessed communion, joy, and bliss with God. Hence they are able with glad eyes to behold the face of God in holiness and righteousness and by the power of the Holy Spirit to endure the infinite fiery love of God, so that they do not perish or die from it but, as stated, are heartily quickened, strengthened, and gladdened by it.

The face of God is a true salve and comfort to the eyes of the elect in that life.

Gen. 32:30; John 14:8

The loving and wondrously kind face of God is a true *collyrium,*[18] a salve and comfort to their eyes; no intinction of strawberry or other prepared salve, ointment, lozenge, or powder can so strengthen a man's failing sight on earth and make his sad eyes so magnificent, alert, pure, clean, and keen as the face and being of God (who is Love itself) refreshes, enlightens, and cleanses the eyes of the elect in heaven. There with gladness they see the clear, bright light of the majestic glory of God face-to-face, and their soul is preserved, and with the apostle Philip they all with one accord declare: "We see the Father and are content."

The children of God will never weary of contemplating the divine Being.

And while in time we become weary and sick of and fed up with everything on earth (according to the saying: "All that is rare is dear; what is common is worthless"), the being and face of God is so very friendly, beautiful, and lovely that angels and men never grow weary or sick of it, but always see new beauty, new gladness, new comfort, new brightness, and new wonder at which their heart leaps for joy, and their eyes are eternally cleansed by it.

As the elect see the face of God, so God in turn sees them with joyful eyes.

Ps. 45

At the same time, God also keeps His eyes open, and as His children behold Him fervently without pause and out of heartfelt love never grow weary or sick of this contemplation, so He in turn looks at them with perpetual joy and finds His heart's pleasure in their beautiful form. And as they are thoroughly pure as angels, holy, unstained, and without sin so that they love their Maker, Redeemer, and eternal Comforter with perfect love, with all their heart and with all their soul and with all their mind, and as this fervent love toward God gleams and shines out of their eyes and all their members, so the King of heaven and earth takes great pleasure in this radiance and shining of His elect, counts them as the apple of His eye, and treats their appearance, beauty, and being as dearer, more precious, and more delightful to Him than the beautiful form of the sun, the moon, and all stars in heaven with their light, radiance, and brightness.

(6) In heaven, God and His elect hold sweet conversation.

In the sixth place, the love of God and the counter-love of His subjects in that world is not a mute love but is publicly demonstrated with gracious conversation, loving discourses, and joyful voice and confirmed with clear songs of praise so that the whole of heaven resounds with it.

18 I.e., a cleansing lotion used as an eyewash.

How sweetly and graciously God speaks to His children.

Ps. 60:6; Isa. 43:21; 54:5; 62:3; Song 4:11; Eph. 5:27; Song 6:4, 10

"God speaks in His holy place," says David, "and I rejoice." And that must have a wondrously comforting and wondrously lovely sound when God causes His voice to pierce the heart of all the Church Triumphant and speaks to them more tenderly than any father on earth, more graciously than any mother, more lovingly than any bridegroom, and more sweetly than any brother or sister, and says, "I have prepared you for Myself, that you should recount My glory. Behold, I, your Maker, am your Husband and your Redeemer, the Holy One of Israel, who is called the God of all the world. You are called My desire and are a beautiful crown and a royal diadem in My hand. I have prepared you for Myself, that your lips may be as dripping honey, and honey and milk may be under your tongue, that you may be indeed beautiful, without blemish of sin, without spot, and without any deficiency, beautiful as Tirzah, comely as Jerusalem, that you may break forth as the morning, beautiful as the moon, flawless as the sun, and terrible as the host arrayed for battle."

The elect thank God without ceasing and glorify Him.

Isa. 6:3

What great joy and bliss there must be where the whole heavenly host answers Him with jubilation, where angels are singing *nova cantica*,[19] and where the bells are ringing *in regis curia*, where they cry out one to another with a loud cry: "Holy, Holy, Holy Lord God of Sabaoth," and before the high majesty of God everyone from among the children of light, out of fervent love, humbles himself, pours out his heart with joy toward Him, and speaks as follows:

How the Church Triumphant glorifies her God.

Ps. 104:1–2; 45:2; 89:17; Song 5:11, 13–14; 6:2; Ps. 45:8; Song 5:16, 10

"O Lord my God, You are very glorious. You are clothed with beauty and majesty, and light is Your garment which You wear. You are the fairest among the children of men, and gracious are Your lips. You are our glory and strength, and by Your favor You have exalted our horn. Your head is the finest gold. Your cheeks are as the flourishing spice garden of the apothecary. Your lips are like roses, which drip with flowing myrrh. Your hands are like rings of gold set with turquoise. Your body is like pure ivory adorned with sapphires. All Your garments are myrrh, aloes, and cassia, when You come forth from the ivory palaces in Your beautiful splendor. Your throat is sweet and altogether lovely. You are forever my eternal Friend, chosen out of many thousands.

19 Here and following, the Latin phrases, meaning "new songs" and "in the King's court," respectively, are from the mixed-language hymn "In dulci jubilo" (H. Suso, 14th century), st. 4, lines 4, 6 (Wackernagel, *Das deutsche Kirchenlied* 2:486, no. 646). This hymn is a recurring theme in Nicolai's book, including the hymnody at the end.

The Church Triumphant's holy humility before the majesty of God.

1 Chron. 17:16–17; Ps. 8:4; Gen. 32:10; Jer. 31:3; Ps. 30:11; 21:6; Luke 1:49; Ps. 89:15–16, 1; 34:1

"But who am I, Lord God, that You have brought me thus far? that You regard me in the shape of a man, who are the Lord God on high? And what is man that You are mindful of him? and the son of man that You care for him? I am not worthy of all the mercy and all the faithfulness that You have shown me—that You have loved me with an everlasting love and with great loving-kindness have drawn me to Yourself; that You have girded me around with gladness and made me most blessed forever; that You have set a crown of gold upon my head and made me glad with the gladness of Your countenance; that You, who are mighty, have done to me such great things, and holy is Your name. O blessed, therefore, is the people who can shout for joy—those who rejoice in Your name every day and in Your righteousness are glorious. I will sing of Your grace forever and make known Your truth with my mouth to all generations. I will praise You at all times, and Your praise shall continually be in my mouth."

God's living voice causes joy in heaven and gives pleasure beyond all measure.

John 3:29; Eph. 6:17; Matt. 4:4; John 18:37; Heb. 4:12; Ps. 19:10; 25:12–14

This and similar heavenly discussions, conversations, and discourse are stirred up by the Holy Spirit and continue forever. And it is good to consider that if John the Baptist on earth could rejoice so greatly because of the voice of Christ, and if the written Word of God, grasped in faith by the power and working of the Holy Spirit, is so mighty, so lovely, and so cheering to the orthodox in this world that it overcomes all tribulation of body and soul, scorns Satan, drives out death, sweetens the bitterness of the cross, gladdens the heart, pierces it like a two-edged sword, is loved more than silver and gold, and is, as David says, sweeter than honey and the honeycomb—oh, then how many thousand times lovelier, more glorious, and sweeter must God's Word sound in that life, where God Himself speaks and with unspeakable sweetness causes His joyful voice to go forth from His gracious mouth into the ears of all angels and men.

On earth, we tire of conversation at last.

Eccl. 12:12

Indeed, on earth, as Solomon writes, much preaching makes the body weary. And even when best friends gather together and the time passes easily during their gracious conversation because of their great enjoyment, so that a day seems to last scarcely an hour, yet eventually they grow weary so that they must cease and go their separate ways.

In that life, where God speaks all things, they never tire of God's voice.

But the voice of the living God in that life becomes more and more dear, and the elect children of God never tire or grow weary of it. From God's mouth they continually hear new joy, new good tidings, new mystery, new delight for the soul, and new revelation, especially the heavenly wisdom of the eternal birth of the Son of God, of the eternal procession or eternal going forth of the Holy Spirit, of the eternal election of grace, of the wondrous creation of heaven and earth, and of the personal union of the two natures in Christ, of the work of redemption, of the almighty governance of all creation, of the heavenly goods, heavenly glories, heavenly pleasures, and the like, at which they marvel with joy and from which they derive powerful comfort, strength, life, health, and vigor.

(7) Out of great love God rests in His children, and they in Him.

Ps. 132:8; Isa. 66:1–2; Rev. 14:13

In the seventh and final place, the love and counter-love in God and His elect in heaven is full of eternal, joyful rest because God keeps an eternal Sabbath or day of rest in His children, and their love also rests in Him forever.

Human love and desire in this world are insatiable and can find no perfect rest in earthly pleasure.

A man's heart is like a boiling pot which is always bubbling, foaming, and running over with desires and fond affections that can never be truly quenched or sated in this world. For all that pleases on earth, such as food, drink, gold, silver, perishable honor, temporal splendor, beauty of the body, lust of the eyes, the body's pleasure, and the like—although men seek and strive after these things, they are not that perfect good in which the heart finds its perfect rest, that it may cease to boil and be completely at peace and desire nothing higher or greater. The first thing that pleases people when they are still children is beauty, then follows desire for marriage. In the marital estate they seek riches; in riches, increase of possessions as well as temporal honor and glory. And this thinking, seeking, and desiring have no measure or end since all perishable goods are finite goods—poor patches and beggars' rags, which cannot quench and satisfy the heart to perfect contentment.

God is the highest good in the world, and in Him the heart of the elect has perfect rest.

But in that life, one sees in God a good in which the heart has its perfect contentment and in which love finds its perfect rest. For there love and counter-love mightily and inseparably bind and connect God and His elect as one, and God is the most beautiful and fairest in the eyes of His children, the kindest and most graceful in their ears, the sweetest in their mouth and on their tongue, the most precious and valuable in their hands, the most encouraging and gladdening in their hearts, and the most lovely and most powerful in all their members so that they do not desire or will to be alone without God for one moment, and God in turn does not will or desire to leave them for one moment. God rests eternally in His elect, and they rest eternally in Him.

The Second Property of Eternal Life: Honor and Glory of the Elect in Heaven; They Are Like God

1 John 3:2; Rom. 8:29

The second property of eternal life is the honor and glory of heavenly love and counter-love in God and His elect, and this glory is that the elect are similar and conformed to our dear God in heaven. "We shall be like Him," says St. John, "for we shall see Him as He is." Likewise, St. Paul: "Those whom He foreknew, He also predestined to be conformed to the image of His Son."

Triumphant Christians in eternal life are similar to the divine Being.

1 John 3; Song 1:1–4; 8:6; Deut. 6:5; Isa. 49:16; Rev. 1:16; 1 Cor. 8:3; 13:12; Ps. 40:8; Jer. 23:5–6; Isa. 6:3–6; Eph. 3:10; 2:21; Rev. 21:22; Isa. 46:3; 1 Cor. 3:9, 16; 6:15

Yet in what way are they like God? Answer: God is Love itself, says Scripture. From this it follows that, since all godly, elect citizens of heaven in that world bear the image of God, they must be bright and clear seals of the most holy and most pure love of God, and as He gives light and shines into them, so they likewise reflect His radiance and light back to Him. (1) He is Love itself and loves His children in heaven with unspeakable love. So, too, they in turn love Him with all their heart and with all their soul and with all their mind. (2) He knows them as if they were stars drawn in His right hand. And as He knows them, they in turn know Him perfectly according to the measure given them. (3) Likewise, all that He wills, they also will. (4) He is wise, righteous, holy, and undying; such are they also. (5) He is Himself their temple in which they hold together with one accord as members of one body. And they in turn are also His temples and palaces in which out of great love He resides and rests.

In that world, the blessed are like our Savior, Jesus Christ.

Matt. 16:24; Heb. 1:3; John 1:12; Ps. 17:15; Isa. 8:18; Heb. 2:10–13; Isa. 63:8; Matt. 12:49–50; Luke 20:36; Rom. 8:16–17; Titus 3:7; 1 Pet. 3:9; Ps. 2:8; 45:16; 110:4; Rev. 5:10; Heb. 7:15–28; 8:1–2; 9:11–15; Rev. 5:10; Isa. 61:6; 1 John 3:1–2; Col. 2:9; John 3:4; 1 Cor. 6:20; 2 Cor. 6:16; Ps. 45:10–17; John 17:2, 22; 16:22, 33

Above all, they are similar and conformed to our only Redeemer and Savior, Jesus Christ. (1) For Christ is the Son of God, the brightness of the glory of the Father and the express image of His being. So through Christ they, too, are children of God, awakened and reborn according to the image of God. "Behold, here am I," says Christ, "and the children whom God has given Me. They are My people, and children that are not false. They are My brothers and sisters." (2) He is an heir of eternal life: so also through Christ they are heirs of all heavenly goods. (3) He is King and reigns forever; so also He has made them kings that they might sit with Him on His throne and wear crowns of righteousness. (4) He is a

Priest forever and appears eternally before the face of God; so also they through Him are made priests, that they might behold the face of God with joy eternally. (5) In Him dwells the fullness of the Godhead bodily and the Holy Spirit without measure. So also they through Him are temples of God and dwellings of the Holy Spirit. (6) He loves them as their Brother and Bridegroom. So also they in turn love Him, His brother and sister and heavenly Bride. (7) He deals with them in a wondrously loving manner and dwells in them. They in turn also deal with Him in the same manner and are perfectly one with Him. (8) He lives forever, and through Him they also live forever.

Glory of the elect in heaven based on love and counter-love.

Augustine, Manual, ch. 19[20]

All this glory of the children of light and their likeness to God which they possess is based on holy love and counter-love. "God the Father," says St. Augustine, "is Love, God the Son is Love, and God the Holy Spirit is the Love of the Father and of the Son. This charity and this love seek in us a thing like itself, namely, Love, by which we are united, connected, and bound together with God as through a kinship or consanguinity."

The entire Holy Trinity confirms the glory of the elect.

And this relationship, likeness, and glory of heavenly love and counter-love is eternally validated and confirmed by God the Father, God the Son, and God the Holy Spirit.

Heavenly adoption.

In the Church Postil for Pentecost Monday.[21] *— Likewise, tom. Witt. Germ. fol. 309*[22]

For God the Father sees all the elect in Christ and through Christ and through His only-begotten Son gives them a noble, precious name, calling them His children forever. "This comfort," says Dr. Luther, "is too great, the joy too high, the blessedness too exalted, and yet the heart of man is too small and narrow," and "the miserable beggar's bag of our old flesh" is too sleepy and lazy to grasp this with thoughts and words and to lay hold of it with the heart. Again: "The glory of the matter is so great that it does not pierce our heart. For it is too far from sense and too high above a man's understanding, that our poor, stinking sack of worms should come so far as to behold this magnificent glory of God forever and continually before our eyes."

20 Author uncertain, *Manuale* 19 (PL 40:959).

21 Although Luther's postil for Pentecost Monday treats John 3:16–21, the first quotation in the following paragraph is from Luther's April 22, 1538, Easter sermon on John 20:16–17: cf. AE 77:25 (= WA 21:214; 46:332).

22 The second quotation in the following paragraph comes from Luther's sermon on John 17:24 (Oct. 31, 1528): cf. AE 69:115 (= WA 28:195–96). This is also used by Christophorus Irenäus in his similarly named *Spiegel des ewigen Lebens* (Ursel: Nicolaus Henricus, 1589), published a decade before Nicolai's first edition.

Glory of the heavenly adoption.

Certainly, it is a surpassing glory that men dwell in heaven and are described as children not of the Roman emperor nor of the king of Persia nor of any other earthly lord but of the eternal, almighty God, and are called heirs of God and sons and daughters of God. The world boasts of its glory and thinks it a magnificent nobility and great honor when someone is the son of a famous king or emperor. And it would be an even higher thing if someone could truly claim to be the son of a holy angel.

The heavenly adoption is accompanied by the most loving works of the entire Holy Trinity.

But what is all this compared to the eternal life in heaven, where blessed men are children and heirs of the lofty majesty of God? This adoption is wondrously lovely and wondrously comforting and soars on its wings and rises high above all the pomp and glory of the world, inasmuch as it has the most gracious, most lovely, and most tender works of the entire Holy Trinity. For God the Father treats His elect more lovingly than any father on earth can; God the Son, as a dear brother and heavenly bridegroom; and God the Holy Spirit as a true comforter and bringer of joy.

I. How God the Father shows Himself to His elect children in heaven.

Eph. 3:14–15; 1 John 3:1; 4:19

There the Father's face radiates and glows better than that of fathers, mothers, or angels, that is to say, a thousand times more loving, tender, and joyful than if the angels in heaven and all parents, fathers, and mothers on earth could melt their tenderness and natural love together and show them simultaneously to one little child so as to gladden him in a truly angelic and fatherly and motherly way. For God the Father is Love itself and a truly loving Father toward all who are called children in heaven and on earth. But the elect, as children of God, resemble their heavenly Father, and as the Father loves them better than fathers, mothers, men, and angels, so they also love Him with perfect counter-love according to the measure given them, in a sincere and childlike manner.

This is, moreover, a true, heavenly joy that lasts forever and never ends. The fervent eyes of God the Father forever lighten and shine and flash with majestic and fervent love, and He reveals the fullness of this great love and divine brightness in His Son, and through the Son He shines on the hearts of all the elect citizens of heaven, acknowledges them all as His children, and sees in them, as in a clear, spotless mirror, the beautifully formed reflection of His divine being, which is called Love. The blessed, as glorified children of God, surrounded with divine brightness, in turn behold with glad, pure eyes the face of the Father as He is in Christ, His Son, the wondrously comforting Being who is called Love itself or the Father's Love.

II. How the heavenly Bridegroom Jesus Christ reveals Himself to the Church Triumphant in heaven.

Second, our Lord and Savior Jesus Christ, in whom God the Father and the whole fullness of the Godhead dwells bodily, also burns with unspeakable love and kindness for men. He acknowledges the blessed children of God as His dearest brothers and sisters and causes the all-triumphant, rejoicing Christians to be His most beautiful, most precious, and most noble Bride.

Glory of the heavenly Bridegroom and His heavenly Bride.

Col. 2:2; Rev. 1:14; Ps. 73:25; 45:9;[23] [Isa. 62:4;] Song 4:9; 6:4

There His eyes are pure fiery beams of love and fiery darts of love, or flames of the sweetest and most unspeakable kindness, with which He comfortingly wounds, comfortingly fills, and comfortingly turns to Himself the glorified eyes of His dear brothers and His dear sisters. And in turn they behold Him in such a way that their eyes, heart, mind, and sense and all their members burn with chaste, fervent, fiery, unfeigned love for Christ and desire nothing in heaven or on earth more dearly than Him. At this love the heavenly Bridegroom greatly rejoices and boasts before all the holy angels that the rejoicing heavenly Church is truly His betrothed Hephzibah, Bride, and beloved, who ravishes His heart with one of her eyes and with one chain of her neck, and her eyes make His eyes burn, and they are lovely to Him as Jerusalem and terrible as hosts arrayed for battle.

The blessed communion of Christ with His elect Bride in eternal life may be compared to no physical joy on earth.

Ps. 45:2, 13–14; Isa. 61:10

No natural friendship between brothers and sisters on earth, nor any earthly love between bridegroom and bride, can compare with this heavenly fellowship, this day of eternal joy, and this everlasting wedding feast. Likewise, the entire appearance and manner of the heavenly Bridegroom is far more pleasant, beautiful, and kind than the majesty, pomp, and prestige of a royal bridegroom with his royal bride and maiden in a great palace and finely built hall on earth. And as the great King of heaven and earth is a magnificent Bridegroom and the fairest of the children of men, so He adorns the Church Triumphant, His precious Bride, so that to His eyes she appears many hundred thousand times more beautiful, more magnificent, more glorious, and more lovely than a royal bride on earth dressed in wrought gold, a crown of gold, garments of needlework, pearls, necklaces, and graceful form, in which she pleases her king and wins his heart.

The dear citizens of heaven are all with Christ and through Christ glorified children of God in that life and eternal fellow-heirs of all heavenly goods. In addition, they are powerful kings and priests before God, who have overcome death, devil, and hell by the blood of the innocent Lamb, and reign with Christ

23 Luther: "the bride"; KJV and ESV: "the queen."

forever, having put on the garments of salvation and being dressed with the robe of the righteousness, as a bridegroom adorned with priestly finery and as a bride prepared in her chamber. They wear the crown of eternal life and dwell forever with Christ in one indivisible life.

III. How the Holy Spirit manifests Himself to the children of God.

The Holy Spirit gives people fervent tongues so that utterly lovely conversations are heard in heaven.

Gal. 5:22; 1 Cor. 3:16; Eph. 1:14; Isa. 65:13–14, 19, 24; Acts 2:3–4

Besides this, the heavenly Paraclete, God the Holy Spirit, makes Himself comfortingly seen and heard with His precious fruits, such as love, peace, and joy, which He there works in the elect children of God perfectly and without means and dwells in them and is Himself the eternal pledge, seal, and deposit[24] of their eternal blessedness and adoption, that they may shout for joy with good courage, have fiery tongues, and speak joyfully with God and God with them. And their most gracious conversation without doubt concerns the glorious deeds of God's kindness and the heavenly adoption, in which God tells the blessed children very tenderly how He made them out of great love, redeemed them through Jesus Christ out of great love, and elected them for eternal life out of great love. For these great benefits the blessed children thank their heavenly Father and their dearest Bridegroom as well as the holy, precious Comforter, and glorify the Holy Trinity with their eternal *Te Deum*, hymns of praise, and songs of joy.

The Third Property of Eternal Life: God's Sweet Inhabitation or Indwelling in His Elect

Lev. 26:12; 2 Cor. 6:16; 2 Pet. 1:4

The third property is God's sweet indwelling in His elect children. As it is written: "I will dwell in them," says God, "and walk in them and will be their God, and they shall be My people." The means of this indwelling is love and counter-love, or that heartfelt knowledge wherein God lovingly knows His own and is in turn lovingly known by them. As St. Peter says, that by knowledge of Him who called them, the children of light become partakers of the divine nature. And several times St. Paul calls them temples of God since out of great love the entire Holy Trinity, God the Father, God the Son, and the Holy Spirit, dwells in them.

How deep the love of God and of His elect extends in eternal life.

1 Cor. 8:3; John 14:21

Therefore, I must call that a heavenly delight and sweet knowledge or strong, piercing love in eternal life where God so knows those who love Him that He actually resides and dwells in them. Therefore, when we read beautiful passages

24 *Arrha*, i.e., earnest money.

of Scripture—such as when St. Paul writes, "If any man love God, he is known of God"; and Christ says, "He who loves Me will be loved by My Father; and I will love him and reveal Myself to him"; again: "And My Father will love him, and We will come to him and make Our dwelling in him," etc.—then we do well to stop and ponder what manner of knowledge and love this may be, and how high it extends with its power and virtue above all earthly and natural love and knowledge, seeing that it attains to their mutual inhabitation or indwelling of one another.

No earthly love or earthly friendship can extend so deep as the love of God for His elect.

For where on earth do we find such love or such knowledge and confidence between parents and children, man and wife, bridegroom and bride that in the power of such love anyone might actually possess his friend's heart and occupy it as his possession? The natural love imprinted on parents and children is so great that, when a mother sees her weak, ailing infant wrestling with death and lying in anguish and distress, she would gladly, if it were possible, tear a piece from her own heart and out of motherly love share it with the infant and add it to his tender little heart, that she might save his health and life. But this is impossible and cannot work, even if the mother's love were a thousand times stronger. Likewise, even in a godly, successful marriage, man and wife are, according to God's chaste ordinance, one flesh and one body by marital cohabitation. Nevertheless, this love does not extend to the point of enabling one person to share his heart, his soul, and his life with the other so as to dwell in the other, and that both may become one by such indwelling.

God dwells in His elect and they are one spirit with Him.

1 Cor. 3:16–17; 6:17; 2 Pet. 1:4; Rom. 8:9–11, 38–39

Our dear God has reserved such power for Himself alone, and He demonstrates it most powerfully in that world where He heartily loves, knows, and embraces His children; He is in turn so heartily known and embraced by them that by means of this piercing love He resides and dwells with great pleasure in each individual as in His own glorious palace, temple, and pleasure-house, so that they are with Him as one spirit, and no power can separate or sunder them. From this it is to be concluded that if any pleasure, joy, and attractiveness of love between parents and children, man and wife, bridegroom and bride, brothers and sisters appears in this transitory life, yet God's inhabitation or indwelling in the blessed children of light above by far and ineffably exceeds and surpasses all such loveliness, joy, and delight.

The indwelling of God in His elect is a deep mystery and yet wondrously comforting.

2 Cor. 6:16; Eph. 3:9; Rom. 8:9–11; John 6:56; Ps. 17:7, 15; 31:1, 20, 23–24; 1 Cor. 15:28; Rev. 21:3–4

And here we might justly wonder at this great mystery—that the depth of the Godhead in that life (for which all orthodox believers in this world long from their heart) reveals Himself so lovingly and dwells in the elect as in His temple, rooted in their heart by fiery love, so that they, being always led by the Spirit of God, are eternally in God and God eternally in them. Their heart trusts Him and confides in Him with all its power and with all its ability, and what they await from Him they find in truth to their eternal amazement, eternal boast, and eternal glory. And He is eternally their eternal good, inasmuch as He occupies and fills them eternally with the riches of His heavenly goods as His holy instruments and houses of delight.

The power of the saving faith.

Rom. 10:17; John 14:23; Rev. 3:20–21; [Matt. 11:12;] John 6:47–58; Ps. 22:4; Rev. 3:7; John 6:54–56

This power is indeed ascribed to saving faith (which is only a part and piece of the true knowledge of God) in this world, that it lays hold of Christ along with His heavenly goods and that our dear Savior with the Father and the Holy Spirit comes to stay with us through the Word and dwell in us through faith. Indeed, faith is likened to a mouth which eats and drinks, and the body and blood of Christ is the food and drink of that mouth. Therefore, whoever trusts our Savior and believes the Gospel takes the kingdom of God for himself by force and lays hold of Christ, and this taking and blessed laying hold pleases our trusted Savior so heartily well that He gives Himself to the believer for his very own and out of great love comes to stay with him as though He caused Himself to be eaten and drunk, according to His words, where He says, "He who eats My flesh and drinks My blood has eternal life, and I will raise him up at the Last Day. For My flesh is the true food and My blood is the true drink. He who eats My flesh and drinks My blood abides in Me and I in him."

Christ dwells in our hearts through the Gospel in this world, where faith is only in part. How much more gloriously, then, must God dwell in His saints above?

1 John 4; 1 Cor. 13; 1 John 3; Ps. 17; Deut. 6

Behold, out of great love the Son of God draws so close to us, even in this life, when our faith, our science, and our knowledge are only in part and a frail beginning. Now, therefore, if a Christian on earth, with such incomplete ability, takes his dearest Savior to and into himself when he eats and drinks spiritually, so that by such partaking he receives strength, power, and life and can then forcefully defy the devil and all enemies visible and invisible and say, "He who is in me is greater than he who is in the world"—if, I say, our incomplete ability does such things, what, then, does perfect love do above in heaven, where the children of God know their heavenly Father and Christ, the heavenly Bridegroom, fully, not through a glass darkly, but in manifest revelation, and see Him face-to-face and love Him fully with all their heart, with all their soul, and with all their strength? Truly, there God must dwell in His children in a wondrously loving and wondrously comforting manner so that from this indwelling of God's they receive many hundred thousand times greater power, greater joy, and greater glory.

The final cause,[25] or the goal, of God's indwelling in His Christians is that He may rest in them, and they find rest in Him.

In addition, it is wondrously comforting when we consider the reason why our dear God dwells in His saints above in an essential manner and is also Himself their habitation in which they join as one like members of one body. He is Love itself and burns with love toward His children and kindles them with perfect counter-love, which they have for Him. And it is the nature, character, and property of love that the more strongly one loves, the more he inclines to and yearns for that which he loves and by which he is loved in turn, and cannot be satisfied until they both grow into a single entity and become perfectly one. Only then has love reached its desired goal and found that in which it may rest.

The noble love and rest of God in His triumphant Christians explained by a comparison.

Eph. 5:31–32; Rev. 21:2; 14:15, 17; Ps. 132:13–14; Isa. 66:23

We have an example in those young people who wish to enter into the estate of marriage. The greater love becomes, the more they long for each other and do not cease until they, bridegroom and bride, are betrothed and then take each other in marriage. Then they both rest in love and are man and wife, one flesh and one body, according to God's chaste ordinance. In this way also God loves His elect in heaven and is loved by them in turn. He is Himself their temple in which they dwell eternally, and they in turn are His temples in which He also dwells eternally. And the end of this indwelling is sweet rest for both parties so that angels and men rest eternally in God, and God eternally in them. Hence David says, "The Lord has chosen Zion and has delight to dwell therein. This is My rest forever; here will I dwell, for it is pleasing unto Me." And Isaiah calls eternal life one Sabbath after another, that is, an eternal day of rest, where God rests in His Church Triumphant and the jubilant Church likewise rests eternally in God.

25 The same as an "end," that is, an aim, purpose, or goal. An end is the cause for which a doer acts or that for whose sake something happens.

God's rest in His spiritual temples as well as the sweet rest of the blessed citizens of heaven is to be preferred above all the peace and rest of the world.

But think, dear friends, what noble and sweet rest this must be where God, out of great love, dwells and rests in angels and men as in His palaces, and angels and men in turn find rest in God, their eternal rest. All worldly love, all nuptial love, all marital love, and all manner of the joy, glory, and restfulness of love and rest on earth are of no value next to this heavenly wedding feast and the eternal Sabbath in eternal life, when the true blessed rest flourishes and blossoms eternally and God pours the fullness of His great love into His children, rests in them Himself, and causes them in turn to rest in Him so that all their members, thereby lovingly strengthened and gladdened, rest in Him, and they neither seek nor desire anything more lovely, more lofty, more noble, more excellent, or more pleasant.

Benefit and fruit of the divine inhabitation.

John 15:5; Gal. 5:22; Rom. 14:17

And all this—the fact that God out of great love dwells and rests in His elect, and they in turn rest gently and lovingly in Him and rejoice in Him eternally—this inhabitation or indwelling of God in His saints also produces great benefit and many heavenly fruits. As Christ says, "He who abides in Me, and I in him, the same bears much fruit." And what kind of fruit this is St. Paul explains, writing that "the fruit of the Spirit are peace, joy, kindness, goodness," etc., and that the kingdom of God is righteousness and peace and joy in the Holy Spirit.

Fruit of inhabitation explained by a comparison.

Ps. 1:3; Jer. 17:8; Ps. 92:11–13

From these words it is to be concluded that just as a good tree planted by the stream of water puts forth buds, flourishes, and bears fruit in due season, and just as the soul of man is not idle in its body but occupies and fills the whole body with its operation and vital power through different offices, so that the eyes see, the ears hear, the nose smells, the mouth speaks, the tongue tastes, and all the members move—so also God dwells and rests in His heavenly children, the noble temples and spiritual palaces, so that from this indwelling they are filled with all divine virtues, filled with love, filled with righteousness, filled with goodness, filled with peace, and filled with all heavenly joy.

The Fourth Property of Eternal Life: In That Life, God Is All in All

1 Cor. 15:28

The fourth property is described and indicated by the holy apostle Paul when he says that in that life, God is "all in all"; in other words, God is the noblest, best, and highest good that fills all the senses, thoughts, and desires of the heavenly citizens to the full so that they see nothing dearer, hear nothing dearer, taste nothing dearer, feel nothing dearer, and speak of nothing dearer than the Almighty who loves them, who is Love itself and out of great love dwells in them.

In the world, all is vain, so the heart can never find perfect rest and quiet there.

In this world, all is utterly vain, and every enterprise is so full of toil and unrest that no one can express it. Even when a man sits at home and has external peace from friends and neighbors who surround him and live around him, yet his heart surges within him and is like a great, stormy sea, full of restless and tempestuous thoughts.

Great vanity of human desire and feelings in this world.

Eccl. 12:8

The eye is never sick of seeing and the ear never sick of hearing. A covetous man is continually desirous of money, and the more he amasses, the more his heart desires. Kings, princes, counts, and noblemen commonly seek to expand their domains and to acquire one territory after another. The youth are eager to listen when they are told of marriages, courtship, and young men and maidens. Others delight to travel around the world and gaze upon distant kingdoms, the beautiful lands of the Orient—Arabia, India, Persia, and Egypt—and Africa and the American continents, and the newly discovered islands as well. And yet all earthly seeking never makes a man say, "Now it is enough. Now I have found the treasure in which I will rest forever. Now I am completely satisfied. Now I desire nothing more. Now my eyes, my ears, and my heart are gladdened and sated to perfect contentment so that I may not wish or desire anything higher or nobler, and this truth holds firm: 'Vanity of vanities!'"

Whence it comes that no human heart can find continual and perfect rest in the world.

Prov. 27:20; 3; John 14:8; Ps. 17:15; 116:7; 16:9; 73:25–26

This all comes from the fact that earthly kingship, pleasure, splendor, honor, glory, silver, gold, treasures, and riches are finite goods, that is (as stated above), poor pieces and patches that cannot satisfy the heart of man and his five senses nor furnish them with perfect rest. Therefore, Solomon says, "Hell and destruction are never full, and the eyes of man are insatiable." But God alone is the infinite, immeasurable, and ineffable Good, namely, Love itself. And since, in His great love, He takes special delight in being visible to the children of men in eternal life and in dwelling with them, this indwelling gives a sweet, perfect rest to both parties, so that the ineffable love of God rests lovingly in His elect, and they in turn rest gently and pleasantly in God, saying with the apostle Philip, "Now it suffices us"; and with King David, "Be at rest, O my soul, for the Lord is my good and my portion." "O Lord my God," say all men, "now I am satisfied because I see

Your face, and now I care nothing for heaven and earth because I have You and because You are my portion and the comfort of my heart."

Testimony of St. Augustine, Manual, ch. 29[26]

Of this blessed rest St. Augustine writes very pleasantly in his *Manual*: "Surely," he says, "this is a true rest of the heart, when it wholly turns and is absorbed through desire into the love of God, nor hungers after anything else, but has its sweet and blessed delight in that which it embraces and in this delight finds its joy. And if, through vain and worthless thoughts, or else preoccupied by other things, it should be drawn away a little from this love, it hastens back again with great speed, esteeming it as exile to go anywhere else rather than to tarry and stay there. For just as there is no moment or hour in which a man does not enjoy and make use of the kindness of God, so there should be no moment or hour that passes in which he does not have his dear God present in his heart and mind."

Testimony of Johannes Ludovicus Vives in The Truth of the Christian Faith, *book 1*[27]

Likewise, Johannes Ludovicus Vives writes aptly of this, saying, "The best and noblest work of the will of man is in love. But love has delight and desire in acquiring the beloved treasure for itself and enjoying it. And once a man's will has obtained it, it rests and is happy. Now, according to the nature of how what he loves and desires ought to be used, so will it be good to him, and so will he also have to think himself. He cannot be perfectly happy unless he enjoys the greatest good, which may satisfy and fulfill the breadth of his love or his desire. Now, nothing can fulfill this desire but God alone. For all other things by which the will and desire of man may be incited and allured are too base, too weak, too brief, too fickle, and too paltry. Therefore, he finds perfection only in the enjoyment of God and in union with Him." Likewise: "All other goods cannot satisfy us. They vanish from our grasp while we possess them, and while they please us, they are too inconstant and dissolve so that the true good that we seek cannot be taken hold of in them.[28] Likewise, our union with God, by which we would be perfectly blessed, cannot find occasion in this life. Therefore, there is another life in which it is found. For in this life, on account of the great darkness of our flesh, we cannot know or love our dear God so fully as necessary. We are called away from this knowledge and this love by the body when it hungers or thirsts or is sleepy, sick or suffering, or weary. Thus we fail to enjoy perfectly these goods of God also. Indeed, the stronger love is, the more sharply we are tormented by the sting of desire. But when we have laid aside the body or when it has been changed, then we will see God far more clearly, love Him far more strongly, be united with Him most intimately, and enjoy His unspeakable goods."

26 Author uncertain, *Manuale* 29 (PL 40:963–64).

27 Juan Luis Vives (1493–1540), *De veritate fidei Christianae libri quinque* (Basel, 1543), pp. 33–34.

28 The Latin text of the first part of the quotation is given in the marginalia.

Orderly contemplation of God's being all in all.

We can ponder well the whole mystery of God's being all in all if we examine in an orderly manner, one after the other, man's five senses and inner powers of the soul and search God's Word to see how our dear God lovingly fills and quickens all things with His being and with joyful participation in His great, unspeakable kindness.

I. Concerning sight: God is the most beautiful good that the elect see in that life.

1 Cor. 13:12; Ps. 17:15; 1 John 3:2; John 14:9–11; 1:1–18; Col. 2:9; John 17:5; Ps. 89:15–16; Rev. 22:5; Isa. 60:19–20; Ps. 36:9

First, concerning the eyes, it is certain that the elect in the heavenly paradise see God face-to-face, not through a glass darkly as in this world, but in His great majesty and glory without veil or covering. They behold the most worthy Trinity with unveiled face and see the Father in the Son and the Son in the Father and the Holy Spirit in the Father and the Son. They also behold the personal, united natures in Christ, how the Word was made flesh and how the fullness of the Godhead dwells bodily in Jesus, the Son of the Virgin Mary. They see His glory which He had with His heavenly Father before the world began. They walk in the love of His countenance and rejoice in His name and are glorious in His righteousness. Neither is there any night, nor do they have need of lamps or of the light of the sun, for God the Lord lightens them, and His glory shines upon them, so that in His light they see light and are heartily gladdened, refreshed, and satisfied by it and desire to see nothing higher.

No glory on earth can so comfortingly gladden, satisfy, and fill a man's eyes as the face of God in heaven fills the eyes of His children.

1 Kings 10:9; Additions to Esther 15:9–14; Matt. 12:42; Eph. 1:18; 2 Cor. 1:20

The queen of Sheba calls those men and servants blessed who stood continually before Solomon and saw his glory. King Ahasuerus comforts his troubled spouse, godly Esther, and when he looks at her kindly and asks, "What troubles you, Esther? I am your brother; fear not," she answers, "When I saw you, it seemed to me that I saw an angel of God. Therefore, I was afraid of your great majesty; for you are terrible, and your countenance is full of glory." But what is this glory compared to the glory of the eternal heavenly fatherland which God, as the Father of mercy and God of all comfort, has made clean from all wrath and terror and filled with utter safety and joy, and where He causes Himself to be seen face-to-face in the most lovely manner and smiles kindly at His children, along with all the holy angels, so that they would not take the whole wide world in exchange for a moment of such glory?

St. Augustine in his Meditations, ch. 27[29]

Oh, how heartily and deeply St. Augustine longed for this blessed light, that he might behold God face-to-face in joy! "For," he says, "this (earthly) light, which is shut up in place, ended by time, varied by the interruption of night, and which we have in common with insects and beasts, in comparison to that supreme Light, is rather to be called 'night' than 'light.'"

Augustine in the Soliloquies, ch. 28.[30] *Heb. 4:13; 2 Cor. 6:14*

"O most ancient Light," he says further, "who shone on the mountains of eternal days before all other lights and to which all things were known and apparent before they ever began—O Light, who hates every spot, You who are the purest and cleanest Light: tell me, what pleasure do You find in man? And what communion has Light with darkness? For where is Your pleasure in man? And to what purpose do You have this pleasure in man? And to what end did You prepare for me a worthy sanctuary of Your majesty, that You should come to me and have the delight of love in me?

Likewise, in Soliloquies, ch. 36.[31] *1 Cor. 13:12; Gen. 15:1; Rev. 2:10; Isa. 35:10; 51:11; 2 Tim. 4:8; Phil. 4:7*

"When we come to You, O Fountain of wisdom, to You, O incorruptible Light, and to You, O ever-burning Light, and see You not as through a glass darkly but face-to-face—then will our heart's desire be satisfied with good things, then will it encounter nothing that it desires but You, O Lord, O highest Good, who will be the reward of all the godly and their crown of glory and their everlasting joy upon their heads, because You pacify them inwardly and outwardly with Your peace, which passes all understanding. Then will we see You rightly, then will we love You rightly, then will we praise You rightly.

Description of that eternal, blessed Light which the elect in heaven see.

Ps. 36:9

"Then in Your light will we see the Light. For 'with You is the fount of life, and in Your light will we see the Light.' But what sort of Light is that? It is an immeasurable Light, a spiritual Light, an incorruptible and incomprehensible Light. Indeed, it is an imperishable Light, an ever-burning Light, a Light that no man can approach, an uncreated Light, a Light of truth and a divine Light, that also lightens the eyes of the angels, that gladdens the beautiful youth of the saints, that is a Light of lights and a living spring. All this You are, O Lord my God. For You are the Light in which we see the Light, namely, we will see You in Yourself and in the bright glow of Your countenance when we shall see You face-to-face.

29 Author uncertain, *Meditationes* 27 (PL 40:922).

30 Author uncertain, *Soliloquia animae ad Deum* 28 (PL 40:886).

31 Author uncertain, *Soliloquia animae ad Deum* 36 (PL 40:895–96).

What it means to see God face-to-face.

1 Cor. 13:12

"Yet what does it mean to see You face-to-face but, as the apostle explains, to know You even as I am known? I will know Your truth and Your glory, that is, Your face. I will know the power of the Father, the wisdom of the Son, and the grace of the Holy Spirit, as well as the single and undivided being of the most high Trinity.

What kind of glory the contemplation of God is.

Phil. 4:7

"This knowledge and contemplation of God is the highest good; it is the joy of all angels and all the saints. Indeed, seeing God is the reward of eternal life, the boast of the heavenly spirits, eternal joy, and the true crown of glory. It is the true prize of blessedness, the true rest and repose, the beautiful peace, and joy within and without. More than this, it is the paradise of God, the heavenly Jerusalem, the blessed life, the fullness of blessedness, eternal joy, and the peace of God that passes all understanding.

Seeing God is perfect blessedness.

Num. 18:20; Deut. 18:1; Josh. 18:7; Ps. 16:6; 73:26; Gen. 15:1

"This is the true, full blessedness and man's perfect glory: that he would see the face of his God, that he would see Him who made heaven and earth, that he would see his Creator who made him and redeemed him and glorified him. He will see his Maker and know Him visibly; he will love Him and embrace Him with heartfelt love; he will praise Him and possess Him with worship. For He, God Himself, will be the inheritance of His people. He will be the portion of His holy nation, of the people which He has redeemed. He will be their salvation which they possess, and He Himself will be their recompense and their reward which they await. 'I am,' He says, 'your very great reward'" (even as great lords are accustomed to bestow great honor).

St. Augustine's understanding of how our dear God is the highest good.

Isa. 40:10; Gen. 15:1; Isa. 65:6; 2 Tim. 4:8; Rev. 3:11; Matt. 5:12; Luke 6:23, 35; Ps. 27:1; John 1:9; Isa. 60:1; Ps. 45:14

"Truly, O Lord my God, You are very great above all gods, and Your reward is a great reward. For You, being great, do not come with a little reward, but as great as You are, so great also is Your reward, since You are no different from the reward. You Yourself are the crowner and the crown. You Yourself are the promisor and the promise. You are the giver and the gift. You Yourself are the rewarder and the reward, even eternal salvation. Now, therefore, O Lord my God, my crowner, my crown, and the wreath of my hope, adorned with great glory: You are the gladdening Light, the renewing Light, and the beautifying adornment. You are my great hope and the desire of the heart of all the saints, and their desired one.

John 17:3

"To see You, dear God, is the perfect reward, perfect recompense, and perfect joy that we await. And this is eternal life, says Your wisdom, this is eternal life, that we know You, the true God, and Him whom You have sent, even Jesus Christ.

To have God and to see God is eternal life.

John 17:3; Ps. 31:19; 24:6; 27:8

"Therefore, when we shall see You, the only God, the true God, the living God, the almighty, invisible, uncircumscribable, and incomprehensible God, and Your only-begotten Son, who is of one substance with You from eternity, even our Lord Jesus Christ, whom You sent into the world for our salvation in the power of the Holy Spirit—when we see You, O true God, threefold in persons and one in substance, and You, the only holy God, apart from whom there can never be any other God, then we will have what we now seek: the eternal life and eternal glory which You have prepared for those who love You and which You have laid up for those who fear You and which will be given to those who seek You, who seek Your face continually." Thus far Augustine.

II. Concerning hearing: In heaven, God's is the most joyful voice, which cheers and satisfies the ears.

Ps. 51:8; 85:8

Second, God also satisfies and fills the ears of His elect, and His voice is the most lovely and most gracious which they hear. For they hear joy and bliss, as the Lord Himself says, and peace preached to His people and to His saints. And this gracious voice of His is the loveliest music so that no harps, no drums, no trumpets, pipes, lutes, citharas, stringed instruments, cymbals, or similar melodious instruments can gladden the ears of man in so wondrously lovely and comforting a manner as the voice of God when He causes Himself to be heard as the eternal Father, heavenly Bridegroom, and true Comforter of souls.

God the Father with His fatherly voice truly cheers all ears of His dear children in heaven.

Ps. 60:6; John 14:10; Heb. 1:1–2; John 3:16; Jer. 3; Isa. 60:21; Eph. 1:4–6; Isa. 63:16; 49:10

What can sound more comforting than when the heavenly Father Himself speaks and comforts His children as a mother comforts someone? When the Father lets His fatherly countenance be seen in the Son and speaks through the Son and says to every elect person, "I so loved you that I gave you My only-begotten Son. I have loved you forever and ever. Therefore, I drew you to Myself out of utter loving-kindness. O My precious son and dear child, you are the branch of My planting and the work of My hands for My own glory. Through Christ, My Son, I chose you before the foundation of the world was laid, and through Him I appointed you for adoption to Himself, according to the good pleasure of My will for the praise of My glorious grace, through which I made you acceptable in the Beloved, that you may be eternally holy and blameless before Me in eternal love. O My dear child, I am your true Father and your Redeemer; from everlasting this is My name. You will be forever glad and rejoice at what I do. You will neither hunger nor thirst, and no heat or sun shall sting you. Now shall the heavens shout for joy, and the earth be glad, and the mountains shall sing praises with the shout of joy because I comfort you."

The Son of God also causes His voice to be heard in heaven.

John 1:18; 15:15; 10:13–15; Isa. 49; John 14:2; Hosea 2:19; Matt. 7:7–8; Hag. 3:4–5; Hosea 15; Isa. 25:8; John 16:22; Rev. 7:17; Jer. 31:13; Isa. 61:3, 7; 65:18; Rev. 3:5; John 12:26

Likewise, it must strike the ears in a wondrously lovely manner when Christ, sitting in the Father's bosom, Himself speaks, saying, "Out of great love I gave My life for you. I took you as a captive from the giant of hell. I loosed you as the plunder of the strong man. And here in My Father's house, where there are many mansions, I have prepared a place for you and taken you for Myself, that you may be where I am. I betrothed you to Myself in eternity. I have married Myself to you in righteousness and justice, in grace and mercy. I will keep with you the faith and grace which I swore to your fathers long ago. Therefore, shout aloud and cry out, be glad and rejoice with your whole heart. I have redeemed you from hell and delivered you from death. I have swallowed up death forever, and I will wipe every tear from your face. Now your heart shall rejoice, and your joy shall no man take from you. Now I will lead you rightly to the living fountain and give you beauty, the oil of joy and beautiful garments. Now you shall eat and drink and rejoice and shout for joy with good cheer. And I will confess your name here before My Father and His angels, and you will see how My Father will honor you because you served Me and followed after Me."

The comforting voice of the Holy Spirit in eternal life.

1 Cor. 3:16; Ps. 132:14; John 16:7; Eph. 1:17; Zech. 12:10; John 6:63; Acts 2; John 16; Rom. 8:9, 11; Eph. 1:14; 2 Sam. 23:4; 1 Cor. 2:10; Zech. 9:9; Rom. 8:15; Gal. 4:5–6; Rom. 14:17; Gal. 5:22–23

In the same way, the voice of the Holy Spirit will be wonderful, wondrously sweet, and wondrously comforting when these words of His are heard: "Your body, your members, and your spirit are My temple and My resting place forever. Here I will dwell, for it gives Me great pleasure. I am your Paraclete, your Comforter, your Seal and the Guarantee of your eternal redemption and of your eternal life, the Spirit of grace and of prayer, the Spirit who gave you life, the Spirit of the Father and of the Son, the Spirit of wisdom and of revelation, as the light of the morning when the sun rises, of the morning without clouds, when from the brightness after the rain the grass grows on the earth. I search out all things, even the depths of the Godhead, and reveal it to you, that you may know how richly you have been graced by God. Oh, rejoice greatly and shout for joy! For I am not a spirit of bondage, that you should be afraid, but a Spirit of sonship, and I cause My fruit to appear in you as nothing but love, utter joy, utter peace, utter kindness and goodness."

The joy of Christians at the voice of God.

Ps. 97:8; 60:6; John 3:29; Song 5:2, 16; Ps. 45:2

What, therefore, does the Church Triumphant do in response to this supremely gracious voice of her God? "Zion hears," says David, "and is glad, and the daughters of Judah rejoice" because "God speaks in His sanctuary." She hears the voice of her Friend who knocks and praises His throat, because it is sweet and altogether lovely, and His gracious lips, because they are like roses which drip with flowing myrrh.

III. Concerning gladness of mouth: In heaven, God is the highest good of which one speaks.

Ps. 126:2; Matt. 12:34; Ps. 116:17–19; Rom. 10:10

Third, their mouth is also full of laughter, and their tongue is full of praise because there is nothing in all of heaven which they, the triumphant Christians, so highly exalt, glorify, extol, and honor as the mighty, omnipotent God, their eternal Father, and Jesus Christ, their eternal Bridegroom, and God the Holy Spirit, their eternal Comforter. Their heart is full of joy and burns with perfect, holy love toward the entire Holy Trinity. And whereof their heart is full their mouth overflows so that with joyful voice they extol, praise, honor, and glorify our dearest God forever.

How Christians in heaven praise God.

Ps. 75:1; Rev. 15:3; Hab. 3:3; Isa. 12:2–4; Ps. 150:1–5

"We give thanks to You, O God," they say. "We give thanks to You and proclaim Your wondrous works. Great and wonderful are Your works, O Lord, God Almighty. Righteous and true are Your ways, O King of the saints. The heavens are full of Your praise, and the earth is full of Your glory. O God, You are our salvation, and we are safe and do not fear. You are our strength and our song, and also our salvation. With joy, therefore, will we draw water from the wells of salvation and give thanks to You, O Lord, and declare that Your name is exalted. We praise You in Your sanctuary; we praise You in the firmament of Your power. We praise You in Your acts; we praise You in Your great glory. We praise You with trumpets, psalteries, and harps; we praise You with drums and the dance. We praise You with strings and pipes; we praise You with clear cymbals and sweet-sounding cymbals."

IV. Concerning taste: In heaven, God is a fountain and water of life.

Ps. 34:8; Rev. 2:17; Ps. 36:8; Song 5:1; Isa. 55:2

Fourth, they also taste how friendly the Lord is and eat of the hidden manna and are become drunk with the riches of the goods of His house, and He gives them to drink with pleasure as with a river. "Eat," He says, "O My beloved ones, and drink My joy and be drunk; eat the good that your souls may become fat in pleasure."

The Church Triumphant's joy and pleasure in heaven.

Matt. 8:11; Eph. 5:18–19; Isa. 55:1–2; Luke 1:15, 46–57; Ps. 103:5; Col. 3:16; Rev. 2:17; John 6:35, 41, 49–51; Isa. 40:29; Song 2:3; Ps. 103:5

They follow this joyful voice and forever sit at table with Abraham, Isaac, and Jacob and all the godly patriarchs and thus are eternally beautiful, lovely, and fat in pleasures, and not drunk with earthly wine, which leads to disorder, but filled with the Holy Spirit and with the water of Life so that they shout for joy and with good cheer, and their soul praises the Lord, and their spirit rejoices in God their Savior. They speak to one another with psalms and spiritual songs, singing and making melody in their heart to the Lord. And as He Himself is their manna, bread of heaven, and water of life, they receive from Him at all times new strength and new power, as though He quickened them with flowers and refreshed them with apples. Their youth is renewed as the eagle's, and they know of no dying or sickness.

The heavenly eating and drinking is incomprehensible.

Who now will tell us how this eating and drinking takes place in that life? Truly, it is a deep mystery that cannot be fathomed in this life, but it will be when we come to that world and know all these things as a present reality.

Eating and drinking in the heavenly paradise is not just believing in God but tasting His great loving-kindness through love.

Ps. 119:103, 105; John 6:40, 54–56; Ps. 22:26; 1 Cor. 6:13; 13:12

Yet we are able in some measure to ponder it if we let the Word of God be a lamp to our feet and a light to our paths. For, first, it is certain that eating the body of Christ spiritually and drinking the blood of Christ spiritually in this life is nothing else than believing in Christ and taking hold of Him with heartfelt trust so that He dwells and lives within us by faith. Now, in that life, faith and hope cease and only love remains. From this it follows that in heaven, tasting, eating, and drinking God's goodness cannot be understood as partaking by faith, but as a partaking which happens in the fiery coal of a pure, fervent love; namely, instead of the belly and earthly food (which are done away there), God causes Himself to be embraced by the children of light with perfect, heartfelt love, and by this love of His He makes them actually to be partakers of the sweetness of His essential Love and of His loving Essence, as though out of great love and kindness He gave and proffered Himself to them to taste, to eat, and to drink and thereby worked heavenly power and joy in them.

In eternal life, there is no interest in earthly food and drink.

Likewise, our dear God tastes so lovely to them, so sweet and so pleasing, that they desire no bodily food or earthly drink, no sweetmeat, no wine, nor any perishable refreshment instead of Him. God alone is their sweetest food and their sweetest drink, as St. Augustine writes so pleasantly of it and directs all his heartfelt longing toward it.

Augustine, Manual, ch. 12[32]

"O Lord my God," he says, "O Sweetness of love (or, sweet Love) and lovely Sweetness: let my body eat You and all my members be filled with the nectar of Your love and kindness, that from these my heart may exhale a fine hymn: O my God, You are Love itself, You are my honey and milk, my sweet honey and my white milk. You are the true food for all who are spiritually mighty. Make me to grow and increase in You, that I may eat You with a hearty mouth. You are my life by which I live. You are my hope to which I hold and my glory that I long to acquire. O God, hold my heart, govern my sense, guide my understanding, lift up my love, raise my mind, and draw the mouth of my spirit up to the streams of the heavenly waters," etc.

God is the sweetest and loveliest thing that His children taste in that life.

Thus our dear God, or essential Love (which God is called), is not only the most beautiful sight in heaven which the eyes see and the most joyful sound which the ears hear and the loveliest subject spoken of with tongues of men and angels, but He is also the sweetest and loveliest thing that they taste and eat and drink.

God finds in His children in eternal life that He in turn is pleased by them as a food.

Ps. 50:13–15; Heb. 13:15–16; Song 5:1

Now, therefore, as the great King of heaven and earth causes His unspeakable loving-kindness to be tasted and partaken of, so He finds in His heavenly Hephzibah or heavenly Bride that she is to Him in turn as a pleasant food, as milk, as honey, and as a sweet offering, namely, the praise offering and the bulls of her lips, and how her whole heart is inflamed with fires of love and directed so toward Him that she, the chosen Bride, so soars in Him, loves in Him, dwells, rests, and rejoices in Him, and so pleasingly serves Him as if she proffered Him her breasts and gave Him honeycomb and honey to eat and wine and milk to drink.

32 Author uncertain, *Manuale* 11–12 (PL 40:956–57).

The heavenly supper of joy.

Isa. 25:6; Song 2; Isa. 55:1; 65:13; Song 2:3–5

And this is the true supper of joy of which the bride in the Song of Songs boasts, saying, "I sit in the shade of Him whom I desire, and His fruit is sweet in my throat. He leads me into the wine cellars, and His banner over me is love. He quickens me with flowers and refreshes me with apples, for I am sick with love."

V. Concerning smell: In heaven, God is a fragrance of eternal life.

Song 1:3; Ps. 45:7–8; 133:2; Exod. 30:25; 2 Cor. 2:14–16; Phil. 4:18; Ps. 141:2; Exod. 30:34–35

Fifth, the name of God in His heavenly paradise is also like an ointment poured out, great in power and lovelier than any oil of gladness, any myrrh, any aloes or cassia (which fragrant spices are extolled in Scripture) may be, and costlier than the balm that flowed down from the head of Aaron into his beard and robe, which was prepared from the noble spices, such as myrrh, cinnamon, calamus, cassia, and oil from the olive trees according to the manner of the apothecary. He is an eternal fragrance of eternal life and causes His good ointment to exude a sweet smell. And as He is the sweetest fragrance to His children, so with their holy love they are in turn to Him a costly and sweet fragrance and incense offering and smell to Him lovelier than all the spices of balsam, stacte, galbanum, and pure frankincense so combined and prepared according to the manner of the apothecary that it should be called the holiest incense of all.

Smell of eternal life in the heavenly paradise.

Song 1:12; Ps. 45:8; Song 5:13; 4:10–11, 13–16

Scripture says that when the King turns, His spikenard gives forth at once His sweet fragrance. And His garments are utter myrrh, aloes, and cassia, His cheeks like a flourishing spice garden of the apothecary, and His lips like roses which drip with flowing myrrh. Likewise, the fragrance of the heavenly Bride is better than all spices, and her garments are like the fragrance of Lebanon. Her plants are like an orchard of pomegranates with pleasant fruits, with cypresses, with spikenard, spikenard with saffron, calamus and cinnamon, with all trees of frankincense; myrrh and aloes, with the best spices of all, as the fount of a garden and the well of living waters which flow from Lebanon. So also the Holy Spirit comes, always awaking like the north wind and coming like a south wind and blowing through the heavenly garden so that its spices drip eternally. With these and similar words the Scripture speaks of this mystery. Let us leave it there until we attain to its true understanding in eternal life.

VI. Concerning touch: In heaven, God lets His children feel Him, and He kisses them tenderly.

1 John 1:1; Gen. 15:1; Isa. 49:16; 41:10; 54:10; Zech. 2:5; Isa. 51:16, 11; Song 8:6–7

Sixth, to these are added the fact that in heaven our dear God, as the Word of life, also causes Himself to be felt since He truly embraces His elect and triumphant Christendom there and kisses them with the kiss of His mouth, saying, “I am your shield and your very great reward; and I have engraved you in My hands. I will strengthen you and help you. I will uphold you with the right hand of My righteousness. My grace shall not depart from you, and the covenant of My peace shall not fail. I am a wall of fire round about you, and I cover you under the shadow of My hands, that delight and joy may take hold of you, and sorrow and sighing be far from you. Therefore, set Me as a seal upon your heart and as a seal upon your arm. For My love is strong as death, and its jealousy is firm as hell. Its coal is fiery and a flame of the Lord, so that many waters cannot quench love, neither can the floods drown it.”

However, this embracing, kissing, and sensation of touch does not take place in a bodily manner since God, as Spirit, is not felt as are created bodies, but it is a deep and very pleasant mystery of which we speak with human words according to the precedent of Scripture and take our reason captive, that we may save the right understanding until that life, when we will understand it perfectly and receive it truly.

How the elect of God in that world rejoice at the kiss of their heavenly Bridegroom.

Gen. 4:1; 32:26; Mic. 4; 5:2; Jer. 31:3; Song 8:6; Isa. 12:2; Ps. 73:25; Song 6:3; 7:10; Eph. 1:13–14; John 10:28; Rom. 8:38

Yet at this most tender, everlasting kiss, the elect magnify the Lord, and their soul rejoices in the living God. “O blessed am I,” says the heavenly host, the elect Bride, to her King of glory and eternal Bridegroom, “that I have the man, the Lord! I will not let You go, O Ruler of the whole world, whose issues are from everlasting, who has loved me forever and ever and out of great love have drawn me to Yourself. Therefore, I will follow Your Word and set You as a seal upon my heart and as a seal upon my arm. And if I have You, O Lord my God, my salvation, my strength, and my song, I care nothing for heaven and earth. For You are mine, and I am Yours. And I am persuaded, assured, and guaranteed forever by Your Holy Spirit, that no man can pluck me out of Your hand—neither death nor life, nor height nor depth, nor power, nor things present, nor things to come.”

The heavenly embrace lasts forever.

This heavenly embrace, kiss, and communion of God with His elect children does not cease, nor does it meet with any satiety or excess, but gives pleasure eternally and is far higher, nobler, and more glorious than what can be grasped and fathomed in this world with human senses.

VII. Concerning the highest love: God is Love itself, and in heaven He satisfies all the love of angels and men.

Seventh, there is nothing surpassing all this which the blessed inhabitants in the heavenly Jerusalem heartily love or are able to love more than our dear God, who is Love itself and is able to satisfy to contentment and to fulfill all the love of angels and men with a wondrously comforting glance from His loving essence, so that they neither wish for nor desire anything higher than Him. Therefore, although in heaven there is also a perfect love of neighbor among the children of Light, so that one loves the other as himself, yet their fervent love toward God has the advantage so that they exalt to the highest degree and far prefer their almighty Lover above all creatures and love Him with all their heart, with all their soul, and with all their mind while they are all heartily loved by Him and He, out of great love, dwells in them as His stately palaces and sun-bright temples.

Augustine in Manual, ch. 18[33]

The soul of men is formed in the image of God, and in that life bears the heavenly image perfectly so that they in turn perfectly love their dear God (who is Love itself and by whom they are heartily loved) according to the measure given them. And as St. Augustine says, "If the soul is able to aspire to the nuptial joy of the Son of God and to enter into marital union with God and to take up the gentle yoke of love with the King of all holy angels—it is love that does this all, according as the soul shows that it is similar and conformed to the image of its dear God and wills what He wills and is minded as He is minded. This love toward God is chief among the affects and powers of the soul and subjects to itself all other affects, powers, and movements so that it alone may rule and grasp and possess the highest Good only, namely, our dear God. Thus is the soul united with God through love, and heartfelt love and counter-love make from the two one spirit, and in that the soul loves its Maker, heavenly Bridegroom, and eternal Comforter forever, all affects, all powers, and all thoughts of the soul must serve this purpose and be subject to pure, holy love."

VIII. Concerning the most blessed knowledge: In heaven, God is the most blessed Good, which the angels and men know with joy.

Ps. 25:14; 51:6; 1 Cor. 13:12; Jer. 31:34

Eighth and last, God is also the highest Good with His wisdom, which the children of eternal life desire to understand and are eager to know according to the measure given them. For there they have not only the firstfruits nor only a tenth part, but the whole harvest of the Holy Spirit so that they truly see and know the mystery of the Holy Trinity, the work of their wonderful creation, gracious redemption, and most blessed sanctification. The mysteries of God are open to

33 Author uncertain, *Manuale* 12 (PL 40:959).

them, as is His secret wisdom, and He causes them to know His covenant, not through a glass darkly, but in the light of the present, heavenly revelation, with living voice, so that no one says any more to another, "Know the Lord," but all know Him at once, both great and small.

The true knowledge of God in that world gives ever-increasing pleasure to the elect.

1 Pet. 2; Ps. 142; Sirach 24; Prov. 3

And the longer they scan with amazement the depth of the heavenly wisdom of God and consider it, the more they desire with all holy angels to look into it, never tire of it, never have enough of it, never grow sick of it, even though this lofty, deep, broad, wide, and immeasurable wisdom according to its infinite abyss remains incomprehensible, unfathomable, and impossible to measure or quantify. Yet it may to some degree be found, so that the highly enlightened children of God draw and grasp from this abyss as much as is necessary for them and see that the depth of the Godhead is utter essential love and look into it as into a fiery furnace, coal, and burning of this love, which fills the heavens and the earth. They have fundamental knowledge of their dear God with the depth of His wisdom and boundless mercy and trust Him eternally with great joy and bliss, as their almighty Lover, and know Him perfectly even as they are known by Him.

Brief summary of how God is all in all in eternal life.

Behold, dear friends, this is how our dear God above is all in all, where He resides, dwells, and rests in His elect children. He quickens, delights, and gladdens all their members, senses, heart, mind, and thoughts and is the most beautiful sight that eyes see, the most joyful sound that ears hear, the best fragrance that they smell, the noblest subject of which they speak, the sweetest savor that they taste, the loveliest sensation that they feel, the friendliest thing that they love, and the deepest depth on which they continually ponder, although this seeing, hearing, tasting, speaking, smelling, feeling, etc., all takes place according to an incomprehensible heavenly manner and our flesh and blood cannot fathom this great mystery.

St. Augustine must have pondered this mystery with great diligence.

There is no one among the holy fathers who so diligently researched this blessedness and hidden good as St. Augustine, who now and again speaks as pleasingly and comfortingly about it as if he had stood with the holy apostle Paul in the third heaven and had seen and experienced everything manifestly. This is why he prays so earnestly and heartily that our dear God with His lovely goodness would fill, possess, and gladden all his thoughts, heart, mind, and sense.

Prayer of St. Augustine in Soliloquies, ch. 1[34]

"O dear Lord," he says in his *Soliloquies*, "let me know You even as You have known me. Let me know You who are the Power and Virtue of my soul. Show

34 Author uncertain, *Soliloquia animae ad Deum* 1 (PL 40:863–65).

Yourself to me, O Lord, my Comforter, and let me see You, who are my Light and the comfort of my eyes. Come, O Joy of my spirit; come, O Joy of my heart. Let me love You, O hearty Life of my soul. Appear to me, my great Delight and my sweet Comfort. O Lord my God, my Life, O perfect Glory of my soul, let me find You, the highest Desire of my heart, and let me hold You, O eternal Love of my soul. Oh, let me embrace You, my heavenly Bridegroom, who are my highest rejoicing within and without. Let me possess You, O eternal Blessedness, let me possess You in the midst of my heart, O blessed Life and highest Sweetness of my soul!

God is the highest Good of the heart, the ears, and all thoughts.

Ps. 96:1–2; 18:2; [98:7]

"Let me love You, dear Lord, my strength, O Lord, my rock and my fortress and my deliverer. Let me love You, O God my helper, my mighty tower, and my sweet hope in all my affliction. Let me embrace You, O precious Good without which nothing good can be. Let me enjoy You, O most Excellent, than which nothing is more excellent. Open the innermost depth of my ears with Your Word, which is more piercing than any two-edged sword, that I may hear Your voice. Thunder down from above, O Lord, with Your mighty and powerful voice. Let the sea roar, and all the fullness thereof. Let the field rejoice, and all that are therein. Enlighten my eyes, O incomprehensible Light. Send forth Your beams and scatter them, that they may not see vanity. Let lightnings abound and frighten them, that the waters may be seen to pour and the foundation of the earth may be discovered.

The best object and good of the eyes, the sense of smell, taste, and all man's senses, is God.

"Give me, O invisible Light, eyes which see You. Create in me a place of rest, O Fragrance of life, that I may smell You and that I may hasten after You in the fragrance of Your anointing. Make whole the tongue of my heart, that I may taste You and know and distinguish how great and how manifold is Your sweetness, O Lord, which You have hidden and laid up for those who are fully in Your love. Give me a heart that ponders You, a mind that loves You, senses that recall You, a right understanding that takes hold of You, and a reason that clings to You mightily as the dearest and highest Good and loves You prudently, who are Love most prudent.

God is a life-giving Life. God is all in all.

"O God, my Life, for whom all things live, my Life from which I have life; who is my Life by which I live and without which I die; my Life by which I am raised up to life and without which I pass away! O my Life, by which I rejoice and without which I am afflicted! O my living Life, my sweet Life, and my dearest Life, which I can never forget: tell me where You are and where I shall find You, that I may decrease in myself and increase in You and stand upon You! Oh, be close in my mind, close in my heart, close in my mouth, close in my ears, and close with

Your help, for I am sick with love and must die if I do not have You with me, and if I simply think of You, I am as it were awakened from death.

St. Augustine has a heartfelt longing for God.

Exod. 33:20; Deut. 6:5

"Your fragrance quickens me, and Your remembrance strengthens me, but I am satisfied when Your glory, the life of my soul, appears. My soul burns with love and grows sick with remembrance and heartfelt longing for You. When will I come at last and appear before You, O God, my Joy? Why do You hide Your countenance, O my Joy through which I rejoice? Where can it keep itself so hidden—that fairest thing for which I yearn so deeply? I draw in Your fragrance and live from it and rejoice at it, but I do not see You. I hear Your voice and am quickened by it. But why do You hide Your face? Perhaps You say, 'No man shall see Me and live.' Oh, my dear Lord, then let me die, that I may see You, and let me see You, that I may die to this world. I do not wish to live; I wish to die; I desire to be released and to be with Christ. I long to die, that I may see Christ, and I renounce living, that I may live with Christ.

St. Augustine desires simply to leave this world that he may be with God.

"O Lord Jesus Christ, O Jesus, receive my spirit. O my Life, receive my soul. O God, my Joy, draw my heart to You. O my sweet Food, let me eat You. O Lord, my Head, govern me. O Light of my eyes, enlighten me. O God, my Psalm, gladden me. O my Fragrance, make me to live. O Son of God and Word of God, quicken and refresh me. O Lord, my Praise, gladden the soul of Your servant, and come to stay with it, O my Joy, that it may be joyful in You. Come to stay with it, O highest Sweetness, that it may taste Your sweet bounties. O eternal Light, arise and shine upon it, that it may see You, know You, and love You."

The Fifth Property of Eternal Life: Perfect Love of Neighbor

Lev. 19:18; Matt. 22:39

The fifth property of eternal life consists of the love of neighbor and is to some extent similar to the first property, in which the heavenly love of all the elect toward God is noted, even as, according to Christ's word, the second chief commandment of the Law ("Love your neighbor as yourself") is similar to the first principal mandate (that we should love God).

Living eternally with God in heaven means existing in eternal love with God. Therefore, the eternal life of angels and men is also a life of love.

For as eternal life, as stated above, is properly a life of joyous love, where God loves His children heartily and is also heartily loved by them in turn, and inasmuch as the Law fundamentally and chiefly deals with nothing else than love and is nowhere fulfilled to a greater extent or more effectively than in heaven, it follows that just as angels and men live there forever with God in perfect love, so that they love God with all their heart, with all their soul, and with all their mind, so also the life that they live with one another must be nothing else than utter love, utter blessed faithfulness, utter friendship, and utter everlasting joy, pleasure, and glory.

How tenderly and sincerely the angels and men love one another in heaven.

Isa. 60:18; 1 Cor. 13:4–5; Ps. 133:2–3

Therefore, when it is asked what the holy angels and blessed men above in heaven do with one another and how they live, we may safely answer and say that they love one another as themselves and thus know of no hatred, no war, no strife, no division, and no discord. No one is envious or boastful, no one is puffed up, no one acts immaturely, no one seeks his own advantage, no one is easily provoked at another, no one seeks to do harm, but all are perfectly kind and gracious to one another. It is a pure, fervent, heartfelt love among them, a pure joy and sweet unity that gladdens their heart and softens all their members more than the precious balm that flows down from the head of Aaron into his whole beard and upon his garments and more than the dew that drops from Hermon upon Mount Zion, because the founder of their gracious unity is God Himself, and they are strengthened and bound in compact forever with His Holy Spirit, and He inhabits His dear, like-minded children with His blessing and life forever and ever.

The great heavenly brightness, honor, and blessedness of the blessed angels and men in that life.

Matt. 13:43; Dan. 12:3; 1 Cor. 12; Rom. 12

In them a heavenly brightness is also seen so that, by the majestic inhabiting or indwelling of the Holy Trinity in them, they shine like the bright sun, although one has a preeminence or an advantage in honor above another according to the various operations and various gifts of the Holy Spirit, precisely as one turquoise outsparkles another, and the sun shines brighter than the moon, and the moon brighter than the stars, and one star has greater brilliance than another. Neither does any division or ill will arise over this, nor does anyone envy his neighbor on account of his special preeminence and advantage, but they stay together in unanimity so that each one rejoices at the other's honor, beauty, and gifts as much as if they were his own, and each wishes the other his glory as much as if it were his own.

Answer to the question whether the elect in heaven also know one another.

They love one another. Therefore, they also know one another.

1 Cor. 13:8

And it is wrong to dispute a great deal here and to raise questions whether the glorified children of God and citizens of the heavenly Jerusalem know one another so that everyone recognizes who the other is. For who would doubt it in the least, since Scripture testifies that the heavenly life is utter love? "Love," says St. Paul, "never ceases. Prophecies will cease, and tongues will cease, and knowledge"—knowing in part—"will cease." Now, then, if love never ceases, it lasts forever. And if the contract or covenant of love revealed by the Law is kept perfectly firm and indissoluble in eternal life, what kind of love and unity or joyful communion would the saints enjoy if one did not know the other?

Love comprehends two virtues within itself: knowledge and concord.

Indeed, it is the nature, character, and property of all love to encompass and comprehend within it especially these two virtues, which are knowledge of minds and agreement of will. For where friends love one another, they must know one another and be of the same mind so that they do not act contrary to one another.

From the love of neighbor in heaven it first follows that they know one another.

Now, because the love of neighbor is nowhere in the whole wide world observed so strongly, so gloriously, and so perfectly as in eternal life or in the heavenly paradise, where the blessed angels and men heartily love one another and in that love abide eternally, it therefore follows irrefutably that this love and such a life encompasses and includes with it the beholding and knowledge of persons, and that the angels must be known to men, and men to angels, and likewise one angel to another, and one man to another, a hundred thousand times better, more exactly, and more properly than husband and wife, parents and children, brothers and sisters, bridegroom and bride, neighbors, friends, and relatives in this world either know or have ever known one another.

All the elect know one another in heaven, even those who did not know one another in the flesh in this world. The elect see and know their God in heaven; likewise, in God they also know themselves from one another.

Matt. 17:3–4; 8:11; 1 Cor. 2:10–13

There Moses knows Elijah and Elijah knows Moses, even though in this life neither had seen the other with the eyes of his body nor known him bodily. Likewise, although the godly, believing centurion in Capernaum (who sought Christ in his trouble) never saw the holy patriarchs and prophets on earth in the flesh, nevertheless in that life he sees and knows them and sits at table with Abraham, Isaac, and Jacob. Likewise, the dear angels and blessed men there all know one another because they are filled with the Holy Spirit, to whom nothing is hidden and who searches out all things, even the depths of the Godhead. And here I can rightly conclude from the greater to the less: If the Holy Spirit is in the elect and dwells in them as in His living temples with such power, efficacy, and brightness that they have fully illuminated and most enlightened hearts and discern the depths of the Godhead with joyful amazement and eternal joy (which is a great and excellent glory), then in God, the almighty and eternal Light, they must truly know one another as well, and in the radiance of the glory of God each angel must know all the angels, and along with the angels, all men. Likewise, each man must have distinct knowledge of all men, and in addition to men all angels (despite the fact that there are many thousand times a thousand of them), and know how to name each of them by name.

Those who did not know one another on earth know one another in heaven; therefore, familiar friends, such as parents, children, etc., also know one another.

Now, if the elect who lived at different times on earth and never knew one another in the flesh know one another in heaven, then also friends and loved ones, such as godly parents and children, husband and wife, bridegroom and bride, brother and sister, relatives and neighbors who were together in this world and dwelled amicably and peaceably together in love and loss, can surely not be unknown to one another in that eternal life.

The loving knowledge of neighbor in heaven is a thousand times stronger, friendlier, and greater than it could be on earth.

Indeed, it is possible to say with indubitable truth that their knowledge on earth was utter patches, pieces, rags, and botchery compared to the blessed heavenly knowledge and recognition, with which they know one another a thousand times better, more exactly, and more properly, love one another a thousand times more strongly with fervent, heartfelt love, and embrace one another more tenderly than anyone in this world could imagine. The love of neighbor there is in full force and in full, lovely glory, as though they well and dwell in one another, and yet there is no undercurrent of sinful concupiscence, immoral passion, or swinish Epicurean[35] lust in it, but all is utter chastity, utter self-control, utter pure love, pure knowledge, honor, holiness, and glory. For here on earth they were still sinners, but there they live and love one another without sin. And in this pure love they find heavenly joy and heavenly happiness and know of no time, so that because of their great love, joy, and bliss, a thousand years are to them as a day, and what is a day in heaven would make a thousand years on earth.

From the love of neighbor follows the concord of the godly.

Next there necessarily follows from this love that they are all of one mind, and no one acts contrary to any other. Accordingly, what Moses, Enoch, Elijah, the patriarchs, prophets, and fathers of the Old Testament desire, the apostles and Christians of the New Testament also desire. God's will precedes and shines before them all, and in accordance with His guiding will, the will of them all is one will and one intention, and the whole sum of this will is that they love God with

35 A follower of Epicurus (341–270 BC), the chief representative of hedonism among the Greeks. Notorious for mockery of traditional religion and piety and dismissal of the idea of life after death, by the sixteenth century the epitaph "Epicurean" was popularly applied to those who sought material pleasure and free reign to passion.

all their heart, with all their soul, and with all their mind and, second, that they love one another as themselves.

In heaven, the children of light hold together very lovingly and are filled with all virtues.

[Matt. 12:34]; Ps. 103; Isa. 8; Eph. 4; 1 Cor. 13; Phil. 4:8–9

Accordingly, what the children of light desire in their concord they also do in concord, and their heart is filled with concordant love and concordant joy, and whereof their heart is full, their mouth overflows, so that they speak unceasingly of eternal life and of the supremely sweet love of God toward them, as well as of their counter-love to Him. In love they embrace one another amiably with kind and gracious words, cling amiably together, hold friendly conversations, and sing and rejoice forever to the Lord of Sabaoth, giving thanks to their God, praising their Maker, honoring their Father, extolling their heavenly Bridegroom, all obeying the Holy Spirit who dwells in them, and they are filled with perfect love for God and unfeigned love toward neighbor and filled with all honor and virtue, filled with righteousness, filled with chastity, filled with truth, filled with moderation. They speak whatever is true, whatever is honorable, whatever is just, whatever is chaste, whatever is lovely, whatever has a pleasant sound, and if there is any virtue or any praise, it is found mightily in them and is richly seen, heard, and observed in their words and works.

The Sixth Property of Eternal Life: Perfect Oneness, Where God Is as One Body and One Spirit with His Elect

The sixth and final property of eternal life is perfect union or unity, whereby God, angels, and men, through the indissoluble covenant of love, are all as one spirit and one body with one another on account of their powerful bond, since they are all very lovingly filled and thoroughly possessed and indwelt by the Holy Trinity and are all one in God, and God one with them, precisely as all the members of a man are one body with the head and cling unanimously together.

Proof of the sixth property.

1 Cor. 6:17; Eph. 4:15; 1 Cor. 12:12; John 17:22

To this union St. Paul refers when he says, "He who is joined to the Lord is one spirit with Him." Again: "Let us be perfect in love and grow in all points in Him who is the Head, even Christ, from whom the whole body is joined together and one limb clings to the other through all the joints, by which one assists the other, according to the work of each member, in its measure." And once again: "Just as there is one body, and yet it has many members, and all members are one body, even though they are many, yet they are one. So also Christ." "I have given them the glory," says Christ to His heavenly Father, "which You gave Me, that they may be one, even as We are one: I in them, and You in Me, that they may be perfectly one." And shortly before that: "That they may all be one, just as You, O Father, are in Me, and I am in You, that they also may be one in Us."

No human union or unification on earth can be as strong and as loving as to compare with the heavenly fellowship and unification of the angels and men with God.

Oh, the wondrously lovely and wondrously comforting union and unification described here with altogether wonderful words! On earth it is counted a joy, pleasure, and glory and may certainly be a joy, pleasure, and glory, and a desirable life, when husband and wife lovingly and graciously agree in chaste, marital love and are one flesh and one body; likewise, when parents and children out of innate, natural love cling together as one family, and brother and sister as one blood, etc. But what are all these unifications and natural bonds compared to the heavenly union and marriage wherein God, angels, and men are called one spirit, one body, and a perfect oneness? Surely, this heavenly union must be many thousand times stronger, more valuable, more precious, and more desirable than are all human unions on earth. Surely, it must contain nothing but utter heartfelt joy, utter boundless loveliness, utter unspeakable rejoicing, and utter heavenly pleasure.

Heavenly fellowship is described by Christ with admirable words.

John 17:22

We can note and observe this from the precious words of our Lord Christ when He graces this heavenly bond, union, and perfect oneness with a splendid name and calls it the glory of God: "I have given them," He says, "the glory which You gave Me, that they may be one, even as We are one."

Here consider, dear friends, the divine glory, how Christ and the Father are one. Then we will approach the second mystery all the more closely and understand all the better the heavenly union of the elect with God.

How the three Persons of the Godhead are one.

God is essential Love, and by means of the character of love He is active with love within Himself, as a living fountain in which utter works of love, such as begetting, being begotten, sitting in the bosom, and proceeding forth, are evident in the Father, the Son, and the Holy Spirit. And as the essential Love in itself suffers no essential distraction or division, therefore the Father, the Son, and the Holy Spirit (despite the fact that they have distinct properties) are not three gods but only one God, and one essence in three persons. And this *Unum*, One, or essential One, is within itself only glory, only joy, only life, and only pure pleasure because it is utter Love and the source of love. In addition, Christ is also one with the Father according to conferred glory. For, according to His human nature, He is the temple of the entire Trinity in whom the whole fullness of the Godhead dwells out of unspeakable, wonderful love, and not without great joy and glory.

The heavenly union of God and His elect may be compared with the divine unity of the Father and of the Son.

Retain well this mystery, and consider further how great a glory that must therefore be where God, angels, and men are one, and not in a simple earthly manner, as husband and wife become one flesh and are called one body, nor as parents and children are one family, or brothers and sisters are one blood—but so perfectly one that this unification can to some degree be compared to the union which Christ has with the Father.

Sense and meaning of the words of Christ when He prays that His disciples might be perfectly one even as He and His heavenly Father are one.

Namely, our Lord Christ wishes to show that there is nothing higher, nobler, lovelier, or better to imagine or find than the only God, who is Love itself and springs from eternal Love and is in His essence filled with works of essential Love, in that the Father begets out of love, the Son is begotten out of love, and the Holy Spirit proceeds from Them both out of love. And although through these works of essential Love three Persons can be recognized, nevertheless all three are one essence and belong to essential Love, which is called God, and is a deep glory, an unspeakable sweetness, and an eternal, perfect pleasure in itself. Furthermore, after this unity and after the unification of Christ with the Father, there is no glory to be found that may compare to this mystery and divine glory to any degree except the heavenly fellowship of God with His elect angels and men, whereby they are all perfectly one through perfect love and counter-love. Here God enfolds, encloses, and surrounds all His children with the fiery hedge wall of His burning love so that with one accord they rest in Him and praise Him eternally, and He in turn dwells, resides, and rests in them as His own possession. This, then, is such a glory that the blessed citizens and fellow lodgers in the household of God would not exchange it for the whole world—indeed, for the heavens and the earth.

How St. Paul expounds the sixth property of eternal life.

St. Paul likens this union and fellowship to a body having many members, yet those members are all one body only. So also God, angels, and men are like one man or one body.

The mystery of many members of one body explains the mystery of the perfect union or unity of God and His elect in eternal life.

Isa. 64:8; Zech. 2:8; 1 Cor. 3:22

What, then, do the members of one body do? They are joined to one another and come to the aid of one another as if he were their own. If the feet are wounded and injured, the heart is afflicted as if the feet were a part of the heart. If the head is weak, every member suffers with it just as if the head were its own. This all comes from the fact that they are one body and are all inhabited throughout by one soul. In the same way, the children of eternal life in heavenly paradise, as members of one body with the Holy Spirit (who is one), are also thoroughly absorbed and, as it were, possessed. God is the Head and says of them, "They are all Mine. He who afflicts them afflicts Me." Likewise, every man says, "All is mine. God is mine, the patriarchs, prophets, and apostles, Paul, Apollo, Cephas are all mine." So also without doubt every angel says, "God is mine, and all angels and men are mine, and there is nothing in heaven that is not mine."

If one rejoices, all rejoice, and if one man or one angel met with an adversity, misery, or accident (though this does not happen in all eternity), God Himself would feel it at once as if the apple of His eye had been touched, and the whole host of heaven, all angels and men, would feel sincere compassion through the stirring of the Holy Spirit, as if it happened to each of them. Then they would all, as members of the body, mourn one another's plight, spring to their aid, and not rest until the misery had been relieved. Now, there is absolutely no such danger to worry about in heaven. I give this example only for clarification, to show how the blessed union, bond, and unity of our dear God and His dear angels and men in heaven is immeasurably strong and powerful and how they burn with fiery love, with love's flames, love's brightness, and love's glory.

I. The blessed men in heaven are perfectly one with God.

There the elect and blessed men are one and as one spirit with the omnipotent and living God, whose image they bear, and are like Him in that they love Him as their Lover and know Him as their Knower, will what He wills, and are wise, righteous, holy, and immortal as He also is. They are also similar to and conformed to the image of our only Redeemer and Savior, Jesus Christ, and are with Him and through Him children of God, priests of the Most High, and glorified princes of heaven, who in Christ and with Christ appear before the face of the Father forever, wearing crowns of righteousness.

II. They are perfectly one in God with the holy angels.

Matt. 22:30; 18:10; Ps. 103:20; Isa. 6:3

They are also united and perfectly one in God with the holy angels, whom they are like, so that they have no more need of any bodily eating and drinking, nor do they marry nor are they given in marriage after the earthly manner, but with the angels feel utter heavenly pleasure, have equal joy and equal blessedness, see with them the most loving being and countenance of the Holy Trinity, and sing to Him the heavenly hymn of joy: "Holy, Holy, Holy Lord God of Sabaoth."

III. They are also unified and perfectly one in God among themselves.

Likewise, the elect men also keep unity among themselves and are as one body, perfectly one in God and similar and conformable to one another, equal in love, equal in knowledge, equal in will, equal in joyful contemplation of God, equal in blessedness, and equal in unspeakable joy. They love one another as themselves, they know one another as themselves, and one wills what the other wills also. Father, mother, wife, child, brothers, sisters, patriarchs, prophets, apostles, and all the elect are there all like-minded, concordant in the Holy Spirit, and joyful in the Lord. With one accord they love the whole host of the holy angels as themselves, and with one accord are loved in turn by the angels as if they themselves were angels also, and they together, both angels and men, have the same pleasure, same joy, same blessedness, and same life.

In eternal life there is no sadness or misery.

Rom. 6:23; Rev. 21:4

They know of no sadness, no sorrow, no anguish, pain, or disease, and no one laments to another his trouble, danger, or mischance, since they are complete in love and do not revile, injure, or persecute one another. So also God does not permit death (which is the wages of sin) in any way to intrude on the heavenly paradise with its diseases and days of woe, inasmuch as His saints there live without sin and are not poisoned with any sinful thoughts, much less with gross transgressions, disgraces, and vices.

In heaven there is no hunger or thirst, but God is all in all.

Isa. 49:10; Rev. 7:16; 1 Cor. 15; Ps. 17:15; 22:26; Isa. 65:13; Song 5:1; Ps. 36:8; Isa. 55:1; Eph. 5:18–20

In addition, they feel no hunger or thirst but are satisfied with heavenly goods. And although they may not eat and drink of any earthly bread, buns, wine, beer, or malmsey,[36] nevertheless they eat together of the love of God so that they are satisfied and drink so that they are quenched. They sit at table and their hearts are glad. For God Himself is their food and drink. He is all in all, and no food, no confection, no drink, no medicine, no incense on earth (as stated above) can be so valuable and pleasant to mortal man, but God Himself is in His elect angels and men, feeding them a hundred thousand times more delectably and sweetly with the abundance of His house so that they are satisfied with heavenly pleasures, and He fills them with His Spirit so that they speak to one another in psalms and hymns and spiritual songs, singing and making melody to the Lord in their heart, and giving thanks continually for all things to God and the Father in the name of our Lord Jesus Christ.

36 A strong, sweet wine.

CHAPTER V

HOW ST. AUGUSTINE DESCRIBES ETERNAL LIFE

Augustine, Manual, ch. 3.[37] *Dan. 12:3; Matt. 13:43; 22:30; 1 Cor. 15:44; Rev. 20:14; Ps. 92:12–13; 37:29; 17:15; Isa. 65:13; Ps. 36:8; Isa. 6:2–3; Ps. 103:20–21; 36:8b*

"WHAT IS it that you love, O flesh," says Augustine, "and what do you desire, O my soul? There in that life is all that you love, and there is all that you desire. If you delight in beauty, there 'the righteous will shine as the sun.' If you wish to be quick or if you delight in strength and the freedom of the body without all hindrance and handicap, there 'they will be like the angels of God.' 'For it is sown a natural body and is raised up a spiritual body,' not spiritual in essence but according to power. If you long for a lengthy and healthy life, there will be healthy eternity and eternal health. 'For the righteous will live forever, and the salvation of the righteous is from the Lord.' If you would fain be filled, there 'they will be satisfied when the glory of the Lord appears.' If wine cheers you, there 'they will be given to drink of the rich goods of the house of God.' If beautiful, sweet-sounding music appeals to you, there the angels sing to our dear God without ceasing. If you wish for no impure but only pure pleasure, there 'the Lord will give you to drink of the river of His pleasures.'

Heavenly love, wisdom, friendship.

Prov. 8; Jer. 31:3; Ps. 73:25; 1 Cor. 13; Ps. 133:1; John 13:14; Eph. 4:3; Rev. 3:21; 5:10; John 14:12; Phil. 4:13; Ps. 118:14; 145:19

"If you long for wisdom, there God's wisdom will show how wise it is in them. If you long for friendship, there they will love God more than themselves and one another more than themselves, for God will love them more than themselves, and they in Him will love Him and through Him will love one another, and when He loves Himself, then through Himself He will also love them. If you long for unity, there they will have one will, since the will of them all will be nothing but the supreme will of God. If you long for power, there they will be almighty

37 Author uncertain, *Manuale* 34 (PL 40:966).

according to their will even as God is almighty according to His will. For just as God can do all that He wills through Himself, so they also will be able to do what they will through God. For just as they will will nothing but what He wills, so He will will all that they will, and all that He wills must come to pass.

Heavenly honor, riches, and security.

Matt. 5:9; John 1:2; Ps. 82:6; Rom. 8; Gal. 4:5–6; 3:26–29; Ps. 23; 37; John 10:28; Rom. 8:35–39

"If you long for honor and riches, there God will place the godly and faithful servant over many goods. Indeed, they are to be called children of God, and gods themselves, and will be the heirs of God and fellow heirs of Christ. If you long for indubitable and constant security, there they will be safe and sure that they will never be lacking this good—so safe and sure are they that will never lose it, and that the benevolent God will never, against their will, take this good away from those who love Him, and that no one is stronger than God such that he might separate God and them or tear one from the other. Now if this good is so glorious and so great, how glorious and how great must that joy be?"

There is utter joy of love in eternal life. The love of neighbor is perfect in heaven.

Augustine, Manual, ch. 35[38]

"O human heart," says Augustine further, "you destitute heart, you poor heart, melted by utter affliction and misery and burdened with misery! How greatly you will rejoice when you may be filled with such precious goods! Inquire of your most extreme and deepest thoughts, whether they are able to fathom and grasp the joy of this heavenly blessedness! Now imagine that one of your dearest friends (who are as dear to you as you yourself) also had the same blessedness as you. Then your joy would be a double joy, for you would rejoice no less for his sake than you rejoice for your own sake. Likewise, if two or three or even more of your best friends were also partakers of the same good, then you would rejoice over each one as greatly as over yourself, since you would love each one as yourself.

Glory of love and love's joy in heaven.

"What glory then there shall be in that perfect love of so many holy angels and men (which are innumerable), where no one will love the other less than himself! For each will rejoice over his own joy and over every neighbor's prosperity precisely as if it belonged to himself. Yet consider, if the human heart cannot sufficiently rejoice over its own salvation, prosperity, and blessedness, but is far too narrow and slender for the purpose, how shall it then grasp and comprehend the multitude and the vastness of so many other joys belonging to men?

38 Author uncertain, *Manuale* 35 (PL 40:966).

How the elect in that life love God with all their heart, all their soul, and all their mind is inexplicable. Thus far the words of Augustine.

"Indeed, consider how joy as a rule agrees with love, so that you would rejoice over your friend's salvation, good, and prosperity just as highly and as much as you love him. Accordingly, everyone there in eternal life and blessedness will love our dear God without any measure and above all things, more than he loves himself and more than he loves all his neighbors as well as himself. From this it follows that he will also rejoice at God's honor, majesty, and glory without any measure far more than he rejoices over his own glory and over the glory of all angels and men. And if the elect will love God with all their heart, all their soul, and all their mind such that all their heart, all their soul, and all their mind are far too small to dignify this love, nevertheless, they will rejoice with all their heart, all their soul, and all their mind at the fact that all their heart, all their soul, and all their mind are still too small sufficiently to attain to the fullness of this joy."

Glory of the heavenly union.

Col. 3:14

In short, they all rejoice from their heart and are all perfectly one through the bond of perfection, which is love, as St. Paul says, and this perfect union, covenant, and fellowship, on account of the fervent love and counter-love, is full of majestic brightness, full of comfort, full of heavenly pleasure, and full of the great splendor of great glory, of the great joy and bliss, the likes of which no eye has seen, no ear has heard, and no carnal heart on earth has ever been able to imagine or conceive.

The glory of eternal life cannot be imagined, much less described.

Augustine, Meditations, ch. 27[39]

"Who can adequately describe or imagine," says St. Augustine again, "what an innumerable multitude of blessed spirits and heavenly hosts stand before the face of God Almighty? What an eternal feast of the contemplation of God it is! What joy without ceasing! What burning of love that never torments but gladdens! What desire there must be in them to see God, that they may be satisfied with beholding, and they are satisfied with desire and heartfelt longing, yet such that their longing is nevertheless not a sinful lust resulting in punishment, and are so satisfied with the contemplation of God that they are not wearied by it! Who can adequately describe how blessed they are to possess eternal blessedness? How gloriously they must be united with the true Light, inasmuch as they have become lights themselves!"

39 Author uncertain, *Meditationes* 27 (PL 40:921).

Augustine, Meditations, ch. 25.[40] *Song 4:7; Eph. 5:27; Ps. 45:10–11, 2*

"O Jerusalem, holy city of God, most beloved Bride of Jesus Christ! I love you with my heart and most heartily long for your beauty! Oh, how splendid, how glorious, and how majestic you are! You are all beautiful, and there is no spot or blemish in you. Oh, rejoice and shout for joy, beautiful daughter of the Prince, for the King desires your beauty, and the Fairest of the children of men loves your noble ways!

Joy of the Church Triumphant at her heavenly Bridegroom.

Song 5:9–10; 2:3; 5:4; 3:1 [,4]

"'But what is your beloved more than another beloved, O fairest among women?' 'My beloved,' you say, 'is white and ruddy, most excellent among many thousands. As an apple tree among the wild trees, so is my beloved among the sons. Behold, I sit beneath the shade of Him whom I desire, and His fruit is sweet to my throat. My beloved puts His hand through the hole of the door, and my body trembled for Him. By night on my bed I sought Him whom my soul loves: I sought Him and found Him.'

St. Augustine's heartfelt longing for the heavenly Bridegroom and His paradise.

Song 7:12

"O Jerusalem, I, too, have found Him and hold Him and will not let Him go until He brings me into His mansion and into His heavenly chamber. There, my dear mother Jerusalem, you will give me your breasts to drink from more abundantly and perfectly so that I shall never hunger or thirst for eternity. Oh, how blessed my soul will be, and again blessed forever and ever, when I shall see your glory, your blessedness, your beauty, your gates, your walls, your streets, your numerous mansions, your noblest citizens, and your most almighty King in His splendor!

Description of how beautiful and how glorious the heavenly city of Jerusalem above is.

Rev. 21:16–21; Tobit 13:18; Ps. 122:6–7; 76:2

"Your walls are made of precious stones, and your gates are fashioned from the finest pearls, and your streets are of pure gold, and in them a joyous *alleluia* without interruption is chanted. Your houses and habitations are founded on square stones built of sapphires and covered with tiles of gold, into which no unclean person enters, and in which no blemished person dwells.

Song 7:6; Isa. 60:19; Rev. 22:5

"O Jerusalem, my mother, how beautiful you have become, and how pleasant you are with heavenly delights. There is no hardship in you, such as we exiled children of Adam must suffer in this world and see in this troubled valley of sorrows. In you there is no darkness, no night nor changing of seasons. Neither is

40 Author uncertain, *Meditationes* 25 (PL 40:919–20).

there any candlelight nor sheen of the moon nor glimmer of stars, but the Lord Jesus Christ, God of true God, Light of true Light, and the Sun of righteousness, gives you light forever.

Glorious and very loving fellowship of God and His elect in eternal life. The king. The angels. The citizens. All the elect. The prophets. The apostles. The martyrs. Confessors of the truth. Men. Women. Young men. Maidens.

"The white and unspotted Lamb of God is your bright and most beautiful Light. Indeed, He is your sun and your brightness, that you may behold this most beautiful royal possession and glory without interruption. He, the King of all kings, sits in the midst of the city, and His children stand round about Him. There the choirs of angels make their joyful voice to be heard. There the assembly of heavenly citizens makes itself seen. There is the sweet jubilation of all the elect, who have been delivered from this troubled world into Your joy. There are seen the judicious prophets, the twelve apostles, and the victorious host of innumerable martyrs. There appear together the holy, precious confessors of the truth. There are the holy hermits and the holy ladies who overcame the lusts of this world. There are the young men, children, and maidens who disposed their time with holy living. There are the sheep and lambs which opposed the snares of worldly passions. They frolic all together in their dwellings, and each one has his distinction of glory, and yet they all share the same joy.

Perfect love rules and reigns in heaven.

"There complete and perfect Love has dominion since God is all in all, whom they behold continually, and as they behold Him continually, they burn with love for Him, they love and praise Him, they praise and love Him, and all of their work is to praise God unceasingly, without interruption and without toil.

Blessedness of the elect souls in heaven.

Ps. 42:2; John 17:24, 5; 12:26; 14:21

"O how blessed and again how blessed I will be forever and ever when after the release and laying aside of this body I shall hear the heavenly anthems of joy which are sung by the citizens of the heavenly fatherland, and the hosts of the blessed spirits in honor of the King! O how blessed and amply blessed I will be when I shall sing with them and stand there before my King, before my God, and before my Captain, and see Him in His glory as He has promised me, saying, 'Father, I will that they also whom You have given Me may be with Me where I am, that they may behold My glory which I had with You before the world was founded.' And in another place: 'Whoever would serve Me, let Him follow Me; and where I am, there shall My servants also be.' Again He says, 'Whoever loves Me will be loved by My Father, and I will love him and reveal Myself to him.'"

Augustine, Manual, ch. 17.[41] *Ps. 87:1–3*

"O my soul, come, and let us all turn our thoughts to the heavenly city where we are enrolled and appointed as citizens. Let us (as much as possible) as fellow citizens of the saints and fellow residents of the household of God, as heirs of God and fellow heirs with Christ, consider well the glorious condition of our widely renowned city and say with the prophet David: 'She is founded firmly on the holy mountains. The Lord loves the gates of Zion more than all the dwellings of Jacob. What glorious things are spoken of you, O city of God.'"

Augustine, Spirit and Soul, ch. 60.[42] *Tobit 13:16*

"O dear God, when shall I see that glorious and beautiful city of which it is written: 'The gates of Jerusalem are built out of sapphire and emerald, and out of precious stones round about all her walls'?

St. Augustine's longing for the heavenly city of God.

"O holy city, beautiful, glorious city, I hail you from afar! Dear, precious city, all my longing is for you, O dear, O beautiful, O beloved! I cannot forget you. You have possessed my heart. How heartily eager I am to be in you and as a citizen to have my existence within you. But that cannot happen to me while I dwell in the flesh and drag the old, callous flesh along with me.

Comforting description of the city of God.

"O how desirable and blessed a city you are! All your walls are of one stone only. God the Lord Himself is your keeper and defender. Your citizens within you all rejoice and are happy at heart. For how can they mourn as they look at you face-to-face continually? In you is no corruption, no defect, no aging; no anger, wrath, quarreling, discord, division; but perennial peace and unity, glorious honor, eternal joy, bliss, glad shouting, and exultation; everlasting youth, and beautiful virtue. . . . In you is salvation and blessedness, life and unity, peace and concord. In you is God, in whom the elect have all (that their heart desires).

Glorious things of the city of God.

Ps. 87:3, 7

"'Glorious things are spoken of you, O city of God! The habitation of all who rejoice is in you.' In you is no fear, no sadness, no sorrow. All that we wish and desire is received in You in abundance and with exceeding joy.

Glory of the citizens of the city of God above, where God makes Himself to be seen and makes all His own to be perfectly one in Himself.

John 17:21

"Indeed, all your citizens and inhabitants receive an overflowing measure and joy for which they rejoice very greatly in love, unity, and kindness. All the elect

41 Author uncertain, *Manuale* 17 (PL 40:958).

42 Pseudo-Augustine, *De spiritu et anima* 60 (PL 40:824–25).

are one, even as the Lord Christ prayed for them, which unity He also obtained in His prayer when, among other things, He prayed: 'Grant, dear Father, that as You, O Father, are in Me, and I in You, so those also whom You have given Me may be one in Us.' Therefore, the whole blessed city rejoices, and all that is in that city is jubilant and happy at heart. The blessed Bride takes pleasure and joy in her Bridegroom's speaking lovingly to her, embracing her tenderly, kissing her graciously; and it is her pleasure and joy in turn to praise and adore her dear Lord and Bridegroom forever and ever."

What Benefit This Description of Eternal Life Provides

Our godly ancestors, parents, children, friends, and acquaintances (whose souls rest in the Lord) are even now in eternal life.

2 Tim. 4:7; Rev. 3:11

Here, then, we have the brief and thorough report concerning the most blessed fatherland and joyful paradise of eternal life. Here we have the heavenly Jerusalem, the city of God, and the hall of peace. Before us have gone all our dear friends, father, mother, husband, wife, children, brothers, sisters, and all acquaintances who in this world held faith in the Lord Christ and valiantly fought the good fight and blessedly finished their course. Oh, the noble crown that is set upon them there by the great King of heaven and earth, now that they have gained the victory! Oh, the blessed joy and bliss that they see, feel, taste, hear, and experience from their joyful contemplation of God and their everlasting fellowship with all holy angels and all the elect patriarchs, prophets, and apostles, and all the elect citizens in the heavenly Jerusalem! Oh, the blessed rest! Oh, the eternal love of God! Oh, the great glory and the joyful life with which they are accordingly refreshed and comforted forevermore!

What we Christians would all do with one another if we understood the doctrine of eternal life rightly.

I rejoice from the bottom of my heart (I say again) and my soul rejoices in the Lord whenever I ponder this heavenly fatherland. And I have no doubt that if only this precious, lofty mystery and comforting teaching were implanted truly deeply within us and engraved on the tablet of our heart, we would spend the days of our life with no other thoughts in the wide world so much as with the sweetest thoughts of eternal life. Of that subject we would always be speaking, singing, and writing, preaching, and having discussions so that even each night in slumber and dreams, no other thought would appear and confront us but these.

Oh, how glad we would always be in hope, and from great joy and glad and jubilant zeal always be striving and seeking the heavenly Jerusalem, the city of God, and the dwelling of the Church Triumphant, that we might arrive there at the first opportunity! Oh, how we would make supplication and sigh unto God to that end and care nothing for all the world's splendor, honor, and pleasure, but in our thoughts, our faith, and our hope be in heaven continually!

Godly widows and orphans and all Christians who mourn the mortal departure of their godly friends and family can draw very rich comfort from this doctrine.

Dear troubled widows and orphans, godly parents and children, brothers and sisters, and all loved ones in Christ who mourn the mortal departure of your friends and relatives who have blessedly fallen asleep in the Lord: Oh, what rich, precious comfort you would draw from this sweet doctrine if you let it stir your heart! For although you are deeply troubled, and your eyes shed tears at the rift that death has made with your friends and family, and death has, as it were, taken away a piece of your heart precisely where love was the greatest—nevertheless, you would rejoice at the fact that your friends and family are with God in the heavenly paradise if you also (God willing) are soon to come there and see them again and know one another a thousand times better and love one another a thousand times more than you ever did on earth. For eternal life in that world is utter heavenly love, a life of pure joyful love, and utter heavenly pleasure, where God causes His essential love to be seen, and that love is heartily requited by His children. There the love of neighbor also is perfectly pure and without sin, and they love one another as themselves. And why else has our dear God taken your friends and family and set them apart from the world and separated them from you by temporal death but that you might turn all your thoughts from the earth up to heaven? He desires that we should turn our heartfelt longing toward Him and life everlasting, that we may all come together again in holy love, love's joy, and love's glory.

What young men and godly young women would do if they understood this doctrine rightly. Holy love's burning of the believing souls for the heavenly Bridegroom, Jesus Christ. Heartfelt longing for the heavenly wedding feast of eternal life.

Isa. 34:16; 1 John 5:1; John 13:1; 15:12–13; Rom. 8:28–32; 1 John 4:7–21

Young men and young women, if you could truly grasp and comprehend the joyful article of eternal life, you would likewise dismiss all yearning for worldly pleasure and concern yourselves with holy, heavenly love and sing utterly spiritual wedding hymns of Christ, the fairest of the children of men, and of His eternal wedding in the paradise of eternal life. Then you would say to your soul: "O my soul, the King of heaven and earth, Jesus Christ, sues for your hand—even the fairest of the children of men, who has gracious lips and is King of all kings and Lord of all lords. O my soul, He who made you is your Husband and your Bridegroom and is called Love itself, and when you were condemned to hell in your sins, He loved you even unto death, and out of great love for you He died, that you might be delivered from death to eternal life. And now out of great love He causes you to be called by His Word, that you might believe in Him and set your heartfelt trust in Him. Then out of great love He will take you after this life up to Himself in the paradise of His Father, and there in the great and glorious assembly of His holy angels celebrate an eternal and joyful marriage feast with you. O my soul, how beautifully, kindly, and lovingly God the Father, and the Son in the Father, will look and smile at you there and out of great love comfortingly fill, possess, and indwell you with His Holy Spirit, as if you were one body, one spirit, one mass, so that in exchange for this glory, joy, and delight you would not take all the pleasure and joy of the world! Therefore, O my soul, if you wish to love something from your heart, do not love the world nor all that is in it, but let your love be directed to the most beautiful, most amiable, most lavish and most splendid King of glory, to the God of heaven and earth, who will satisfy your heart to contentment, which no earthly splendor, joy, or pleasure can do."

How kings, princes, and lords would think if they understood the doctrine of eternal life rightly.

Ps. 42:1–2; 24:3–4; 82:3–4

In the same way, O kings and princes and rulers of the earth, if this article were truly familiar to you, you would concern yourselves with heavenly thoughts and say with King David: "As the hart pants after fresh water, so my soul cries out for You, O God. My soul thirsts for God, for the living God. When shall I come there, that I may see God's face?" In the blessed consideration that eternal life is a life of fervent and unfeigned love, you would heartily love God above all things, and after Him your subjects, and with this love you would exhibit the beginning of eternal, heavenly life. Out of fervent, heartfelt love for God you would defend the right and pure teaching of the Gospel in your cities, towns, villages, churches, and schools. You would make the gates wide and lift high the doors of the world that the King of glory may enter in unto you. Out of true, fatherly love you would do justice to the poor and the orphan and help the miserable and needy. You would, as children of light, cast off all worldly splendor and pride, seek after love, peace, and unity, not oppress land and people with new burdens and new taxes, but as princes of the kingdom of heaven you would burn with holy, heavenly love and shine forth and manifest Christian love in all your governing.

Diligence and care of all orthodox Christians who have rightly taken up the doctrine of heaven and eternal life.

Luke 10:39; Matt. 6:33

O Christians of high and low estate, nobility, townspeople, and peasants, husbands and wives, rich and poor, great and small, old and young! You would not involve yourselves and become so wrapped up in worldly dealings and worldly business, in the cares of sustenance, in temporal goods, riches, splendor, grandeur, and fleeting delights! With Mary you would stay with God's Word at the feet of Christ and choose the best portion which cannot be taken from us. Oh, how you would seek the kingdom of God and His righteousness! How sincerely you would love the almighty and loving God and think with all diligence how you might simply grow and increase in His love and in knowledge of Him daily! Oh, what a love of neighbor there must also be among you, that one should love the other as himself and let go of all rancor, hatred, wrath, bitterness, spite, and hostility!

Comfort for all miserable brothers of the cross from the article of eternal life.

2 Cor. 4:17–18

Likewise, all you poor, needy Christians, who in this world must pass through the valley of sorrows and pour from your eyes the fountains of sadness: oh, that you might know and understand this noble article of eternal life rightly! How happy you would be in hope and how patiently you would bear the Lord Christ's easy yoke which He has laid upon you! You would forever be mindful of eternal life and the heavenly fatherland and with the holy apostle Paul would say, "Our tribulation, which is temporal and easy, provides an eternal glory of immeasurable weight for us who look not to what is seen, but to what is unseen. For what is seen is temporal, but what is unseen is eternal."

CHAPTER VI

FOUR BENEFITS AND USES OF THE ARTICLE OF ETERNAL LIFE

TO PUT it briefly, we would all highly gladden one another at all times with this comforting doctrine of eternal life, and throughout our time on earth we would employ it for four different benefits and purposes. First, we would use it to admonish ourselves to walk constantly in holy love toward God and neighbor. Second, we would draw from it living and constant comfort in all manner of cross and tribulations. Third, it would give us glad instruction, that we might learn out of fervent hope in the fatherland to die to the world. Fourth and finally, we would let ourselves by moved by it to pray that we might have an eternal longing for God and sigh for eternal life.

The First Benefit and Use of the Article of Eternal Life: The Contemplation of Eternal Life Gives Incitement to Love

To speak of these four points in an orderly manner, I have no doubt, first, that if we truly remembered from holy divine Scripture what kind of conduct and life the elect lead in heaven, we would ponder it with all diligence, that our life in this world might (so far as possible) be similar to, and conformed to the image of, life in that world. Now, eternal life in that world and in the heavenly Jerusalem, for which we all have an ardent longing, is nothing other than an eternal wedding feast and a life of eternal, fervent love between God and His elect. When a Christian dies and passes through death into eternal life, the soul comes, as it were, to a joyful wedding feast and into a paradise where everything shines and burns with sweet, unspeakable love and with holy love's joy, love's power, and love's glory. So also we await the new heavens and the new earth at the Last Day, in which righteousness dwells, which righteousness will be utter, pure love between God and His dearest angels and men.

We are to learn to conform ourselves to the nature, manner, and quality of eternal life while there is time.

We would ponder this diligently at all times without ceasing, and, while there is still time, we would learn to conform ourselves to the nature, manner, and quality of heavenly life and to guard ourselves against all ungodly hatred, envy, enmity, and devilish works, which are contrary to love and belong not in heaven but in hell. As children of eternal life and as children of light, we would be filled with holy love and with holy friendship and with holy concord, in which we would walk continually and know of no devilish wrath, quarreling, or vengefulness. And just as a man receives the beginning of his life in the womb before he becomes capable of and participates in full life in this world, so also we would by the governance and power of the Holy Spirit begin in this world our heavenly life, which is a life of eternal love, before we are transported out of the realm of faith into the realm of sight.

To love God and one's neighbor is a heavenly life and a heavenly conduct.

1 John 3:14; 1 Cor. 8:3; John 13:35

He who loves God and his neighbor and grows and increases in such love leads a life of paradise on earth and has a heavenly conduct, even though he is still making his pilgrimage and journeying in the flesh. As St. John says, "We know that we have come out of death into life, for we love the brethren." And we would always ponder and consider such a life and walk in holy love if we had any desire to live in heaven and to have fellowship with God and His elect, who by utter love and counter-love are strongly tied and bound together into one body. So also love is the mark by which God knows His own, whether they have a part or portion in eternal life. "If any man loves God," says St. Paul, "he is known by Him." Also Christ says, "By this shall every man know that you are My disciples, if you love one another."

Order of heavenly love: how it is presented to us in the Law.

Oh, how we would let this be first, if only the longing and hope for eternal life burned and welled up in our heart like a fire! And we would constantly think about it and seek above all things that we might first love God with all our heart, with all our soul, and with all our mind and, second, that we might also love our neighbor as ourselves. For the Law prescribes to us this order of love, and this is the eternal, immutable will of God, which suffers no change and is never more perfectly fulfilled than in heaven.

We would turn all our thoughts, heart, mind, and sense to God and always concern ourselves with His love if we were truly familiar with the article of eternal life.

Accordingly, no blood in our veins and no vein in our whole body would stir—indeed, there would be nothing in our soul, nothing in our thoughts, and nothing in our heart that did not glow and burn with fervent, fiery love for God the

Father, for God the Son, and for God the Holy Spirit. Young men and young women would speak, sing, and talk to one another of no love so much as the love with which God loves us and of our counter-love for Him and how out of unspeakable love and kindness God dwells in them and they in Him. Man and wife would unceasingly extol, glorify, and highly exalt the love of God and with their children and servants would seek and desire nothing higher than that they might be a living house-church of God Almighty, and that with their body and soul they might be His possession, His temple, and His dwelling. A poor servant girl or a despised worm, in consideration of this noble article, would always go about leaping for joy and thinking, "What do I care that I am unworthy and despised in the world since God in heaven is my Friend, my dearest Father, my most precious Savior, and my highest Comforter?" In the midst of the cross you would take hearty comfort in the boundless love of God and always be full of heavenly joy and heavenly pleasure and heavenly glory. You would burn with heavenly love day and night and through God's Word would let your heart be wounded with such darts of love that you would feel it in all your members. In addition, you would daily sigh to the Lord your God and pour out your heart to Him with these words.

Prayer of a Christ-believing heart that is kindled with fervent love for God.

Song 5:8; Ps. 17:15

O my dearest God, I am sick with love for You and cannot be content until I behold Your face in righteousness! O my dearest God, let me increase in Your love and knowledge, that I may remain in faith and serve You in spirit always; that here I may taste Your sweetness in my heart and constantly thirst for You. O my dearest God, let me love You with all my heart, with all my soul, and with all my strength, and my neighbor as myself, that in this world my heart may be kindled and set ablaze with the light of heavenly life, which is an eternal life and a life of eternal love in Your paradise.

The fervent love of Christians for God the Father.

Augustine, Soliloquies, ch. 19[43]

"I love You, O Lord my God," my soul says with St. Augustine, "and long to love You with increasing devotion, for in truth You taste sweeter to man than any honey and sustain me more pleasantly than any milk may do and are brighter to me than any light can seem to me. Therefore, I love You above gold and above silver and above all precious stones. All that I begin on earth, that I do, and that I make displeases me and will not succeed, so wholly has love possessed me and the longing that I have for Your sweetness and for the beautiful taste of Your house. O God, noble fire that constantly burns and never goes out nor is extinguished!

43 Author uncertain, *Soliloquia animae ad Deum* 19 (PL 40:880–81).

O noble Love, bubbling over like a boiling pot that never grows cold! Oh, kindle me; oh, let me be wholly set ablaze, that I may love You entirely and all my love be directed only to You. For You are not perfectly loved, but little loved, when someone loves something next to You and not for Your sake alone.

Great benefits of the Father with which His unspeakable kindness is demonstrated.

Job 10:10

"I will love You, O Lord my God, for You first loved me. But where shall I find words adequately to extol and describe Your most excellent love which You have shown me? Countless are the benefits with which You have graced me. When I was nothing, You made me according to Your image, honoring and exalting me among all the creatures which You made." You milked me as milk and curdled me like cheese. You put on me my skin and my flesh. You joined me together with bones and breath. You gave me life and favor, and Your visitation preserves my breath.[44]

God the Father out of great love gives us His Son and the Holy Spirit.

Rom. 4:25; Joel 2:32; Titus 3:5; John 17:3

All this You did out of great love. And when I was dead in trespasses, out of great love You gave me Your dearest Son and caused Him to become man and to die for my sins and to rise again for my justification, that I might believe in Him and through faith be saved. Out of great love, for the sake of Your dearest Son, You also give me the dear Holy Spirit to enlighten, govern, and lead me, that I may rightly know You, the true God, and Him whom You have sent, even Jesus Christ.

Our heart is to burn with fervent, childlike love for God the Father.

John 14:23; Rom. 10:8

Therefore, I love You, O Lord my God, with great love and would gladly love You from my heart still more. Oh, grant me that I may love You always, as much as I myself desire and as much as I ought to love You, that You alone may be the end toward which all my senses and all my thoughts are directed. But where will I find You, my dearest Father, and where will You let Yourself be found except in Your dearest Son? And where does Your Son let Himself be found that I may love Him except in His Word alone? "He who loves Me," He says, "will keep My Word, and My Father will love him, and We will come to him and dwell with Him." This Word is near in my mouth and in my heart. Therefore, grant that I may love You in Your Son and love Your Son in His Word and love His Word in my heart, that I may love nothing, desire nothing, and seek nothing that is fleshly, earthly, or of the old Adam, but that I may love You and have You with Your only-begotten Son with His Word in my mouth and in my heart.

44 Here Nicolai expands on the final thoughts of *Soliloquia* 19.

A godly heart's fervent love for Christ.

Augustine, Manual, ch. 10[45]

"Likewise, I love You, my dearest Lord Jesus! I love You from my heart and wish that I could love You still more and more. Oh, grant me, Lord my God, fairest among the children of men, that I may desire You and love You as much as I desire and as I ought. You are immeasurable and are justly to be loved without measure, especially by us whom You have loved so exceedingly, even into death, and have redeemed us and done such great things to us.

Heartfelt longing for Christ.

"O Jesus, Love ever burning and never extinguished! Sweet Lord Christ, good Jesus, Lord my God, true Love, kindle and inflame my whole self with the fire of Your love, with Your sweetness, and with fervent longing for You. Oh, kindle me with Your loveliness, with Your jubilation, with Your joy, with Your delight, and with desire for You (for this desire is a good, chaste, pure, holy desire), that I may be entirely filled with the sweetness of Your love and thoroughly inflamed and kindled with the fires of Your love. Let me love You, my sweetest and fairest Lord and Savior, with all my heart, all my soul, and all my strength. Let me turn all my thoughts to You so that my heart is pained in my body and I may heartily cry and weep with fervent love for You. Let me perceive You with fear and trembling and have and hold You in my heart, in my mouth, and before my eyes at all times and in all places, that no foreign love may ever usurp and take hold of me."

Augustine, Manual, chs. 3–5.[46] *Song 8:6*

"Oh, come, dearest Lord Jesus, and stay with my soul and prepare it for Yourself, who made it and so dearly bought it, that it may be Your own and that I may set You as a seal upon my heart. I pray You, do not spurn my heartfelt supplication, since before I called upon You, You called me and sought me, to the end that I might be Your own possession and seek You, and having sought You, might find You, and having found You, might love You. Now, therefore, I have sought You and have found You, O Lord my God, and I desire to love You.

Outside of Christ there is nothing to satisfy our heart.

"Therefore, multiply in me a fervent longing for You, and do not deny me that for which I implore You. If You gave me all that You have made, all that would still be unable to satisfy me, Your servant, if You did not give me Yourself. Oh, my God, give me Yourself. Behold, I love You heartily, and if that is too little, let me love You even more strongly. I am surrounded with Your love and burn with fervent longing for You. You have possessed my heart, and I cannot and will not forget You forever.

45 Author uncertain, *Manuale* 10 (PL 40:956).

46 Author uncertain, *Manuale* 10 (PL 40:953–54).

Love for Christ lightens all temporal sorrows and temptations.

"Behold, while my soul sighs for You and thinks on Your unspeakable goodness, I feel the lightening of my sorrow and misery in this world, and the burdens of my flesh do not weigh so heavily upon me as they usually do. Indeed, my confused and restless thoughts relent, and my mortality and my manifold tribulation, sorrow, and misery do not afflict me as they are accustomed to afflict me. Everything is quiet, and all things must hold still. My heart burns, my mind is glad, my memory is renewed, my understanding grows clear, and my spirit is kindled with fervent desire to see You and seeks with great love the invisible bounties of heaven.

Desire and longing of the godly heart to sit at table with Christ in heaven.

"Alas, woe to the poor soul that does not seek or love Christ! How it must faint and wither in its misery! All that a man loves is futile if he does not love You, O Lord my God. He who does not remember to live for Your sake, for Your praise, and for Your honor is nothing and nowhere to be esteemed. He who will not live for You is dead even while he lives, and he who is not wise in You is a fool.

A believing heart is to be entirely devoted to the Lord Christ.

"O most merciful Lord Jesus, I commit myself to You. I devote and deliver myself to You, and through You I am what I am. To You I live, and only in You am I wise. I trust in You, I build upon You, and my whole confidence rests upon You, who will raise me up from the dead, who make me to live and furnish me with rest. You alone do I desire, You do I love, upon You do I call, with You will I remain, with You will I reign, and with You will I be eternally saved. A soul that does not seek You and does not love You loves the world and serves iniquity. It is subject to sins and can never be still and never be safe.

Glorious wish and desire that one may love and praise Christ forever.

"O most merciful Lord Jesus, grant that my senses may forever serve You. On this my troublesome journey and pilgrimage let me constantly sigh after You and let my heart burn with love for You. O my God, let my soul rest in You, and in fainting let it behold You. Let me sing to Your praise with great jubilation, and grant that in this I may find my comfort in my misery and that my mind may turn away from the heat of all worldly thoughts and take refuge in the shadow of Your wings. Let my heart have rest and peace in You, for outside of You is, as it were, a great sea filled with restless thoughts, which are the roaring floods, billows, and waves of water.

St. Augustine has a deep longing for the joyous table of eternal life.

Luke 1:78; John 6:32–35; Rev. 3:20; Ps. 36:8; 1 Cor. 15

"O rich God, who are able to satisfy us so generously with good food of heaven! Feed me also, who am so weary, and set aright my scattered thoughts again.

Deliver me, a poor prisoner, and heal my broken and contrite spirit. Behold, I stand before Your door of grace and knock with my prayer and ask You by Your heartfelt mercy, with which You have visited us, O Dayspring from on high! Command that it may be opened unto me, who am needy, that with free access I may come to stay with You and rest in You and be fed and refreshed with Your heavenly bread. For You are the heavenly manna and living spring of water. You are the Light of eternal glory and all that from which those who love You draw their blessed life.

Prayer that Christ would come to stay with the believing heart and make His home therein.

"O my God, who is the Light of all hearts who behold You and the Life of all souls who love You and the Strength of all minds that seek You: grant me that I may walk in Your holy love. Come, I pray, and stay in my heart and intoxicate it with the streams of Your delight, that it may forget all temporal things and seek after eternal goods. I am ashamed and pained to see and endure what the despicable world perpetrates and achieves. What I see on earth is utter sorrow to me, and what I hear concerning perishing things is hard for me to hear. Therefore, help me, O Lord my God, and grant my heart true blessed joy. Come to me, oh, come to me, and stay with me, and let me see Your face!

The habitation of the human heart is sinful and ruinous, but Christ can purify it and raise it up again.

"And yet my soul is as a narrow house and far too small and narrow to receive You until You come to stay in it, that it may be enlarged by You. It is very decrepit, so repair it and make it ready for Your habitation. I also confess and know that it is polluted with many vices at which Your pure, holy eyes must surely recoil in disgust. But who can cleanse it except You, and to whom shall I bring my complaint but to You alone, Lord Jesus Christ? Forgive me my hidden faults and preserve me from pride.

For Christ's sake St. Augustine desires to die to all worldly lusts.

"O sweet Savior, Lord Christ, good Jesus, grant me out of fervent love and yearning desire for You that I may lay aside and cast off all fleshly lusts and all earthly desires! Let me not obey the flesh's passions, but grant that the flesh may be subject to the soul and the soul to the reason and my reason to Your grace; and let my whole self and all that I am and have within and without be subject to You. Grant me that my heart, my tongue, and all my members may praise You. Enlarge my senses also, and turn the eyes of my heart up to You on high, that my spirit may come to You with nimble thoughts and reach You, who are eternal Wisdom. I ask You also to release me from all the bonds of temporal care, hindrance, danger, and adversity, that setting behind all things, I may hasten to You, be concerned with You only, and wait constantly on You."

Augustine, Meditations, ch. 35[47]

"Ah, sweetest Jesus! Ah, most merciful, most beloved, most precious, most desirable, most amiable, and most beautiful Jesus! Pour deeply into my heart, I beseech You, the streams of Your sweetness and the flame of Your love, that I may desire nothing and think nothing that is earthly, fleshly, and perishable, but that I may love only You and have only You in my heart and my mind. Write upon the tablet of my heart Your will and Your statutes, that I may have You, O Lord, my God and Maker (who are full, immeasurable, and unspeakable sweetness), and Your commandments constantly and continually before my eyes.

"Oh, kindle my soul with Your fire, which You brought down from heaven to earth, that it may burn exceedingly. Oh, kindle me therewith, that with tears I may daily offer to You a broken spirit and contrite heart. O sweet Jesus Christ, gracious Jesus, how greatly I long for You! Therefore, I pray You with all my heart, give me a holy, blameless love for You to fill me, enfold me, and entirely possess me, and give me manifest signs of that love, that my eyes may be two living wells of water and springs of tears, constantly flowing and overflowing, so that my tears may be a testimony to my fervent love for You and reveal openly how greatly my soul loves You and how its tears cannot be contained for its fervent and heartfelt love for You."

Augustine, Meditations, ch. 39[48]

"I know and confess, O Lord my God, that You made me, wherefore I am wholly indebted to You with all that I have. You also redeemed me and were made man for me, wherefore I also owe You even more than I am, if only I had more. I owe You something greater than I am, as much greater as You are greater than I. But behold, I have no more, and without You I have nothing that I could give You. Therefore, take me and draw me to Yourself, that I may be Your own—Your own with true following and Your own with fervent love."

Prayer and heartfelt sigh to God the Holy Spirit.

Likewise, I love You, O Lord God, Holy Spirit, who are the Spirit of the Father and of the Son, and out of great love enlighten me and out of great love make me to live. O true Light, holy Light, wondrously lovely and comforting Light! Come with great power and break into my dark heart, and lighten it with Your radiance and brightness. Wound all my most hidden and inmost thoughts with the arrows of Your love, and kindle them with the burning flames of heartfelt desire and of heartfelt longing for You. Come and dwell in me and make me a residence of God the Father and of His only-begotten Son. Come, most gracious Comforter, come, holy Light, precious refuge, come and give me to drink the rivers of Your pleasures, that I may not taste nor be pleased by the poisonous sweetness of this world.

47 Author uncertain, *Meditationes* 35 (PL:928).
48 Author uncertain, *Meditationes* 39 (PL:938).

Augustine, Soliloquies, ch. 34[49]

"O Lord my God, the light of Your love and of Your knowledge has risen in my heart, for which I am glad. It has risen like the morning star and gladdened all my members. Oh, that it might be filled and have its full brightness! Oh, increase it, that it may grow and wholly encompass me. Behold, I feel great joy in my members. What kind of joy can this be? What kind of fire can this be that so warms my heart? What kind of light can this be that so illumines and lightens my heart?

Prayer and thanksgiving. Our love for God in this world is partial, but in the next life it will be perfect.

1 Cor. 13:12; Ps. 118:15, 24

"Enlighten me, O Lord my God, and purify the eyes of my heart, that I may see You with pure eyes, since no man sees You unless he is pure in heart. Take away and remove from me the scales of my darkness, that I may see You Yourself, and in Your light see light; so will I give thanks to You, O Lord, my eternal Light. Behold, I see You with the eyes of my heart. O God, increase and strengthen this sight in me, that I may remember the wonders of Your right hand, who are so wonderful among Your saints. I thank You, my dearest Light. Behold, I see You, yet through a glass darkly. But when shall it be face-to-face? When shall the day of joy and rejoicing arrive, when I will go into the tabernacles of the righteous and to the house of God, that I may see You face-to-face and that my highest wish and my desire may at last be fulfilled?"

The nature and mind of a true Christian who rightly loves the Lord his God.

Behold, dear friends, it is in this form and with such words that we would pour out our heart to God and have an incessant longing for Him, if only the doctrine of eternal life were rightly planted and inculcated in us!

Amazement of a God-loving Christian at the world's folly and blindness.

Augustine, Manual, ch. 28[50]

"For he who truly loves God always thinks: 'When shall I come to God? When shall I leave the world? When shall I be delivered from my mortal tent, that I may find true and constant peace?' He has continually directed his heart and his longing toward heaven, and there he sits, there he goes, there he rests, and whatever else he does, his heart is never turned away from God. He incites and exhorts all people to the love of God, and he boasts to everyone how sweet the love of God is; and how the love of the world, by contrast, is a bitter and harmful love he demonstrates from the works of all men. He despises all worldly splendor and rebukes temporal solicitude, or care of the belly, and teaches what great vanity it is to put trust in perishable things. He is amazed that people are so reluctant to

49 Author uncertain, *Soliloquia animae ad Deum* 34 (PL 40:893–94).
50 Author uncertain, *Manuale* 28 (PL 28:963).

leave and relinquish a decrepit and inconstant possession, for he thinks that what tastes good to him must be sweet to everyone, and what he loves must please everyone, and what he knows is familiar to all people. He looks continually to the Lord his God with the eyes of faith, and from this spiritual contemplation he is pleasantly and increasingly refreshed. For as he counts God the most desirable object of his affection and praise, so also he finds Him the sweetest object of his ceaseless meditation."

A God-loving Christian is eager to hear God's Word and eager to pray.

In addition to this, out of heartfelt love for God he is eager to hear God's Word; out of fervent love he glorifies the mighty grace and benefits of the entire Holy Trinity. He is eager to pray, and out of true love he is eager to hold converse with God, and his heart speaks with God. He thinks to himself: "God is my highest Friend and my dearest Father. The Lord Jesus is my dearest, most beautiful, and most precious Bridegroom, and the Holy Spirit is my dearest Comforter. The entire Holy Trinity loves me and prepares me for eternal life and waits for me to come to Him in eternal life and into the heavenly paradise of eternal joy. Therefore, while here on earth, I will begin my conversation or conduct with God my sweetest Lover and praise, honor, extol, and glorify Him here as much as I am able until I come to Him from the realm of faith into the realm of sight. Then it will come to full maturity, and I will praise Him perfectly."

How a Christian, contemplating eternal life, loves his neighbor.

John 3:16

Next, he also loves his neighbor, since he leads a heavenly way of life and knows that he has come from death into life. He thinks to himself: "God is love, and eternal life is a life of burning love, for which God made all men. And out of great love He gave His only-begotten Son to the whole world, that all the world might believe on Him and by faith enter into that life. Now, therefore, if eternal life is a life of love, and if I am made for this life by God the Father and redeemed for this life by Christ, as well as sanctified for this life by God the Holy Spirit, why should I not walk in love and heartily love my neighbor, with whom I am to live forever with God above in eternal love and love's glory?"

A Christian follows His Savior, Christ, in love.

Matt. 11:29; 1 Cor. 13:4–8

He looks to the example of Christ and learns from Him to be meek and humble of heart. He is long-suffering and kind; he does not act jealously and does not seek his own way and is not puffed up. He does not act insolently, he does not seek his own, he does not let himself become embittered, he does not seek harm. Where he sees poisonous serpents and croaking toads that secretly sting their neighbor and slander them, it causes him pain, and with his heart he hates what is contrary to unfeigned Christian love. He rejoices when it goes rightly, he reconciles all things, he trusts all things, he hopes all things, he endures all things, and he never lets love cease.

There is pure holy love in the children of light.

In summary, whoever considers aright the article of eternal life and rightly takes it to heart is a child of the Light and walks on earth among men in pure, unfeigned love, as if he were living above in the heavenly paradise among the blessed patriarchs, prophets, apostles, and all elect angels. He is surrounded with holy love, and what he does, what he engages in, what he undertakes all flows from fervent love.

The Second Benefit and Use of the Article of Eternal Life: It Gives Comfort in Cross and Tribulations

Second, all godly and orthodox Christians must confess, and they also feel it strongly in their cross and adversity, that after the knowledge of and confidence in the blood of Jesus Christ and His joyful resurrection, nothing so deeply stirs the heart and promises such blessed comfort and creates such desire and longing today as when the last article of eternal life is daily pondered and constantly discussed with a pious heart.

Tobit, in his domestic cross, comforts himself with this article.

Tobit 2:14, 18; 2 Maccabees 7:14

In this the pious Tobit takes comfort when in his domestic cross he is derided by his own friends and cast off by them with mocking words: "Where now is your confidence in which you gave alms and buried so many dead?" "Do not speak thus," he answers. "For we are children of the saints and look for that life which God shall give to those who remain strong and firm in faith before Him." So also that boy who was terribly tortured and tormented to death by Antiochus, that fearsome bloodhound, seized upon this hope, and when he was about to die said to the king, "It is a great comfort to have the hope that, when men put us to death, God will raise us up again."

In their tribulation, Christians are to ponder eternal life with diligence.

You can imitate these words and blessed thoughts, dear Christian, in your troubles and great afflictions. When it seems to you that all earthly comfort is disintegrating, and your troubled heart cannot be gladdened anywhere, then let this precious article be a refreshing draft for you, with which your soul may put itself at ease and wait for hope in patience.

I. The sorrow of Christians at the mortal departure of their family members.

Sirach 38:16–17

If you are a widow or a poor orphan or otherwise disconsolate and moisten yourself with your own tears at the mortal departure of your closest family members on earth, you are right to weep and right to have sorrow, as Sirach exhorts, saying, "My child, when a man dies, mourn for him and lament him as though great injury were done to you, and wrap his body in a decent manner, and bury him honorably. You are to weep bitterly and be heartily troubled and bear sorrow, after he has been."

How a Christian is to confront this sorrow with this article.

Ps. 43:5; Luke 23:43; Matt. 8:11

Yet if you know that your dearest kinsman has said farewell to the world in true, constant invocation and confession of the name of Jesus and has fallen blessedly asleep in the Lord, you are able to soften your sorrow with this article and say, "Why are you cast down, O my soul, and so disquieted within me? I have not lost a friend but only let him go ahead before me into the eternal, joyful paradise, where all godly patriarchs, prophets, and apostles, Abraham, Isaac, Jacob, Enoch, David, Elijah, John the Baptist, Peter, Paul, and the rest are dwelling. He has been gathered to these blessed fathers and to all elect angels and children of light and now beholds his dear God face-to-face and rejoices with perfect joy for all eternity. My dear soul, you should grant him this from your heart and therefore not be so severely troubled, but rejoice all the more that his grief, affliction, and misery have come to a blessed end. He rests from his labors and would not for a moment exchange his heavenly joy for this whole wide world with all its kingdoms, splendor, power, honor, and glory, nor will he return to us in this wretched, troublesome valley of sorrows."

Godly Christians take comfort in the fact that in heaven they will see their deceased family members again and rejoin them.

2 Pet. 1; Job 19:26–27; Rev. 6:9; 7:14–17; Ps. 36:7–9

But you, O my dear soul, shall come to him soon and see him in unspeakable joy in the midst of the angels and all the elect, when you also have laid aside the mortal tent of your body. "This world lasts a little while, and all things have their time," people say. But hereafter you will not only see your dear family members again but also behold your dear God Himself with your own eyes, and He will wipe away all your tears from your eyes and bring you to the fountain of life, that in His light you may see the eternal light and be given to drink of pleasure as with a river.

Comfort and joy for godly widows and orphans.

Behold, dear Christian, this is the comfort that this article gives, and it arouses even far lovelier and more joyful thoughts, so that you think of your family member who has died in God as having only gone into an wondrously beautiful kingdom far across the great sea, and there come to a very splendid and very joyful wedding feast in a wondrously beautiful city, where he also awaits your arrival and dwells in great riches, great joy, and great glory, which shall last forever and shall have no end. Why would you not rejoice from your heart and wish that you might come there at the earliest moment, the earliest day, and the earliest hour?

II. The cross of Christians who are burdened with enemies, robbers, diseases, and physical trials.

You may well have other pressing trouble, anguish, grief, and misery, such as losing your possessions and livelihood, being plundered, robbed, or deprived of your property and meager portion under a false show of justice. Your honor, respect, and good name may be shamefully tarnished by your adversaries, or you may otherwise be treated with spite and hostility and subjected to persecution, be unable to find justice anywhere, and be forced to dwell in exile here and there. Your eyes may weep many deep pools, you may carry your illness, sorrows, plague, and days of woe on your neck, which leave you no rest or peace but always crack the heart and bear utter despondence and perpetual sighing and weeping.

The article of eternal life is an exquisite cup of comfort for this cross.

2 Cor. 4:17; Rom. 8:18; Matt. 16:27; 11; Acts 14:22; James 1:12; 2 Tim. 4:8; Rev. 3:11

If so, this article again, like a cup of consolation, can give you a refreshing drink so that you say, "It is a great comfort that my cross and my misery will not last forever. For I know that my tribulation, which is temporal and easy, provides me with an eternal and immeasurably weighty glory and is not worthy of the unspeakable glory, joy, and bliss that shall be revealed in me. Why, then, should I not patiently carry after my dear Savior and Redeemer, Jesus Christ, the cross that He has laid upon me? It neither can nor shall be otherwise than as Scripture says—that through many tribulations we must enter into the kingdom of God and that we rejoice in various temptations, knowing that the crown of life shall be given us hereafter. If I suffer a measure of cross and tribulation here, very well! Only a few years, or even a few months, a few days, and a little length of time and I shall no longer be in the world, but in eternal life. Then for my measure of anguish, trouble, and tribulations which I suffered in the world I will receive from my dear God many hundred thousand measures of heavenly joy and eternal glory—indeed, of eternal power and eternal health."

We should gladly suffer all calamity on earth, as long as we are assured of eternal life.

Augustine, Manual, ch. 15[51]

"O my dear soul," says St. Augustine, "why use many words? Even if we were made to feel pain and agony daily—indeed, even to suffer with great torment the flames of hellfire a long time—simply that we might see the Lord Jesus Christ in His glory above and be saved with His saints, we ought to do so and to endure and suffer all that can cause us woe that we might simply partake of that great good and that great glory, namely, to see Christ in heaven.

Our tribulation on earth whets our hunger and thirst for eternal life.

Ps. 31:10; Hab. 3:16

"Come, then! What if the vile demons continually seek after me and continually send their arrows of tribulation against me, my body always suffers hunger, is weighed down with garments, oppressed with wearisome toil, and wasted with much waking? What if this or that man chatters, cries out, beats me, and causes me unrest? What if great cold and frost bend me to the earth and my sadness gives me no peace? What if great heat scalds and pains my head? What if my chest stings, my belly burns, my appearance becomes pale and weak? What if my life ebbs away with pain and my years with sighing? What if my bones collapse and my body turns to dust and ashes? Let the last day of tribulation come! I will gladly suffer all, that I may finally rest and go up to our blessed people."

Benefit and use of the words of St. Augustine.

With such sayings and similar comforting words you can address your distressed soul in the midst of anguish and strengthen it thereby, that you may bear your adversity in the weary pilgrimage and journey of this passing life with all the more strength and patience.

III. Offense of the godly at the prosperity and pomp of the ungodly on earth.

Jer. 12:1–3

You see how the ungodly children of the world, arrant villains, eye-pleasers at court, saintly-seeming fornicators, slanderers, traitorous fellows of Doeg,[52] false brethren, bristling misanthropes, and pseudo-Christians all enjoy prosperity. They are not in danger like others, but you are afflicted daily, and with the prophet Jeremiah you think: "Dear God, why do the ungodly prosper and the scornful have abundance? You plant them so that they take root and grow and bring forth fruit. You cause them to boast much of You, and do not chasten them. But You know me, O Lord, and You see me and try my heart toward You."

51 Author uncertain, *Manuale* 15 (PL 40:958).

52 See 1 Sam. 22:6–23.

Comfort from this article against the aforesaid offense.

Heb. 11:37

Here take the article of eternal life and know that God permits the villains and arrant children of Belial because the fattened hogs always keep living securely and continuing their malicious will with success, because they are to be punished with hell and hellfire. But because the children of light are to be comforted in heaven, they must pass through the valley of sorrow and shed fountains of tears here, even as it has always been for all the elect since the beginning of the world. Some suffered mockery and scourging and bonds and imprisonment. They were stoned, sawn in two, pierced, slain with the sword. They wandered about in furs and goatskins, being destitute, afflicted, and tormented, of whom the world was not worthy. And they wandered in exile, in deserts, and in mountains, and in the dens and caves of the earth.

In this world all godly fathers, like pilgrims and strangers, have always sighed for the heavenly fatherland,

Heb. 11:13–16

"These all," says the apostle Paul to the Hebrews, "died in the faith, having not received the promise"—that is, the promised salvation and glory of eternal life obtained by Jesus Christ and prepared for all the elect from the foundation of the world—"but having seen it from afar, and were comforted by it and content and confessed that they were guests and strangers on the earth. For those who say these things declare that they seek a country. And truly, if they thought this about that from which they came forth"—namely, that this their earthly home was their true country—"they might have had opportunity to have returned. But they desire a better one, namely, a heavenly one. Therefore, God is not ashamed to be called their God, for He has prepared for them a city."

Through cross and all tribulation, the elect are encouraged to die to the world and to turn their heart to the heavenly fatherland.

Accordingly, just as our dear God forcefully attacked this wondrous people and readily raked them over the hot coals of anguish so that they might die to the world from one day to the next and have a heartfelt longing for the heavenly fatherland of eternal life while the ungodly on earth prospered, so today also He causes true, godly, and upright Christians on earth to live in exile so that they must be despised creatures—indeed, the footstool and foot-blister of all the world—and are continually given to drink of the cup of the cross, prepared from bitter gall and the wormwood of tribulation, that they may turn their thoughts away from the world to the blessed paradise of eternal life, constantly thirst for it, and increasingly turn their back on all worldly pomp, temporal goods, and transitory glory.

The world's joy, pomp, and Epicurean life passes away; the eternal good gives true courage.

Therefore, you should not be offended at the Epicurean pomp, happiness, and temporal prosperity of the ungodly, but in joyful contemplation of this article learn to despise them and say, "Dear fellows, things go according to your will for as long as He who dwells in heaven permits your villainous conduct. You may keep mocking God's holy name, Word, and Sacrament, feasting, guzzling, coveting, living in filth and lewdness without any cross and temptation. The pods are for such pigs as these. Before God you have nothing, but are despised and rejected. I do not ask for your happiness, but I know of and wait for another, of which you know nothing at all. So God has promised me that after this life I will live with Christ forever, while you, on the contrary, shall go to the place where laughter is costly. For the end of my faith is called eternal life."

Chrysostom's testimony about the different joys and pleasures of this world and of the one to come.[53]

"Imagine," writes St. Chrysostom, "that a man lives a hundred years in all pleasures and joys on this earth. Even if he lives a hundred or even ten thousand more years, pray, what is that time compared to eternity? If we will rightly consider it, the whole time of this passing life in which we live in joy and pleasure according to our own imagining is, as it were, the fleeting dream of a single night, if we will value and reckon this period against eternity."

IV. Faithful preachers especially are despised and persecuted in this world.

The counsels of the devil and his consorts against a godly preacher who rebukes sin and vice.

Wisdom 2:12–19

Say you are a preacher, and, in return for your faithful teaching, exhortation, and warning, you are forced to receive and suffer many a sting in the heel from Satan and his puffed-up knaves. They undertake these things against you with hidden maneuvers and secret tricks, in which they join forces and say (as the Book of Wisdom reports), "Let us lie in wait for the righteous man. For he gives us great apathy and is contrary to our doings, and upbraids us with our sinning against the Law, and proclaims our ways as sin. He professes to know God and calls himself the child of God; he reproves what we have in our heart. He is harmful to us even to behold, for his life is not like other men's, and his ways are wholly different. He esteems us as worthless and abstains from our doings as from filthiness; he professes that the righteous will have good in the end and boasts that God is his Father. Therefore, let us see if his word is true. If the righteous man is a son of God, He will help him and deliver him from the hand of the adversary. Let us try him with disgrace and torment, that we may see how pious he is and know how patient he is. Let us condemn him to a shameful death; so shall he be known by his words."

53 St. John Chrysostom, *Homilies on Lazarus* 1.11, abr. (PG 48:978).

How Scripture comforts all godly preachers with the article of eternal life.

Wisdom 2:21–22; 3:1–3

Now observe to what end this beating and threatening leads. "Such things they imagine," says Scripture further, "and are deceived. Their wickedness has blinded them so that they do not know God's secret judgment. For they do not have a hope that a holy life shall be rewarded, but esteem as nothing the honor that the blameless souls shall have." And shortly thereafter: "But the souls of the righteous are in the hand of God, and no torment shall touch them. In the sight of the unwise they seem to have died, and their departure is taken as agony and their going forth as destruction, but they are in peace."

Here, dear preacher, you see what glorious comfort the article of eternal life produces. You can say, "Very well, I do not care how hopeless and perverse things become in the world or how long God lets the devil and his hopeless creatures continue to conspire, rage and rave, thunder and storm against me. I will not be stopped because of that, but only act all the more sharply, rebuke all the more earnestly that which should be rebuked, and proceed confidently in my call. My enemies will not carry on their game against me for a hundred years. Only a little while and God will summon me hence, for I am in another world and in a better life, where my fortune will be reversed. I will receive with joy the crown of righteousness from my Captain and Savior, Jesus Christ (under whose banner I fight). And as the hellish Leviathan now soars on high with his judges, and I must lie below, so he and his servants will again lie at my feet, and I will soar on high with Christ, my Savior, and have dominion over them forever.

St. Augustine's comfort in the Book of True Innocence[54]

In this same way St. Augustine takes comfort, saying, "The world may well rage and fume, slander and shame with their tongues, threaten with weapons and arms, and snarl and do what they cannot avoid doing. What is all this compared to the glory which we await in that life? I contrast and weigh what I suffer here against that for which I hope, and although I feel what I am suffering, and do not yet see what I hope for, so also that for which Christians hope in the future is overwhelmingly greater and better than that which has taken us here."

How Dr. Luther was comforted by the hope of eternal life in the midst of his adversity.

Tom. 4, Witt. Germ., fol. 18[55]

Similarly, Luther says, "Should we not value the dear Lord's Word and comfort more dearly and highly than the disgraceful rage, threats, excommunication, cursing, and thundering of any powerless, filthy, stinking sack of worms or pope (or any other ungodly villain and boaster), even if he poured out the dregs and

54 Prosper of Aquitaine, *Epigrammata ex Sententiis Augustini,* or *Liber de vera innocentia* 32 (PL 51:0508B–C).

55 From *Sermon on the Mount* (1530–32), on Matt. 5:12: cf. AE 21:50 (= WA 32:339–40).

the entire hell of his disfavor and cursing as a cloudburst upon us? For I hear that it pleases my Lord Christ so heartily well, and He Himself bids me rejoice at it and promises a fantastic reward: that the kingdom of heaven will be mine and all that Christ and all the saints and the whole Church possesses—in short, such a treasure and comfort that I would not exchange it for all the possessions, joy, and stringed music in the world, even if all the leaves and blades of grass were tongues! Here it is not one Christian—indeed, not one angel—who calls me 'blessed,' but the Lord of all angels, at whose feet both they and all creatures must fall and do worship. Therefore, they must with all creatures, including the leaves and grass, joyfully sing and leap to my praise and glory."

Luther mocks all his enemies on account of the hope of eternal life.[56]

Dr. Luther says further, "What are those who slander and curse me compared to these things, but utter nits and louse-bags—pardon the expression—indeed, far more shameful than anyone can name? If all creatures, the leaves and blades of grass in the forest, and the sand in the sea were tongues, and they spoke utter scorn and contempt, what would that be compared to one word of this Man? For His voice rings so brightly that heaven and earth must be filled and reverberate with it, in comparison to which the sickly demands, scratchings, and sputterings of His enemies disappear."

Account of Duke John Frederick, Elector of Saxony.

Here I must mention the pious elector of Saxony, Duke Johann Friedrich, of most worthy memory, who, when the Evangelical preachers of Augsburg were expelled because of the accursed Interim, sent for one of them and asked how he was. "Gracious lord," answered the preacher, "the emperor has expelled us and forbidden us the whole Roman Empire." At this the elector started to weep, and the tears ran down his cheeks, and he stood and went to the window. But immediately he turned again and asked further, "Did he forbid you heaven as well?" The preacher said, "No." "Ah," answered the elector. "Then there is no distress. Be of good cheer. The empire and heaven must remain ours." Thereupon he had his saddlebags fetched and said, "In here is all that I have on earth. From this I will bequeath to you some travel money. Divide it among your brethren and companions under the cross. Although I, too, am a poor, captive prince, God will certainly restore it to me."

Constant comfort from the doctrine of eternal life for all troubled preachers of the truth.

1 Cor. 15:19; Col. 3:3; John 16:22

In our daily war that we wage against the devil and his followers, we preachers of the divine Word should count the article of eternal life as our highest comfort and say with St. Paul: "If we hope in Christ only in this life, we are the most

56 From *Sermon on the Mount* (1530–32), on Matt. 5:12: cf. AE 21:51 (= WA 32:340).

miserable of all men. But our life is hidden in Christ with God, and we know that when Christ our life shall reveal Himself, we also will be revealed with Him in glory." The Son of God says, "You have sorrow now. But I will see you again, and your heart shall rejoice, and your joy shall no man take from you." We should take these and similar verses to heart and not waver since we know that God Himself shall be our reward in heaven.

V. Comfort for dying Christians from this article.

Furthermore, dear brother, when you wrestle with death and your powers forsake you, you cannot stand another drop, your throat is swollen, your tongue sticks to the roof of your mouth, your speech fails, sight grows dim, hearing fades, and your breath is lost, consider then whether anything anywhere can be more comforting for you than this article, especially when you are preserved with faith in Christ and all your longing is for eternal life.

Godly Christians need not be afraid of death.

Ps. 118:17; 116:16, 8

There is no need for you to fear any hell, any devil, or the hideous visage of death since the Son of God, Jesus Christ, has overcome the devil for your good, conquered and harrowed hell for your sake, and broken the power of death so that it must let you pass through and go from this valley of sorrow into eternal life. "I shall not die," says David, "but live, and proclaim the works of the Lord. O Lord, I am your servant, the son of your handmaid. You have broken my bonds asunder, for You have plucked my soul from death, my eyes from tears, my feet from slipping. I will walk before the Lord in the land of the living."

In contemplation of the article of eternal life, Christians are unfazed when the world threatens them with death.

Luther, tom. 6, Witt. Germ., fols. 365–66[57]

Indeed, if the enemies of the divine truth threaten me with death, what could be more comforting than this article and the fact that Christ says in John 16:33, "Be of good cheer, I have overcome the world." "They threaten us with death," says Dr. Luther. "If they were as wise as they are foolish, they would threaten us with life. It is a ridiculous, laughable threat to frighten Christ and His Christians with death when they are lords and victors over death. It is as if I wished to frighten someone by having his horse saddled and making him ride it. But they do not believe that Christ rose from the dead and is the Lord of life and death. For them He is still in the tomb—indeed, still in hell. But we are defiant and fearless, knowing that He is

57 From Luther's letter to Hartmut von Cronberg, ca. March 1522: cf. Preserved Smith, trans. and ed., *Luther's Correspondence and Other Contemporary Letters* (Philadelphia: Lutheran Publication Society, 1913–18), 2:104 (= WA 10/2:55.3–16).

risen and death is nothing more than an end of sin and of death itself. For life in this flesh still clings to sins and remains in sins, and it cannot be without sin because of the flesh. Therefore, the captive spirit in us cries: 'Come, death and the Last Day, and put an end to sin and death. Amen!' as St. Paul writes in Romans 7 and 8."

Comforting benefit of the article of eternal life.

Behold, so wondrously comforting is the last article of our Christian Creed concerning eternal life, and it refreshes godly hearts to an immeasurable degree in their tribulation, cross, and adversity. For which reason we also, with patient endurance of all temporal misery and despising of all worldly splendor, goods, joy, and delight, would set and direct all our *datum*,[58] senses, thoughts, and desires toward the eternal good, if only we understood it and would let ourselves truly and perfectly grasp and comprehend the joy of that eternal life, which defies comparison to any earthly glory.

The Third Benefit and Use of the Article of Eternal Life: The Article of Eternal Life Teaches Us to Die to the World and to Turn Our Heart toward the Eternal Fatherland

Third, this article gives joyful guidance so that we learn to die to the world daily out of fervent hope for the heavenly fatherland. For what is life on earth but a weary pilgrimage? And what is the world with its glory but a hostel full of the wretched, where beggarly pomp and stinking pride constantly have free course, along with strife, division, envy, warfare, covetousness, and perpetual unrest? Who would desire to stay long in such a hostel when he is assured of heavenly goods and the certain promise of eternal life?

St. Augustine's lament at the vanity of this life in Meditations, ch. 21[59]

"I grow immeasurably sick," says Augustine, "of this life and this weary pilgrimage. For this life is a miserable life, a decrepit life, an uncertain life, a laborious life, and a polluted life. It is the mistress of all wickedness and queen of all arrogance, full of wretchedness and full of error, so that it ought not to be called life but to be called death, in which we die every moment, are subject to manifold deficiencies and miseries, and die in various ways."

How the holy divine Scripture describes the vanity of this life.

Isa. 40:17; Ps. 103:14–15; Sirach 14:15; Ps. 49:10–14; 144:4

Indeed, even if a man has feasted several years in this world, is rich, stately, wise, healthy, and prestigious, and flourishes like a flower in the field, lives a long time, and trusts in his riches, nevertheless he must finally die and lose his life just as much as fools and dullards do and must leave his property to another.

58 Meaning all those things which God has given to us.

59 Author uncertain, *Meditationes* 21 (PL 40:917).

The heart of the worldly is at ease because their chambers are full, from which they can furnish one store after another, so that their sheep bear a thousand, and a hundred thousand in their villages, their oxen labor much, no harm, no loss, nor lament is in their streets, their houses endure forever, their habitations abide from generation to generation, and they have great honor here on earth. But they do not remain long in such dignity but must leave it like cattle. And when they have taken comfort in this good life and praised a man's seeking after good days, they must finally follow their fathers, see the light no more, and take nothing with them in their death. Where is Artaxerxes, who reigned over 172 lands? Where is the mighty king Alexander the Great? Where are the beautiful women Abigail, Abishag of Shunem, Judith, Lucretia, Helen, and the rest?

The wise king Solomon confesses from his own experience how everything under the sun is vanity.

Eccl. 2:4–11

"I did great things," writes Solomon of himself. "I built palaces, planted vineyards. I made myself gardens and parks and planted all manner of fruiting trees therein. I made myself pools from which to water the forest of green trees. I had servants and maidservants and attendants. I had a greater wealth of cattle and sheep than all that were before me in Jerusalem. I gathered to myself silver and gold also, and from the kings and lands, a treasure. I made for myself singers and female singers, and the delight of men, all manner of stringed music, and increased above all who were before me in Jerusalem. Also wisdom dwelt with me, and all that my eyes desired I granted them, and denied my heart no joy so that it was glad from all my labor. But when I looked upon all my works which my hands had done, and the toil which I had had, behold, it was all vanity and sorrow, and nothing more under the sun."

We are to learn to die to the world and to have a longing for God.

But whereas we see, and not only does Scripture teach us but also daily experience attests, that this life on earth is full of toil, full of vanity, and, finally, is concluded with death, what then can serve us better, that we may learn to turn our back to this world and lift our heart to heaven, our eternal fatherland, than this last article of our Christian Creed?

The hope of eternal life should be our constant concern and expectation.

1 Pet. 1:3–4; Titus 2:13

"God calls us," says St. Paul, "to a living hope through the resurrection of Jesus Christ from the dead, to an imperishable and unblemished and incorruptible inheritance which is kept in heaven for you." And St. Paul admonishes us to await this blessed hope: "We are to look," says he, "for the blessed hope"; that is, we are to learn to distinguish this present, perishable life from the imperishable life to come, and turn our back on this present life which is passing away and which we must leave in the end, and take into our sight continually that life to come, hope in it firmly and certainly as that which abides forever and in which we belong. With this blessed hope we are thus to concern ourselves constantly with good works, discipline, righteousness, and godliness, and to dwell in the heavenly fatherland (even though we do not yet see or feel it) far more firmly than we are dwelling and hoping in this present life.

Eternal life is little esteemed and the temporal too much attended.

Luther, in his sermon on the blessed hope, printed in Erfurt, 1565[60]

"Now there are very few people on earth," as Luther recounts in a sermon, "who look for the blessed hope of the imperishable inheritance and kingdom which is to come, and wait for it with as much certainty as they ought, so that they do not dwell so securely in this present life. There are few who look at this temporal life only through a tinted glass and, as it were, blindly, but at that eternal life with clear, open eyes. The blessed hope and eternal inheritance is, alas, too often forgotten. But the temporal life and the perishable kingdom on earth is remembered all too much. The perishable life is kept ever in view, it is the subject of thought and concern and joy, while that imperishable one is turned away from. The former is sought after day and night; the latter, scattered to the wind.

How a Christian ought to look at this temporal and that eternal life.

"Now, surely it ought not to be so among Christians, but quite the opposite. A Christian ought to behold this temporal life only with shut eyes and blindly, but he ought to view the eternal life to come with fully opened eyes and in clear, lucid light. And he ought to be in this life on earth only with the left hand, but with the right hand and with the soul and whole heart he should be in that life, namely, in heaven, and in certain hope wait for it with joy at all times.

Admonition of the holy apostle Paul.

"For thus St. Paul teaches (1 Cor. 7:29–31), where he clarifies what it means to wait for the blessed hope, saying, 'Furthermore, this is the meaning: those who have wives, that they should be as if they had none; and those who weep, as if they did not weep, and those who rejoice, as if they did not rejoice; and those who buy, as if they did not possess; and those who use the world, that they not misuse it. For the substance of the world is passing away.'

What St. Paul actually means by his words.

"With these words, the dear apostle would gladly obscure and cast into darkness this life on earth which we now behold with the eyes of the body, that we may learn to look at it only blindly, as that which is not our true life. By contrast, he would gladly set before us and bring to light that life in heaven for which Christ

60 From Luther's sermon on Titus 2:13–14, August 19, 1531: cf. AE 57:22–25 (= WA 34/2:110–14).

has redeemed us and for which we are baptized and have received the Gospel, that we may learn to tune our eyes, heart, and soul to it and in lively hope await it joyfully. For if we wish to be Christians, our ultimate quest should not be to marry and be given in marriage, buy and sell, plant and build, as Christ says that the ungodly especially shall do before the Last Day (although we must use these things for the needs of the body), but our ultimate quest is to be something better and higher, namely, the blessed inheritance in heaven which does not pass away.

Testimony of St. Paul that this life is our pilgrimage and eternal life our home.

2 Cor. 5:1, 6

"Likewise, he writes in another passage: 'We know that if our earthly house of this tent is broken asunder, we have a building built by God, a house not made with hands, which is eternal in heaven. And above that we yearn also for the habitation which is of heaven.' And shortly thereafter: 'We are of good cheer at all times, knowing that while we are in the body, we are not home with the Lord. For we walk in faith and not by sight. But we are of good cheer, having far more desire to walk out of the body and to be home with the Lord,' etc. Here he makes a distinction between this perishable life and that imperishable one, saying that this life on earth is not our home and our true life on which we have to set our hope. But we are to yearn for the true fatherland and to long for the eternal habitation in heaven.

St. Paul teaches that we have our true citizenship not on earth but in heaven.

Phil. 3:20

"And to the Philippians he says, 'Our citizenship is in heaven, from whence we also await the Savior, Jesus Christ, the Lord, who will glorify our lowly body that it may be made like His glorified body, according to the working whereby He is able also to subdue all things to Himself.' It is as if he would say the citizenship, conduct, and dwelling of us Christians is not in this world, but our citizenship, conduct, and dwelling is in heaven. While we are citizens and dwellers on earth for a while according to the outward existence of the world, nevertheless this is not our true, hereditary, lasting citizenship. Rather, our true citizenship is with Christ in heaven, where we will remain citizens forever, when He shall come from heaven and take us up. Therefore, we are to conform ourselves to this as those who are not of this world nor belong in it, but who belong elsewhere, in another citizenship and kingdom, where we have a lasting existence.

St. Peter calls us strangers and pilgrims on earth.

1 Pet. 2:11

"St. Peter also teaches similarly, saying, 'Dear brethren, I exhort you as strangers and pilgrims to refrain from fleshly lusts.' He calls us strangers and pilgrims to show what our life is on earth and how it should be regarded.

What "stranger" means. What "pilgrim" means.

"'Stranger' means an immigrant or foreigner who is not a citizen by origin or birth in the place where he dwells but has his origin elsewhere. In short, 'stranger' means one who is not native, as the children of Israel were strangers and not native in Egypt, into which they had come from the land of Canaan through the famine, as Moses often reminds them, saying, 'You were strangers in the land of Egypt.' 'Pilgrim' means a migrant who travels through a land and is not in his city or his place where he belongs, but only lodges in a foreign place as in passing, who is not only a visitor, as a foreign person, but also a guest, and has nothing of his own nor hopes to have such in the place of his pilgrimage, but is merely passing through, as the children of Israel were pilgrims in the wilderness.

Why Christians are called strangers and pilgrims.

Job 1:21; Gen. 47:9

"Thus Christians are strangers and pilgrims in this world. They are strangers because, according to the fleshly birth, they came from God into this world, created out of nothing, and do not remain in this world but must leave the world like all other men on earth. As Job says, 'I came naked from the womb; naked I will depart.' They are pilgrims because, according to the spiritual birth, they are guests on earth (when they were reborn from the Holy Spirit through the washing in the Word), and their life is only a pilgrimage, as the patriarch Jacob calls it.

Following St. Peter's teaching, we should view this temporal life precisely as strangers and pilgrims.

"Thus St. Peter wishes to show that we are to view this life precisely as a stranger and pilgrim views the land in which he is an outlander and guest. A stranger cannot say, 'Here is my fatherland,' for he is not a native there. A pilgrim does not intend to remain in the land where he travels or in the inn where he stays the night, but his heart and thoughts are elsewhere. In the inn he only gets his provisions, supper, and sleep and keeps walking on to the place where he is at home. So, he says, you Christians, too, are only strangers and guests in this world and belong to another land where you have a constant lodging and a continuing city for eternity. Therefore, act like strangers and guests in this strange land and inn, from which you receive no more than food, drink, clothes, shoes, and whatever you need for this night's lodging, and so think only of what lies ahead and of your fatherland, of which you are citizens.

"Now this is quick to say but not easily comprehended. For even we Christians who are baptized, hear the Gospel, and have begun to believe still feel that the spirit within us is weak, but the flesh and blood and reason are especially strong, and they always pull us back so that we regard that life as lowly and also sometimes cast doubt on it. Thus, if we would confess truly, we must admit that we seldom think of the fact that we must eventually leave it and relinquish this life."

Lament at our addiction to the world and our world-curious hearts.

By nature we all have hearts that hunger, thirst, and long for the world, and most people go along complacently, seeking peace and a good life, pleasure and joy on earth, are intoxicated with greed, arrogance, and other vices, and are so intimately involved in the world it is as if they would stay here forever and leave heaven to God alone.

The Epicurean children of the world live like pigs and senseless beasts and regard eternal life as nothing.

Therefore, Scripture warns us against such Epicureanism and calls us strangers, guests, and pilgrims to turn our thoughts and senses away from the world, lest we become too deeply immersed in this temporal life, like pigs and senseless beasts, which have absolutely no concern for the life to come. A pig lies in the sty or on the manure, rests and grunts, and thinks only where the corn and bran are, thinks of no death, fears no hell, looks forward to no heaven, but corn and bran are its kingdom of heaven. So are they, too, who think no more than how they can have everything in the world to the full.

We should treat temporal life as if we were a stranger to it and let our thoughts be always directed toward heaven.

As children of light, we should with all diligence seek what is above and so use this world that we do not misuse, and become too deeply involved in, the cares of temporal sustenance and worldly affairs. A Christian should occupy himself with such thoughts and say, "Because I must live on earth as long as God wills, I will eat, drink, marry, plant, build house and home, and have and make use of whatever God grants, not as though it were the true good but as a temporal necessity." And just as a stranger and guest in a foreign land and place of lodging, who intends to leave all these things and to set out with his staff again, so I am always contemplating departure from this world as from the strange land and from the evil, unsafe lodging to the true fatherland of eternal life, where there will be utter safety, peace, rest, and joy forever.

The proper use of this temporal life, lest we forget eternal life.

1 Cor. 7:29–30

If we knew how to act this way and if we rightly perceived the distinction between temporal and eternal life, this article would truly stir our heart, and then, in accordance with St. Paul's admonition, we would turn our back on all earthly affairs, have wives as though we had none, weep as though we did not weep, rejoice as if we did not rejoice. We would view this whole life as a dream and a shadow and with our thoughts be continually above in heaven, speak and sing, seek and think continually of eternal life evening and morning, day and night, so that even in our physical dreams we could imagine nothing else than utter heavenly joy, heavenly glory, and the heavenly fellowship of the holy angels.

The Fourth Benefit and Use of the Article of Eternal Life: The Article of Eternal Life Teaches Us Heartily to Long and Sigh for the Heavenly Fatherland

Lam. 3

Fourth, there is no doubt that if the article of eternal life were deeply embedded in us and deeply stirred our heart, we would have a blessed yearning for heaven and, just as young chickens when they leave the hen always chirp and mourn until they come under the mother's wings, so you would never be able to put your heart fully at peace in this world but would turn to God and sigh for the eternal heavenly fatherland evening and morning and say with the prophet Jeremiah: "My eyes flow and cannot cease, for there is not ceasing there until the Lord looks down from heaven and sees."

How a Christian should constantly shed tears and sigh for eternal life.

Lam. 2:11

Follow this example, dear Christian, and learn to sigh to God so that your hearty longing is directed to no joy or good, no comfort or refreshment on earth so strongly as to God and His heavenly hall of joy. Let tears flow day and night (as the prophet exhorts), like a stream, and do not cease, and let no eye desist. Arise in the night and cry out; pour out your heart to the Lord in the first watch: learn to pray with the prophet David, with the holy apostle Paul, and with St. Augustine, and say:

Prayer in which a Christian pours out his heartfelt longing for the eternal life.

O good and faithful God, who knows me inside and out! O my dearest Father, O Son of God, my dearest Savior, Lord Jesus Christ, O Lord God, Holy Spirit! O Holy Trinity, true God, I wish to know You in that life by sight, who You are; I wish to know You and see You, who are my soul, strength, and might. O my dearest Comforter, show and reveal Yourself to me here in faith and there in sight, that I may see You as the light and comfort of my eyes.

Godly Christians shed tears and sigh for the heavenly fatherland.

Ps. 63:1; Baruch 2:18; Ps. 69:3; Rev. 22:17; Ps. 130:6; Isa. 64:1

My eyes pour out tears to You, early do I wait for You, my soul thirsts for You, my flesh longs for You in a dry and thirsty land where no water is. My soul is vexed and bowed down, and goes in sorrow, and has wept its eyes almost to dryness. I cry out till I am weary, my throat grows warm, and my vision forsakes me because I must wait for You so long. You say, "Yes, I come soon," and let the Spirit and the Bride cry out, "Come," and let him who hears it say, "Come." Therefore, I cry out day and night, and my soul waits from one morning watch to the next. Oh, come, Lord Jesus, come and make Yourself known to me, O highest Joy of my spirit! Oh, that You would rend the heavens and come down, that the mountains would melt before You as hot waters singed by a great, forceful fire!

The heart, thirsty for heaven, waits continually on God.

Ps. 130:6

O dear God, with what anguish I wait for You! My soul waits, and I hope in Your Word. My soul waits for You from one morning watch to the next. I wish to behold You with the delight of my heart. I wish to love You heartily, who are the life of my soul. O Lord, appear to me, who have my great pleasure and joy in You, who are my sweet comfort. O my God and Lord, You are my life and the glory and honor of my soul.

Strength and indubitable hope of a firm faith.

Job 19:26–27; Ps. 17:15; 18:2; 36:7

O dear God, I have You in my heart at all times and sigh for You and have great longing for You. I will meet You one day. One day I will be granted to see You, who are so heartily dear to me. I will embrace and kiss You with joy, O gracious, heavenly Bridegroom! O dear God, who is my highest joy, who is my eternal life and blessedness, my comforting pleasure and sweetness both of body and of soul. I will see You and partake of You manifestly. I will love You, O Lord, who are my strength, my mighty fortress, my refuge, and my deliverer, my only comfort and hope in all misfortune. With great reverence I will honor You, the highest Good, besides which there is no higher or greater good.

God alone is the eternal light.

O incomprehensible and invisible Light, enlighten my eyes and give me such vision that I may see You here in faith from Your Word and there in sight.

Prayer that God Himself would be the highest Good which fills all senses and all human powers.

Song 1:3; Ps. 31:24

O sweet, loving Fragrance of my life, create a fragrance within me that I may smell Your good anointing. Give me a savor that I may know and realize how great Your goodness is which You have concealed from those who fear You and which You show to those who trust in You more than all people. Give me a heart to remember You at all times, a soul to love You, a mind never to forget You, an understanding to know You truly, a sense to long for You and cling to You constantly as the loveliest good, until I come to You and see You before me.

A faithful soul's confession and boast of its God and Savior.

O my Life, from which I and all that lives receive life! Through You I live, without You I die, and when my life ends, through You I will be restored to life and raised up, in You and through You I rejoice, and without You I have no joy or comfort. O living, gracious, loving, and sweet Life, where are You to be found? Show me this through Your Word and Spirit, that I may put my trust not in temporal life but in You, the eternal Good.

Only God quickens, fills, and gladdens all man's senses, desires, and emotions.

Song 2:5; Ps. 17:15; 84:2; Song 6:1; 2 Cor. 2:15–16

O dear God, through Your Word be near me, in my mind, in my heart, in my mouth, in my ears. Hasten to help me, for I am sick with love, and without You I die, and when I remember You, I am as though enlivened again. Your sweet, lovely fragrance refreshes me. I will be satisfied when I awake according to Your likeness. My soul longs and yearns for You, O Lord; my body and soul rejoice in the living God. Where is the fairest and loveliest God for whom I have such deep longing? O dear God, I smell and taste here Your lovely fragrance from Your Word, from which I gain pleasure and joy. While I do not see You, I hear Your voice, from which I am as though enlivened again.

We cannot see God with our sinful eyes, but we will hereafter when we come to Him.

Exod. 33:20; Phil. 1:23

Now, therefore, when I ask You, dear God, why You conceal Your face from me, I receive the answer: "No man shall live who sees Me." If this is the case, O dear God, then I will gladly die that I may see You. I have no desire to live any longer, but I yearn to be released and to be with my Lord Christ. I desire to die that I may see Christ. I am weary and tired of this life and have no desire to live here any longer, that I may live there with Christ forever.

A Christian wishes to die that he may come to God.

Ps. 39:4; Heb. 13:14; Ps. 116:8; 102:6–7; 77:2–3

Come, death! Come, Last Day! Come, last hour of my departure, and take me from the world that one day I may be delivered from the despondent valley of sorrow and go home from this exile to the true fatherland of eternal life. I am a guest and stranger on earth and have here no continuing city, but I seek the one to come. I groan with fervent longing for my God so that my heart faints. I am like a bittern[61] in the wilderness. I am like an owl in the disturbed places. I watch and am as a lone sparrow on the roof. My hand is stretched out at night and does not cease, for my soul will not be comforted.

Augustine, Soliloquies, ch. 35.[62] Ps. 42:1–2; 63:1–2

"As the hart pants for fresh water, so my soul pants for You, O God. My soul thirsts for God, for the living God. When shall I come to see the face of God? O Lord, my God, fountain of life, living spring, when shall I come from the dry and

61 A type of heron, known for its haunting, booming cry. Most Bible translations have desert owl, pelican, or vulture.

62 Author uncertain, *Soliloquia animae ad Deum* 35 (PL 40:894–95).

thirsty land to the streams of Your sweetness, that I may see Your power and Your glory and quench my thirst with the sweet, precious water of Your mercy? I thirst, O Lord. I thirst for You, the living God. Oh, when shall I come, O Lord, my God, that I may appear before Your face?

Comfort of the soul in the midst of its sighing.

[Ps. 42:5]

"But why are you cast down, O my soul, and so disquieted within me? I know that I shall see the precious day—indeed, the precious day of joy and rejoicing, on which we will rejoice and be glad. Ah, that precious time, that glorious, beautiful day that knows of no evening and has no setting, on which I will hear the voice of praise, the voice of rejoicing, and the public praise!

The believing soul finds consolation in the day of its redemption and is glad at its glory to come.

Matt. 25:23; John 16:20–22; Isa. 65:18–19; Ps. 36:8–9; Rev. 20:6; 1 Cor. 13:12; 1 John 3:2

"Oh, that precious day when I will hear the gladsome voice: 'Enter into the joy of your Lord!' Enter into eternal joy, into the house of the Lord your God, where there are great, unsearchable, and extraordinary mysteries which cannot all be expressed! Enter into the joy that knows of no sorrow but is filled with eternal rejoicing. There is utter good and nothing evil. There is all that your heart desires, nor is there anything there that you do not desire. There is true, living life, sweet life, lovely life, and life that is never forgotten and never can grow weary. There is no foe to fight against you nor any sinful lust, but high and certain safety, as well as sure quiet and rest, restful gladness and glad salvation, salutary eternity, eternal blessedness, blessed Trinity—indeed, God, one in substance and three in Persons, the one true God, and the blessed vision of His being, which vision truly is the joy of the Lord your God.

Heartfelt longing for eternal joy.

Ps. 42:2; Exod. 3:3; Ps. 120:5; 42:3; Isa. 28:10

"Oh, joy above joy! Oh, blessed joy far exceeding all transitory joy of the world and without which no constant joy can ever be found! Oh, blessed, precious joy! When shall I come to you, that I may see the Lord my God who dwells in you? I say with Moses, 'I will go and see this great sight.' But what is it that makes me refrain and draw back? Alas, woe is me, that I must be a stranger so long on earth! Alas, woe is me, that I play the pilgrim so long in this world! It is like a groaning in my bones, that they daily say to me: 'Where now is your God?' And that I must continually hear these words: 'Wait here, wait there, wait here, wait there, here a little, there a little.'

Prayer to God the Father.

Ps. 39:7; Phil. 3:21; Luke 12:36

"And now, O Lord, for what do I wait so long, and for whom shall I look so long? Lord God, Father, shall we not wait for Your only-begotten Son, our Savior, Jesus Christ the Lord, who will glorify our lowly body that it may be made like to His glorified body? We Your children wait upon the same Lord, when He shall come from the wedding to lead us there to His marriage feast.

Prayer to God the Son, that He would come soon.

Rev. 22:20; Luke 1:79; Isa. 61:1; Zech. 9:9; Ps. 80:14; 142:7; 42:7–8; 13:1–2

"Come, then, dearest Lord, and delay no more! Come, Lord Jesus Christ, come and fetch us home in peace. Come and lead the captives out of captivity, that we may rejoice with perfect hearts. Come, Lord, our Savior, come, highly desired of all nations, and let Your face shine, and we shall recover. Come, my Light and my Deliverer, and bring my soul out of prison, that I may glorify Your holy name. How long shall I be driven about in the floods of my mortality and cry to You, O Lord, and You do not answer me? O Lord, hear me, a wretched person who cries to You from this great tossing sea of misery in this world, and draw me into the harbor of eternal blessedness.

The believing soul remembers the blessedness of all the elect in heaven.

Ps. 116:7; 1 Cor. 9:24; 2 Tim. 2:10; Acts 14:22; Rev. 7:14–17; Isa. 55:12–13; Wisdom 2:22–23

"Oh, what blessed people they are in truth who have come from the sea of tribulation to the shore of salvation, and from this exile to the true fatherland, as it were from captivity into the heavenly palace, where they now live in blessed and most desirable rest and have obtained the prize of eternal glory which they sought with much affliction here! They have obtained it, and so rejoice with blessed jubilation forever and ever. Oh, what blessed people, indeed, beyond blessed are they who are now free and safe from all evil, from all sorrow, from all anguish and distress, and have attained the incorruptible glory and the beautiful kingdom of eternal life!

Description and blessed contemplation of the kingdom of God.

[Phil. 4:7; Isa. 51:11; Ps. 104:2]

"Oh, what an eternal kingdom that is, and a kingdom from everlasting to everlasting, where shines the light that never grows dim, where reigns the peace that passes all understanding! O precious kingdom in which the souls of the departed saints softly rest, where eternal joy is upon their heads, where they have joy and rejoicing, and where sorrow and sighing are far from them! O how very glorious a kingdom, where You, almighty Lord God of Sabaoth, cause all Your saints to reign with You, dressed in light as with a garment, and they wear upon their heads the noblest crown of their glory, and You let them see You face-to-face, and You gladden them with Your peace that passes all understanding.

Contemplation of the great prosperity deceased godly Christians have in that life.

"There is an immeasurable and infinite joy, a joy without sorrow, there is utter salvation without pain and days of woe. There is the beautiful street on which one walks and never grows weary. There is the light without darkness and the life without the tribulation of death. There is utter good and nothing evil. There all the children of God are beautiful, vigorous, youths and never grow old. There life knows no ending. There the beautiful form of the elect never grows ugly, never shriveled, never pale. Its fervent love is not corrupted, nor does it grow cold. Its health does not change, and its joy is never undone. In addition, they never feel pain, they hear no sighing, they see nothing sad, they have eternal joy, and they fear no calamity, no adversity, and nothing evil, inasmuch as they possess the highest Good, that is, because at all times they see with joy the face of the Lord of all hosts. Therefore, they are blessed and beyond blessed who are redeemed from the shipwreck of this transitory life, and they have passed through death to this great joy.

Our wretched condition on earth.

Sirach 40:1–2

"But alas, how poor and unblessed are we miserable children of Adam, who in this valley of sorrow, as in a tossing sea, must continue to navigate the ship of our life through the many great floods, waves, and roaring billows of exile, and do not know how long it will be and at what time and hour the Lord shall come and deliver us! Our life is here in exile, and our way is nothing but great peril. In the midst of life, we are surrounded by death. There is always care, fear, hope, and, finally, death, both for him who sits in high honor and for him who is least on earth, and for him who wears silk and a crown no less than for him who wears a rough tunic."

Augustine, Meditations, ch. 41.[63] *Lam. 1:16; Ps. 88:9; 102:9; 69:3; 73:25–26; 27:8; 51:11*

"Therefore, I weep and both my eyes flow with water because the Comforter who should relieve my soul is far from me. . . . And what shall I say? What shall I do? Where shall I go? Where shall I look for Him? Where shall I find You? Whom shall I ask? And who will tell the Lord my God, my dearest Friend, that I am sick with love? The joy of my heart has faded, and my laughter is turned into weeping. O God, eternal comfort of my heart and my portion forever! My flesh is dried up, my heart faints, and my soul will not be comforted except by You alone, who are

63 Author uncertain, *Meditationes* 40 (PL 40:942).

my highest sweetness. For what else do I seek in heaven and earth but You only? You do I desire, in You do I hope. You do I seek, and to You my heart says, 'I seek Your face; Your face, Lord, do I seek.' Cast me not away from Your presence.

The persistence of God in His coming and in our redemption.

Ps. 10:14; 27:10; 80:14, 19; Exod. 34:5–6; John 15:11; Ps. 63:1; 42:2

"O most gracious Lover of men! The poor commend themselves to You. You are the helper of the orphans. O my most faithful Advocate, my Mediator and Defender with God the Father! Have mercy upon me, Your forsaken orphan. My father and my mother have forsaken me, and my soul is as a widow. See the tears of my misery and my grief which I offer to You, until You come to me. Oh, then, my dearest Lord—oh, therefore appear to me, and I am comforted! Show me Your presence, and I have what my heart desires; and reveal to me Your glory, and my joy will be perfect. My soul thirsts for You, and my flesh longs for You. My soul thirsts for You, O Lord, the Fountain of Life. When shall I come there, that I may see Your countenance? When will You come, O my Comforter, and how long shall I wait? When shall I see You, O my Joy that I desire?"

Meditations, ch. 37[64]

"I beseech You by Your salutary wounds which You suffered on the cross for our salvation and from which Your precious blood flowed for our redemption—wound this, my sinful soul, for which also You died. Wound it with the mighty, fiery arrow of Your great love and kindness. Wound it with Your Word, which is living and powerful and stronger than any two-edged sword. O my God, choice Arrow and sharp two-edged Sword, who is able with Your power to pierce the mighty armor of the human heart! I beseech You, strike my heart with the arrow of Your love, that my soul may say to You: 'I am wounded by Your love so that from this wound of Your love my tears flow generously day and night.'

We call upon God to direct and turn our hearts to Him.

"Strike, dear Lord, I beseech You, strike my stony and petrified heart with the blessed, powerful spike of Your love, and with Your mighty strength press forcefully and deeply into it, and draw forth the streams of my eyes from my head, and let both my eyes be fountains of tears that flow and run unceasingly from inward desire and longing for the sight of Your beauty, that I may cry and weep day and night, and in this life let no temporal comfort stir my heart until I am granted to see You in the heavenly throne and hall of joy, O most beloved and most beautiful Bridegroom, my God and Lord!

A faithful soul rejoices at its coming glory and the joy of eternal life and thinks of it continually.

"When, together with all Your elect, I shall see Your glorious, wonderful, and

64 Author uncertain, *Meditationes* 37 (PL 40:935–36).

most beautiful face, full of all sweetness, there with my own eyes, and when I shall honor, worship, bless, and adore Your great majesty and glory there in true humility, and when I am filled with heavenly and unspeakable joy and eternal rejoicing, then I will celebrate and shout for joy with all who love You and say, 'Hurrah! Now I have in sight that for which I hoped for so long, and that for which I have so heartily striven I now possess; and what I highly desired, I have received. For now I am in heaven, one spirit and (as it were) one cake with Him whom I loved on earth with all my powers, whom I surrounded with all love, and to whom I clung with all love. Now I praise Him and now I glorify Him and now I adore Him forever, namely, the Lord my God, who lives and reigns from everlasting to everlasting. Amen.'"

Part Two
How God Readies Us for Eternal Life

UP TO this point I have given a brief account of the joy and glory of eternal life, as well as the blessed benefit and use of this precious and lofty mystery. I will now continue with the second part, showing from whom it comes and how we are made ready for it.

CHAPTER VII

WHENCE DOES ETERNAL LIFE COME?

Eternal life comes only from God.

2 Cor. 5:5; Rom. 5:2; 1 Pet. 1:3–4

TO BEGIN, eternal life comes ultimately not from angels or men but from God Almighty, as Scripture expressly informs us, saying, "He who has prepared us for this very thing is God, who has given us the pledge, the Spirit." Likewise: "We glory in the hope of the glory to come, which God shall give." "God, according to His great mercy, gave us new birth in a living hope through the resurrection of Jesus Christ from the dead, to an imperishable and unstained and incorruptible inheritance, which is kept in heaven." It is beneficial for us to know this and to take careful note of it, that we may give God alone the glory, regard heaven as His gracious gift, and ascribe eternal salvation not to our merit or worthiness but to the boundless goodness of God and His unspeakable kindness.

Deut. 33:3; Ps. 144:3; 8:4

Now that must surely be a great, wondrous love and a mystery the height, depth, breadth, and length of which we, Adam's children, can never search out or fathom in this world—that God should so prefer men above all visible creatures: the heavens, the earth, sun, moon, stars, and everything that lives in the air and on earth as well as in the water and in the earth, and make them partakers of eternal life, which happens to no other creature. And therefore we might well exclaim in amazement, "What love God has for people! Lord, what is man, that You take such account of him; and the child of man, that You so esteem him?"

Summary description how God prepares mankind for eternal life.

Wisdom 2; Ps. 100; Gen. 3; Hosea 6; Rom. 6; John 3; 1 Tim. 3; Gal. 3; Isa. 53; Hosea 13; Matt. 19; Rev. 5; Joel 2; John 16; Titus 2; Rom. 10; 1 Cor. 11; John 1; 8; 2 Cor. 5; Luke 21; 1 Cor. 15

Now, dear brother, if you wish to know how and in what form we are made ready by God for that eternal life, this is the brief, summary answer of Holy

Scripture: God the Father first created man for eternal life, but our first parents, Adam and Eve, by their sinful fall abandoned God and through the devil's instigation, deceit, cunning, and envy lost eternal life not only for themselves but also for all their children and descendants. Then God the Father had mercy on our miserable estate and, out of great love, sent His only-begotten Son into our flesh and blood and caused Him to die for our sin, that we might be delivered from sin, death, the devil, and hell unto eternal life. He also gave His Holy Spirit in order that through the Gospel He might gather, enlighten, and sustain us unto eternal life. And so, whoever by faith takes hold of Christ in the Word, He regards him as His dear child, causes him to pass through temporal death to eternal life, and, at the Last Day, will also waken his body again to eternal joy and glory.

In this sketch and summary outline of how God prepares us for eternal life, the most noble works and benefits of God are presented to us, which are full of His boundless love and faithfulness toward mankind.

All works of God which He demonstrates to us for eternal life are an indication of His unspeakable kindness.

For behold, what does God do? Out of great love He made us in His own image. Out of great love He had mercy on our sorrow and misery. Out of great love He came from heaven and became not an angel, sun, or star, but a man—because of His great love for men. Out of great love He dies for us and redeems us from death, the devil, and hell. Out of great love He gives us His body to eat and His blood to drink in the holy, most worthy Supper, that He may dwell in us and we in Him. Out of great love He is present with His holy angels and protects us from the devil and his retinue. Out of great love He gives us His Holy Spirit. Out of great love He causes us to be called to the heavenly wedding feast, and out of great love He saves us.

To what end God shows the works of His great love and kindness to us.

All this He has done for us in order to show His great love and to bring to us eternal life, which is a life of fervent, burning love, that we might live with Him and all holy angels in the kingdom of heaven both now and forever, in utterly holy love and in the eternal joy, bliss, glory, and majesty of that love. Thus eternal life is a present and gift of the great love of God. It springs and flows forth from eternal love and consists of nothing but pure love and will eternally remain a life of love. And that immeasurable love and kindness of God toward men can be sensed and perceived in nothing so exquisitely and powerfully as in eternal life, for which He has out of great love made us, out of great love redeemed us, out of great love given us new birth, and which He causes to be a life of eternal love.

CHAPTER VIII

THE SIX MIGHTY BENEFITS OF GOD BY WHICH HE FURTHERS ETERNAL LIFE

***The outline of the second part of* The Joy of Eternal Life.**

ALL THIS takes little time to say, but it is not so quickly comprehended or taken to heart. For we are by nature sluggish and cold to believe and sluggish to understand what is briefly set forth and presented from holy, divine Scripture concerning this lofty mystery. Therefore, if it is our intent not to skip over it and pass it by hastily, but to consider it carefully with love and delight, we must contemplate six benefits of God's which are pertinent here and consider them in order one by one. (1) The first benefit is identified as creation unto eternal life. (2) The second is called redemption unto eternal life. (3) The third is our rebirth unto eternal life. (4) The fourth is found in the godly Christians' mortal departure and homeward journey from this valley of sorrow into the heavenly fatherland. (5) The fifth benefit shines forth and is apparent in the blessed and joyous condition of the elect souls with God in His paradise. (6) This will be followed by the sixth and final benefit, namely, the resurrection of our bodies to eternal life on the Last Day.

The First Benefit of God: The Making of Mankind unto Eternal Life

Our creation unto eternal life should give us joy.

Let us take up these six benefits from God in an orderly manner and examine them each in turn. And as far as the first is concerned, our heart ought justly to laugh for great joy when we consider only a little the reason and purpose why we originated and issued from the almighty, everlasting God.

Why and for what purpose God made mankind.

Ps. 100:3; Deut. 6:5; Matt. 22:37; Luke 10:27; Mic. 6:8; Rom. 13:8–9; 1 John 3; Wisdom 2:23

"Know that the Lord God is He who made us," says David, "and not we ourselves: as His people and as the sheep of His pasture." But what moved and inspired God to create man in His own image other than His own unspeakable love? For what purpose did He make us other than for love, that we should love Him with all our heart and all our soul and all our strength, and our neighbor as ourselves? And why should we walk in such love except for the sake of eternal life, which is and will be a life of eternal love? "Lord God," says Scripture, "You love all that is and hate nothing which You have made." For You certainly fashioned nothing with hatred in mind. And again: "God created men for eternal life and made him as an image, that he should be as He is."

God made mankind out of love, in love, for love, and for the eternal life of eternal love.

That is truly a love above all love, that the great King of heaven and earth made man out of great love, in sincere love, for fervent counter-love, and for the eternal life of eternal love. Oh, the surpassing love and deep kindness of our God! How sincerely He loves men! What strength, what fire, what wonder, what sweetness of love, that the whole work of our creation should have its origin in love and be perfected in love and concern itself with love and demand nothing else from us but counter-love! What a wonderfully affectionate father God the Father must be and what a wonderfully sweet friend of men! What a powerful and exquisite life of sweetest love eternal life must be as well, since everything has been oriented and directed toward that life by God the Father through His only-begotten Son in the almighty power of the Holy Spirit, as though by love, through love, and in love!

Comparison of a king who out of love begets children and out of great love shows them very great benefits.

This work of God puts me in mind of a mighty king who wishes to marry, builds a thoroughly glorious palace reaching far and wide, engages numerous servants, maintains an enormous court of counts, barons, noblemen, knights, foot soldiers, and all manner of courtiers, then begets children in his own image (who look like him), loves them sincerely, causes them to dwell with him, and makes his princes, counts, barons, and every minister of high or low station wait diligently upon them, but asks nothing of the children except childlike love, that they give him childlike honor and childlike fear as their dear father. Here everyone must say, "The king heartily loves his children. He begot them in love, and out of love he made a place for them in the royal palace, to occupy it with him, and also out of great love commands that the royal children be waited upon by the fine courtiers, princes, counts, barons, noblemen, as well as all the servants, and the life of the king with his children, and of the children with their kingly father, is a life of true love."

The article of the creation explained by excellent comparisons.

Gen. 1:1–19; 2:7, 15; Ps. 115:16; Heb. 1:14; Ps. 103:20; 34:7; Deut. 4:19; Mic. 6:8; Deut. 6:5; Matt. 22:37

It is exactly the same way with creation. Within five days our dear God and heavenly Father fashioned the beautiful edifice of heaven and earth as it were a royal palace and also created angels as heavenly princes, counts, noblemen, and foot soldiers for His service and eternal glory. Next, He made man as His own child, in His own image, and set him as lord over the earth and all that is in it. He also charged His holy angels with the service of men, to wait on them, as well as the sun, moon, and stars, and the whole host of heaven, to serve us all with their light, strength, and effect. And for such immeasurable benefits He required of man nothing but love and made love the chief commandment, that we should live an eternal life with Him in eternal love and let our eternal life be an eternal love.

The cause and purpose for which God made us is love.

Accordingly, nothing first moved God to make man but His own unspeakable love. Out of fatherly love He fashioned for man the great edifice of heaven and earth as though it were a palace and royal residence. Out of great love He made His heavenly spirits and angelic hosts as ministers to wait upon us. Out of great love He created us for no other purpose than that we should love Him, and for no other life than for an eternal life of eternal love. And Moses plainly intimates this purpose of the most blessed creation when he writes that God formed and created man in His own image.

God's image and nature is Love itself.

1 John 4:8

Now, what, I ask, is God's image, God's form, and God's essence? Here St. John answers in an exceedingly comforting way and paints God in detail with living color when he says, "God is love." We should learn from him this perfect way of speaking and diligently keep it, seeing it has such a friendly ring to it and affords great comfort, as we shall see hereafter!

Among all the properties of God, love is the first and foremost, under which all others are simultaneously comprehended.

And among all the properties of God, we are to hold love as the foremost of all so that all the other properties are comprehended and understood under love, for along with the fact that He is love itself, there are also so many various properties ascribed to God, such as eternal righteousness, eternal, infinite wisdom, holiness, omnipotence, mercy, truth, and the like. And it is right to say that God is Omnipotence itself, Truth itself, Mercy itself, Righteousness itself, Wisdom itself, etc. For there is no property of the divine Being that is not the Being itself. And yet out of all the properties, love has the advantage and is like a circle that surrounds and contains within it all other properties since all that God does and works flows out of love, even when He rages, flashes, and thunders according to His righteousness, as Dr. Martin explains with apt clarity in his sermon on love.

The created reflection of God in man before the fall was a virtue which also is called love.

As love is the foremost among all properties of God, so in the Law love is the chief mandate.

Now, therefore, if God is Love itself and nothing but Love, as Scripture testifies, it can be quickly deduced from this what the reflected image of God in man must have been before the fall. Namely, it was a noble, lofty quality or a kind of noble virtue, which, in a word, is called love. Mark this well. God, I say, is essential Love; therefore, the reflected image of God in Adam before the fall was really nothing but a created counter-love. Man burned with pure, fervent love first toward God and then toward his neighbor. And just as God in His revealed Word is given the name of Love, under which name all other properties of God, such as eternal wisdom, power, righteousness, mercifulness, etc., are comprehended, so the image of God, as it is revealed in the Law, is referred to by the word *love*, and this love is the principal mandate or chief commandment which encompasses and, as it were, encircles all other virtues, such as knowing God rightly, praising God, being perfectly righteous and holy, living without sin, and the like, so that they all belong in love or under love.

Human nature also is itself not dissimilar to the divine nature to a certain degree.

In addition, God so provided that man's nature also was in itself not dissimilar to the divine nature, as explained in various ways among the fathers Hilary, Augustine, and other writers, and in our times by Philipp Melanchthon. They cite various examples, one in one way, another in other ways and opinions. But I myself hold that if we simply look at and contemplate the Law rightly as a mirror of divine wisdom, we will find in it this mystery so brightly and clearly uncovered and revealed that godly Christians will take pleasure in this explanation and need no lengthier ones.

In both, namely, in God and in men, a trinity is discernible.

For just as in the Godhead there are three Persons, God the Father, God the Son, and God the Holy Spirit, which all three embrace men with unspeakable love, so the Law commands that man should in turn love God, his Lover, first, with all his heart, second, with all his soul, and, third, with all his strength. Therefore, there is in both God and man a trinity. In God there is the Father, the Son, and the Holy Spirit. In man there is the heart, the soul, and the strength. And both mysteries—the Trinity of God and the trinity of men—have their foundation in God's Word. God loves men and desires to be loved by men in turn as those whom He created according to His image. God the Father, God the Son, and God the Holy Spirit loves us. Likewise, we are obligated to love God in turn with all our heart, all our soul, and all our strength.

How the Trinity of God is reflected in man's nature.

God the Father is like man's heart, God the Son ("of the Father's heart begotten")[65] is like his soul, or the life in his heart, and God the Holy Spirit is like the strength of his heart and soul. Now, when I name the heart, the soul, and the strength of man in order, I nevertheless understand not three men but one man to whom all three—namely, the heart, the soul, and the strength—belong. Similarly, God the Father, God the Son, and God the Holy Spirit are not three Gods but three Persons and only one God.

Two assets belong to the glory of the divine image in man before the fall.

Here you see how man before the fall, both according to essence and according to quality or virtue, was the mirror and image of our dear God. Now, therefore, note further that two great assets belonged to this noble mirror and image: The first asset was called the covenant of God with man. The second was the heavenly life or the indwelling of the Holy Spirit—that God had His residence and dwelling in man as in His temple and house of delight.

The first asset was the covenant of God established with man.

The covenant of love was built into man before the fall.

First, regarding the covenant, we are to know that this was a contract, covenant, and pledge of love. God showed Himself to man as a father, friend, and great lover. Hence man was pledged and bound to Him with holy, perfect counter-love so that he loved his God with all his heart, with all his soul, and with all his strength. And this contract was the first and oldest covenant which was embedded and implanted in man through the creation so that he could keep it rightly and through the wisdom created in him could understand it rightly and would need no earthly teacher. For just as there is a natural inclination in the hen toward her chicks, and in the chicks toward their mother, and just as between parents and children, brothers and sisters, an innate and inherited covenant of natural love (which [in Greek] is called *storgē physikē*)[66] is discerned, so that one heartily loves the other (where things proceed rightly) and they need no instruction nor any written Law—this much they comprehend and keep from their nature. Likewise, Adam and Eve before the fall needed no tablet of Moses nor any written statute on the

65 A reference to the hymn by A. Prudentius (4th century). (See *LSB* 384.)

66 Cf. Cicero, *Letter to Atticus* 125 § 4 (book 7.2).

manner in which they were to love God and their neighbor, since this covenant was created in them, so that in the holiness implanted and infused into them they were able to act accordingly and to reason within themselves that, because God loves them, they must certainly love Him in turn.

How love and counter-love came together before the fall.

In this manner, then, did the two loves come together, the divine and the human, the eternal, essential Love which created all things and the counter-love in man, which was created in time according to the image of God. Then God loved man, and angelically pure man loved his God. God is Being, and man was a pure crystalline mirror of this Being. And where God as essential Love looked into His mirror, and the created mirror gave its reflected light and loved its Lover, so that utterly pure love shone upon both parties, and there was utter love and counter-love.

How love and counter-love in God and man embraced and kissed before the fall.

Therefore, these two loves before the fall embraced and kissed and with great affection clasped each other—the divine and the human, or God and Adam. God loved His reflection, Adam, as a father loves his child and looked upon him as though He were looking at His image in a mirror. For Adam was God's mirror, and when God gazed into this mirror with the rays of love, the mirror produced a reciprocal gaze and reciprocal radiance and shone back with fervent love upon God its Maker (whom it resembled and whom it knew rightly) so that on both sides it gave forth a noble brightness, radiance, and glory of noble love and counter-love.

The perfect love of neighbor in Adam and Eve before the fall.

In addition, Adam loved his neighbor as himself. For when Eve was brought to him, he received her and knew her as his own flesh and blood, and in this no sinful desire was mingled, but the love of both for each other was a chaste love, a holy love, a pure love, and a love that pleased the entire Holy Trinity and was kindled by God Almighty Himself and was affectionately pledged and confirmed by His Holy Spirit as by a mighty bond. And had they continued in their created righteousness, holiness, and innocence, they would have kept their marriage bed in holy love, begot dear, holy children in holy love, and produced a holy offspring and nothing but holy descendants, and with these filled both paradises—first, the Paradise on earth, and then the paradise in heaven.

The second asset was heavenly life.

Adam had two lives before the fall: the natural and the spiritual.

The second asset and property of their heavenly image was the supernatural spiritual life. For man had two lives before the fall. The first was physical and natural, but the second was spiritual and supernatural, or a heavenly and spiritual life.

As far as the first is concerned, it has no need of lengthy description since everyone knows what kind of life man's natural life is. It is a union of body and soul so that the soul dwells in the body as its habitation, and its power is distinctly divided among all members. Besides this natural life, however, Adam and Eve also led a heavenly life, from the inhabiting or indwelling of the entire Holy Trinity in their body and in their soul. For since both God and man burned so affectionately and fervently with love and counter-love for each other, God dwelt through His love in the man and took His Sabbath or His rest in him so that the whole man was not his own with body and soul, but was God's possession, God's temple, God's palace, and God's habitation. Therefore, just as the natural life is a union and communion of body and soul, so the divine life in Adam and Eve was a union and communion with God so that God rested and dwelt in them, and their body and soul were thoroughly possessed with the living God.

Profit and fruit of the heavenly life.

Hence they knew of no death, but were continually strong in body as well as in soul: the body was beautiful, vigorous, and healthy; the soul encountered no anguish, no sadness, no sorrow, no secret suffering or hidden heartache. The life of the body was the soul, and the life of the soul was God Himself, as Augustine and Prosper of Aquitaine express it. And as our body would let itself be governed by the soul, so were both body and soul subject to the divine Being indwelling them and hearkened to the Holy Spirit.

Holy condition of our first parents before their sinful fall.

Gen. 2:19–23

Thus our father Adam also, from such indwelling of God, was holy, righteous, wise, and so well-versed in all things that he knew God rightly and served Him from the heart with joy. Accordingly, he also knew all beasts on earth and all fowl under the heavens and gave to each beast its name. And despite his being asleep when his wife was fashioned from his rib, he nevertheless knew her in the first moment as his flesh and blood and said, "She shall be called woman because she was taken from man." He was intelligent, clever, handsome, strong, unwavering, godly, and knew of no sin or sinful lust. His authority and dominion extended so far that he ruled over the fish in the sea and over the fowl under the heavens and over every beast that crept upon the earth. Everything was necessarily subject to him.

Adam and Eve, before the fall, had in their bodies a glory with which they were dressed instead of clothing.

I also hold that before the fall (when he was still a temple and dwelling place of the Holy Trinity), from this indwelling of God, Adam likely possessed in his body to some degree an outward glory and brightness and was enveloped by it as with a cloud, just as Moses' skin and face shone before the people of Israel when he had spoken with the Lord. For because Scripture testifies that Adam and Eve first saw and learned after the fall that they were naked, which seemed to them so shameful that they covered themselves with fig leaves, it may be that before the fall they shone like brilliant stars or like burning torches and were encompassed, clothed, and, as it were, beclouded by an outward radiance and glow instead of clothing, so that their bodies were seen to be not bare and naked but shrouded with encircling glory and bright clouds, for which reason they also had no need to be ashamed. They were without sin, and God the Lord dwelt so affectionately in them that by it they shone and knew of no sinful bareness in their body.

If Adam and Eve had not sinned, we would have inherited the image of God.

It was such a case with our first parents before the fall, and everything went so pleasantly, gloriously, orderly, and admirably according to God's will, that God in heaven with His holy angels took delight, joy, and sincere pleasure in it.

And no doubt if they had continued steadfast in that love, with diligent, accurate preservation of that noble, heavenly image which was implanted in, impressed upon, and affixed to them by God, they would have had children also not only according to their image but also similar to and uniform with the image of God, so that out of inherited and inborn holiness, we would have loved our heavenly Father together with His only-begotten Son and the Holy Spirit with all our heart, with all our soul, and with all our strength, and each of us the other on the whole earth as himself.

Two goods of the divine image.

This image of God would have evinced itself in all of Adam's children with its two assets or properties, which were mentioned above.

First, the Law and covenant of love would have been inborn in us.

For, first, the covenant or contract and obligation of love would have needed no special revelation from heaven upon Mount Sinai through Moses, or else through another mediator, but just as there are love's kind and tender feelings, love's joy, and a loving inclination between parents and children, brothers and sisters, cousins, aunts, and close blood relatives, on whom *storgē physikē* or blood-love and blood-kinship is impressed and imprinted by nature, so the covenant and the Law of holy, perfect love for God and neighbor would have been passed down to and implanted in us also through our natural birth.

What the circumstances of religion would have been if man had remained without sin.

Oh, how splendid the practice of religion would have been throughout the world, never to have heard of any divisions, unnecessary disputations, or scholastic quarrels! Oh, with what unanimity all the nations in Europe, Asia, and Africa would have loved their Lord with all their heart, with all their soul, and with all their strength!

Oh, how often all Adam's children from every land would have come together with heartfelt joy and rejoicing, that with one voice we might honor, extol, and praise the Lord our God and glorify and increase His great goodness, grace, wonders, and benefits! How there would be only one religion, one faith, one worship implemented everywhere! How pleasantly, how brotherly, how amiably, and how splendidly all nations, all Gentiles, and all men under the sun, such as Germans, Italians, Spaniards, Turks, Moors, Indians, etc., would have agreed together in the faith, in the confession of the truth, and in the Holy Spirit!

How we would have loved our neighbors. The great world would have been full of pure love.

How the love of neighbor also would have possessed and held sway over mankind! Then I would have been able to travel safely throughout the whole world without any danger by land and sea and would have known all peoples in the eastern lands, in the northern domains, and in the territories located to the south and west and been very loved, accepted, and welcomed by every man in all the world as by my loving brother and most familiar friends. We would have known of no war or strife, heard of no bloodshed anywhere, and no other new tidings from any lands, from Moscow, from Turkey, from Arabia, from America, and from the newly discovered islands, would have emerged except utterly fervent, pure love, and to relate how the people everywhere loved God with all their heart, with all their soul, and with all their mind, and one another as themselves, and that there was no other strife but to see how one might excel another in showing honor, in great love, and in unfeigned friendship.

Love would have been pure in man everywhere, without any lust.

Then there would have been no sinful lust. Then groom and bride, as well as young men and maidens, would have loved each other with utterly holy chastity by instigation of the Holy Spirit. Then man and wife would have begotten children in godly happiness and with their children increased the kingdom of God. The natural love between parents and children, brothers and sisters, would have been a pure, holy, perfect love. The holy angels would have attended us with gladness according to God's decree.

Second, every man on earth would have had two lives: one natural and one spiritual.

We would also have always, from the beginning of our birth, led two lives: the natural and the spiritual. The body would have lived at all times without pain and without the tribulation of death naturally and would have been crowned and clothed with another, heavenly life. For God would have dwelt in the body as well as in the soul, as in a beautiful temple, in a wonderfully pleasant and comforting way, and our whole life would have been with God, in God, and through

God; likewise, God's life, God's dwelling, God's Sabbath in us, and accordingly our whole life and conversation among one another on earth, would have been nothing but a life of ardent, burning love and counter-love, or a covenant of love, so that just as God loves us, we, too, (as often stated) would have loved Him in turn with all our heart, with all our soul, and with all our strength, and one another as ourselves.

The splendor of the whole world, if man had not sinned.

The whole world would have been a beautiful paradise full of such children of God and such noble temples of the Holy Spirit that every place throughout the whole earth (wherever I might see any men) would have shone, sparkled, and gleamed as if I saw nothing but heavenly stars or glowing lamps. For out of the affectionate indwelling of the Holy Trinity, we, as the temple of God, would all, like Adam and Eve, have gleamed beautifully and had an outward glory instead of clothes, yet one greater and more than another according to the various gifts and workings of the Holy Spirit.

How splendid it would have been in every place.

The holy angels would, out of great love, have served us with gladness according to God's decree. And there would have continued to be one language in every place so that you would have been able to understand an Indian, Turk, Arab, Muscovite, or one from America just as easily and instantly as the language of your mother. No wars, bloodshed, envy, hatred, or sedition would have been heard of, nor any tempest, accident, anguish, sorrow, sickness, or misery, nor any death or dying. The ground would have borne no thistles or thorns, but only roses, lilies, sweet-smelling herbs, spices, and the most exquisite fruits as quickly in Norway, Moscow, and every northern land as in Egypt, Arabia, and similar far-flung lands of the east. The fowl under the heavens, the beasts on the earth, and the fish in the waters would have been subject to us without any fear or terror.

We would have all ascended alive into heaven.

In addition, when a man had passed his time and finished his course on earth, he would have departed from this world alive with body and soul, without any bodily pain, without sickness, and without the peril of death, and ascended into heaven. He would not have tasted death and not have felt the least affliction, but he would have been taken up out of the earthly paradise into the heavenly paradise. He would have gone forth in a fiery chariot like Enoch and Elijah, surrounded and accompanied by many thousands of angels. He would have bidden farewell to his children, his brothers and sisters, and all his friends who were left behind would not have wept or mourned in the least at his glorious and majestic departure, but they would have rejoiced greatly and shouted with joy. With gladness and jubilation they would have given thanks to the eternal, almighty God for it, in the unwavering confidence that after the fulfillment of their time, they, too, would soon follow and likewise ascend into heaven.

Adam and Eve fell from God.

But because those two from whom we all descend—Adam and Eve—fell and allowed themselves to be woefully turned and led astray by the lustful, accursed devil, they thereby lost God's image, namely, the noble quality of perfect love implanted in them, and instead took hold of despicable Satan's image, that is, anguish and fright, so that instead of noble, holy love for God, after taking the bite of the apple, they had an agonized dread of Him.

How Adam and Eve after the fall became aware that they were naked.

Then they fell and departed from the most ancient and first covenant or contract of love with which they had been pledged to their God, and they loved the creature or creation more than their Creator; they perverted their holy, perfect love into a sinful and damnable lust. On account of this the eyes of them both were also instantly opened (as Moses writes), and they became aware that they were naked. But how did this come about? Answer: The Holy Trinity, God the Father, Son, and Holy Spirit, their heavenly life, withdrew from them so that they were no longer His temples, tabernacles, and houses of delight. And when He removed His residence or indwelling and withdrew from them, they also instantly lost the outward radiance and brightness of their body so that they looked at each other bare and naked with shame and disgrace, and they both, as spiritually dead people, being stripped of the heavenly life, saw well that they were no longer children of light, but masks of the infernal darkness and vessels of the devil's stench. Therefore, being bare and naked, they hurriedly looked for a solution and wove fig leaves together and made aprons for themselves.

In Adam and Eve after the fall, the natural life still remained intact when the spiritual one was lost.

Now the natural life was still intact in them when they were spiritually dead so that they were still able to walk, see, hear, speak, take counsel, and use carnal reason. Nevertheless, they had been entirely and wholly deprived of the divine life (which is the noblest of all) and had perverted the love for God instilled in them into an earthly lust, and saw that their bare and naked members, in contrast to their former splendor, were now to be accounted as nothing other than dead corpses compared to living men and no longer had the same beauty, strength, power, and virtue, nor outward radiance and brightness as before, and therefore fled from God in agony and hid themselves behind the trees. Yet afterward, their body was gradually vitiated by all manner of pain and illness and wore out, until, finally, death came and brought them both under the earth.

We men bear children on earth all by nature of Adam's image.

Now just as Adam after the fall was no longer heavenly-minded by nature, but only earthly- and carnally-minded, he also begot children after the earthly image, and for this reason, we are all conceived in sin and born in sin, and through sin are subject to death. The image of God, which is called perfect love, is of course gone, removed, and extinguished, and the despicable devil's image, which is called sinful lust, as well as the infernal terror at God's judgment, has taken its place. For just as Adam and Eve after the fall fled from God and hid themselves, so we also bear by nature an agonizing terror and abhorrence of the presence of God, and our flesh and blood is afraid of Him as of a consuming fire of a strict judge whom it hates with all its soul.

All Adam's children are an adulterous generation, and after their fall from God courted the devil; yet God has mercy on us.

But here note further what God did for us and to what length His great love and tender loving-kindness moved Him. Imagine a very godly man who, out of true and boundless love, receives back into his grace his wife who has run away and committed adultery—especially if he hears and learns that his sworn enemy enticed her with cunning words and took her away and treated her most wickedly, wooed her for a time, then struck her and trampled her underfoot so that she lay sprawled out and her red blood flowed pitifully from her eyes, ears, mouth, and nose. The husband would learn all this, and even though he could keep silent and by all rights be pleased by the adulteress's torment and affliction, nevertheless out of great, unmerited love and mercy he shows her pity, calls her to himself, and takes her back as his wedded wife.

God calls us by grace back to Himself, like a godly husband who receives his adulterous wife back to grace.

Jer. 3:1, 12

No differently does our benevolent God deal with us when He sees mankind, the adulterous generation, lying under the power of death, the devil, and hell, so that she must readily allow herself to be tortured, tormented, and afflicted by Satan, her infernal lover. At this God, in His great love, is filled with pity, and calls her back to Himself, forgives her sins, and reestablishes with her the covenant of love, according to the parable which He Himself used with the prophet Jeremiah, saying, "If a man divorces his wife and she goes from him and takes another man, may he take her again? Is it not so that the land would be polluted? But you have played the whore with many lovers; yet come back to Me, says the Lord." Likewise: "Return, faithless Israel, says the Lord, and I will not turn My face against you. For I am merciful, declares the Lord, and I will not be angry forever."

Question.

"Indeed," you say, "how could God receive and accept mankind again to grace without injury to His strict righteousness and His Word, in which He had threatened us with death?"

Answer: God finds a way for our redemption so that His righteousness is by no means interrupted.

Rom. 5:10

Answer: While on our part the covenant and contract of love was broken and dishonored, so that we thereby forfeited eternal life, which we could not afterward regain by human powers and means, yet on God's part the covenant was not sinned against since He loved man from His heart and did not give him the least cause to fall away and transgress. God remained constant and unwavering to love at all times, even after our unhappy fall, just as St. Paul writes that God loved us even while we were still His enemies. But that this love might not contradict righteousness, He took thought for a way and means by which righteousness might be satisfied, that He might receive and accept us again into grace and into the covenant of love without injury to righteousness, that we might again become His temples, instruments, palaces, and peculiar possession.

The incarnation and the Son of God's gracious work.

Namely, He caused His only-begotten Son to become man and sent Him as the life of His heart into our flesh and blood and cast on Him all the world's sin, disgrace, guilt, and punishment and caused Him to die and descend into hell, that by faith in Him we might be loosed and freed from sin, death, the devil, and hell and in turn become capable of and participants in the eternal heavenly life.

All this is expounded for us very gracefully and comfortingly in the beautiful hymn "Dear Christians, One and All, Rejoice," when you sing:

> Fast bound in Satan's chains I lay;
>   Death brooded darkly o'er me.
> Sin was my torment night and day;
>   In sin my mother bore me.
>   But daily deeper still I fell;
>   My life became a living hell,
>   So firmly sin possessed me.
>
> My own good works all came to naught,
>   No grace or merit gaining;
> Free will against God's judgment fought,
>   Dead to all good remaining.
>   My fears increased till sheer despair

Left only death to be my share;
The pangs of hell I suffered.

But God had seen my wretched state
Before the world's foundation,
And mindful of His mercies great,
He planned for my salvation.
He turned to me a father's heart;
He did not choose the easy part
But gave His dearest treasure.

God said to His beloved Son:
"It's time to have compassion.
Then go, bright jewel of My crown,
And bring to all salvation.
From sin and sorrow set them free;
Slay bitter death for them that they
May live with You forever."[67]

It is an indescribable, wonderful love that God gave us His Son. A parable of a king who causes his son to die for a criminal.

Who, then, can sufficiently praise this wonderful love and benevolence of our God? Who can fathom the depth, the breadth, the height, and the length of this goodness and of this kindness? If every leaf on the trees, every blade of grass on the earth, every grain of sand in and beside the sea, and every speck of dust in the sunlight had tongues—not merely like Demosthenes, Cicero, and Pericles, but even tongues of angels—it would still be impossible for them with their rhetorical art sufficiently to praise and tell out these bounties. For consider: if you had earned the death penalty, and the executioner was about to pull your skin over your ears or all your veins out of your body with glowing tongs, and a mighty king gave his son for you, caused him to be hideously tormented and mistreated, and adopted you as his son and heir, how could you extol and praise such love enough? You would surely discern and see that not one vein or drop of blood in his whole body was hostile toward you. This is how God acts toward us. When we ought to have been led away by all devils into the pit of hell and been tormented forever with hellfire, He interposed His only-begotten Son for us, drew the thorn out of our foot and pressed it into His Son's foot, adopted us as His heirs, and gave us eternal life.

67 "Nun freut euch lieben Christen gmein" (Luther, 1523), sts. 2–5 (*LSB* 556, public domain).

The bowels of God's mercy.

Luke 1:78

These are the true "bowels of mercy" (as Zechariah says in his canticle), that is, the tender mercy of our God, through which the Dayspring from on high has visited us, that He might appear to those who sit in darkness and the shadow of death and to guide our feet into the way of peace. Therefore, we sing:

Oh, Father's love unknown,
Oh, kindness of the Son,
We would all have perished
For all our awful sin,
But so hath He us cherished,
He gained us joys of heav'n.
Oh, that we were there![68]

Augustine, Meditations, ch. 15[69]

"Oh, immeasurable faithfulness," says Augustine. "Oh, unfathomable love! Lord God, You gave up Your Son that You might redeem the servant! God was made man that lost man might be delivered from the power of the wicked spirits. O dear God and Father, how very kind a lover of men Your Son is, to whose heartfelt love it did not seem sufficient that He should come down and be made man, born of the pure Virgin Mary, unless He might also undergo the death of the cross and shed His blood for us and for our salvation. The faithful God came to us. He came out of His faithfulness and goodness. He came to seek and to save what was lost. He sought the lost sheep, He sought it and found it and, laying it on His shoulders, brought it back to the fold of the flock—the pious Lord and true Shepherd!

The works of great love which God showed us.

"Oh, great love! Oh, great faithfulness! Who has heard the like? Who would not always ponder this heartfelt mercy? Who would not marvel at it? Who would not rejoice highly at the great love with which You have loved us? You sent Your Son in the likeness of sinful flesh, and through sin condemned sin in the flesh (Rom. 8:3), that in Him we might become Your righteousness (2 Cor. 5:21). For He is the true spotless Lamb that has taken away the sin of the world and who by His grievous, bitter death destroyed death and by His rising again has restored everlasting life.

We can never repay our dear God for His ardent love.

"But what can we give or show You in return, O Lord our God, for such great benefits of Your mercy? How can we praise You enough and thank You enough?

68 "In dulci jubilo" (attr. Henry Suso, 14th century), st. 3. (Compare with *LSB* 385, st. 3.)

69 Author uncertain, *Meditationes* 10.15–16 (PL 40:911ff.).

Even if we were as wise and strong as the holy angels, we would produce nothing worthy to repay such great faithfulness and great goodness of Yours. Indeed, if all our members were changed into tongues, we would still be far too lowly to honor and extol You with indebted praises.

How highly God exalted our flesh and blood in Christ, His Son.

"For beyond all reason is Your unspeakable love, which You have shown us unworthy ones solely out of Your goodness and benevolence. For Your only-begotten Son, our God, took not angels but the seed of Abraham and was made like us, yet without sin. Therefore, assuming not an angelic nature but a human one and glorifying it with the white robe of the resurrection and immortality, He exalted it above all the heavens, above all choirs of angels, above cherubim and seraphim, and set it at His right hand. There angels praise it, dominions worship it, and all the virtues of the heavens fear this man who is God.

How highly all godly Christians are exalted in Christ Jesus.

"Now, therefore, I set on Him all my hope and all my trust. For in this Christ Jesus, our Lord, is a portion of every one of us, that is, the flesh and blood of us all. Where, therefore, that portion of myself reigns, there I believe that I, too, shall reign. Where my flesh is exalted, there shall I also be made glorious. Where my blood has dominion, there will I also have dominion. And although I am a sinner, I have no doubt about this communion of grace. Likewise, although my sins prevent me, nevertheless my substance and being in Christ commands and demands this glory. And although my transgressions shut me out, yet the relationship or communion of nature cannot thrust me back. For God is not so harsh and unmerciful that He should forget man and that He should not remember that which He bears in the unity of His person and which He assumed for my sake and requested for my sake.

In Christ Jesus we find our salvation and blessedness.

"Truly kind and very good is our God, and He loves His flesh, His members, and His body. In our God and in our sweetest, kindest, and most gracious Lord Jesus Christ, in whom we are arisen and are now ascended to heaven and now sit together in the heavenly places—in Him, I say, our flesh loves us, for we find and have the noble prerogative and marriage of our blood in Him. For we are His members and His flesh, and He is our Head, from which the whole body consists (Eph. 5:23; Col. 2:19), as it is written: 'Bone of my bones and flesh of my flesh' and 'The two shall be one flesh' (Gen. 2:23–24). Likewise: 'No man ever hated his own flesh, but he nourishes it and cares for it. This mystery is great. But I speak of Christ and the Church' (Eph. 5:29, 32).

Thanksgiving to God.

"Therefore, with lips and heart and with all my strength, O Lord our God (of infinite mercy), I give You praise and thanks for all Your mercy with which You have wonderfully deigned to assist us poor, lost sinners, through Your Son, our Savior and Redeemer, who died for our sins and rose again for our justification and now, living forever, is seated at Your right hand, where He represents and pleads for us (Rom. 8:34)."

Augustine, Meditations, ch. 17

"Now, therefore, dearest Father, forasmuch as You have shown us so great a benefit through Your Son, who in His Word says explicitly: 'No man comes to Me unless the Father who sent Me draws him' and: 'No man comes to the Father except through Me' (John 6:44; 14:6)—therefore, I beseech You and humbly ask You, draw me to Him always, that He may draw me to You, where He is seated at Your right hand, where there is eternal life and eternal blessedness, perfect love without fear, and eternal day, the one Spirit in all, the highest and most certain security, secure rest, restful joy, joyful prosperity, prosperous eternity, eternal blessedness, and the blessed sight of Your face, and the praise of You, who with Your Son, and He with You, live and reign in the communion of the Holy Spirit, true God, forever and ever. Amen."

The end of our creation and of the mercy of God is eternal life.

1 John 4:8–9; John 3:16; Rom. 5:8; 6:23

The first thing to note and retain on this point is the end to which God created us and gave us His only-begotten Son, which was not temporal riches, power, pomp, and prosperity, but eternal life. As Scripture says, "God is love. In this the love of God toward us was made manifest, that God sent His only Son into the world that we might live through Him. God so loved the world that He gave His only-begotten Son so that all who believe in Him will not perish but have eternal life. God glorifies His love toward us in that Christ died for us while we were still sinners. Much more, then, will we be preserved from wrath since we have been justified by His blood. The gift of God is eternal life in Christ Jesus."

The Second Benefit of God: Our Redemption to Eternal Life

The work of the redemption is ascribed to the Lord Christ.

After the work of the great love and kindness of our heavenly Father, who created us for eternal life and, when we were lost, sent us His only-begotten Son that by Him we might regain the salvation that we lost, there follows the second benefit, which is, briefly put, redemption. And as creation is ascribed to God the Father, so the work of redemption is attributed to His dear Son, our Savior, Jesus Christ.

God's Son is made man, suffers, dies, descends into hell, rises from the dead, ascends into heaven, and thereby obtained for us eternal life.

For behold, what does the Son of God do? Out of love and kindness He was made man, out of love He takes upon Himself all the sins of the world, all the sorrows of the world, and the curse of the Law. Out of great, fervent love He allows Himself, for our sins, to be crucified, put to death, accursed, and weighed down with the unbearable wrath of His Father, that He might redeem us from death, the devil, and hell and reconcile us to His heavenly Father. Here indeed was the

. . . wondrous fray—
When life and death contended.
But it was life that won the day,
And death, devoured, was ended.
Holy Scripture plainly saith
How death was swallowed up by death
And put to scorn and mock'ry.[70]

Christ overcame him and crushed the head of the serpent and stormed, conquered, destroyed, and razed hell. On the third day He rose again from the dead, ascended into heaven, and sits at the right hand of the Father Almighty, where out of great love He now represents us before His Father so that all who believe in Him will not perish but have eternal life.

How children and the unlearned can learn and retain the whole work of our redemption.

You children and unlearned are able to learn and retain this well from your Christian hymn, where you sing (continuing):

The Son obeyed His Father's will,
Was born of virgin mother;
And God's good pleasure to fulfill,
He came to be my brother.
His royal pow'r disguised He bore;
A servant's form, like mine, He wore
To lead the devil captive.

To me He said, "Stay close to Me,
I am your rock and castle.
Your ransom I Myself will be;
For you I strive and wrestle.
For I am yours, and you are Mine,
And where I am you may remain;
The foe shall not divide us.

70 Compare with "Christ Jesus Lay in Death's Strong Bands" (Luther, 1524), *LSB* 458, st. 4.

"Though he will shed My precious blood,
Me of My life bereaving,
All this I suffer for your good;
Be steadfast and believing.
Life will from death the vict'ry win;
My innocence shall bear your sin,
And you are blest forever."[71]

The surpassing love of the Son of God for mankind.

Yet consider, children of light, what marvelous love and unspeakable kindness there must be in our pledged Redeemer and Savior, Jesus Christ, that this great God honors us sinful earthworms so highly above all the stars of heaven, above sun and moon, even above all angels and heavenly hosts, and so vastly prefers us that He does not become a moon, a sun, a star, or even an angel, but a man, and a virgin's Son, and out of great, unspeakable love comes heartily to the aid of our distress, our sorrows, and our misery and for our sakes dies a bitter, contemptible death.

Symbol of the Egyptian bird, the pelican.

As the Egyptian bird called the pelican, when it sees its young lying stone-dead, slain by the serpent, wounds itself and out of heartfelt love pecks its own breast and sheds blood with which it sprinkles its young and restores them to life—so this heavenly Pelican loves us men as His own blood-relatives, not with normal love, but with a wondrous, passionate love. He loves us into death, even the death of the cross (Phil. 2:8)—indeed, into the depths of hell and into the anguish and torment of hell, since He suffered death, hell, and the anguish of hell because of our sin and spilled His crimson blood on the tree of the cross, that we might be redeemed and restored from eternal death to eternal life. That is what I call love and mercy!

Xerxes wept for his great host in contemplation of their death. Far more was the Lord Christ moved to compassion by our misery.

It is written of King Xerxes that when he waged the great war against the Greeks and had collected 1,100,000 men, he climbed a high mountain, and when he looked down on the great multitude, he began to weep bitterly. When he was asked why he was weeping, he is supposed to have answered, "Ah, should I not weep? I see the great host and consider that none of them will be alive after a hundred years." Much more was the Son of God moved to pity for the whole wide world since so many hundred thousands of thousands of men were to be cast away and condemned. And because He lets Himself be put to death for that very reason and sheds His blood for our redemption, who does not see then that He must love us heartily and faithfully? Rather, it seems (as Johann Tauler writes)

71 "Nun freut euch, lieben Christen, gmein" (Luther, 1523), sts. 6–8 (*LSB* 556, public domain).

as if the heavenly Father thought more of us or, indeed, as much of us as of His only-begotten Son and that the Lord Christ thought more of us or, indeed, as much of us as of Himself and that the holy, divine Majesty was neither able nor willing to do without us.

Two points to be considered here: first, the treasure obtained; second, God's hand, in which the treasure is given to us.

Now, that we may understand this noble, sweet mystery fruitfully and appropriate it more richly, we must here pay close attention to two points. First, we must ponder what kind of treasure or what kind of good it is that the Lord Christ has obtained for us and for which we were redeemed by Him, that we might receive it and possess it. Second, we must also become acquainted with His hand, in which the salutary and precious good which He merited is given, offered, and presented to us by Him.

Christ, with all His goods, is Himself our treasure.

1 Cor. 1:30

The treasure obtained is, in a word, our salvation. And by this is understood the Lord Christ Himself with all His goods and gracious benefits, even as He is from God made to us wisdom and righteousness and sanctification and redemption. Whoever knows Christ rightly and takes hold of Him rightly in faith takes hold of the fullness of the Godhead, the Father, the Son, and the Holy Spirit, the true treasure, the eternal life, and the everlasting good. Whoever has all that his heart desires in this world but does not have Christ is poor, naked, and bare and has less than nothing. Conversely, whoever has nothing of his own in the world but believes in Christ is richer than the king of the Turks and has a treasure surpassing silver and gold.

Testimony of Holy Scripture.

Ps. 73:25–26; Phil. 3:8; Matt. 6:20

"If I have You only," says David, "I care for nothing in heaven and earth. Although my body and soul should fail, yet You, O God, are the comfort of my heart and my portion." Likewise, Paul writes, "I count all as loss compared to the excelling knowledge of Jesus Christ my Lord, for whom I have reckoned all as loss, and count it as dung, that I may win Christ." Likewise, shortly after that: "Not that I have seized it already or am already perfect. But I pursue it, that I might also seize it, according as I have been seized by Christ Jesus." This is the blessed treasure that "neither moths nor rust can consume and that thieves cannot steal."

We are to picture Christ as a tree of life.

Rev. 2:7; Hosea 14:8; Song 2:3

A simple Christian layman can picture the whole mystery of this noble, lofty treasure aptly and take it to heart with blessed application if he imagines and allows Jesus Christ or the salvation obtained by Christ to be nothing other than a whole tree with all that belongs to it, which are the roots, the trunk, and the delectable fruit. For Christ is indeed the tree of life mentioned in St. John's Revelation. "I will be like a green fir tree," He says in the prophet Hosea, "on Me your fruit shall be found." And in the Song of Songs, the Christian Church sings of her heavenly Bridegroom: "As an apple tree among the trees of the wood, so is my beloved among the sons. I sit under the shadow of Him whom I desire, and His fruit is sweetness to my taste."

In Christ, the tree of life, we find three kinds of goods: (1) root-goods, (2) trunk-goods, and (3) fruit-goods.

Now then, just as these three parts belong to the tree: first, the root; second, the trunk; and, third, the fruit—so we find on the tree of life, that is, in our Lord and Savior, Christ, three goods also, which you may also call, first, root-goods; second, trunk-goods; and, third, fruit-goods.

Description of the root-goods.

The root-goods are the first benefits which our Lord Christ obtained for us and makes the foundation, ground, and root of all other goods. Therefore, just as the tree must first be established and the roots placed into the ground before it can grow and its fruits be enjoyed, so no one can partake of the trunk-goods or the fruit-goods of the noble tree of life unless he has first laid hold of the roots and rightly grasped the foundational goods in faith.

Three root-goods.

Of these root and foundational goods there are chiefly three, and they are, first, the righteousness revealed in the Gospel; second, the true peace which exists in our reconciliation with God; and, third, the victory which Christ has won against the devil.

The first root-good is the righteousness that avails before God.

Rom. 10:4; Gal. 4:4; 2 Cor. 5:21; Rom. 8:3

The righteousness revealed in the Gospel is the first foundational good and includes within it the fulfilling of the Law, that Christ took upon Himself all the world's sin, debt, and transgression, and with His holy life, conduct, obedience, works, and His harsh, bitter death paid our debt and fulfilled the Law for us. Of this Scripture says, "Christ is the end of the Law. He who believes in Him is righteous." "God made His Son subject to the Law, that He might redeem those who were subject to the Law." Likewise: "He made Him who knew no sin to be sin for us, that in Him we might become the righteousness that avails before God." And again: "What was impossible for the Law (since it was weakened by the flesh) God did, and sent His Son in the likeness of sinful flesh, and through sin condemned sin in the flesh, that the righteousness demanded by the Law might be fulfilled in us."

What evangelical righteousness is.

Matt. 19:16–26; 22:37–40; Deut. 26:16–19; Rom. 1:32; 2:7–8; Ps. [14]:3; Rom. 10; Ps. 44:26; John 13:1; 2 Cor. 5:15, 19; 1 Cor. 1:30; Isa. 61:10

In this verse of Scripture, saving righteousness is described for us. And this is its meaning, that we may appropriate it rightly: The Law requires of us perfect obedience, so that we love God with all our heart, with all our soul, with all our strength, and everyone his neighbor as himself. He who does this has eternal life. He who transgresses is accursed and belongs in hell. Now, we are all transgressors and have all sinned. Therefore, the Law demands that we all be punished and will allow no one to heaven since none of us has kept it. Christ, however, fulfilled the Law and paid for us *actively* and *passively*, that is, with actual obedience and by suffering the punishment. For He does the will of the Father for us and loves us even into death, and He bears our sin and lets the curse of the Law come upon Him, though He did not deserve it, and after the Law is hereby fulfilled and appeased, the Lord Christ gives us His obedience to be our righteousness, our adornment, and, as it were, a beautiful garment with which He covers our sin, provided we take hold of it and put it on by faith. As Isaiah says, "I rejoice in the Lord, and my soul is joyful in my God, for He has dressed me with garments of salvation and clothed me with the robe of righteousness."

Our second root-good is reconciliation with God or the true peace which the world cannot give.

The second foundational good is the heavenly and truly golden peace, namely, our reconciliation with God Almighty, and consists in the forgiveness of sin, that for the perfect sacrifice of His dearest Son, our Lord and Savior Jesus Christ, God most graciously causes His righteous wrath to vanish and depart and will no longer remember our sins forever.

Testimony of Holy Scripture of our reconciliation.

2 Cor. 5:19; Col. 1:19–20; Heb. 8:12; 10:17; Ps. 103:8, 10–12; Mic. 7:18–19

"God was in Christ," says the apostle, "reconciling the world with Himself, and not counting their sin against them. For it pleased the Father that in Him all the fullness should dwell, and all things by Him should be reconciled to Himself, whether things on earth or things in heaven, having made peace through the blood of His cross. I will have mercy on their trespasses and sins," says God, "and will no longer remember their iniquities." In Hebrews 8, the apostle relates this to the reconciliation accomplished by Christ. And pertinent here is what David says: "Gracious and merciful is the Lord, patient and of great goodness. . . . He does not deal with us according to our sins, nor reward us according to our iniquities. For as high as heaven is above the earth, so high does He cause His grace to abound upon those who fear Him; as far as the east is from the west, so far does He cause our transgressions to be removed from us." Likewise, Micah says, "Where is there such a God as You, forgiving sin and pardoning iniquities to the remnant of His inheritance, who does not keep His wrath forever? For He is merciful. He will have mercy upon us, blot out our iniquities, and cast all our sins into the depths of the sea."

The third foundational good is our victory over death, the devil, and hell.

The third root-good or foundational good is the gracious heavenly victory, the fact that our Savior, Jesus Christ, for the comfort and salvation of us miserable children of Adam, overcame the devil, death, and hell, along with the whole world, and gives us His victory, that we may take comfort in it and know that no one can pluck us out of His hand.

Testimony of our victory through Christ.

Isa. 9:4; 1 Cor. 15:56; Heb. 2:14; Luke 11:21–22; Col. 2:15; John 14:30; 16:33; Luke 11:20

He has broken the yoke of our burden, the staff of our shoulder, and the rod of our oppressor, says Isaiah. That is, we were burdened with death. "The sting of death is sin, and the strength of sin is the Law." But God's Son took on our flesh and our blood, "that through death He might take the strength of him who had the power of death, that is, the devil." For the devil was a strong man armed, and as long as he keeps his palace, his goods are in peace. But Christ, the stronger one, came upon him and overcame him and took from him his armor in which he trusted and divided the spoils. "He spoiled the rulers and authorities and made a show of them openly, making them a triumphal procession through Himself." And He apportions this victory (that He overcame death, the devil, hell, and the whole world) to us in His Gospel, when He says, "The prince of this world is coming and has no claim on Me." "Be of good cheer, I have overcome the world." "If by the finger of God I drive out devils, then the kingdom of God is coming to you."

Description of the trunk-goods.

When these three root-goods have been grasped and taken hold of by faith, they are followed by the heavenly trunk-goods, which spring up from the first and are like a trunk upon its roots. And these trunk-goods include in themselves these treasures and benefits which far surpass and highly excel all the world's pomp, happiness, riches, honor, and majesty and are not to be gained or bought with any silver, with any gold, with any pearls or jewels—indeed, not with any kingdoms on the whole earth. But whoever sees Christ, the tree of life, and has first grasped and taken hold of the root-goods in Him can also come to the second set and become a partaker of them in like manner.

There are three trunk-goods.

Now, of these trunk-goods also there are three, just as there are of the root-goods, and they are (1) the blessed adoption of sons, (2) the heavenly bridal delight, (3) and the glory of the spiritual temple. Note this well, you who are unlearned, and imagine them just as if you saw three large boughs on some tall, noble trunk which you must first reach before you can get to the fruit-goods on the branches.

The first trunk-good is the blessed adoption.

1 John 3:1; Rom. 8:15–17; Gal. 3:26; John 1:12

The first trunk-good is the blessed adoption, in which God the Father, for the sake of His dearest Son, our Lord and Savior Jesus Christ, receives and adopts us as His children. He wills to be our dear Father, and we are to be His children and the dear brothers and dear sisters of His only-begotten Son. "Behold," says Scripture, "what love the Father has shown us, that we should be called the children of God! You have not received the spirit of bondage, that you should have to fear again, but you have received the spirit of adoption, by which we cry, Abba, dear Father. The same Spirit bears witness with our spirit that we are the children of God. And if we are children, then we are also heirs, namely, heirs of God and joint heirs with Christ. You are all God's children through faith in Christ Jesus. For as many as have received Him, to them He gave power to become the children of God, even those who believe in His name." Therefore, Christ also is not ashamed to be called our Brother.

John 20:17; Matt. 12:50

"Go," He says to Mary, "to My brothers and say to them, I go up to My Father and to your Father, to My God and to your God." "For he who does the will of My Father in heaven, the same is My brother, sister, and mother."

Dr. Luther explains the first trunk-good very splendidly.

Tom. 4, Witt. Germ., fols. 522–23[72]

"Anyone who could simply believe this comforting promise," says Dr. Luther on this point, "would already be in paradise in heaven. What would such a heart (that believes in these words) have to fear, or what would it worry about? It would have to say, 'I will worry about nothing since I have such a Brother.'"Likewise: "Would to God we simply knew a little about this so that it did not sit on top of our heart like foam on the water. For if this teaching truly sinks into someone's heart, all suffering and calamity are a jest to him, as we see in the dear virgin martyrs Agnes, Agatha, etc., who were fourteen years old and yet (as we read of them) went joyfully leaping into death, just as if they went to a dance. Where does a young maiden get such courage? From the fact that they believe and regard as true the fact that they will be joint heirs with Christ. This causes a Christian to be so taken in by faith that he forgets all misfortune."

72 From *Sermon on Mary Magdalene* (1530): cf. AE 56:328, 330–31 (= WA 32:82.7–11, 88.10–11).

Fol. 524[73]

Likewise: "Dear Lord God, there is nothing more to it than to grasp it and simply wait and let it be given him. So simply believe in the Word and be proud, be boastful and defiant on it. For that treasure is certainly worthy of boasting and defiance. Christ will be your Brother, and God will be your Father, and all angels will be your friends, and the sun and moon and all the stars will laugh and rejoice with you, hell will be all shut up, and there will be nothing but the fatherly and gracious will of God. Behold how beautifully and pleasantly the Lord Christ can speak!"

The second trunk-good is the heavenly bridal delight.

Hosea 2:19; Isa. 54:5; Eph. 5:28, 31–32

The second trunk-good is the heavenly bridal delight and consists in the fact that our Lord and Savior Jesus Christ will be our Bridegroom and will acknowledge us who believe in Him as His spouse and chosen Bride, even as He has here and there likened the kingdom of heaven to a wedding and called Himself a bridegroom. "I will pledge Myself to you forever," He says. "I will be betrothed to you in righteousness. Yea, in faith will I betroth Myself to you." Likewise, Isaiah writes, "He who made you is your husband, the Lord of Sabaoth is His name, and your Redeemer, the Holy One in Israel, who is called the God of all the world." Likewise, St. Paul: "Husbands, love your wives, just as Christ also loved the Church." And shortly thereafter: "For this reason shall a man leave his father and mother and cleave to his wife, and the two shall become one flesh. This mystery is great, but I speak of Christ and the Church."

How Luther explains the second trunk-good.

Tom. 4. Witt., fol. 569.[74] *The unspeakable grace and gift of believers.*

On this, Luther writes very pleasantly and says, "It is a great and unspeakable grace and gift, as St. Paul calls it, which God has given Christians, even if it has no attraction in the eyes of the world. For consider yourself what honor and glory it must be that Christ, God's Son, descends so low and so kindly joins Himself to us, that He lets Himself not only be called our Lord, indeed, and Father, Brother, and Friend, etc., but, using the name of highest love and closest friendship on earth, He will be and be called our Bridegroom and be one body with us (as we say of husband and wife) or, as Scripture says, one flesh and one bone with us, which is said of no other relationship or friendship. In this way He wished to show Himself to us in the most loving and friendliest way and offered and promised His highest love, that we should be called His dear Bride and with all confidence should and could call Him and claim Him as our dear Bridegroom."

73 From *Sermon on Mary Magdalene* (1530): cf. AE 56:332 (= WA 32:90.15–22).

74 From Luther's sermon on Eph. 5:22–23, April 24, 1536: cf. AE 57:234 (= WA 41:552.33–37, 553.12–20).

Christ is one body with His Church.

Likewise:[75] "I cannot see this glory and adornment which is applied and attached to you by Christ, nor can you yourself (except as you grasp it by faith), and if we could see it and feel what we have in it, I believe we would already be in heaven. For what greater joy and blessedness could a man have than if he could rest assured and have no doubt about it and with all his heart exclaim: 'Christ is one body with me and shares with me all that He has and can do, as a bridegroom does with his bride, where everything is shared and there is one body, possession, and honor, and they are divided in nothing.'

Marriage binds and keeps everything together.

"All other friends and estates separate and divide themselves: children from their parents, brothers and sisters from one house and property. But this estate binds and keeps everything together in such a way that they leave father and mother and all things and join themselves with another—even their own life, if it is true marital love. Christ, says St. Paul, has done the same to His Church. He has loved her and given Himself for her, that we might become one body with Him and have all things in Him and that we might appropriate Him and all His glory which He has in heaven and take comfort in it as our own possession.

The grace that we find in Christ is unspeakable.

"Oh, what a great, glorious thing this is! Who can sufficiently describe and comprehend or ponder the fact that a poor sack of worms, conceived and born in sin, should come into such glory as to be called a bride of the Majesty in heaven, namely, of the Son of God, and that He should unite Himself with us so that all that He is and has is ours; and that all that we are and is in us He also will be in turn? But what is He? He is the fair Bridegroom, eternal righteousness, eternal strength, and eternal life—in short, eternal, incomprehensible good that no heart can ever sufficiently grasp or consider and both angels and men may gaze upon forever—while we poor, miserable creatures are full of sin and filth, entirely corrupt from head to toe, subject to the devil, and judged under God's wrath to death and condemnation.

Immeasurable love of Christ toward us poor sinners.

"Therefore, it must be an unspeakable grace and fervency of love that He should descend so far and so willingly give Himself to us and spend so much to bring us to Himself and not be ashamed to shed His precious blood and to suffer contemptible death in order that we may be called His Bride and possess His goods of eternal righteousness, freedom, blessedness, and life instead of the sin, death, and power of the devil, in which we lay."

75 From Luther's sermon on Eph. 5:22–23, April 24, 1536: cf. AE 57:234–35 (= WA 41:554–55).

The third trunk-good is our temple honor.

The third trunk-good we may call our "temple honor" or "temple glory," namely, that God for the sake of His Son, Jesus Christ, honors us so highly and makes us His temples and dwellings of the Holy Spirit, that He may be perfectly one with us and we with Him, and He may have in us His residence, seat, Sabbath, and eternal rest of joy.

Testimony of Scripture.

John 14:23; 6:56; Eph. 3:16; 1 Cor. 3:16; 6:19; 2 Cor. 6:16

"He who loves Me," says the Son of God, "will keep My Word, and My Father will love him, and We (namely, the Father and I) will come to him and make Our dwelling with him. He who eats My flesh and drinks My blood abides in Me and I in him." Likewise, the apostle writes, "God grant you strength according to the riches of His glory that you may become strong through His Spirit to your inward being, and that Christ may dwell in your heart by faith." Likewise: "Do you not know that you are God's temple, and the Spirit of God dwells in you? Do you not know that your body is a temple of the Holy Spirit, who is in you, whom you have from God, and you are not your own? For you have been dearly bought. You are temples of the living God, as God says, 'I will dwell in them, and walk in them, and will be their God, and they shall be My people.'"

We were created and redeemed to be God's temples.

We should carefully consider these mighty, glorious, highly important, and comforting words, which say that the entire Holy Trinity will be ours and dwell in us. For in the beginning, our dear God prepared man's body and soul to be His own palace, and when poor, miserable man lost that life through sin, and God's blessed house was changed into a filthy nest of demons, God's Son could not tolerate it, but had zeal for the house of His inheritance and cast out the infernal serpent's dish and adder's brood and still casts it out daily by His Word and Spirit and sprinkles us with His blood in faith so that we in turn become a clean and pure dwelling of the entire Holy Trinity and let Him and His Spirit mightily take possession of and occupy us.

What kind of glory it is that God dwells in us.

Rom. 8:31; 1 John 4:4

You would highly rejoice and boast and be defiant if your territorial prince came with great goods and stayed at your place, took lodging with you, nourished you grandly, and promised and pledged strong and powerful protection against the enemy. How much more comforting is it, however, that the true, eternal, immortal, everlasting God (who has the power to command or forbid all devils and the whole world) will take up residence and dwell in you with His power and grace? What is more gladdening, what is more pleasant, what is more profitable and bearable than such a kind inhabitation, wherein I hear that my body and soul are to be the temple and palace not of a holy angel or of an earthly light, but of the high and holy Trinity? Here we may say, "If God be for us, who can be against us? He who is in us is greater than He who is in the world." For where the eternal living God is, there the holy, heavenly ministers and divine spirits must be admitted as well! There it teems and surges with nothing but angels all around us, who for God Almighty's sake attend us and keep us in all our ways.

The three trunk-goods are distinguished in an orderly way according to the three persons of the Godhead. Why the three trunk-goods are distinguished thus.

These are the salutary trunk-goods obtained for us by Christ and earned with His grueling sweat and blood. They are distinguished according to the order of the Holy Trinity so that the adoption properly relates to God the Father, then our heavenly bridal delight to God the Son, and our holy temple honor to God the Holy Spirit. Not that in this each Person has His own separate work that He works and carries out by Himself alone without the participation of the others, for in each trunk-good the entire Holy Trinity is present. When God the Father adopts us as His children, He does so through His Son, and in addition puts in our heart His Son's Spirit of adoption. So, too, in our heavenly marriage, the heavenly King holds the wedding for His Son, and the Holy Spirit accompanies as a bond of love and knits Bride and Bridegroom firmly together with a burning flame of love. Likewise, when the Holy Spirit dwells in us as His temple, He comes sent from the Father and the Son and comes simultaneously with them, so that all three of them reside and rest in us. Now, the three trunk-goods are ascribed distinctly, one to the Father, the second to the Son, and the third to the Holy Spirit, because the blessed adoption especially relates to God the Father, the Bride especially to God the Son as the true Bridegroom, and the temple honor to God the Holy Spirit.

Description of the fruit-goods.

Now these trunk-goods are followed by the fruit-goods, which are peace and joy in the Holy Spirit, heartfelt love for God, heavenly strength and comfort, and kindness to one's neighbor. Thus a believing Christian delights in the Lord, is equipped with divine strength, encouraged, courageous, and unfearing against the devil, death, and hell and the whole world, takes comfort in the overabundant grace and mercy of God, relies on God the Father, Son, and Holy Spirit, praises and glorifies Him with joyful lips, prays and calls upon Him from the heart, despises all worldly pomp, arrogance, and vanity, and turns all his thoughts toward the fatherland of eternal life.

The fruit-goods hang on two branches.

Rev. 5:9–10

These fruit-goods of the noble tree, moreover, hang upon two branches, which diverge and spread out from the lofty trunk. The first branch is called the "royal wedding"; the second is called the "priestly dignity." To these two branches and two kinds of fruit-goods St. John's Revelation bears witness that the elect in heaven call upon the Lamb of God and say, "You were slain and have purchased us by Your blood from every tribe and tongue and people and nation and have made us kings and priests to our God, and we will be kings upon the earth."

The first branch on the tree of life is our royal wedding.

The royal wedding is the first fruit-good and branch on the noble and sweet tree of salvation, namely, the kind of lordship wherein a godly Christian has dominion over death, the devil, and hell and by sharing in the power and grace of our Savior, Jesus Christ, is very powerful and a great victorious prince who in faith overcomes the devil, the world, and all manner of tribulation just as if he were moving a mountain and accomplishing far greater deeds, such as if he could cleanse lepers, wake the dead, and do similar wonders.

What Scripture testifies concerning our royal wedding.

Rev. 3:21; Mark 11:23; Matt. 21:21–22; Mark 9:23; John 14:12; Rev. 2:26; 1 John 5:4; 4:4; 1 Cor. 6:2; Phil. 4:13

To this royal wedding the Lord Christ testifies when He says, "He who overcomes, to him will I give to sit with Me on My throne, just as I have sat down with My Father on His throne. Have faith in God. Truly, I say to you that he who says to this mountain, 'Arise, and cast yourself into the sea,' and does not doubt in his heart, but believes, what he says shall be come to pass." "All things are possible for him who believes." "Truly, truly, I say to you, he who believes in Me will also do the works which I do and will do greater ones than these, because I go to the Father." "He who overcomes and keeps My works until the end, to him will I give power over the nations, and he shall shepherd them with an iron rod, and like a potter's vessel shall he shatter them." "Everything," writes St. John, "that is born of God overcomes the world, and our faith is the victory that has overcome the world." "Children, you are of God and have overcome them. For He who is in you is greater than he who is in the world." Likewise, St. Paul says, "Do you not know that the saints shall judge the world?" "I can do all things through Him who strengthens me, even Christ."

Works and wonders of Christians.

Tom. 4, Witt. Germ., fol. 240[76]

On this point Luther writes, "The world gapes only after that which seems high and great, rich and powerful, and which goes along in majesty and pomp, and yet it cannot recognize where it gets it from. But if you are baptized (says Christ) and believe in Me, you are the man who has and can do far more and greater things—yea, who can do precisely those works and even greater ones than I now do. For I will make you who believe in Me such lords that your works shall avail and do more than any king's or lord's on earth. For you shall achieve and accomplish whatever you wish and help to govern with Me both spiritually over souls unto salvation and also bodily obtain and preserve through your prayers everything on earth."

The Christian's boast and glory.

Likewise:[77] "What else would I prefer, if I knew for certain that I could save a man from death? What compares to the fact that through Christ I shall and can comfort and save hearts and consciences and pluck them from the jaws of the devil and help all men with my prayer? If all the world's gold and silver, authority and honor lay before me in a heap, I would surely regard it as coal compared to that and spit on it."

Christians have all things and are lords over all lords, and yet beggars on earth.

Likewise:[78] "[Christ] does not say, 'If you believe in Me, you will acquire and possess great treasure of gold and silver, cities, palaces, lands, and kingdoms.' For by that Christians are not yet helped; rather, that we are to have authority over sin, death, and the devil. As He says to the apostles (Luke 10:19): 'Behold, I have given you authority to tread upon serpents and scorpions and over all the power of the enemy, and nothing shall hurt you. For I have put the Word in your mouth, which is My Word, and I have given you Baptism, which is My Baptism, and by them will I demonstrate My almighty power.' Because we have such treasure, then, we have all things and are lords over all lords. We may be beggars on earth (as Christ Himself also was), but before God we are covered with all goods."

The authority which believers have in Christ.

Likewise:[79] "It is as if Christ says: 'Through the authority which I will have on the right hand of the Father, in the same divine majesty, and openly glorified as true God and the Lord of all creation, I will work in you who believe in Me, who have My Word, Baptism, and Sacrament and who cling to them. And as I am the

76 From *Sermons on John 14–16* (1533–34): cf. AE 24:83 (= WA 45:536.16–25).

77 From *Sermons on John 14–16* (1533–34): cf. AE 24:83–84 (= WA 45:536.31–37).

78 From *Sermons on John 14–16* (1533–34): cf. AE 24:84 (= WA 45:537.15–27).

79 From *Sermons on John 14–16* (1533–34): cf. AE 24:85–86 (= WA 45:538.19–26).

Lord over sin, death, hell, devil, world, and all things, so shall you also be, so that you can claim for yourself the same authority. Not that you have it by your own worthiness or from your own power, but only because I go to the Father.'

Small and insignificant works of Christ done among His people the Jews.

"'And precisely for this reason (He says) I go to the Father, that I may begin and accomplish this. For I am now so weak because I am still walking here below on earth in this flesh and still do small and insignificant works, such as raising a few from the dead or helping a handful of Jews, and I must now let Myself be crucified and put to death. But afterward, when I have been crucified, dead, and buried, I will make a leap from death, from the cross and tomb, to eternal glory and divine majesty and authority and will then (as He says elsewhere) draw all things to Myself, so that all creation shall be subject to Me, so that I can say to you apostles and Christians: O Peter, or Paul, go and cast the Roman empire into a heap, if it will not accept My Word and obey Me.'"

Christians' royal actions and miracles.

Therefore, whoever believes in Christ and trusts in His true Word is a mighty king, a lord over all earthly lords who do not know God, and a conqueror of death, the devil, hell, and the whole world, able to do great wonders. He can powerfully cast down false doctrines, error, and idolatry along with their whole rabble (be they emperors, kings, princes, and similar potentates), overcome all tribulation strong in the Lord, put all devils to flight by hundreds and thousands, put all enemies to derision, despise death, and have no care for all the world's wrath, terrors, and threats. "If a plague will come," says David (Ps. 112:7–8), "he is not afraid. His heart hopes in the Lord without wavering. His heart is confident and unfearing until he sees his desire upon his enemies."

List of honorable, mighty deeds.

Heb. 11:33–35

Pertinent here is what is told in Hebrews regarding the faithful fathers of the Old Testament, "who by faith subdued kingdoms, wrought righteousness, obtained promises, stopped the jaws of lions, quenched the force of fire, escaped the edge of the sword, were made strong out of weakness, became powerful in battle, laid low the enemy's host. Women received back their dead from resurrection."

The second branch on the tree of life is our priestly dignity.

1 Pet. 2:9; Rom. 12:1; Isa. 61:6

The second branch on the tree of life is the priestly dignity, that all who believe in Christ have free access to God, to whom they offer their bodies as a sacrifice, converse with Him, declare His praise and virtue, as St. Peter writes, "You are," he says, "the chosen generation, the royal priesthood, the holy people, the people of the possession, that you should declare the virtue of Him who has called you out of darkness to His wonderful light." Likewise, St. Paul: "I admonish you, dear brothers, through the mercy of God, that you devote your bodies as a living sacrifice, which is holy and pleasing to God, which is your reasonable act of worship." "You shall," says Isaiah, "be called priests of the Lord, and you will be called servants of our God."

We who believe in Christ are all priests of God.

Gal. 5:24

With these and similar testimonies, Scripture reminds us that we believing Christians are all priests of God through Christ, our High Priest, who through the sacrifice of His body not only reconciles us with God but also has obtained this priestly dignity and anointed and consecrated us to it in Baptism with the Holy Spirit, that we should also make sacrifices after His example. Now, we offer Him our body not by being crucified and put to death bodily as He did, but we offer ourselves with the spiritual mortification of our sinful thoughts, desires, words, and works. As St. Paul says, "Those who belong to Christ crucify their flesh together with their lusts and desires."

The priests' two offices of prayer and sacrifice.

Praying and offering sacrifices were the two chief offices of the Levitical priests in the Old Testament and depicted the spiritual priesthood of the Christian Church, where both belong to all of us Christians, who are all consecrated as priests through Christ and are to pray constantly and all to offer sacrifices daily to our dear God.

What the prayer of Christians is.

Rom. 5:1; John 14:13–14

And what is prayer, properly speaking, but conversation with God, with whom we speak in Christ's name at His command and promise, bring before Him the concerns that weigh on us, ask Him for His help, and do not doubt that He will hear? "We have peace with God," says the apostle, "through our Lord Jesus Christ, through whom we also have access in faith." So, too, the Son of God says, "I go to the Father, and whatever you shall ask in My name, that will I do, that the Father may be honored in the Son. If you shall ask anything in My name, I will do it."

What the sacrifice of Christians is.

Ps. 51:16–17; Heb. 13:15; Phil. 4:18; 2 Tim. 4:6

Accordingly, we offer our dear God not goats, calves, oxen, or other senseless beasts, which were only shadows and figures in the Old Testament, but we offer Him our bodies with their wicked passions and desires, which are the true wild, goring oxen and harmful beasts, if they are not put to death. We offer our heart through the fire of divine wrath or through true remorse and repentance, which makes the wrath of God burn again in us as a fire so that we recoil from it and fall from self-security to fear of Him. As David says, "Burnt offerings do not please You. The sacrifices of God are a broken spirit; a broken and a contrite heart, Lord God, You will not despise." We offer our lips when we praise Him and comfort our neighbor, as it says in Hebrews: "Let us through Him offer the praise offering to God continually, that is, the fruit of the lips which confess His name." We offer sacrifices to Him also with works of Christian love and mercy, as St. Paul acclaims when he says in Philippians, "I am filled, having received through Epaphroditus what came from you, an acceptable sacrifice, pleasing to God." Likewise, we offer our whole body when it is chastised not only to obey God but also for patience, when it is attacked with sickness or with death, as the apostle says, "I am already being offered, and the time of my departure is at hand."

The tree of life with its goods is a summary of all Christ's benefits.

Behold, dear friends, here we have the tree of life, the Lord Christ Himself with all His goods which He has obtained and earned for our good, namely, the whole tree with its root-goods, trunk-goods, and fruit-goods. And I have no doubt that whoever diligently inculcates in himself this pattern, concept, and correct order of the precious goods which we have obtained learns to know Christ rightly, to grasp Him rightly, and to take hold of Him entirely, so that he knows to what end he serves Him and what sort of rich treasures and benefits he finds in Him. All this you can easily ponder and speak of, preach and teach at length to others, if only the noble tree, with its roots, trunk, and fruit, is not forgotten.

Of the hand of God, with which the heavenly goods are offered to us.

Rom. 10:6–9; Deut. 30:14; [Rom. 10:9]

After this it is also necessary to note and observe what sort of hand God lowers from heaven, with which He offers and extends to us these goods. For whoever desires them must above all things know where Christ is to be met with and where He wills to have Himself found. On this point, then, the holy apostle Paul gives us very good guidance and says, "Say not to your heart, who will ascend into heaven? (This is nothing else than to fetch Christ down.) Or who will descend into the deep? (This is nothing else than to fetch Christ from the dead.) But what does it say? 'The Word is nigh, namely, in your mouth and in your heart.' This is the Word of faith which we preach. For if you confess with your mouth that Jesus is Lord and believe in your heart that God raised Him from the dead, you will be saved."

Two hands, one giving and one receiving.

Here in this mystery, we are shown two different hands which come together, namely, a giving hand and a receiving hand.

The giving hand of God is the Gospel with its attached seals, which are Baptism and the Lord's Supper.

The giving hand is God's Word or the Holy Gospel with its most worthy Sacraments and seals attached, being Baptism and the Supper, in which the Lord Jesus Christ, out of great, burning love, causes His precious benefits (which have been mentioned in order) to be presented and offered to us. He Himself is also present in both natures in this entire transaction, where His Word is preached and the Holy Sacraments are apportioned, and through faith comes to dwell in us together with the Father and the Holy Spirit so that we abide in Him and He in us. In addition to this, in His holy, most worthy Supper, along with the spiritual partaking, He also gives us to eat and to drink His true body and His true blood, that we may constantly remember Him and never forget His grueling, bitter death and the goods which He so dearly won.

The Lord Christ shows us unspeakable love in the work of redemption.

But who can sufficiently extol, glorify, and declare our Savior Jesus Christ's infinite kindness and love for mankind, which He so richly shows and demonstrates to us in all His works? For out of great, burning love He took upon Himself our flesh and blood. Out of true love He died for us. Out of great love He obtained for us the most worthy, salutary goods (which are the righteousness of faith, peace with God, victory and conquest over the devil, blessed adoption, heavenly bridal delight, holy temple honor, royal lordship, and priestly dignity) and out of unspeakable love causes them to be richly put forth and presented to us all and is Himself present in them, that we might receive and possess Him with all His treasures.

Christ out of great love gives us His body to eat and His blood to drink.

To all this is added the fact that He does not stop there, but also out of great, burning love gives us His body and His blood to eat spiritually and bodily: spiritually in faith and bodily with our mouth. Why does He do this? Answer: While God is Love itself, yet according to His bare essence He is also a consuming fire to the sinful children of Adam, kindled and fed in wrath through our transgression. Hence we are by nature timid before and painfully afraid of God's majesty, as if it were a burning and consuming fire. But now that we are reconciled to Him through Christ, He has let go of His wrath and is our Friend again, and to show us His fervent love, and that we need not be afraid of Him, Christ gives us His body and His blood to eat and to drink spiritually and bodily, that He may be with us and we with Him as one cake and one mass.

To what end we are fed and given to drink Christ's body and blood.

He does this out of great, fervent love. Out of love He gives His flesh to eat and out of love He lets His blood be drunk, that we might discern from this how much God loves men and how, laying aside and relenting from His righteous anger, He desires in His love to be perfectly one with us and to unite and bind us to Himself in the most intimate manner possible, that we may constantly remain in Him and He in us forever. Oh, unspeakable love, at which we will never be able to marvel enough! And this is why we ought justly to hold the most worthy Supper in honor and to visit it frequently. And this is the mystery which the squinting sectarian spirits—Calvinists and Zwinglians along with the Anabaptists[80] and Schwenkfelders[81]—do not understand or perceive. Therefore, they let go of the incarnate God and try to deal with the bare Godhead (which is a consuming fire) apart from Christ's flesh and blood. A God-pleasing Christian, however, observes the words of the Supper and in accordance with the literal sense clings simply to Christ's body and blood so that he does not burn his fingers on the bare Godhead, but sees Him as He is revealed in the flesh and in heartfelt love gives His body to eat and His blood to drink.

The receiving hand is our faith.

The receiving hand is our faith, which grasps the Word of the Gospel and in the Gospel the tree of life with all its root-goods, trunk-goods, and fruit-goods, so that they are applied and appropriated to us. And here faith also (when it grasps the tree of life) is like a fruitful tree. When it sees and knows the great love and kindness of our Lord Christ, it cannot keep it hidden but must extol and glorify the whole work of redemption with the salvific treasure and dearly won goods, then it praises Christ its great lover and heartily longs to love Him, cries out to Him, sings to Him, beseeches Him, confesses everything to Him, and speaks:

A fervent prayer in which a faithful heart praises and addresses Christ and joyfully applies and appropriates to himself the goods dearly won by Christ.

Augustine, Meditations, ch. 35[82]

"O Jesus, my redemption, my love, and my heart's desire, true God begotten of God, assist me, Your servant. I call to You, and with a loud cry I cry to You from my heart. I call You into my soul, that You would come into it and prepare it for Your dwelling, that You may possess it without any wrinkle and without spot. For a pure dwelling befits You, the purest Lord of all. Therefore, sanctify me as Your vessel which You have created. Cleanse from all malice, fill it up with Your grace, and keep it full, that I may be a temple worthy of Your indwelling here in time and hereafter in eternity.

80 Anabaptists rejected especially infant Baptism and emphasized as well the internal working of the Holy Spirit apart from the external Word.

81 The followers of Caspar von Schwenkfeld (1489–1561), an early adherent of Luther's teaching, believed that Christ brought His humanity with Him from heaven; advocated a merely spiritual eating of Christ's heavenly body in the Lord's Supper; and also separated the internal working of the Holy Spirit from the external Word.

82 Author uncertain, *Meditationes* 35 (PL 40:928–30).

We are to praise and glorify Christ far above all creatures.

"O sweetest, kindest, most loving, dearest, most precious, most desiring, most lovely, most beautiful Lord Jesus! You are sweeter to me than honey, You are whiter to me than milk and snow, You are more delicious to me than wine and malmsey, and You are more precious and dearer to me than gold and jewels—indeed, dearer than all the riches and all the honors of the whole wide world. What do I say, O Lord my God, my only hope—what do I say of Your great mercy? What do I say, O Jesus, who are my unfailing and blessed sweetness? What do I say while I say this? I say what I can, yet I do not say what I ought. Oh, that I might speak of You as shouting and rejoicing choirs of the angels speak of You! Oh, how gladly I would turn and direct my senses, powers, and thoughts to the end that You might be worshiped and glorified! Oh, how devoutly in the midst of the Christian Church I would sing without ceasing the angelic hymns of heavenly melody to the praise and glory of Your name!

Although we cannot praise the Lord sufficiently here, we should still begin to do so.

"But because this is impossible for me to do, should I therefore be silent? Woe to all who are silent concerning You since You open the mouths of the mute and give skillful tongues to infants and nursing babes! Woe to those who do not speak of You since even with eloquent tongues they are mute if they do not speak of Your praise! But who can praise You worthily, O unspeakable Power and eternal Wisdom of the Father? Although I am unable to find a word with which I might describe You adequately, O almighty and all-knowing Word, yet I will speak of You what I can until You call me to come to You, where I can speak of You as is fitting and as I ought. And, therefore, I humbly beseech You to regard not so much what I say now as what I desire to say.

A faithful heart desires to praise Christ.

"For with great desire I desire to speak of You what I ought to speak and what is fitting to speak, since praise and glory befits You, and You deserve all honor. Therefore, You know, O Lord my God, searcher out of all things, that You are more precious and dearer to me than heaven and earth and all that is in them. For I love You above heaven and earth and above all that is in them. Indeed, all that is transitory, if it is not loved for Your name's sake, should not be loved at all."

The reason a believing Christian praises and blesses his Savior.

(And why should I not love You before all things since You, out of great, burning love, have done so much for my sake, who are mighty and whose name is holy? You, out of great love for me, died and became my Redeemer, my Helper, my Protection, my Savior, and my Refuge. You are to me a tree of life, and, with Your grueling, bitter death as well as with Your victorious resurrection and ascension, You have obtained and won for me the comforting root-goods, the glorious trunk-goods, and the splendid fruit-goods. You give me Your righteousness, Your peace, and Your victory: You provide for me the blessed adoption of eternal life, You are my heavenly Bridegroom and fashion me into a temple and dwelling of the Holy Spirit. You have made me a king and a priest for the Lord my God, that I might rule and reign with You forever.)[83]

We should love Christ heartily.

"Therefore, I love You, my God, with great love and eagerly wish that I could love You more deeply and strongly. Oh, grant me always to love You as much as I wish and as often as I should, that You alone may be in my mind and in all my thoughts. Let me think of You during the day without ceasing, let me be aware of You in my sleep during the night, let my spirit address You and my heart converse with You. Let my heart be lightened with the light of Your countenance, and by Your governing and leading let me go from strength to strength, and at last let me see You, the God of all gods and the King in Zion (Ps. [84:7]), here as through a glass darkly, and hereafter face-to-face, that I may know You even as also I am known (1 Cor. 13:12).

Prayer to Christ for true love for Him.

"'Blessed are the pure in heart, for they shall see God' (Matt. 5:8). And: 'Blessed are they who dwell in Your house, O Lord. They will be praising You forever' (Ps. 84:4). Therefore, I beseech You, O Lord, through all Your grace and mercy by which we have been delivered from eternal death, that You would soften my hard, stony, rocky, and iron heart with Your most holy and potent anointing and heat and thoroughly roast me with the penetrating fire of Your love, that I may be at all times a living sacrifice before You. Grant that I may always have before Your presence a broken and contrite heart, soaked through and sprinkled with many fervent tears (Ps. 51:17; Isa. 57:15). Grant that in Your love I may wholly die to this world and out of great fear and love for You forget all temporal things, so that for the sake of temporal things I neither mourn nor rejoice, nor indeed love them; but through love and loss, let me not be blinded or frightened.

The Lord Christ must Himself work in us so that we love Him.

"And since Your love is as strong as death (Song 8:[6]), I beseech You, let the fiery and honey-sweet power of Your love pull my heart, mind, and senses away from all that is under the sun, that I may truly cling to You only and may feed myself with the eternal, constant remembrance of Your loveliness. From the heavens let there come down, O Lord my God, from the heavens let there come down into my heart Your loveliest fragrance! Oh, let Your honey-sweet love enter into me! Let the savor of Your goodness and Your wondrously unspeakably sweet fragrance, which stirs up in me an eternal desire for You, come to me and be in my

83 Here Nicolai interjects in the prayer.

heart as a living spring of water springing into eternal life. You are immeasurable, O Lord, and therefore You are to be loved, extolled, and praised without measure by those whom You have redeemed with Your precious blood.

The children of light should learn of fervent love from the children of this world.

"Oh, most goodly Lover of mankind, oh, most clement Lord and fairest Ruler, to whom the Father has committed and delivered over all judgment (John 5:22): You have judged according to Your most wise judgment, and regard as right and fitting that, just as the children of this world, out of deep love for the night and darkness, cling with all diligence and strength to passing riches and fleeting honor and seek and love them, so we, Your servants, ought much more to love You, our God, through whom we have been created and redeemed. For if one human being can love another with such great love that the one cannot do without the other's presence, and if a bride so clings to her groom with ardent heart and mind that for her great love she cannot find peace or rest but is anxious and troubled when he is away from her (Hosea 1; Ps. 45)—O dear God, how much greater ought that love, diligence, and zeal be with which my soul (which in faith and in grace You have betrothed to Yourself) should love You in turn, O true God and most beautiful Bridegroom, who have so greatly loved us and graced us and for our sakes performed so many and such great deeds?

All earthly and transitory love of this world cannot gladden the heart so much when the love of our Savior, Jesus Christ, is in a man's heart.

"Earthly and transitory things may well have their joy and their pleasure and their love. But they do not give pleasure in such a manner as You, O Lord our God, in whom the righteous man rejoices from his heart, since Your love is a gentle love and a sweet love. For the hearts which You occupy You fill with Your goodness, Your loveliness, and Your rest. By contrast, the love of the world and of the flesh is doubting and perturbed, and where it enters the soul it tolerates no peace there, for there it stirs up various suspicions and various perturbations. But You are the only pleasure of all believers, and fittingly so. For with You there is powerful rest and life without terror and without tribulation. Whoever enters into You, good Lord, enters into the joy of his Lord (Matt. 25:21) and will no longer fear, but finds himself blessed in the blessed place, saying, 'This is my rest forever. Here will I dwell, for I have chosen it' (Ps. 132:14). And again: 'The Lord is my shepherd; I shall not want. He feeds me in a green pasture' (Ps. 23:1–2).

We should never forget the benefits and kindness of Jesus Christ.

"O sweet Christ, O good Jesus, I beseech You, fill my heart constantly with unspeakable love and with the eternal remembrance of Your name so that I constantly burn like a fiery flame in the sweetness of Your love and that many waters may never extinguish the burning of this love (Song 8:7). Make me, dearest Lord, to love You truly and in heartfelt longing for You to lay aside the burden of all carnal desires and the most burdensome load of all temporal passions which afflict and oppress my poor soul, that I may run after You in the noble fragrance of Your anointing and by Your leading come shortly to You, where I will be satisfied with the pleasant sight of Your most beautiful countenance (Ps. 17:15; Ps. 43).

There are two loves: one good and one evil. Love for God is good, but love for the world is evil.

"For there are two loves: one good and the other evil, one sweet and the other bitter; and these two have no concord in one heart. Therefore, if anyone loves something above You, O Lord my God, Your love is not in him. O Love of sweetness and sweetness of love, noble Love, not tormenting but gladdening me! Pure Love, remaining chaste and pure forever! Fiery Love, burning constantly and never extinguished! Sweet Christ, good Jesus, very Love, my Lord and God! Kindle my whole self with Your fire, with Your love, with Your sweetness and delight, with Your joyfulness and exultation, with Your passion and desire . . . that being filled with the sweetness of Your love and set ablaze by the flame of Your charity, I may love You, my God, with all my heart and with all the powers of my soul, having You in my heart, on my tongue, and before my eyes at all times and in all places, lest any false, adulterous love steal into me.

Conclusion of the prayer.

"Hear me, O Lord Jesus, hear me, O blessed Light of my eyes, hear what I ask, and grant that what I ask, You may hear. O faithful and merciful Savior, do not stop Your ears against me because of my sins; but because of Your great goodness receive the prayers of Your servant, and grant me the fulfillment of my petition; for You rule and reign with the Father and the Holy Spirit forever and ever. Amen."

The end of our redemption through Christ is eternal life.

With this and similar prayers a Christian ought to exercise his faith diligently as a receiving hand and take hold of the Lord Christ, his highest Friend and true tree of life with all His goods, and appropriate them to himself. Here observe the end of your redemption and the reason for which the Son of God did so much for your sake and obtained so many noble goods for you. For by this He seeks nothing other than eternal life, that you may be saved and have eternal communion with the entire Holy Trinity in heaven and live in eternal, burning love with God the Father, with God the Son, and with God the Holy Spirit.

The Third Benefit of God: Our Rebirth unto Eternal Life

Now there follows the third benefit, namely, our rebirth to eternal life. And this rebirth is a work of unspeakably great mercy and kindness of our God and consists of the fact that He calls sinners as spiritually dead people through the Word and Sacraments, gathers them, and enlightens them through the preaching of the Law. When they have been sufficiently stricken and crushed with it as with a hammer, He comforts them with the Gospel, stirs up faith, and through faith accounts to them the righteousness, innocence, and victory merited by our Lord Christ. He receives them into grace, acknowledges them as His inheritance, gives them the Holy Spirit, and governs and leads them according to His Word; He keeps them under the cross for the mortification of the old Adam, the testing of the faith, the furtherance of prayer, and new obedience; and He takes them at last from this valley of sorrow to Himself in the heavenly paradise and fatherland of eternal life.

Testimony of the Holy Spirit.

John 1:13; 3:5–7; 1 Pet. 1:3–4

Of this mystery Scripture testifies in many places, saying that the children of God are born "not of the blood nor of the will of the flesh nor of the will of a man, but of God." Likewise: "Truly, truly, I say to you, unless a man be born of water and the Spirit, he cannot enter into the kingdom of God. That which is born of flesh is flesh, and that which is born of the Spirit is spirit. Do not marvel that I have said to you, 'You must be born again.'" St. Peter says, "God gave us new birth according to His great mercy, according to a living hope through the resurrection of Jesus Christ from the dead, and according to an imperishable and unblemished and incorruptible inheritance that is kept for you in heaven," etc.

In rebirth, God's kindness and love for man are richly commended and put before our eyes.

Wisdom 7:1–2

Now, that you who are unlearned may properly absorb this noble and very comforting teaching and take it to heart, it should firstly be known that in this once more God's unspeakable love which He has for us men is richly manifested and, as it were, painted and delineated in living color. For bearing and begetting children is the work of love and springs from natural love and natural desire, as Solomon puts it in the Book of Wisdom when he says, "I was molded as flesh. In the time of ten months I was curdled together in blood of the seed of man by the pleasure of concurring sleep." Accordingly, if God also treats birth this way by giving men new birth, He must indeed have wondrous love for people and a truly fervent longing for our salvation.

How the lofty mystery of rebirth may be understood and grasped to some degree. Comparison with natural birth.

By comparing natural birth and supernatural, heavenly birth, we may also deduce and understand to some degree with what motherly love and with what affection and in how exceedingly salutary a manner our faithful God fulfills and accomplishes in us the high work of rebirth.

For just as a man is initially formed in the womb as in a narrow lodging and microcosm and prepared for this larger world, so that he reigns, dwells, and lives therein, so also in this larger world, he is given a new birth by God, newly formed and equipped for heavenly life, and is more pleasant, more beautiful, and more glorious, namely, for heavenly paradise and the fatherland of eternal joy, so that he is to live and reign above in heaven forever in unspeakable joy and glory with Christ and all the elect. And just as in the womb he begins to live and move in a natural way so that he does not come into the world dead, but brings life with him from the little, narrow lodging into the larger world, in which he is strengthened, draws breath, and is perfected, so he obtains and receives the beginning of heavenly life in this world on earth and brings it with him through death into heaven, where he lives a perfect life full of all joy and blessedness.

Contemplation of all the causes and circumstances of our rebirth.

But here we must examine rightly, and contemplate in order, the causes and circumstances of this noble mystery, namely, (1) who the Father and Architect of this rebirth properly is; (2) what moves Him to this work; (3) who the mother or pregnant bearer might be; (4) what sort of womb this bearer has in which this work is performed; (5) what seed the mother receives; (6) what outward instrument is used for this; (7) how precisely the whole work of holy rebirth proceeds in the spiritual womb; (8) how long it takes; (9) what end it receives; (10) to what purpose a man is reborn and what good this does him; (11) what the reborn man is called in Scripture; and, finally, (12) how a Christian in this world should count his heavenly rebirth more important than all else. Let us weigh each of these twelve points in order.

I. The principal efficient cause.[84]

To begin, the Architect, or Father, Author, and Initiator from whom rebirth comes, is not an angel nor a mere man nor some other frail creature of heaven or earth, but the eternal, almighty God Himself, as Scripture expressly testifies that the children of God are born not of the will of a man but of God.

Rebirth is ascribed to the Holy Spirit.

And the work of rebirth is ascribed particularly to God the Holy Spirit, not that the Father and the Son are isolated, separated, or excluded from this work, but because the Holy Spirit is properly sent by the Father and the Son for this purpose and performs the work of His sending according to the will of them both. Therefore, we must learn to distinguish the three principal beneficial acts of God as creation, redemption, and rebirth in such a way that, although God the Father, Son, and Holy Spirit are together for every work, nevertheless creation

84 Something by means of which something else happens and on which the effect of that happening depends; that which brings about an effect.

is attributed and ascribed to God the Father, redemption to God the Son, and rebirth to God the Holy Spirit.

II. The impulsive cause.[85]

1 Pet. 1:3; John 3:16

But what in particular can move the eternal, almighty God to show us poor worms such a great benefit? Truly, our worthiness and good works do not do it since we are by nature dead to all good and with our sins have earned nothing else than God's wrath, death, hell, and all calamity and invited these upon our neck. Rightly, however, does St. Peter say that God gave us rebirth according to His great mercy, as also the Lord Christ testifies that God sent and gave the world His Son out of love.

It was out of pure loving-kindness and mercy that God was moved to give us rebirth.

Eph. 2:5–9

For just as a good, merciful father, if he sees his son lying completely dead before him, regardless of the fact that the son stabbed and murdered or killed himself with a knife, he would be moved to heartfelt pity and sorrow, and if he could he would employ every remedy, way, and means that the son might live again—so also us, for "when we were dead by the transgression of sin and were by nature children of wrath, God revealed the riches of His mercy through His great love with which He loved us. For while we were dead in sins, He made us alive together with Christ; and with Him raised us up, and with Him seated us in the heavenly places in Christ Jesus: there we are saved by grace through faith, and this not from ourselves, it is God's gift, not from works, lest anyone should boast."

III. Who the spiritual mother is.

"Yes," you say, "if God Himself is the Father and initiator who begets us again according to His will, what sort of wife does He have who conceives, bears, and is the mother of the reborn children?"

The secondary cause: The spiritual mother is the Holy Christian Church.

Isa. 54:1–7

You answer: The mother is the Holy Christian Church, which although she seems to the world a poor, paltry flock, and what is more, a barren woman, and, as it were, a lonely and forsaken widow, yet God Almighty, her Husband and heavenly Bridegroom, causes her to conceive, and she is never without children, neither will she cease to give birth until the Last Day. "Exult, O barren one," the Holy Spirit says to her, "you who do not bear. Rejoice with exultation and shout

85 That which impels a principal efficient cause to act. This impulsion comes either from inside or outside the principal cause.

for joy, you who are not with child. For the solitary has more children than she who has a husband, says the Lord. Make the place of your tent broad, and spread out the carpets of your habitations. Spare not, lengthen your cords, and make fast your stakes. For you shall break forth on the right and on the left, and your hand will inherit the Gentiles and dwell in the desolate cities. Fear not, for you shall not be ashamed. Be not afraid, for you shall not be put to shame, but you will forget the shame of your maidenhood and no longer remember the reproach of your widowhood. For He who made you is your Husband (the Lord of Hosts is His name) and your Redeemer, the Holy One in Israel, who is called the God of all the world. For the Lord caused you to be called a forsaken woman and afflicted at heart. And as a young woman that is rejected, says your God, I have forsaken you a little while, but with great mercy will I gather you."

By the woman with child in the prophet Isaiah, the Christian Church is understood.

Rev. 12:1–6

Here by the travailing woman with child, the Christian Church is understood, which by faith carries the Lord Christ spiritually in her heart, calls upon Him, confesses Him openly before the world, and always bears children through Baptism and through the preaching of the Holy Gospel, although not without cross nor without great sorrows, according as she is at all times forced to suffer vehement resistance, blows, and persecution from the devil and his bride, that is, the world. Therefore, St. John, in his Revelation, also sees the Christian Church as a pregnant mother who carries a little child in her womb, is constantly in travail, and is harshly attacked by the hellish dragon. Yet God Almighty protects her and always prepares for her a place in the wild, desolate world, where she may be nourished and rule in the midst of her enemies.

IV. What womb the Christian Church has wherein we are conceived and born.

John 5:39; Ps. 17:4

Her womb in which she conceives is God's Word comprehended in the prophetic and apostolic Scriptures of the Old and New Testament, insofar as this still rings in her ears and wells in her heart, along with the use of the holy, most worthy Sacraments. For in that Word she finds the dear Child, Jesus Christ, as He Himself says, "Search the Scriptures, for you believe that in them you have eternal life. And it is they that testify of Me." All orthodox Christians and children of light hold to this Scripture and to this Word, as though they are wrapped in them and, as it were, lying concealed in the womb, as David says, "In the word of Your lips I keep myself from the works of men, from the way of the murderer."

God's Word is the womb.

Isa. 46:3–4

Now forasmuch as the Christian Church is Bride of God and her word comprehended in Holy Scripture is nothing other than God's Word, therefore this Word is also called the womb and matrix of God, as when God says by the prophet Isaiah, "Hearken unto Me, O house of Jacob, and all the remnant of the house of Israel, you who are borne by Me in the womb and are carried by Me in the matrix."

Testimony of Luther, tom. 1, Witt., fol. 220.[86] *Mathesius, 23, Trinit.*[87] *Isa. 46:3–4*

"Faith," says Dr. Luther, "makes children of God who are born through the Word, which is the matrix in which we are conceived, carried, born, and reared." Likewise, Mathesius writes, "A child lives in the womb and is sustained by the mother, grows and increases day by day, even though it is small and weak under the mother's heart and hardly moves or stirs. Likewise, we, too, are born anew in the Word, through the Word we begin to believe, in the Word we are sustained, and those who remain in Christ the matrix and in His Word grow and increase continually and live and move in it, as the verse says:

> We live in the Word as an embryo closed in the womb.

Holy Baptism is the door and entrance into the Holy Christian Church.

John 3:3

And here Holy Baptism, especially when young children are brought to Christ and incorporated into the Christian Church, is the veritable first door, portal, and entrance into the maternal womb of the holy Church. For because the Son of God openly testifies that he who is not born again of water and the Spirit does not enter the kingdom of God, it follows conversely that by the sacrament of Baptism, from the power or operation of the Holy Spirit, children truly enter it—that is, they have access and entry into the kingdom of God and become children of the Most High, members of the Christian Church, and fellow heirs of eternal life in faith.

V. What the seed of the Christian Church is.

The material cause.[88]

1 Pet. 1:23; James 1:18; Titus 3:5

Accordingly, God's Word is not only the womb in which we are spiritually conceived and born again but also the seed itself from which we receive our new

86 From *Lectures on Galatians* (1531): cf. AE 26:391 (= WA 40/1:597).

87 See *Syrach Mathesii*, vol. 2 (Leipzig, 1588) ch. 38, sermon 16, fol. 135r.

88 The same as "matter," which is that from which something arises or of which it consists. A material cause receives and sustains a form, thus producing an actually existing being. For example, the material of a sculpture of Martin Luther could be stone, wood, metal, clay, or the like.

beginning. "You are born again," says St. Peter, "not from perishable seed but from imperishable, namely, from the living Word of God, so that it abides forever." Likewise, St. James: "He begot us according to His will through the Word of truth, that we should be the firstborn of His creatures." Of the Holy Spirit St. Paul testifies, saying, "According to His great mercy He saves us through the washing of rebirth and renewal by the Holy Spirit, whom He poured out on us abundantly through Jesus Christ, our Savior."

God's Word is simultaneously our womb and our spiritual seed.

1 John 3:9

But to understand how the Word of God may be at the same time the womb in which we are conceived and reborn as well as the seed itself from which we take our heavenly origin, it is necessary that we rightly note this distinction. For if, when that Word sounds in our ears, we think of ourselves in the midst of such ringing, reverberation, and public handling of the Word as being locked and shut up within a strong fortress against the devil, the world, and all false doctrine and refuse to be lured out of it, but stop our reason, eyes, and ears against the devil's rumbling and tempest—then such ringing and public use of the divine Word and its attendant Sacraments are like the womb of God and like the womb and matrix of His Church, in which He develops and carries us. But if it is preached and, by the power and operation of the Holy Spirit, goes into the ears and enters the heart so that it converts a man, kills the old Adam, kindles faith, strengthens it, wakens new obedience, governs his life, and frightens him away from sin, vices, and wickedness—here it is as a life-giving seed from which God gives us new birth so that we become new creatures which do not intentionally sin. As St. John says, "He who is born from God does not commit sin, for His seed abides in him, and he cannot sin, because he is born of God."

How a Christian should regard God's Word as very important.

Therefore, a godly Christian ought to treat God's Word as so important that he keeps himself locked and enclosed in it as an infant in the womb, and then that he lets himself be led only by God's Word and its attendant Sacraments as the seeds of his rebirth by which he is begotten, reborn, governed, led, and directed.

The seed of the holy divine Word is also to be our spiritual food and sustenance.

Ps. 131:1–2; 19:10; 119:50

In addition, just as in the womb an infant receives not only his origin and beginning but also (while he is formed and prepared therein) his food, energy, and increase, so we, as newly conceived children of light, in the Holy Scripture as in the spiritual womb of the Christian Church, are also to let the Word of God, the seed and beginning of our rebirth, be our spiritual food and nourishment and by no means to search outside of the revealed Word for higher things and for other, stronger food, but only to satisfy, appease, and strengthen our souls with God's Word. As David sings and says, "Lord, my heart is not proud, and my eyes are not haughty, neither do I walk in great things which are too high for me. When my soul is seated and quieted, then was my soul weaned, as one is weaned from his mother." "Your statutes are sweeter to me than honey and the honeycomb." "This is my comfort in my affliction, for Your Word quickens me."

VI. What instrument God uses for the work of rebirth.

The assistant causes.

Now, for the spreading and propagation of this heavenly seed the almighty God also uses outward instruments, namely, preachers and ministers of His Holy Word, so that they are like vine branches, conduits, and external means through which the Spirit of God makes Himself heard and spreads and scatters the imperishable seed of the Gospel in the midst of the hearers.

Preachers and ministers of the Gospel are organs and instruments of God Almighty.

Matt. 10:19; Mark 13:11; Luke 21:14; John 15:26; Jer. 1:7; Hosea 12:10; 6:5

The Lord Christ testifies to this when He very comfortingly says to His disciples, "It will be given to you in that hour what you shall say: 'I will give you mouths and wisdom.'" "Do not worry about what you shall say, nor meditate beforehand, but what is given to you in that same hour, speak that." Likewise: "The Spirit of truth, who proceeds from the Father, will testify of Me, and you also will testify." And to the prophet Jeremiah, the Lord God says, "You shall go where I send you and preach what I command you. Lo, I put My Word in your mouth." And in the last place: "I speak to you the prophets, and it is I who give so many prophecies and through the prophets reveal Myself." Likewise: "I hew them by the prophets and slay them by the word of My mouth, that Your judgment may come into the light."

Godly preachers have the glory of making their hearers spiritually reborn.

1 Cor. 4:15; Gal. 4:19

Therefore, when a preacher stands in the pulpit, preaches God's Word, abides by Scripture, introduces it rightly, and explains the Gospel intelligibly so that it is attended with fruit and taken to heart; likewise, when he administers the holy, most worthy Sacraments and gives the Supper—there is a true instrument of the Holy Trinity, lending his tongue to the Holy Spirit, and in Scripture he is given the glory of begetting spiritual children as a spiritual father, of which St. Paul is not ashamed to write openly, saying to the Corinthians, "I admonish you as my dear children. For though you have ten thousand instructors in Christ, you do not have many fathers. For I have begotten you in Christ Jesus through the Gospel." And to the Galatians he says, "My dear children, whom I am again bearing in anguish until Christ is formed within you."

Apostles, preachers, and schoolteachers are fathers.

Luther, tom. 2, Witt. Ger., fol. 239[89]

Luther explains this last verse in the following words: "The apostles, all godly preachers, and schoolteachers also are, in their own way, our parents. For just as by natural birth we inherit our physical form from our parents, so such men also are of service that our hearts and consciences may gain a proper form within us. And that proper form which a Christian heart is to have is faith or confidence in the heart, by which we take hold of Christ and cling to Him alone and nothing else. Whatever heart accordingly has such faith that we will be accounted righteous before God for Christ's sake has its proper form after Christ and is like Him.

How the proper form of testimony is prepared.

1 Cor. 4:15; 2 Cor. 3:3

"Now, this form is prepared through the preaching office, as Paul says to the Corinthians: 'I have begotten you in Christ Jesus through the Gospel so that you have known Christ and have believed in Him'; likewise: 'You are a letter of Christ's, prepared by the preaching office and written by us, not with ink, but with the Spirit of the living God.' For there the Word proceeds from the apostle's mouth and touches the hearts of the hearers, the Holy Spirit accompanying it and causing the Word to be fixed in the heart in the way it is preached. In this sense, every godly teacher is a father. For he, as through the preaching office, begets and prepares the proper form of a Christian heart."

VII. The formal cause[90] of rebirth.

Now from this it is possible to recognize and deduce to some degree the formal cause of rebirth, that is, the rebirth itself, namely, how this work takes place and what form it assumes.

How the whole work of rebirth properly takes place is hidden to reason.

John 3

And here we come right to the kernel and marrow of this noble, lofty mystery, for which Nicodemus with his learned reason and power of thought is unable to prepare himself, nor conform to it, but regards it as impossible that a man should be born again. And to confess rightly and to speak the truth, there are very many such "Nicodemians" in the Reformed Church today, who believe no more of this mystery than they can grasp and fathom with reason. Indeed, we must all confess

89 From *Lectures on Galatians* (1531): cf. AE 26:430 (= WA 40/1:649.19–30).

90 A formal cause gives being, or "form," to an effect by forming a material. For example, the form of a sculpture of Martin Luther is its artistic shape, not what it is made of. The same idea can be applied to nonartistic things as well. For example, the "form" of fire could be a chemical reaction that releases great amounts of light and heat, no matter what is burning or what color the flame.

that it lies far too deeply concealed to our five senses and human wisdom and that our flesh and blood cannot speak or reveal this to anyone.

Natural birth happens in a marvelous way, but much more does the supernatural birth.

Eccl. 11:5

But if we are forced to marvel at natural birth and are never able to fathom all its causes adequately, how should we then have any understanding or comprehension of the supernatural, heavenly, and divine work of rebirth? It is impossible, and, in this life, it will certainly remain as Solomon correctly writes and says, "As you do not know how your bones are fashioned in the womb, neither can you know the work of God."

Comparison of birth and rebirth.

Yet we ought to endeavor to learn to know and retain as much from it as God's Word reveals to us. And that this may happen, let us compare and contrast the work of natural birth and the supernatural rebirth.

Description of natural birth.

Ps. 139:14–16; Job 10:10–12

Of natural birth, we know that a man is miraculously formed and prepared in the womb by God. As David says, "You were over me in the womb. I thank You that I am wonderfully made. Wonderful are Your works, and that my soul knows right well. My bones were not concealed from You when I was made in secret, when I was formed below in the earth. Your eyes saw me, when I was still unfinished, and all my days were written in Your book, which were yet to be and when there was none of them." Job says, "Have You not poured me out like milk and curdled me like cheese? You clothed me with skin and flesh; You bound me with bones and vessels. You granted me life and favor, and Your providence preserves my breath."

Description of the supernatural rebirth.

The supernatural and heavenly rebirth happens far more wonderfully and takes place in the spiritual womb, namely, in the midst of the ringing, reverberation, and rule of the divine Word (where this rules and governs publicly with its two attached seals), driven and fulfilled by the power and operation of the Holy Spirit. For the public voice, public preaching, and public use of the Word are like a rushing wind that rushes over, embraces, covers, and encloses men everywhere on the field of this life as a jail and narrow womb, so that man does not know how he is: now beaten and struck to the ground by the Law, now quickened by the Gospel, now again cast down and afflicted, yet he hears nothing from God's Word but that it must be so. He hears this Word as a rushing of the wind and feels the wind's various powers and operations, such as terror, anguish, comfort, joy, and then again sadness and misery. But reason is confounded by this and made an utter fool, unable to understand or establish from whence the heavenly wind (namely, God) comes with these various operations through the rushing of His Word, what He intends by it, and to what end it is finally directed.

Testimony of the miraculous rebirth.

John 3:6–8

Such is the situation with our own rebirth, to which the Lord Christ also refers in His conversation with Nicodemus, saying, "What is born of the Spirit is spirit. Do not marvel that I have said to you, 'You must be born again.' The wind blows where it will, and you hear its sighing, but you do not know from whence it comes and whither it is going. So is everyone who is born of the Spirit."

To the formal and proper work of rebirth belong seven aspects.

Simple men, retain this well and consider it carefully so that this salutary teaching may become familiar to you and stir your heart. Holy Scripture does not stop here but goes on and further shows all the formal parts, elements, and aspects of this mystery, namely, how it regularly takes place when God makes a poor sinner to be reborn and readies him for eternal life. Of these aspects there are in every case seven, of which the first is called *vocatio*, calling the sinner. The second is called *contritio*, the hammer blow of the Law. The third is called *justificatio*, justification. The fourth is called *exaltatio*, raising up. The fifth is called *renovatio*, renewal, or effecting new obedience. The sixth is called the cross, which also God uses for this noble, lofty work. Lastly, the seventh is the complete preparation, preservation, and sustaining to eternal life.

(1) The first aspect of rebirth is the* vocatio *or call through the Word. The office of preachers and hearers.

First, regarding the *vocatio* or the call, God causes His Word to be preached and the Holy Sacraments to be distributed and thereby calls and attracts the sinner to Himself, desiring that he should hear the Word and meditate on it diligently. By these He then enlightens the heart, dispels the inborn darkness, and kindles a new, heavenly light so that the man begins to perceive and understand what is preached and how it reveals God in the Word. And it is precisely to this end that the preaching office with the administration of the most worthy Sacraments is instituted, so that by these God wills to be efficacious and to enlighten attentive hearers.

Matt. 28:19; Acts 20:28; Heb. 13:17; Col. 3:16

To preachers it is said, "Teach all nations and baptize them in the name of the Father and of the Son and of the Holy Spirit, and teach them to keep all that I have commanded you." "Attend to the whole flock among which the Holy Spirit has set you as bishops, to feed the congregation of God, which He has purchased by His own blood," etc. And to hearers: "Listen to your teachers and obey them.

Let the Word of Christ dwell among you richly in all wisdom. Teach and admonish one another with psalms and hymns and pleasant spiritual songs, singing to the Lord in your heart."

Power and operation of the* vocatio *or call. God enlightens by the Word.

Isa. 55:10–11; Eph. 5:14

Accordingly, where there is pure teaching, pure preaching, pure admonition, and diligent attention, heavenly enlightenment does not remain absent but follows powerfully. As those beautiful promises say, "As the rain and snow fall from heaven and do not return, but moisten the earth and cause it to be fruitful and to flourish, so that it gives seed to sow and bread to eat, so shall the Word also be that goes forth from My mouth. It shall not return to Me empty but shall do what pleases Me and shall succeed in that for which I send it." Likewise: "Let him who sleeps awake, and rise from the dead, and Christ shall shine upon you."

Acts 16:14

We have a notable example in Lydia, the seller of purple, of whom Luke reports that she listened to Paul and the Lord opened her heart that she might attend to what was spoken by St. Paul.

***(2) The second aspect of rebirth is* contritio.**

Then, before the rest, comes *contritio*, that is, the hammer blow of the Law, when God, through the preaching of the Law, causes a man to be confronted with his inborn sinful nature, as well as his actual crimes and vices, together with the curse and eternal punishment which he has merited, and has these impressed upon him, thereby striking him to the ground, as it were, so that he is terrified at heart, laments, and must despair of all his powers, works, and means and count them as futile.

God commands the Law to be preached.

Isa. 58:1; Jer. 6:27; Ezek. 3:11; Deut. 27:26; Ps. 14:3; Rom. 3:10–12, 22–23, 19–20

"Cry out with confidence," says the Lord to the preacher, "spare not. Lift up your voice like a trumpet and make known to My people their transgression, and to the house of Jacob their sins." "I have set you as a tester of metals among My people (which is so hard), that you may learn and try their way." "Say to them: 'Thus says the Lord God, whether they hearken or forbear.'" "Cursed is he who does not fulfill all the words of this Law, to do according to them." "They have all turned aside and together become corrupt. There is none who does good, not even one." "There is no distinction. They are all together sinners and lack the glory that they are to have before God," "so that every mouth may be stopped, and all the world be held accountable to God, for by the work of the Law no flesh may be righteous before Him. For by the Law comes knowledge of sin."

Fruit and operation of the Law.

Jer. 23:29; Rom. 7:7–10

The Holy Spirit uses this preaching of the Law to bring hearers to the knowledge of their sins and to drive them out of their damnable complacency into fear, so that they have remorse and sorrow for their sins, despair of their own powers, works, and abilities, fear God's wrath, and humble themselves before Him. God works these things through the Word of the Law, just as though He were burning them with fire and striking with a hammer. As He says in the prophet Jeremiah: "Is My Word not like a fire and like a hammer that breaks the rock?" Thus St. Paul writes, "I would not have known sin except through the Law. For I would not have known lust if the Law had not said, 'You shall not covet.' But sin, taking opportunity by the commandment, produced in me all manner of coveting. For apart from the Law, sin was dead. Now, I was once alive without the Law. But when the commandment came, sin revived, and I died. And it was found that the commandment, which was given to me for life, resulted in death for me."

(3) The third aspect of rebirth is the justification of a poor sinner before God.

Third, there follows here the *justificatio* or the gracious justification of a poor sinner before God, and this consists of God's causing the Gospel of Christ to be preached to poor sinners (whose hearts are heavy with sin and severely afflicted by anguish) and having it proclaimed to them that Christ took upon Himself the iniquity of the whole world and died for our sins and rose again for our justification, that He fulfilled the Law for us, stilled the Father's wrath, razed hell, and overcame the devil. Through this preaching, He comforts afflicted sinners, works and kindles faith in them, accounts to them Christ's righteousness, forgives sin, and quiets their conscience so that they rest and are content.

God causes the Gospel to be preached to us, wherein the righteousness of Christ, His Son, is offered to us.

Rom. 10:8–9; 2 Cor. 5:18–21; 1 Thess. 5:9; Rom. 10:4

To this comforting office of the Gospel Scripture testifies in many places. St. Paul says, "This is the word of faith that we preach, for if you confess Jesus with your mouth, that He is Lord, and believe in your heart that God has raised Him from the dead, you will be saved." Likewise: "God gave us the ministry of preaching reconciliation. That is, God was in Christ reconciling the world to Himself, and not reckoning their sins to them, and instituted among us the word of reconciliation. Now, then, we are ambassadors in Christ's stead, for God exhorts through us. Therefore, we now pray you in Christ's stead, be reconciled to God. For He made Him who knew no sin to be sin for us, that we might become in Him the righteousness that avails before God." "For God has not appointed us for wrath, but to possess blessedness through our Lord Jesus Christ." "Christ is the end of the Law: he who believes in Him is righteous."

Absolution, Baptism, and the Supper belong together with the Gospel.

Matt. 18:18; John 20:23; Acts 2:38; 1 Cor. 11:24–26

To this office of evangelical preaching there also belongs Holy Absolution, or the Key of Loosing, instituted by Christ when He says, "What you loose on earth will be loosed in heaven also" and "Whose sins you remit, they are remitted to him." The same holds for the Holy Sacraments also. For we are baptized for repentance and for the forgiveness of our sins. And in the most worthy Supper we are fed with Christ's body and given to drink of His blood in remembrance of Him, that we might take comfort in His precious merit and believe the forgiveness of sins.

By the outward use of the Gospel and Sacraments, God works faith in us.

John 6:29; Col. 2:12

Therefore, where this office of preaching together with the Absolution and administration of the most worthy Sacraments is practiced diligently and poor, contrite hearts with spiritual hunger and thirst attend eagerly to them, God, through this outward use of the Gospel, kindles faith in them so that they believe the Gospel and confide in Christ. And accordingly the faith in us is not by human power nor our own ability, but God's gift and God's work, as it is written: "This is the work of God: that you believe in Him whom He sent." Likewise: "Acknowledge what is the surpassing greatness of His power in us, who believe according to the working of His mighty power, which He wrought in Christ when He raised Him from the dead and seated Him at His right hand in heaven." And again: "You are buried with Christ through Baptism, in which you are also risen through faith, which God works, who raised Him from the dead."

Through faith, the Lord Christ's righteousness and innocence is reckoned to us and our sin is covered.

Rom. 4:5–7; Ps. 32:1; John 3:17

Now when this faith longs for and confides in the evangelical promise, takes hold of Christ with His merit, and clings to His righteousness, then God reckons to us the righteousness of His Son by faith, covers our sins with it, and will no longer remember them forever. So the holy apostle Paul testifies to this, saying, "To him who does not deal with works, but believes in Him who justifies the ungodly, to him is his faith reckoned for righteousness. Even as David also says that blessedness belongs to that man alone to whom God imputes righteousness without the addition of works, saying, 'Blessed are they whose unrighteousness is forgiven and whose sins are covered. Blessed is the man to whom the Lord imputes no sin.'" Likewise, Christ says, "God did not send His Son to judge the world, but that the world through Him might be saved. Whoever believes in Him will not be judged."

(4) The fourth aspect of rebirth is our heavenly exaltation.

The fourth aspect of heavenly rebirth is the gracious exaltation: that God not only justifies us by faith but also, in the Gospel, causes us to be presented with and offered the blessed adoption to eternal life and the heavenly bridal honor, that by faith we might be His children and the chosen Bride of His beloved Son. Moreover, as a surety and certain pledge of this He sends the Spirit of His Son into our hearts, that we might be His possession and a temple or dwelling of the entire Holy Trinity.

Glorious promise that God will be our Father and Christ our Bridegroom.

Jer. 31:1; 2 Cor. 6:18; John 1:12; 20:17; Hosea 2:19; Isa. 62:4–5

Regarding this exaltation or raising to a high rank, the words of His promise are thus: "I will receive you and be your Father, and you shall be My sons and daughters, says the Lord Almighty." "As many as received Christ, to them He gave the power to become children of God." To Mary Magdalene the Lord Christ says, "Go to My brothers and say to them, 'I am ascending to My Father and to your Father, to My God and to your God.'" And of our heavenly bridal honor He says, "I will pledge Myself to you forever, I will be betrothed to you in righteousness. Yea, in faith will I betroth Myself to you." "You shall be called 'My delight is in her,' and your hand 'Espoused,' for the Lord has delight in you and your hand has a spouse. For as a young man loves his young woman, so your children will love you; and as a bridegroom rejoices over the bride, so will your God rejoice over you."

Promise of the faithfulness of the Father and true love of the Bridegroom.

Ps. 103:13; Isa. 66:13; 49:15; Matt. 28:20; John 15:26; 16:13

We are also told in the Gospel that God the Father will show us faithfulness surpassing that of a father and mother, and the Lord Christ will show us the true love of a bridegroom: "As a father has mercy on his children," we sing with the prophet David, "so the Lord has mercy on those who fear Him." He says, "I will comfort you as one's mother comforts him." "Can a wife forget her little child and not have mercy upon the son of her womb? And although she forgets him, yet I will not forget you." Likewise, Christ, our heavenly Bridegroom, promises that He will not forsake His Church, but will dwell with her until the end of the world and that He will send her the Holy Spirit from the Father, who will lead and guide her into all truth.

God works faith so that it embraces this heavenly exaltation, and His Holy Spirit seals it in us.

There are exceedingly precious treasures and an honor above all worldly honor and glory, that God the Father will be our Father, and God the Son our Bridegroom, and God the Holy Spirit our Comforter. He not only causes these benefits to be presented to us, but, if we attend to the Word, He also awakens faith so that a Christian embraces and takes hold of them with the same faith with which he previously received the forgiveness of sins and the righteousness of the dear Gospel. And thus the entire Holy Trinity comes to us by faith and dwells in us, namely, the Father as our dearest Father, the Lord Jesus Christ as our dearest Bridegroom, and the Holy Spirit as our highest Comforter, who is additionally the seal and pledge of our salvation so that we have no doubt about this tremendous promise.

Testimony of Scripture.

1 Cor. 6:15; Gal. 3:27; 1 Cor. 3:16; Gal. 4:6; Rom. 8:15–16; Eph. 1:13–14

Pertinent here are the passages: "As many of you as are baptized have put on Christ." "Do you not know that you are members of Christ?" "Do you not know that you are God's temple, and the Spirit of God dwells in you?" "Because you are children, God sent the Spirit of His Son into your hearts, who cries, 'Abba, dear Father.'" "You have not received a spirit of servitude, that you must again fear, but you have received a spirit of sonship, through which we cry, 'Abba, dear Father.' The same Spirit bears witness with our spirit that we are God's children. And if we are children, then we are also heirs, namely, heirs of God and fellow heirs of Christ." And again: "If you believe, you have been sealed with the Holy Spirit of the promise, who is the pledge of our inheritance for our redemption, that we should become His possession to the praise of His glory."

The fruit of our exaltation.

This heavenly exaltation produces joy and very great comfort in all anxiety, sadness, and misery and gives strong courage so that a believing Christian need not fear before God as before an enemy and torturer, but trusts Him in a childlike manner, relies on Christ as a bride relies on her bridegroom, and confides in the Holy Spirit as his highest friend and most powerful comforter.

(5) The fifth aspect of our rebirth is spiritual* renovatio *or renewal.

In the fifth place comes *renovatio*, that is, spiritual and heavenly renewal, when God, having justified His children in faith through the imputed innocence of His Son and having received them as His children, bridal temple, and possession, also kindles new obedience in them, so that by the power and working of the Holy Spirit, after they have received the forgiveness of sins and obtained the joy of their precious, heavenly redemption, they begin in turn to love God and their neighbor, to hate sin, to resist the devil, the world, and their own fleshly desire, and to live according to God's commandments.

Divine promise that God will listen to and govern the heart of His Christians.

Ezek. 36:26–27; Jer. 32:39; John 15:4–5

The promise that God has made about this is: "I will put a new heart and a new spirit in you, and I will take away the heart of stone from your flesh and give you a heart of flesh. I will put My Spirit into you and will make you such people as walk in My commandments and behave and do according to My statutes." "I will give them one heart and way, that they may fear Me all their life." "Abide in Me, and I will abide in you. As the branch can bear no fruit of itself unless it clings to the vine, so you cannot unless you abide in Me. I am the Vine; you are the branches. Whoever abides in Me, and I in him, the same brings forth much fruit. For without Me you can do nothing."

Spiritual renewal is God's work in us and a fruit of our justification and exaltation.

1 Cor. 6:19–20

Now, when you have been sprinkled with the blood of Christ by faith, believe the forgiveness of sins, trust God the Father with childlike trust as your true Father and the Lord Christ as your Redeemer and dearest Bridegroom and God the Holy Spirit as your only and highest Comforter, who dwells in you and possesses you as His own temple and residence, you should know that where God resides and dwells, He is not idle but active and produces fruit, which springs forth and grows. Therefore, when He dwells in you also and takes root in your heart through faith, He produces fruit, stirs up new movements in you, and incites you to good works, just as if you had no power over yourself, but a ruler dwelt in you to whom you had delegated all that you do or do not. As St. Paul says, "Do you not know that your body is the temple of the Holy Spirit, whom you have from God, and you are not your own? For you are bought with a price. Therefore, glorify God in your body and in your spirit, which are God's."

Good works are fruit of faith and testimonies of our new Christian life.

And these workings and movements are sure testimonies of the new life in us, just as a child stirs in the womb and the mother can deduce and conclude from that that she has a living infant within her.

Holy Scripture bears witness to this teaching.

Rom. 8:14; Gal. 5:22–25; Eph. 4:22–24; John 15:35, 12–17

"Those whom the Holy Spirit drives," says Scripture, "they are the children of God." "But the fruit of the Spirit is love, joy, peace, patience, kindness, goodness, faith, gentleness, chastity—against such things the Law is not. But those who belong to Christ crucify their flesh together with lusts and desires. If we live in the Spirit, let us also walk in the Spirit." "Therefore, lay aside, according to the former conduct, the old man who is corrupted by lusts in error, and be renewed in the Spirit of your mind, and put on the new man, who is made according to God in perfect righteousness and holiness." "By this," says the Lord Christ Himself, "will everyone know that you are My disciples, if you love one another." "This is My commandment, that you love one another as I have loved you. No man has greater love than he who lays down his life for his friends. You are My disciples, if you do what I command you. I say henceforth not that you are servants; for a servant does not know what his master is doing. But I have said to you that you are friends. For all that I have heard from My Father I have made known to you. You have not chosen Me, but I have chosen you and appointed that you should go and bear fruit, and that your fruit should remain, so that whatever you ask the Father in My name, He will give it to you. And these things I command you that you may love one another."

Our new obedience and works of faith are the quickening of a living infant in the womb.

Rom. 8:1–13

Therefore, just as a human being in the womb (as soon as life is kindled in him) begins to stir, and although such a beginning is frail, tender, and of little account, yet he increases therein from day to day and grows in powers until he comes out of the cramped, narrow lodging into this world, then his life is perfect, and he moves fully in all his members—so the children of light also have only the first-fruits of the Spirit, and with their new obedience and good works which they do in faith, out of love toward God and neighbor, they embark upon the spiritual life. They also grow and increase therein until they die to this world through temporal death and are taken up into the heavenly paradise. Then the eternal life stirs with full force so that they love their Lord God with all their heart, all their soul, and all their mind, and their neighbor as themselves.

(6) The sixth aspect of rebirth is the dear cross.

The sixth aspect of rebirth is the holy cross, when God causes various kinds of tribulation, anguish, distress, and misery to befall His children that He may thereby diminish and put to death the lusts of the flesh and the old Adam in them and test, sharpen, and strengthen the faith kindled in them and give them cause for prayer, for humility, for patience, and all Christian virtues and make them similar and conformable to the image of His Son, Jesus Christ, to His glory and honor.

God Himself puts the cross on us.

Matt. 16:24; Rev. 3:19; Matt. 20:23; Sirach 2:1–4; Ps. 68:19; 75:8

Of the cross itself, how it is imposed by God and how all godly Christians are to accept and bear it patiently, the Lord speaks in His Word thus: "If anyone will come after Me, let him take up his cross and follow Me." "Those whom I love I discipline." "My cup you shall indeed drink, and with the baptism with which I am baptized you shall be baptized." "My child, if you would be God's servant, prepare yourself for temptation. Hold fast and endure, and do not waver, that you may become ever stronger. Whatever you encounter, endure it, and be patient in every manner of sorrow." "God lays a burden upon us," says David, "but He also saves us." "For the Lord has a bowl in His hand and it is filled full with strong wine, and He pours out of the same."

***What is meant by the word* cross.**

Matt. 10:22; John 16:2; Mic. 4:6; Job 1:12; 2:6; 16:11

Now this word *cross* means all kinds of tribulation, affliction, and sorrow which a godly man encounters; likewise also enmity and persecution, when God ordains and allows His Church to be afflicted and persecuted by the devil and by the world in the most pitiful manner. As Christ says, "You must be hated by everyone for My name's sake, and they will put you into exile. But the hour is coming that whoever kills you will suppose he is doing God a service thereby." "God causes affliction," says Micah, even as God Himself says of Job and Satan, "All that Job has is in your hand, only lay not your hand upon him." Afterward, however, He says, "Behold, he is in your hand, yet spare his life." Then Job writes, "The Lord has delivered me over to the unrighteous."

Yet at the same time, our dear God does not mean evil or mischief for His children when He holds them under the cross and visits them with adversity, but by these things furthers the whole work of salutary rebirth, that it may have free course and be brought to completion.

Testimony of Scripture.

Jer. 30:11; Ps. 90:7–8; Isa. 48:10; Ps. 66:10; Isa. 26:16; 1 Cor. 11:32; Rom. 6:6; 5:3–5

For, first, He uses it to lead them to the knowledge of their sins; as He Himself says, "I will discipline you with moderation so that you do not regard yourself as innocent." Likewise, David says, "Your anger causes us to perish, and Your wrath causes us to depart suddenly. For You set our iniquity before You, our secret sin in the light before Your face." Second, He uses it to test and strengthen faith, as it is written, "I will refine you . . . and make you chosen in the furnace of affliction." "O God," says David, "You have tried and refined us as silver is refined." Third, He then uses it to incite them to prayer, as Isaiah says, "Lord, when there is tribulation, You are sought; when You discipline, they cried to You anxiously." Fourth, the cross is also a salutary defense against sinful lusts. For "when we are judged, we are disciplined by the Lord, that we may not be condemned with the world." And "our old man is crucified, that the sinful body may cease, that we may no longer serve sin." Fifth, in addition to all these, "tribulation brings patience, and patience brings experience, and experience brings hope, and hope does not make ashamed."

(7) The seventh aspect of rebirth is complete preparation.

Finally, the seventh aspect belonging to the work of rebirth is complete preparation: that God not only initiates the conversion and the new birth of His Christians but also completes the entire work, provided His revealed ordinance is followed.

God's promise.

Isa. 46:3–4; John 14:16–17; 10:27–28

"You are borne by Me in the womb," He says, "and are carried by Me in the matrix. I, even I, will bear you to old age and until you grow gray. I will do it, I will raise you and bear you and deliver you." "And I will ask the Father, and He will give you another Comforter, to remain with you forever, even the Spirit of truth." Likewise: "My sheep hear My voice, and I know them, and they follow Me, and I give them eternal life, and they will never perish, and no man shall pluck them out of My hand."

1 Pet. 1:5; 1 Cor. 1:7–9; 1 Thess. 5:24; Phil. 2:13; 2 Thess. 3:2–3

To this promise St. Peter looks when he writes, "You are preserved by God's power through faith unto salvation." St. Paul also does the same here and there in his epistles, saying, "Only wait for the revelation of our Lord Jesus Christ, who also will keep you firm until the end, that you may be blameless on the day of our Lord Jesus Christ. For God is faithful, by whom you are called to the fellowship of His Son, Jesus Christ, our Lord." Likewise: "He is faithful, who calls you, who will also do it." And in another place: "For it is God who works in you both to will and to do according to His good pleasure." Again he says, "Faith is not a thing of any man, but the Lord is faithful, who will strengthen you and preserve you before the wicked."

The whole work of rebirth happens marvelously.

Behold, dear brother, such are the circumstances with the true course and business of rebirth, and thus must the whole work be assigned and ascribed to no other in heaven or earth but to our dear God alone. For as a tender infant in the womb does nothing of itself, nor can add anything to its being conceived and kindled with natural life, but lets itself be formed and fashioned and hence receives its life so that it begins gradually to move and stir—so also a Christian in this world is carried in the Word of God, as though enclosed in His womb or in the matrix and womb of His Christian Church, and cannot out of his own human power acquire spiritual life, but must let himself be prepared for it by the Gospel, enlightened, and kindled with saving faith, that he may thus begin to live spiritually and let the movements or motions of this life be seen publicly in a godly conduct of Christian virtues.

VIII. How long rebirth takes.

2 Cor. 5:4–9

If you wish further to know how long this rebirth takes before it is completed, St. Paul answers, saying, "While we are in the tabernacle (of our life), we have longing and are burdened, for we would rather not be unclothed but further clothed, that the mortal might be swallowed up by life. But He who prepares us for this is God, who has given us the pledge, even the Spirit. But we are always confident, knowing that while we dwell in the body, we walk with the Lord. For we walk in faith and not in sight. But we are confident and have far more desire to walk out of the body and to be home with the Lord. Therefore, we are also diligent, whether we are at home or on pilgrimage, that we may be pleasing to Him."

Our rebirth continues from Baptism until death.

From these words it is clear and plain enough that in this temporal life our rebirth, as long as we make use of it, does not reach a conclusion but continues from Baptism until death. During this time we must continually be called, enlightened, chastened, comforted, governed, and led by God's Word and under the cross, as in the school of discipline, confess to our dear God what we have learned from His Word, how strongly we trust in Him, how we depart from sin, repent, and occupy ourselves with works of Christian love.

Error of the Papists concerning our rebirth.

And this particularly is to be noted and retained in opposition to the Papists, who maintain that in Baptism rebirth is entirely completed, and children are completely released from all sins, so that in their flesh nothing sinful remains any longer. This error arises from blind ignorance since they do not rightly perceive or understand the mystery of rebirth: for this does not happen all at once in a flash or the blink of an eye, just as a man also is not naturally conceived, formed, and born all in the same hour, but everything has its time, its limit, and its progress. Through Baptism our spiritual mother, the Christian Church, conceived us by the Holy Spirit, and we are accordingly carried in our mother, that is, in God's womb and in God's matrix, and therein are being formed and fashioned into God's children until, by temporal death, He separates us from this world and brings us into eternal life. Meanwhile, we must continually hear God's Word, continually mourn our sins, continually pray for forgiveness, and constantly exercise ourselves in the faith, fighting against sin, praying, and walking in new obedience.

IX. What end rebirth receives.

Now, the end of this whole salutary work is temporal death, by which God tenderly releases His children from all sorrow, distress, and adversity so that the soul ceases to sin, becomes pure as an angel, and leaves the decrepit lodging of its body for the fatherland of eternal life. But the body rests under the earth until the Last Day; then it will rise again without any blemish or deficiency, in perfect glory, power, and majesty, be united with the soul, go forth to meet the Son of God in the clouds of heaven, and be with Him forever.

St. Paul longs for the end.

Rom. 7:24; 6:7; Phil. 1:23

For this end the holy apostle Paul heartily longs when he says, "Poor man that I am, who will deliver me from the body of this death?" "He who has died is justified from sin." "I have a desire to depart and to be with Christ." But of this we will hear further instruction hereafter.

X. The fruit and use of rebirth: For what purpose a man is reborn and what benefit rebirth brings.

1 Pet. 1:3; 2 Cor. 4:17–18; Col. 3:2; Rev. 2:10

Concerning the fruit of our rebirth, it is eternal life. For the Father of our Lord Jesus Christ (as Scripture testifies), "according to His great mercy, gave us rebirth to a living hope through the resurrection of Jesus Christ from the dead to an imperishable and unblemished and incorruptible inheritance that is kept for us in heaven." "Therefore, our affliction, which is temporary and light, produces an eternal and immeasurable glory for us, who do not look to what is seen but to what is unseen, and seek that which is above and not that which is on the earth." "Be faithful unto death," says the Son of God, "and I will give you the crown of life."

We are to esteem rebirth highly because of its noble fruit and benefit.

We must note this carefully so that we may the more highly esteem God's Word, the use of the most worthy Sacraments, the Absolution, the most worthy Supper, the exercise of the faith, prayer, and the true fear of God. For to what purpose are we baptized? Why do we go to church, hear God's Word, believe the Gospel, and cultivate Christian conduct? What fruit and benefit do we derive from this? For agriculture, for the outward operation of a household, for political government and management, for buying and selling, for sowing, planting, and for similar business we surely have no need of Baptism, preaching, the Supper to instruct us in church how to carry on such affairs and temporal offices. For the heathen, Turks, and Tatars can do so just as well as we, even though they do not receive rebirth. What is ultimately sought after in our believing the Gospel and being reborn is eternal life and the imperishable, unblemished, and incorruptible inheritance which is kept for us in heaven.

The name of the reborn.

Acts 11:26; Deut. 7:6; 2 Cor. 6:18; Gal. 6:1; Col. 3:12; 1 Cor. 3:16; John 8:36; 10:4–17; 15:15; Eph. 2:19; Matt. 7:17–18; 25:34, 40; etc.

In addition, those who are reborn receive the noble, precious name of Christ and are called Christians after Him. They are also called children of God, people of God, the possession of God, brothers and sisters of Christ, as well as His disciples, His sheep, His members, His friends, fellow citizens and fellow lodgers in God's household, new creatures, new men, righteous, holy, free, spiritual, taught by God, the blessed of the heavenly Father, good trees, and temples of the Holy Spirit.

Where we get the glorious and excellent name.

What, then, can sound more pleasant, friendly, and comforting than that we are new creatures, children of God, brothers and sisters of Christ, temples of the Holy Spirit, and heirs of God? And where do we get such honor and glory but from rebirth?

Luther, tom. 1, Witt. Ger., fol. 220[91]

"Whoever is a child," says Dr. Luther, "is also simultaneously an heir, for birth entails the right that a child is simultaneously an heir. But no one acquires heirdom by his works or merits, but birth alone brings it to him, so that in this way the inheritance is not won but only given; that is, although a person may labor, worry, and do what he can, he will not become the heir. What makes him an heir, rather, is that he is a child born in the inheritance; for a child certainly contributes nothing to being born, but only endures it and often survives it with the mother.

How we inherit the eternal riches of heaven.

Isa. 46:3–4[; Rom. 8:17; Heb. 2:14–15]

"In this way we inherit the eternal riches of heaven, such as forgiveness of sins, righteousness, the glorious resurrection, and eternal life, not through our adding anything, but apart from all our doing, we allow it to be given us and receive it from God through Christ. Here there is nothing that advances our cause. By itself, faith takes hold of the inborn promise. Thus as a child in the worldly realm and the household becomes an heir only by his being born into the hereditary estate, so here faith makes those children of God who are born by the Word, which is the matrix in which we are conceived, carried, born, and raised. Now, therefore, just as we become children of God by this birth that God accomplishes without our adding to it, so we also become heirs by the same means. And if we have become heirs, we are free from death, the devil, etc., and have righteousness and eternal life."

The name that the reborn have also tells what they truly are.

And hence we are not merely called children of God, heirs of God, and fellow heirs of Christ, but we also are such things in truth and possess the property along with the name, despite the fact that it does not appear to sight in this world but lies hidden in the Word and is only grasped by faith. In short, whoever believes the Gospel, trusts our Savior, Jesus Christ, and is instructed, governed, and

91 From *Lectures on Galatians* (1531): cf. AE 26:392 (= WA 40/1:597).

reborn by the Word, is in truth a child of the Most High, a brother or sister of the Lord Christ, one blessed of the heavenly Father, and an heir of eternal life.

XI. How a Christian in this world is to esteem rebirth.

Finally, because this rebirth is for no other creature under the sun but us men only, and the highest blessedness of all Christians on earth depends on it, esteem it highly, dear brother, and make sure that you do not intentionally or maliciously resist our dear God, who out of great, fervent love has given you rebirth and readied you for eternal life.

A Christian in this world is to adhere carefully to God's Word.

You know how the man must initially be formed and readied in the womb and kindled with life before he appears to the world alive and becomes a partaker of the air. So let God's Word also be your spiritual mother in this world, and in this spiritual womb let the Spirit of God govern, instruct, and ready you as a new creature. Then you can think thus and say, "Come, then! In this world God is bearing me unto eternal life, and from my Baptism until death I am being borne by Him in the womb and being carried by Him in the matrix, namely, in His Word, in which He forms me anew and makes me spiritually alive. Therefore, I will diligently go to church, diligently hear God's Word, and diligently meditate on it and take it to heart, that God may do His work in me and prepare me for blessedness."

A child in the womb is marvelously nourished and does not quibble but lets himself be formed, nourished, and made ready.

We also know how a child in the womb, before he comes into the world, is marvelously nourished by the maternal seed and strengthened thereby until, through natural birth, he presses out of the narrow, cramped lodging into the world. His nourishment meanwhile comes through the narrow holes and orifices which scientists call *cotylidones*, and he does not worry himself with careful thoughts about how this may happen, does not ask for strong drink and food which the people in the world use, nor are his thoughts focused on the wide earth and how people may dwell and live upon it. Indeed, if he tried to go out into the world before birth (before it is the right time) and see his father's face, and he succeeded in doing so, it would cost him his life for which both mother and child exist. Therefore, he keeps himself still in his narrow little house, trusts the seed of his creation, is content with the proffered nutrition and sustenance, and lets himself be nourished, strengthened, and sustained by it.

As a child in the womb lets himself be nourished by the maternal seed, so a Christian in this world lets himself be fed and spiritually nourished with God's Word.

Do likewise, dear brethren. From your Baptism until death keep yourself enclosed in God's Word like a child in his mother's womb. There let the Gospel be your milk and sustenance. Likewise, when you hear that in the most worthy Supper the Son of God bids you eat His body and drink His blood with the visible elements of bread and wine, believe the words simply, as they read, and by no means doubt with the thoughts of clever reason how this could ever be. Guard yourself against the Calvinists as well as the Schwenkfelders, Anabaptists, and other Enthusiasts[92] who neglect the Word and speculate how they may take hold of God in His bare majesty. What is more, they do not allow that the fullness of the Godhead of Christ dwells in His assumed flesh, but wish to deal with it outside of the flesh. They also speak of His eternal foresight, election to grace, and similar mysteries not as He has revealed Himself in His Word, but according to the thoughts of their clever reason.

Warning against all the blindness of the Enthusiasts.

Exod. 33:20

Therefore, guard yourselves against them, and do not desire in this world to see God in His bare majesty, for this is not the time. As He Himself says, "No man shall live who sees Me." But if you wish to be certain and sure of your salvation, only pay attention to the Word in the Gospel. Look at Christ, how He is conceived, born, crucified, died, risen again, ascended into heaven, and exalted to the right hand of God, and what He said and instituted. There become a child, take your reason captive to the obedience of Christ, and cleave to the revealed Word, and you will remain sure and undeceived.

Luther, tom. 3, Witt. Germ., fols. 14–15[93]

Dr. Luther also gives this advice, saying, "Just as the divine essence is incomprehensible and cannot be grasped or circumscribed by all the world or by any creatures, so also it is not bearable or tolerable for our human nature to try to search out and fathom His incomprehensible and infinite being, majesty, and glory with the senses. Therefore, if you wish to deal prudently, safely, and without danger to your conscience and salvation, refrain from such speculation and searching, and learn to grasp our Lord God in the manner which Scripture teaches, as written in 1 Corinthians: 'Since the world through its wisdom did not know God through His wisdom, it pleased God the Lord through foolish preaching to save those who believe therein' (1 Cor. 1:21)."

92 During the Reformation, "enthusiast" or "fanatic" (*Schwärmer*) was a term used for all those who sought the Spirit without the means of the Word (Bible, preaching) and Sacraments and thus rejected the spiritual power of the external Word. Sacramentarians, Anabaptists, and even the radical elements of the Reformation, such as Thomas Münzer and his followers, fell under this banner.

93 From *Lectures on Galatians* (1531): cf. AE 26:29 (= WA 40/1:77.20–26).

Where God is to be sought and found. We are not to deal with God outside the humanity of Christ.

And shortly thereafter:[94] "If you contemplate or dispute with yourself where God is to be found, who justifies sinners and makes them godly and receives them to grace, then make sure that you know of no god nor esteem any god except the man Jesus Christ, but only take hold of Him and continue clinging to Him with your heart and freely let go of all thoughts and speculations about His majesty. For as Solomon says, 'He who searches out heavy things, for him it will be too heavy' (Prov. 25:27). What I say here, I have experienced, and I know that it is true. But the enthusiastic spirits, who try to deal with God apart from this man Christ, do not believe me in this. Christ says it Himself: 'I am the way, the truth, and the life. No man comes to the Father except by Me.' Therefore, without this way, which is Christ, you will find no way, but utter hypocrisy and falsehood; no life, but eternal death."

As an infant in the womb grows and increases in natural life until it becomes mature and the right age for birth, so a Christian in the world must grow and increase in the spiritual life until death.

2 Pet. 1:3–8

Furthermore, be diligent, as long as you live on earth, that you may grow and increase in the spiritual life, that is, in faith, in love, in knowledge of God, and in all manner of virtues, precisely as an infant in the womb, having been kindled with natural life, also grows from day to day in powers and becomes continually stronger until the hour of his birth. Then he presses out from his narrow little house into this world and then breathes in the air for life, so that his life is a complete and perfect life. In the same way, be constant in the exercise of the faith with watching and prayer and all things that pertain to the spiritual life as long as, in this world, you are being carried in our dear God's Word as in the matrix, and He will at last richly grant you the entry from this valley of tears to the eternal kingdom of His Son, Jesus Christ.

Scripture exhorts us to the spiritual life.

2 Pet. 1:10–11; 1 Thess. 5:11; Col. 3:14–16; Phil. 1:9–11

To this Scripture here and there exhorts us, saying, "Dear brethren, be all the more diligent to make your calling and election sure. For if you do so, you will not err, and in this way, you will be richly rewarded with entry into the eternal kingdom of our Lord and Savior Jesus Christ. Therefore, exhort one another and edify one another. Put on love, which is the bond of perfection, and may the peace of God reign in your hearts, to which you also are called, into one body, and be thankful. Let the Word of Christ dwell among you richly in all wisdom, teaching and admonishing one another with psalms and hymns and spiritual,

94 From *Lectures on Galatians* (1531): cf. AE 26:29 (= WA 40/1:78.14–23).

pleasant songs and singing to the Lord in your heart." Likewise: "I pray that your love may increase more and more in all manner of wisdom and knowledge, that you may prove what is good, that you may be pure and without reproach until the day of Christ, filled with the fruits of righteousness which come by Jesus Christ (in you) to the honor and worship of God."

Exhortation to all manner of virtues which belong to the spiritual life.

Follow these and similar exhortations well, dear Christian. Be eager for God's Word as an infant for his mother's milk. Depart from sin, be heartily converted, listen gladly to the preaching of the Gospel, use the Supper often for the strengthening of faith, fear God and love Him above all things, and love your neighbor also; do not follow sinful lusts. Have no fellowship with the ungodly, be patient in the cross, resist the devil, the world, and your own flesh, in faith attend to your vocation, and take heed to your salvation with fear and trembling.

Exhortation to prayer.

Furthermore, be constantly joyful in the Lord, and give thanks to Him without ceasing. Pray and cry to Him diligently (after He, in fervent love, has begun this salutary work of rebirth in you) that He would also kindly finish it and prepare you completely for entrance into the heavenly paradise.

Prayer of reborn Christians.

Glory and praise of God's great grace.

Ps. 8:4; Eph. 1:3–8

Say: O dear God, what is man that You are mindful of him, and the child of man, that you come to his aid? O dear God, Father of my Lord Jesus Christ, how richly You bless me with all manner of spiritual blessings in the heavenly possessions through Christ! You chose me through Him before the foundation of the world was laid, that I should be holy and blameless before You in love. You also appointed me to adoption to Yourself through Jesus Christ, according to the pleasure of Your will, to the praise of Your glorious grace. O gracious Father, how glorious is Your grace, through which You have made me acceptable in the Beloved! Oh, what a noble redemption I have in Your Son through His blood, namely, the forgiveness of sins, according to the riches of Your grace, which has been richly bestowed on me in all manner of wisdom and knowledge!

1 Pet. 1:23, 4; Isa. 46:3; Eph. 2:5, 10; 1:9, 13

O Lord my God, heavenly Father, how great is Your goodness, that You have given me new birth in this world, not from perishable seed, but from imperishable, namely, from Your living Word (which endures forever), to an imperishable and unblemished and incorruptible inheritance that is only preserved in heaven! O my dear God, how heartily I rejoice that from my Baptism until the grave I am borne by You in the womb and am carried by You in the matrix. I was dead in sins, but You make me alive in Christ and set me together with Him in the heavenly places. Great and exceeding great is the precious grace of rebirth, that You cause me to be Your handiwork created in Christ Jesus and that You cause me to know the mystery of Your will according to Your pleasure. Seal me also with the Holy Spirit of the promise, who is the pledge of my inheritance for my redemption, that I may be Your possession to the praise of Your glory.

Thanksgiving and prayer for increase of faith.

Ps. 116:12; 51:15; Eph. 1:18–19; Gal. 2:20; John 6:29; Eph. 1:19–20, 14

O my dearest God, how shall I repay You for all these benefits which You show me? Oh, open my lips, that my mouth may show forth Your praise and my tongue proclaim Your righteousness. And enlighten the eyes of my understanding, that I may increase in the spiritual and godly life and may know what is the hope of my calling and what are the riches of Your glorious inheritance in me and what is the surpassing greatness of Your power in me. For I live, and yet not I, but Your Son, Jesus Christ, lives in me. For the life that I now live in the flesh, I live by faith in Your Son, who loved me and gave Himself up for me. And it is Your work that I believe since I believe according to the working of Your mighty power, which You worked in Christ when You raised Him from the dead and set Him up at Your right hand in heaven.

God must be the Alpha and Omega, the beginning and the end, of our salvation.

Eph. 3:15; Isa. 4:9:15; Luke 17:5; Eph. 3:16–18

O Father of my Lord Jesus Christ, You, who are the true Father of all who are called children in heaven and on earth; who are far less able to forget Your newborn children than a mother to forget her little child, that she should not have mercy on the son of her womb: O heavenly Father, increase my faith. Oh, give me power according to the riches of Your glory to become strong through the Spirit in the inward man, and grant that Christ may dwell in my heart by faith and I may be rooted and grounded in love, that I may comprehend with all the saints what is the breadth and length and depth and height and may know that to love Christ is far better than to know all things, that I may be filled with all manner of God's abundance!

Prayer to be sustained unto eternal life.

Phil. 1:6; Isa. 66:9; 2 Cor. 4:7; Ps. 17:8

My dearest God, who has begun this good work in me, I implore You also to complete it until the day of Jesus Christ. Give birth to me, even as You cause others to open the matrix; and You who cause others to be born, do not remain closed for me! Your Son, Jesus Christ, Your Holy Spirit, and Your Word are my highest treasure, and I have this treasure here in an earthen vessel, that the surpassing power may be Yours and not mine. Therefore, strengthen and sustain me unto eternal life, and keep me as the apple of Your eye, that here I may increase in knowledge of You and, finally, when the hour of death arrives, I may leave this valley of sorrow unhindered by the devil, the world, and all temptations and come to You in the eternal paradise. Grant this to me, O gracious Father, through Jesus Christ, Your Son, in the power of the Holy Spirit. Amen.

The Fourth Benefit of God: A Dying Christian's Blessed Journey Home from This World to Eternal Life

Of our final deliverance.

The fourth benefit of God depends on the third and is properly nothing other than the completion of the most salutary rebirth, when God delivers His elect children from all evil of body and soul and, finally, when the hour of death has come, summons them from this valley of sorrows, takes their souls through temporal death from this world to the paradise of eternal joy, and causes their bodies meanwhile to rest and slumber under the earth until the Last Day.

Narrow gate to life. Comparison of this world and the next.

Luther, tom. 6, Witt. Germ., fol. 145[95]

"Here, then, there arises the narrow gate and the slender path to eternal life," as Dr. Luther writes, "which every person must happily ponder. For even if this way is in truth narrow, nevertheless it does not last long, and the process here is no different from a child's being born from the little dwelling of the womb, with danger and anxiety, into the wide heaven and earth, that is, into the world. In the same way, a man goes through the narrow gate of death from this life into eternal life. And although heaven and the world which we now inhabit are very different and far apart, nevertheless everything is far narrower and smaller compared to the heaven to come than the womb is compared to the sky.

Death of the saints.

"Therefore, the death of the dear saints is called a new birth, and their feast in Latin is called their *natale*, the day of their birth." For when we die here to this world, we are born into the next life. But the narrow gate and the slender way and the anxious sorrows in the throes of death cause us to prefer to remain here in this world of temporal life and to think that the next life is narrow, but all that is to be done is for us to venture freely upon death and to press through the narrow gate of death into eternal life, as a child from the womb.

95 From *Sermon on Preparing to Die* (1519): cf. AE 42:99 (= WA 2:685.22–30; 686.1).

Example of physical birth.

John 16:21

And so, from the example of the physical birth of a child, we must learn to die, even as Christ also comforts His disciples thereby, where He says, "A woman, when she is giving birth, has sorrow, for her hour is come. But when the child is born, she no longer thinks of the anguish because of the joy that a man is born to the world." So also in death, we must consider the anguish and know that afterward there will be a large, broad space and eternal joy.

How our spiritual rebirth is rightly to be understood from the example of physical birth.

The Holy Christian Church is the pregnant mother, a dying Christian is the child which is to be born of that mother, the Word of God is the womb in which the child lies enclosed and shut up, his old Adam, or his flesh and blood, is the afterbirth or the caul (which physicians call *chorion* and *secundina*[96]), with which the living child is surrounded in the womb. And natural death is the departure, or like the arrival of the infant from his mother's womb into this world.

(1) Comparison of the Christian Church on earth with a pregnant woman.

Gal. 2:20

Now, then, as the woman first goes about pregnant with a child which she carries in her womb, and the child in the womb is also pregnant with his life, which he desires to bring from his narrow, slender lodging out into the wide world, so the Church of Christ in this world always and daily goes about pregnant with spiritual children, which she conceives by the Holy Spirit through Baptism, and carries them in the Word of her Bridegroom, Jesus Christ, as though in her own womb, in which they are formed, newly born, and every day are more and more prepared and made ready for eternal life. And these children are also themselves pregnant with the spiritual life, where Christ, with the Father and the Holy Spirit, dwells in their hearts through faith, so that from this they have new heavenly powers and movements, as seen in St. Paul when he says, "I live, and yet not I, but Christ lives in me."

A child in the womb yearns for birth; so a Christian yearns for the deliverance of his body.

Rom. 8:23–28

What, then, does a living child do in the womb? He has the firstfruits of his life and yearns for the completion, that he may be brought out of the *secundina* and narrow caul and pregnant mother and be delivered into the wider world. In the same way, an orthodox Christian, in whom the Holy Trinity dwells and lives by faith, always has a heartfelt longing for the eternal fatherland. Therefore, the

96 Both of these terms refer to membranes of the placenta.

apostle says, "We who have the Spirit's firstfruits long also for the adoption and wait for the redemption of our body. For we are saved, and yet in hope, but the hope that is seen is not hope, for how can one hope for that which is seen? But if we hope for that which we do not see, we wait for Him with patience."

(2) Comparison of our body with the skin of a child in the womb.

Then in the second place, the *secundina*, or the skin and caul with which the infant is wrapped and encircled in the womb, has *orificia*, or holes and pathways, (as scientists indicate) by which the child draws the air and sustenance that he may live, grow, and increase.

In the same way, a Christian on earth has his body and the outward instruments of his senses—the mouth, the eyes, and the ears—that with them he may serve our dear God, hear the Gospel, see the Sacraments instituted by Christ, and speak continually of Him and His surpassing benefits, since the Holy Spirit is given through these means. For through diligent hearing and meditation on God, as well as the outward and proper use of the holy and most worthy Sacraments, God enlightens hearts, converts them, and awakens faith, which He also strengthens, comforts, and enlarges by these means, that it may thereby be quickened and increase in the spiritual life.

(3) A child in the womb longs for deliverance.

In the third place, when the child in the womb increases in his form and bodily powers and approaches natural birth, the skin or caul, the *secundina*, with which he is surrounded, becomes too small for him and increasingly more burdensome, so that he desires to get out and longs to be delivered.

Thus the children of light in this world also long to be delivered from this valley of sorrow to eternal life.

Wisdom 9:15; 2 Cor. 5:7–8; 4:16

It is no different for the orthodox Christians and children of light in this world when the spiritual life in them grows and increases while the old Adam and the decrepit body are conversely burdened with all manner of woeful days, cross, and distress. Then they are in anguish and desire to get out into the spacious fatherland of eternal life. For "the mortal body," says Scripture, "burdens the soul, and the earthly tabernacle presses the scattered mind." And yet, say the children of God, in whom Christ dwells by faith and stirs, "we walk in faith and not in sight. And now therefore we are confident and have far more desire to walk out of the body and to be home with the Lord. Therefore, we are not weary, but although our outward man is wasting away, yet the inward man is renewed from day to day."

Cyprian, in his sermon On Mortality.[97] *2 Cor. 5:8*

Our body on earth is indeed far more a prison than a pleasant dwelling of the soul, especially when it is sapped and wearied with daily sorrow, affliction, and misery. Therefore, we may certainly say with St. Cyprian: "If, in your house, the walls wavered, shook, and tottered because of their age, and the whole building were so weak and rotten that it could not stand but must collapse, would you not get out of it in all haste?" So, too, if you were lying in a stinking, dark prison in which you must endure great peril from snakes, toads, basilisks, and dragons which daily leapt at your throat and ate from the bowl with you, would you not be eager to leave, especially if a royal palace were prepared for you instead of a jail and all that your heart wished for and desired were given? Because our old Adam is no less burdensome and difficult in this world than a collapsing house to its resident or a stinking jail to its prisoner, therefore godly Christians have a longing rather to be away from the body and at home with the Lord.

Rom. 7:24; Phil. 1:23; Ps. 143:6; 142:8; 2 Pet. 1:14

For this we have examples in St. Paul and other saints mentioned here and there in Scripture. St. Paul says, "Poor man that I am, who will deliver me from the body of this death?" "I have a desire to depart and to be with Christ." David cries, "O dear God, I spread my hands out to You. My soul thirsts for You as a dry land. Bring my soul out of the house of bondage, that I may give thanks to Your name." Likewise, St. Peter: "I know that I must soon put off my tent, even as our Lord Jesus Christ has revealed to me."

(4) Comparison of the sorrows of the Christian Church, our spiritual mother, with the sorrows and crying of a woman with child.

In the fourth place, a mother is anxious and fearful when she is about to give birth, and she cries and calls out until the fruit of her womb is delivered by the gracious help of God and the child is born into the world.

Likewise, the Christian Church on earth, our spiritual mother, is constantly pregnant with children of light, who are carried in her womb, that is, in the Word of God, and is daily in the midst of her travail, namely, when orthodox Christians take leave of the world and blessedly die in the Lord. Then the pregnant Church cries and calls out in her Our Father, "Dearest Father, Thy kingdom come! Deliver us from all evil!" This Our Father is the common cry of the mother and is graciously answered every day, since not one day passes in the world when Christians do not die and by temporal death are carried out of this valley of sorrow in faith and born into eternal life.

97 Cyprian, *De mortalitate* 25 (PL 4:600B).

Comfort for a dying Christian.

In addition, a dying Christian should count it a great comfort that, in the time of his homeward journey out of this misery, all of Christendom, like a pregnant woman giving birth, is in travail, and that the collective Our Father, prayed and spoken here and there in the churches of God, is like an anxious mother's cry to God Almighty to come to the aid of the dying Christian. Therefore, he should also count himself included in the Christian intercession of all godly men in churches and public assemblies and not doubt that the prayer will surely be answered by God Almighty according to His promise.

(5) The whole creation is compared with a pregnant woman because it serves the Church.

Rom. 8:19–22

In the fifth place, it is pertinent here that not only the Christian Church with God's children in this world is pregnant like a fruitful mother, but also the whole edifice of heaven and earth acts like a pregnant woman and longs to be delivered. For so the holy apostle Paul writes, saying that "the anxious expectation of creation waits for the revelation of the children of God. Since creation is subject to vanity against its will, but because of Him who subjected it to hope. For creation also will be freed from this service of the perishable existence, to the glorious freedom of the children of God. For we know that all creation longs with us and is continually in anguish."

The distinct mysteries should be marked diligently.

Whoever would rightly understand this mystery must mark the distinction in the manner in which these three—the whole creation, the Christian Church on earth, and every orthodox Christian—are likened to a groaning woman with child.

The whole creation, the Christian Church, and a child of the light are all three like a pregnant mother in some way.

First, you see this great edifice of heaven and earth that surrounds us like a round sphere and encloses mankind—all Adam's children who dwell on earth—in its midst. Here we are surrounded and enclosed on every side with the air and the high, arching firmament of heaven and are carried in the midst of it like many children in the maternal womb. For here the whole created order of heaven and earth, with all that is in them, must serve us like a mother, since the sun, moon, stars, air, sea, and land together with all mindless beasts and every growing thing are made for the use and service of man. And since God calls, gathers, and enlightens a Holy Christian Church among men at all times, which is constantly lying under the cross and most fiercely persecuted by the devil, tyrants, and false brothers, therefore St. Paul likens creation, that is, the whole edifice of heaven and earth, to a pregnant mother carrying the Christian Church like an infant in her womb and longing to be delivered for the sake of the wicked, whom she must serve against her will and would gladly be released from such vanity, that the Christian Church might indeed depart from this house of anguish and valley of sorrow as a child from the womb and go home to eternal life.

The Christian Church is pregnant with the children of light.

Second, in the midst of the anguished creation, the Holy Christian Church also (as stated above) is pregnant and through temporal death bears godly souls daily from this valley of sorrow into the spacious fatherland of eternal joy. And here the sense is that living Christians are like the members of a pregnant woman's body, and the dying Christian like a child that is born into the world. Now, just as a mother's members are in great anguish and toil that the child may be delivered and come into the world, so also living Christians come to the aid of the dying man with their Our Father and earnest prayer to God, that the dying man may pass from this world by death to eternal life. Therefore, as long as an orthodox Christian is walking on earth, he is a member of the Church Militant and with his diligent prayer helps his neighbor who is departing from this valley of sorrow. Then, when he himself is about to die, he is like an infant, and then the other members come to his aid in the same manner, that he may depart blessedly. And this bearing of spiritual children goes on from one age to the next and will go on till the Last Day, so that with devout intercession to God and with godly admonition, consolation, and warning, one man will, as it were, bear another into eternal life; and as he has given birth, so he in turn will himself be born into eternal life.

Every orthodox Christian is spiritually pregnant with Christ, his Savior and Redeemer.

Rev. 12:2

Finally, the Lord Christ dwells and lives in the hearts of all Christians by faith so that every Christian who believes the Gospel is called the temple of God, and out of this indwelling of Christ he leads a heavenly life, speaks continually of Christ, remembers Him day and night, and openly extols, praises, glorifies, and confesses Him before the world in every distress and tribulation, precisely as though he were pregnant with Christ and were carrying the infant Jesus in his womb. And this mystery is depicted to us in the Revelation of St. John in the woman with child who cries out and is in travail and has great agony for giving birth.

The whole creation, the Christian Church, and a child of the light—all three are in some way pregnant and similar to pregnant mothers.

Here you see what nature and distinct aspects this whole mystery has, namely, how the great edifice of heaven and earth is like a pregnant woman carrying the Church Militant on earth like a child in her womb; second, how the Church Militant also is pregnant and has a womb, which is God's Word, in which nothing but children of light are formed and shaped; and, finally, how the godly Christian in this womb also is pregnant with a heavenly life, which he leads in faith, and longs for it, that he may leave the kingdom of sight. Here, then, one pregnant work encloses and surrounds the other, and the one lies hidden in the other. If you believe in Christ, the kingdom of God is inside and within you, just as life is in the tender infant. And you act in God's Word (which is preached publicly in the church) not otherwise than as a living infant acts in the womb. What does the Christian Church do then? She walks and makes her pilgrimage on earth in the midst of the work of nature and surrounded by the air and the lofty edifice of heaven. Here, then, the whole edifice of heaven and earth is like a round sphere. But God governs the whole work and is like a matriarch promoting this birth in every place.

God compares Himself with a pregnant mother.

[Matt. 23:37;] Isa. 66:9; 46:3

And this is supported not a little by the fact that the great King of heaven and earth compares Himself with a mother hen. And the prophet Isaiah says, "Shall I cause others to open the matrix and not Myself give birth? Shall I cause others to give birth and Myself remain closed?" "You are borne by Me in the womb, and You are carried by Me in the matrix."

(6) As a man removes the old skin in birth, so must he also lay aside the tent of his body in death.

Isa. 26:17–18

In the sixth place, when a man is born and emerges from the womb into the world, he must give up his old skin. For the afterbirth or the caul, called the *secundina*, with which he was surrounded and enveloped in the maternal womb, then dies from him. So it is also with a dying Christian. By God's power, he passes from this world into eternal life, yet in the process he must relinquish the old Adam and his flesh and blood so that his body dies and decomposes under the earth. Therefore, as a man is born into the world with sorrow, so also he departs it with sorrow. And here belongs what Isaiah says: "As a pregnant woman, when she is about to give birth, has anguish and cries out in her sorrow, so is it also in Your sight. Then we are also pregnant, and we are afraid so that we scarcely draw breath."

The body is laid under the earth like a grain of wheat.

1 Cor. 15:43–44

But it is very comforting that our body is not to remain under the earth forever, but it lies there like a grain of wheat, which, on the Last Day, will flourish and come forth again with joy. For as Christ died and rose from the dead, so also will all who believe in Him be raised from death to eternal glory. Therefore, "the body is sown corruptible and will rise incorruptible; it is sown in dishonor and will rise in glory; it is sown in weakness and will rise in strength; it is sown a natural body and will rise a spiritual body."

(7) As a midwife comes to the aid of the weak infant, so God with His hand comes to the aid of the dying Christian and the departing soul.

Ps. 31:5

In the seventh and final place, the midwife comes to the aid of the pregnant mother in the giving of birth and delivers the infant. So also God, with His hand, comes from on high like a heavenly midwife to the aid of the dying Christian and takes hold of the departing soul, that it may not sink down into the pit of infernal anguish and agony but be taken up into the high paradise of eternal blessedness with joy. Therefore, David says, "Into Your hands I commend my spirit. You have redeemed me, O faithful God," as though he would say, "Dear God, I am contending with death and must leave the world. My body is collapsing, my powers are waning, and my soul is going out from me. Here it is like an infant that is born into the world and cannot help in the great anguish unless the midwife with helping hand does what is needed and is present. So, dear God, may You also take my poor soul with Your fatherly hand and raise it and take it up, that it may not perish in the earth but rise on high and be taken into eternal life."

Testimony of Luther.[98]

Luther also understands this mystery this way in his explanation of that verse of the fourth psalm: "I lie down and sleep entirely in peace, for You alone, O Lord, help me to dwell safely" (Ps. 4:8). "The prophet," he says, "here uses a subtle expression: 'The Lord holds me'—wherein he shows that one who dies is not forsaken by the Lord but is sustained from above, just as though God stretched forth His hand and laid it on him, so that he does not fall but rather is delivered and lifted up. By this he expresses and depicts properly and masterfully the manner of a dying man and of God who sustains him. For a dying man seems to be perishing and is swallowed up, but God's hand draws near him from above and sustains him so that he cannot perish but rather is lifted up to life, and thus, while to the world's eyes and his own he may die, yet to God he is sustained and supported."

The death of Christians is the new birthday of their soul.

Behold, dear brother, this is how it is with a dying Christian when he takes leave of the world and goes forth into the blessed fatherland of eternal life: which procession and homeward journey is truly a new birthday, and the whole process of this homeward journey can be learned nowhere better than in the example of a child's bodily birth.

98 From the German translation of *Labors on the Psalms* (1519–21), on Ps. 3:6, WA 5:90.18–35.

A godly Christian should diligently imagine the process of our rebirth and Christian dying not otherwise than as a birthday.

So much instruction has, God be praised, been written in many books concerning the manner of preparing for death on the basis of holy, divine Scripture that I regard it as unnecessary in this place to rehearse it at length. Only be careful, dear Christian, to retain the whole process of your rebirth, and imagine it diligently as it has been depicted and briefly suggested here in its various aspects. And as long as you live on earth, have no other conception of yourself than as if you are, from the time you received Baptism until your last hour of death, lying enclosed in God's Word as in a womb and are submitting there to be born, formed, and fashioned by the almighty power and working of the Holy Spirit for another life of which the blind, complacent world, Turks, Jews, and pagans, know nothing.

As long as a Christian lives on earth, he is to keep himself shut up in God's Word as though he were carried in the womb.

Matt. 18:3

Here yield to the Holy Spirit in His Word, attend the sermon, and let the Gospel ring richly in your ears. Believe the voice of our Lord Jesus Christ simply, and by no means allow foolish, senseless reason to seduce you from God's Word with carnal thinking. Guard yourself against the Papists, Calvinists, Anabaptists, and all enthusiastic spirits, who quibble with Christ in the Gospel and so pierce, torment, and torture the text of Scripture with their glosses that the seed from which you are to be reborn cannot be called a pure seed, but a seed mixed with noxious tares and deadly poison. Therefore, be on guard, and act like a little child. As Christ says, "Unless you turn and become as children, you will not enter the kingdom of heaven."

We should constantly pray for a blessed death. Brief form of a prayer for a blessed departure from this valley of sorrow.

Say: Ah, my most beloved treasure, Lord Jesus Christ, precious crown! I have longed for You, and as a deer pants for running water, so my soul thirsts for You. I pray You by Your harsh and bitter death to comfort me in my last, mortal breath. And lighten the eyes of my heart when my eyes are broken and I see no more, when all human help fails me and my mind no more avails me. Let me never perish in the bitter throes of death. Let me never waver at the fiery pit of hell. Let me never wander from the comfort of true faith! Grant that past the thick, black clouds of gloom and darkness I may see Your kind, consoling eyes of grace. And give Your holy angels charge over me, O highest Refuge, to keep me and bear my soul into Your bosom, where, untouched by pain, it may rest from all its labors. And if in my human frailty some impatient word or action should escape me, cover it over with the cloak of Your grace, and in my weakness be strong and mighty, that I may never turn my heart away from Your merit, sweat, and blood, but long for and confide in it until my final breath and so pass through death into life and remain with You forever. Amen.

How a Christian should act in the last throes of death.

Now, therefore, when death comes, treat it this way: act as if you are boarding a ship and sailing across a stormy sea to a fair land where all things live from great joy and glory.

Our death is like a roaring, rumbling sea, but God's Word is our ship in which we must cross it.

Death with its hellish temptations and the anxious and sorrowful contemplation of our manifold sins, the wrath of God, and the frightening power of the devil are together like the great sea that rages and roars on every side with terrible blasts, billows and waves, and torrents of water. But the Gospel of our salvation, forgiveness of sins, and deliverance from death, along with the articles of our Christian Creed, are the ship that we must board with fearless, undaunted confession and in the name of God venture over the great sea of death until we reach the heavenly fatherland.

A Christian is not to fear the great sea of death, but to trust in the spiritual ship.

Isa. 43:1–2

While to our reason the sea may seem very large and frightening and the ship very weak, small, and lowly, yet as one who would cross the Rhine or the Danube does not regard the great water, but relies on the ship, though it may be small and lowly, and trusts the skipper to bring him across with success—so, dear brother, you are not to regard how great the sea of death is and how it roars on every side, but to trust the ship of God's Word and the evangelical promises, in which Christ, the ship's patron, Himself is present and says, "Fear not, for I have redeemed you. I have called you by your name, for you are Mine. For when you pass through the waters, I will be with you so that the rivers shall not overwhelm you."

How it happens that countless thousands of men are turned awry in death and go ill. Those who are damned abandon the ship of the Gospel.

And by this you can mark how it happens that so many thousands of men are lost and, when they die, do not pass into life everlasting, but drown in the sea of death and go to the pit of hell. For the Turks, Jews, and pagans, as well as the works-righteous, Papists, and Anabaptists, abandon the ship and try to swim across with good works. The Sacramentarians,[99] the Arians,[100] and similar

99 "Sacramentarians," such as Ulrich Zwingli, Andreas Bodenstein von Karlstadt, and their followers, defined Christ's humanity in such a way as to deny the possible presence of Christ's body and blood in more than one place (particularly in the blessed bread and wine of the Lord's Supper).

100 Arians believed that Christ was only the highest creature and not true God. This teaching of the Alexandrian presbyter Arius (ca. 280–336) was condemned at the Council of Nicaea in 325.

frivolous spirits act like presumptuous people who refuse to take a seat in little boats or ships when the water rages and storms, but stand on the proud, high feet of their reason and rock the ship with all manner of glosses[101] until they take a fall and plunge overboard into the water. So do all the dying who in the last struggle of death take no note of the evangelical words of comfort, but only consider the multitude of their sins, the terrible rays of God's wrath, the power of the devil, the might of death, and the horrible anguish of hell and thereby depart in a wretched state. These all abandon God's Word, the true ship, and preoccupy themselves with the tumultuous sea outside of the Gospel until they drown in it and perish.

Warning to all dying Christians against perilous shipwreck.

Therefore, make sure, dear Christian, especially when you struggle with death in the final moments, that you do not immerse yourself in sorrowful speculations and thoughts outside of the Gospel. Temptations will not remain absent. Even in that moment your sins, crimes, and vices, as well as the image of the wrath of God, of the curse of the Law, of the specter of death, of the power of the devil, and of the torment of hell, will awaken, and all kinds of depressing thoughts may strike: "Am I elect to eternal life? Oh, many thousands of men are damned and perish! Am I among them, I wonder?" etc.

Against the tempests of death, a dying Christian should enclose and wrap himself in nothing but evangelical words of comfort.

John 3:16

But here quickly take hold of evangelical words of comfort: "God so loved the world," etc., or the articles of the Christian Creed. Wind yourself up in them and envelop yourself with strong memory, just as though you pulled a great pile of sheets around you and over you and under you in the middle of the ship against all stormy gales of the sea and against the tumultuous wailing, roaring, and raging of the tempest, and lie down, wrapped up in the sheets, that you may not hear it. By no means stand up in the ship on the feet of your human reason, nor gape far out at the towering waves and billows which rise up around you, but, as stated, set and lay yourself down in the midst of the ship, enclose yourself in the Word, and let nothing but Christ's birth, death, resurrection, and ascension reign in your heart.

Comparison with an infant delivered from the womb to the world.

John 5:24

What does a man do when he is delivered from the womb to the world? Surely, if he could use his reason and consider how it were possible that he should pass

101 A "gloss" is a translation or explanation of a text, especially of a verse of Scripture. In this instance, these explanations that rely on reason, rather than the Word of God, ultimately endanger the believer and capsize faith.

through the small, narrow door to the world, he would worry himself to death and not come alive to earth. But as there is no presumptuous thinking, no worry, no fear, but utter childlike simplicity, and the tender life that he received in the womb does not cease nor end until he comes into the world and receives his perfection there—so you also must become a child if you wish to enter the kingdom of God and have nothing to do with sad thoughts of death. Simply believe the Gospel, and let this faith be your only life. Exercise, train, and advance this life with the ceaseless contemplation of the precious merit of Jesus Christ until you have passed through the narrow gate of temporal death to eternal life. "Truly, truly," He says, "I say to you, whoever hears My Word and believes in Him who sent Me has eternal life and comes not into judgment, but he has passed from death to life."

How a man in the ship does not recoil at or fear the wind and waves very greatly as long as he has a good skipper. So also, in our mortal distress, we are to trust in Christ.

Ps. 89:15

Therefore, reject all suggestions which you encounter from death, sin, the devil, the Law, and hell, and let only the Son of God, with the blood that He shed and the anguish that He endured in hell, answer for you. Act like a man who sits below in the ship and lets the wind of the sea, the waves and great billows rage and storm as they will. He lets the skipper worry about it and meanwhile sits, sings, and is content. In the same way, keep yourself in the ship of the Gospel and your Christian Creed, trust Your Savior, and in the throes of death let your heart (and if possible, your tongue) be filled with the sound of the joyful hymns of Christmas and Easter: "From heaven above to earth I come,"[102] "Now sing we, now rejoice,"[103] "We praise You, Jesus, at Your birth,"[104] "Christ Jesus lay in death's strong bands,"[105] etc. Oh, that is exceedingly great balm to the suffering heart! And, oh, how blessed are the people who can shout for joy in this way!

Dr. Luther's advice to a dying Christian.

Dr. Luther also gives similar advice, as may be seen in an exposition of Psalm 23 from the year 1530:[106] "'And though I walk in the dark valley, I fear no calamity,' etc. From this verse," he says, "they are taught very well with what disposition, mind, and thoughts one should commit oneself to death: namely, not thinking of nothing at all, but only of the Lord Christ. For the verse says, 'For You are with me'; that is, 'I think of You and put all confidence and faith in You, and so ponder nothing else.' For blessed are those who thus shut their eyes and do not ask to see

102 "Vom himmel hoch da komm ich her" (Luther) (*LSB* 358).

103 "In dulci jubilo" (*LSB* 386).

104 "Gelobet seist du, Jesu Christ" (Luther) (*LSB* 382).

105 "Christ lag in Todesbanden" (Luther) (*LSB* 458).

106 From Luther's *Scholae* (1513–16), originally in Latin (WA 31/1:467.24–36), here from the German version, furnished by Veit Dietrich's heirs, Walch 4:2228–29, retranslated in StL 4:1632.

the place where they are to go, but examine themselves with all their trust and mind upon Christ in the midst of the darkness of death, for they die in the Lord."

Tom. 7, Germ. Jen., fol. 59.[107]

Likewise: "When the time comes to enter the next life and to leave this one, you must take this way alone or forever perish. For 'I am the way,' He says, 'by which one comes to the Father, and there is no other. I am the truth and the life, and there is no other.' Here you must go your way, clinging to this man, and continue firm in the faith and confession, using these continually in suffering and death and saying, 'I know no other help or aid, no salvation or comfort, no way or path, but only my Lord Christ, who for my sake has suffered, died, and risen, and ascended into heaven. With this I abide and pass through, though nothing but devils, death, and hell be beneath and before me.' For this is the true way and bridge, more solid and certain than any building of iron or stone, and heaven and earth must sooner break than that this should fail or deceive."

Tom. 8, Jen., on the words of John 8:51: "Truly," etc., "if anyone shall keep My Word"[108]

And again in another passage: "We must die and suffer death, but this is a wonder: that whoever clings to God's Word shall not feel death, but depart as in slumber, and so it should not be said, 'I die,' but 'I am forced to sleep.' But whoever lets himself be found outside the Word must die in anguish and forever perish and be damned. For this nothing helps. Therefore, the best thing is not to dispute it at all, but with all your heart to say, 'I believe in Jesus Christ, the Son of God. I know nothing more, nor do I wish to know more.'"

Tom. 3, Jen., on Jer. 23, concerning Christ's kingdom, etc.[109]

Likewise: "Behold, what riches are had by a Christian, who, because he has Christ Himself, can never die. What, then, shall death or sin wield over a Christian in the throes of death? Nothing. Death will be laughter to him, nor will he care about sin, for neither sin nor death nor devil nor hell nor anything can bring a charge against Christ, whom each possesses. Therefore, when death comes to a believing Christian, that Christian says, 'Welcome, dear death, what good do you bring? What do you seek here? Do you not know whom I possess? Christ is my righteousness. Pray, come and take it from me. If you take it from me, I'll go with you. Yet you are certain to leave it.' In this way Christians bid defiance to death and say with St. Paul: 'Where, O death, is your sting? Where, O hell, is your victory?' (1 Cor. 15:5). And as he says further: 'Christ is my life, and death is my gain. If I die, I have gain, for I come all the sooner to life' (Phil. 1:21). Here you see what death achieves among Christians. He is their gain. They lose nothing in him, but rather in biting them he finds his death." Thus far Luther.

107 From *Sermons on John 14–16* (1533–34), on John 14:6: cf. AE 34:36 (= WA 45:493.13–25).
108 From Kummer's collection of Luther's *Table Talk*, WA TR 4:539, no. 4835.
109 From *Sermons on Jer. 23:5–8* (1526): cf. AE 56:200–201 (= WA 20:574.21–34, 575.10–11).

A Christian should consider in good time what words he will use at the hour of death to take his leave of the world.

For these reasons, it is not unfitting that a Christian consider in good time what joyful words he will use at the hour of death to take his blessed leave of the world and to depart for heaven. I recall, nor does it rarely occur to me, how heartily a bride rejoices when she is to be brought to her bridegroom and how the children in strange lands shout for joy when they are to go home and return from distant countries to their beloved fatherland. In the same way, and yet far more so, should a dying Christian rejoice from his heart to pass through temporal death from this miserable valley of sorrow into the paradise of God.

A Christian wish for a blessed dying hour.

My faithful God, grant that in contemplating with strong faith the death of Christ and the present redemption I may overcome all sorrow, sadness, and misery and in the midst of death rejoice heartily at eternal life, not otherwise than as if I had it already in sight—even as children highly rejoice when, returning from foreign lands, they first see again from afar the high towers, steeples, and walls of their native land that they love so much.

A form of joyful address with which a dying Christian is to cheer himself heartily.

In addition, dear Christian, take heed to the time and then, when the hour of death arrives, say, "O rejoice, my dear soul, and take joy in God your Savior, that your grief, affliction, and misery should come to a blessed end! Oh, happy am I that the wearisome pilgrimage of my sorrowful life on earth should cease now at last! Oh, welcome, blessed hour of my departure from this wicked, evil world! I am so weary of the useless, vain fretfulness of this life and so weary of the tedious pilgrim way, and I rejoice with all my heart to be delivered from the mortal tent of my body, as from a dark, reeking inn and foul house of bondage."

In death, the dying Christian is close to the heavenly paradise.

Now at last I near the dear fatherland of eternal life and feel as though I see from afar the heavenly Jerusalem, the beautiful city, with her lofty spires, with her towers excelling, and her gates of gold. O beautiful Jerusalem, city of the living God, my eternal fatherland, how heartily I long for you! Even now I am coming, and this is the day of my exodus from the world, the day of my arrival in the heavenly paradise, and the day of my new birth, when my soul is born from the realm of faith into the realm of sight.

A Christian dies to the world and comes to the blessed harbor of eternal life.

Farewell, O world, with your haughty splendor, with your great vanity, with your perishing goods, and with your beguiling happiness! You have vexed me long enough! Long enough have you afflicted, tormented, and deceived me and filled me with cares! This is my final struggle with which I complete and overcome all my labor, all my danger, all my cares, and all my tribulations. My redemption draws nigh. The dawn of my eternal salvation, of my eternal joy, and of my eternal blessedness breaks forth. And forasmuch as my life was until now a restless and anxious voyage on the tumultuous sea and on the wild ocean, I come at last (to God be praise and thanks) to the true harbor and ship out of the world into the heavenly Canaan and into the true land of joy, where all things live by joy, where the Sun of righteousness shines forever and the light never wanes and no night, no darkness, no anguish, no death, and no sorrow is felt.

The spiritual joy of a dying Christian. We are to hasten from the Egypt of this life through the Red Sea of death into the heavenly Canaan.

Oh, rejoice, my soul, you chosen bride of Jesus Christ, who bought and purchased and won me so dearly with His crimson-red blood! Behold, He, your dearest Redeemer, your highest Friend and noble Bridegroom, is here with His holy angels. The great Prince of heaven is present to take you home from this valley of sorrow into His Father's kingdom. Oh, rejoice, my soul, and tarry no longer nor stay in this wicked, contemptible world. Make haste to go forth with Lot from Sodom, and by no means look back. What else is the world than a Sodom and a Gomorrah? And what more is your life on earth than slavery in Egypt? So, O my soul, depart from Sodom and withdraw from Egypt. Make haste through the Red Sea of temporal death, where Jesus Christ, with the rod of His cross, has divided the floods of hell and the fearsome waters of anguish so that you can pass through in safety unscathed. Make haste, and do not look back, that the Pharaoh of hell, wretched Satan, may not seize you with worldly passions and world-loving thoughts. Make haste to enter the heavenly Canaan, where the mountains are flowing with milk and honey.

It was for eternal life that a believing Christian has been created, redeemed, sanctified, and chosen.

Ps. 118:17

O my soul, God the Father made you for eternal life, Jesus Christ redeemed you for eternal life, God the Holy Spirit sanctified you for eternal life, the Holy Trinity chose you for eternal life. You are prepared for the kingdom of heaven, chosen for the kingdom of heaven, and reborn for the kingdom of heaven, and your citizenship is above in heaven. There you will dwell for eternity and find your eternal joy. Therefore, simply let all your thoughts be turned there, and with confidence lay aside the unclean and whole oppressive burden of your flesh. If the deliverance seems hard to you and the exodus from this life pains you, O my dear soul, be at peace! It is your new birthday, when you pass from this wearisome world into eternal life. Therefore, restrain yourself a little while, and yield to your Deliverer and Savior, who will soon release you. You shall not die, but you shall live and declare the works of the Lord.

How a dying Christian should take leave of his mortal body.

Wisdom 9:15; Sirach 10:12; Isa. 26:20

But you, O my body, shall rest in the earth, to slumber on until the Last Day. For many years now I have had too much to do with you and wasted much precious time with you in vain. So burdensome and obstructive have you been that my heart neither lifted itself up to God nor thought on the eternal good as much as it ought. Forasmuch, then, as it is God's will that you shall return to the earth, and the many diseases, sorrows, and calamities, as it were messengers and harbingers of death, have now repeatedly knocked on your door and summoned you—come then! Obey the Lord your God, and go beneath the earth into your chamber of rest and shut the door behind you and wait a little while, till on the Last Day God shall wake you and call you forth again.

Comfort from the article of the resurrection of our flesh.

1 Cor. 15:49; Job 19:26; Ps. 17:15; Eph. 5:30

Until now you have borne the likeness of the earthly Adam, but then you shall bear the likeness of the heavenly One, and in your flesh you shall see the face of God when you awake according to His likeness. And although you are scattered like dust, you belong to the Lord Christ and are bone of His bone and flesh of His flesh. Therefore, you cannot perish, but when He shall call you, you will appear again, made whole and strong and perfect.

Comfort from the fact that the whole creation and Christ Himself feel compassion for the dying.

Rom. 8:22; Heb. 4:15; Zech. 2:8; Luke 2:29–32

Why, then, should I recoil and not rather rejoice at my redemption? At the moment I may be sapped of strength and sick unto death, but it will not last for long. The whole creation groans with me and longs for its redemption. And why do I speak of creation? Christ Himself, my Redeemer and Savior, feels compassion for me, and I know that the apple of His eye is now being touched because of my weakness so that He cannot watch it for long. Come, then, O death, and release me. You are not fearsome to me, but a pleasant guest and, through Christ, a gate from this world into the heavenly fatherland.

Serene am I in heart and mind,
Still and peaceful,
Just as God hath promised me:
Death, thou'rt become my slumber.[110]

110 From "Mit Fried und Freud ich fahr dahin," Luther, st. 1 (cf. *LSB* 938).

Comfort from the unspeakable joy of eternal life. Christ calls in His Gospel.

Isa. 64:4; 1 Cor. 2:9; Matt. 11:28; 23:37; John 10:27–28; Luke 23:43

No eye has seen and no ear heard and in no heart of man has entered the great, unspeakable joy to which I now shall pass from this miserable valley of sorrow.

O where are joys, O where?
Where, if they be not there?
There are the angels singing
New heavn'ly hymns and fair,
And there the bells are ringing
In courts of royal air.[111]

There the entire Holy Trinity, God the Father, God the Son, God the Holy Spirit, calls me. And I hear now the voice of my Savior, Jesus Christ: "Come, poor, weary, and laden, come, and I will refresh you. Come, I will gather you as a hen gathers her chicks under her wings. Come, My dear sheep, and follow Me. I will give you eternal life, and no one shall pluck you out of My hand. Truly, truly, I say to you, today you will be with Me in paradise."

The dying Christian answers his Savior with joy.

Rom. 8:38; John 10:28; Ps. 25:1–2; 70:1; 31:5

Yes, come, my dearest Lord Jesus! I come, O my dearest Friend, and am certain that neither death nor life, neither angels nor principalities nor powers, neither things present nor things to come, neither height nor depth, nor any other created thing, can separate me from Your love. O Jesus, my trusty Brother and my heart's precious crown, although I must leave the body, yet I know that no one shall pluck me out of Your hand. I am so heartily weary of this life, and I long for You. O my God, I trust in You. Make haste to deliver me soon. Into Your hands I commend my spirit. You have redeemed me, O faithful God.

Bidding farewell to the world.

2 Tim. 4:7; Ps. 116:8–9; Num. 6:24–26; Ps. 121:8

With that, good night, O world! Good night, O father, mother, wife and children, brother and sister! Farewell, hearth and home and all that is in the world! With peace and joy I now depart. I have fought a good fight; I have finished my course. Now up, carry on, O my soul, and let yourself be delivered from death and your eyes from tears and your feet from falling, that you may walk before the Lord in the land of the living. Now may God the Father, God the Son, and God the Holy Spirit accompany me and the holy angels receive me with hearty joy and rejoicing. The Lord bless me and keep me; the Lord lift up His countenance upon

111 From "In dulci jubilo" (attr. H. Suso, 14th century), st. 3 (cf. *LSB* 386).

me and give me His peace; the Lord preserve my going in and my going out from henceforth and even forever. Amen, amen.

We are to glorify Christ in our death.

2 Tim. 4:6; Phil. 1:20; John 21:19

Whoever dies and takes his leave of the world in this manner not only makes a blessed journey but also glorifies and honors God with his death, even as all Christians justly ought to do. Of this we have an example also in the holy apostle Paul, when he calls death an offering: "I am already being offered," he says, "and the time of my departure is at hand." Yet in what way is it an offering? In this way: he says, "Christ will be highly glorified in my body, whether by life or by death." Likewise, when our Lord Christ prophesies to His disciple Peter concerning his future bonds, cords, and captivity, St. John writes that the Lord said this to show by what death Peter would glorify God.

What thoughts a Christian should think about death and all manner of distress.

In short, a Christian is to be joyful in Christ, so honoring, confessing, and glorifying Him that he can, as St. Paul says, even boast or be joyful and glory in it when things go badly, and his heart may only think thus: If he is poor, yet he has a great treasure; if he is lying in prison, yet he is a mighty prince and lord; if he is weak and sick, yet he is strong; and likewise, if he is shamed and disgraced, yet he soars in utter glory; and if he must die presently, yet he will become a new, living man. In short, he may take utterly new heart and courage and make it altogether new for him on earth and so begin here a prelude of the existence to come, when all things are brought to light and are made just as new as he now envisions and imagines by faith according to his new existence.

How the patriarchs in the Old Testament took comfort.

Tom. 1, Witt. Ger., fol. 431[112]

So did the dear fathers do as well, clinging firmly to their Lord Christ. Of this Luther writes with great comfort, and I quote his words here: "They used to sing this song:[113] 'How precious in the sight of God is the death of His saints' (Ps. 116:15). Likewise: 'Their blood is counted precious in His sight' (Ps. 72:14) and 'He remembers and makes inquisition for their blood' (Ps. 9:12).

How reason views death. How faith views death.

"Thus the pious hearts speak, and from such words they devised a great many sermons (although they are only put briefly and only written as a *thema* or conclusion of their sermon), for it gives very powerful and rich comfort with which

112 From *Two Sermons at the Funeral of Elector Duke John* (1532): cf. AE 51:245–48 (= WA 36:258–61).

113 Antiphons on these text were sung for the feasts of Holy Innocents, All Saints', and various apostles and martyrs.

a heart can be propped up because from this they forcefully conclude: "Dear sir, it may seem very different to you and appear to your eyes as if the death of the saints is sheer downfall and destruction and as if they are forgotten and silenced and have no God who defends them because He did not defend them while they were living, but allowed them to die so miserably, such as those who were torn apart, devoured, burned alive, and ground to powder. Thus reason cannot say otherwise than that their death is a pitiful, miserable, shameful matter. Yet in the sight of God (say the dear fathers) you should certainly reckon that when a saint (that is, every Christian) dies, he has been offered as a very precious, excellent offering—the most pleasant and sweetest fragrance of incense and the best and loftiest divine service that may be rendered to Him.

It seems as though God does not care about the saints, but when they are dead, He champions their cause.

"For He does not think so much of the living saints as of the dead ones. Indeed, while they are living, He lets them go along in such weakness and misery and be tortured with sin, world, devil, and death, as if He did not see and did not wish to help them. But suddenly when they are out of the eye of people and now a stinking, rotting carcass (which no one can stand) or turned to ashes and scattered like dust so that no one knows what became of them and are utterly gone and forgotten from the world, as those who have nothing more to hope for—only then do they begin to become a valuable thing in God's sight, and not only sheer life, but a priceless treasure which the Majesty Himself counts precious and highly esteems and can boast of nothing more valuable. And the more they are forgotten by the world, the more highly He champions their cause and boasts of them.

He who inquires after blood. God champions the cause of Abel dead more than when he was still alive.

"Of this you have a fine example in the first two brothers (Gen. 4:9–10), when that rogue, Cain, secretly murdered and buried his brother, went his way, wiped his mouth, thinking no one would know and the matter would stay concealed, as though Abel had no one who cared about him. And when God asked, 'Where is Abel your brother?' he acted so holy and pure that he even boasted that he was not obligated to care for him, saying, 'What do I know? How can I be my brother's keeper?' But then He who is called 'He who inquires after and avenges the blood of His saints' said, 'Your brother's blood cries to Me in heaven.' Who asked God to speak this way now? Can He not forget it now that Abel is dead and gone? Must He still call from heaven and cry over the blood, as though it is so important to Him that He cannot tolerate this or remain silent? He could certainly have prevented it before; or else spared him, since Cain was now alone and had no brother or heir. Instead, He punishes him so horribly that he is cast out by his parents and even the earth is cursed on his account. That is what you call jealously defending the blood that was wasted. He did not show such zeal and care when Abel was still alive, except that He took pleasure in his sacrifice. But now that Abel is gone and lying under the earth, all of a sudden he is living and speaking in heaven so that God Himself preaches on his behalf and raises such a cry in all the world that both Abel and his murderer must forever stand as an example in Scripture and never be extinguished.

How the fathers viewed and judged the examples of Scripture.

"Behold, this is how the dear fathers viewed these examples and from them took their sayings that the saints who are dead must certainly live before God and come forth again far more glorious than before. For He does not defend the cause of any living beast or livestock or what has no hope, nor of tyrants and the ungodly who perish in the devil's name, but of His needy saints who die in so wretched and shameful a manner, and regards that death far more precious than the whole of their life. For they cannot be without sin, even though this is under forgiveness and under Christ. Yet it is nothing compared to a man leaving this life and dying to sin and the world so that then God opens both of His eyes and all the angels must be present and attend to him, under and over and all around him, provided he is clothed with the Baptism of Christ and with faith and God's Word, that he may be numbered with those who are called the saints of God.

Saints of God, saints of the pope.

"For you know of course (God be praised) what is meant by 'the saints of God'—that Scripture means not the saints above in heaven, the saints who are made by the pope, whom we are supposed to invoke and fast for and celebrate their days and set them as mediators; nor those who have hallowed themselves, like Carthusians,[114] discalced Franciscans, and other monks or secular brethren and such devils who of their own accord seek to be holy through their own works; but those whom God has hallowed apart from all their works and their doings, by whom they are baptized into Christ's name, sprinkled and washed clean with His blood, and graced and adorned with His dear Word and gifts of the Holy Spirit, all of which we have not begotten nor can beget, but must receive from Him by pure grace. But he who does not have these but seeks other holiness is an utter stench and abomination to God, as he who denies that this washing by the blood of the innocent Lamb does not hallow and cleanse.

The death of those who fall asleep in Christ is precious in God's sight.

"Those, then, who are such baptized Christians, who love His Word and cling to it firmly and die in it—whether they be hanged or tortured or burned or drowned or die from the plague or a fever, etc., simply include them in Christ's own death

114 Founded by Bruno of Cologne (ca. 1030–1101) in 1084 in Grand Chartreuse, France, Carthusians are a famously strict religious order that requires silence, labor, and contemplative prayer.

and resurrection and promptly speak upon them the text: 'The death of the saints is precious and worthy before the Lord' such that He regards it as an excellent, beautiful treasure and priceless jewel on earth. Although the devil kill you in your bed or the hangman on the gallows, it is decided that such a death is a holy death and esteemed so precious in His sight that He will not leave it unavenged, but summon to judgment the devil who murders you and afflict him with everlasting torment, sentence sin to beheading, bury death in hell, and avenge all things by which His saints have been made to die."

The Fifth Benefit of God: The Glorious Condition of the Elect Souls with God in His Paradise

Estate and condition of a Christian who dies blessedly in the Lord.

Hereupon follows the fifth benefit of God, which deals with the eternal, unspeakable honor, glory, and joy of which our forefathers who fell asleep blessedly in Christ now partake in yonder world, no longer in faith but in sight. For as soon as a Christian dies in the Lord, while the body is interred in the earth and takes its rest in its narrow cottage and decays and turns to dust until the Last Day, yet the soul that is sprinkled with the blood of Christ by faith and cleansed from sins then ascends from the mouth up to heaven and is gathered with all the elect of angels and men, with whom they live and dwell in perfect gladness with God, awaiting with joy the Last Day.

Various opinions or ideas and inquiries concerning the condition of the elect.

Now, how all this happens and what are all its aspects and all its forms, we cannot search out, much less establish, with carnal reason and inquisitiveness. Painters tend to depict a babe flying up from the mouth into the lofty clouds, and this is supposed to indicate a living soul leaving its body and ascending into heaven. Of this kind there are also a great deal of other presumptuous ideas, guesses, and speculations. For as the soul is an invisible spirit, it cannot be seen or perceived with the eyes of the body what kind of existence it has, how it makes its exit from the mortal tent of its body, and where it dwells. And yet many wish to know this, especially those whose friends, husband, wife, children, brothers, sisters, etc., have died. The greater the love was on earth, the more strongly they remember them, and if there were a sure report about it, they would not be reluctant to hear it.

How people easily err to the left or to the right in this mystery.

But here we must heed not the dreams of our flesh but the Word of God and be careful not to stray far to the left or the right. Those who turn aside to the left are the Epicureans and crude sons of the world, who claim the soul dies with the body and dissolves like thin air, or else lies asleep, snoring until the Last Day, so that nothing may be asserted of its salvation or damnation. To the right the presumptuous go in confusion, who set aside God's Word and yet make grand assertions as to the condition of the souls of the saints and their spacious heaven, precisely as if God gave them a special revelation. Here we must watch ourselves closely and stick to God's Word as the only middle road if we wish to avoid deception and to seize on the doctrine of this mystery rightly.

What Holy Scripture testifies of the condition of the elect.

Matt. 10:28; 22:32; Luke 23:43; Wisdom 5:15–16; 3:1

My confession, teaching, and belief on this is that the souls of the righteous live forever and know no more of anguish or sorrow after temporal death. "Fear not," says the Lord, "those who kill the body and cannot kill the soul." "I am the God of Abraham, the God of Isaac and Jacob. But God is not a God of the dead, but a God of the living." "Truly, truly, I say to you, today you will be with Me in paradise." Likewise: "The righteous will live forever, and the Lord is their recompense, and the Most High cares for them. Therefore, they shall receive a glorious kingdom and a beautiful crown from the hand of the Lord." And again: "The righteous souls are in the hand of God, and no torment touches them."

The souls of the elect continue after their departure from this world into the heavenly paradise and there lead a true life of paradise.

Luke 23:43

For this reason, I heartily believe and hereby confess orally and in writing, that the souls of the elect are not snuffed out like a light nor do they dissolve like thin air or a vapor nor lie snoring and sleeping until the Last Day, as the Dormitantians[115] raved, but that they live and that their life is a peaceful life, full of all comfort and every heavenly pleasure, and that this life begins after death, as Christ says to the thief: "Today you will be with Me in paradise." A dying Christian ought to make use of these words and learn well to extend and expand them: "'Today, today,' says the Son of God, as if He would say, not only on the Last Day shall your life of paradise begin, but even today, in one or three or four hours, as soon as you die and the soul is separated from your body. Then your soul will not snore and sleep, nor remain straying and wandering between heaven and earth, but will be at once with Me in paradise and enjoy the glory, joy, and life of paradise with Me."

The heavenly life of paradise is the life of a wedding feast.

Matt. 25:1–30

In the second passage, this life of paradise is called a wedding feast, at which Christ rejoices with His elect children of light, who have fallen blessedly asleep

115 I.e., psychopannychists, or those who believe in "soul sleep," that the human soul is totally unconscious between temporal death and the resurrection of the dead on the Last Day.

in the Lord, and to it He has also summoned from this valley of sorrow all who await His coming with believing hearts as if with burning lamps. For He compares Himself with a bridegroom who knocks at midnight and whom His godly Christians go out to meet like wise virgins with burning lamps and go in with Him to the wedding feast, and He exhorts us to constant readiness and expectation of His coming, saying, "Be like those men who wait for their lord, when he shall emerge from the wedding, so that when he comes and knocks, they open up to him at once. Blessed are those servants whom the Lord, when He comes, shall find watching. Truly, I say to you, He will gird Himself up and will seat them at the table and go before them and serve them."

How the communion of the elect souls with Christ in heaven may be explained to a certain extent.

From these and similar words we gather that the blessed condition and communion of the elect souls in Christ in heaven can be explained and depicted to a certain extent by a likeness, if only attention is given to the description of a paradise and a wedding feast.

Now the word *paradise* is commonly understood as a pleasure garden in which are found all sorts of stately trees, precious fruit, fragrant herbs, and beautiful lilies, roses, and flowers, as well as fine garden houses and booths, artfully trimmed with all manner of foliage. For when one enters this horticultural splendor, especially after winter has ended, in the season when flowers appear, and sees in the midst thereof the budding and blossoming trees, all set in good order and closely clustered as in a pleasant green wood, and the fine structures of graceful booths, fine, lofty arches, walking paths, rivulets, fish ponds, shady bowers, and the like, and hears the nightingale, the lark, and other pleasant birds singing incessantly; likewise, when one sees nothing but great nobles and stately people sitting at table therein, walking around, eating, drinking, singing, dancing, playing on instruments, citharas, bells, fiddles, cymbals, etc., and making merry in highest honor, then such a pleasure garden is rightly called a paradise, and the joy seen therein, the life of paradise.

What the term "wedding feast" means.

But where wedding feasts and nuptial honors are mentioned, we properly understand such terms in no other way than as the great, honorable day of a bridegroom with his bride, as well as the glad company and assembly of honorable and finely dressed people who join the bride and groom in being merry, eating, drinking, and singing and having hearts filled with joy.

The elect souls with God in paradise are again in that estate of perfect blessedness in which Adam and Eve were before the fall.

Now, although heaven, to which all godly souls go from this world, is no earthly paradise nor worldly Elysium and land of joy of which the poets tell fables, but rather a place of gladness the likes of which no eye has seen, no ear heard, and no heart of man experienced; and although the elect souls there do not celebrate an earthly, bodily wedding feast, but there discover utterly indescribable heavenly joy and glory—nevertheless it is called a paradise and a wedding feast to indicate that a faithful Christian's soul after death is instantly returned the state of perfect blessedness in which our first parents, Adam and Eve, lived before the fall, when the earthly Paradise was their fatherland, and in it they celebrated their wedding feast with holy joy. For what we lost in the first Adam, who was earthly, we find richly and abundantly again in Christ, as in the heavenly Adam, and possess it in this world in faith, but instantly after death we are with Him and see it before our eyes.

What kind of life our first parents had before the fall.

But what kind of life did our first parents have before the fall but a true life of paradise, joy of paradise, and communion in God, like a joyous wedding feast, where they were God's temple, God's bride, and God's possession? They dwelt in the beautiful, noble pleasure garden which God Himself had prepared for them, in it celebrated their wedding feast, and they both were God's dwelling and living mirror, or reflection of His divine being, so that they acted with utterly fervent love and loved their God with all their heart, all their soul, and all their mind, and after that they loved each other as themselves.

The life of Christians after their temporal death is a holy and joy-filled life with God.

Behold, such was the life that Adam and Eve led before they sinned and before death entered the world! And according as our Lord Christ has blotted sin out and taken from death its sting and, as the heavenly Adam, brought us comfort by finding again and purchasing dearly the life and blessedness which we lost, how else can or should an elect soul view his blessed departure from this world (if it has overcome sin and death in faith) except as a wonderfully comforting life of paradise, where it is brought to the heavenly Adam as a newborn Eve and celebrates sheer heavenly joy and a heavenly wedding feast with Him? Surely it will and must feel precisely as if you had left this valley of sorrow by temporal death and suddenly entered a beautiful pleasure garden for a wedding feast, where for indescribable joy, pleasure, beauty, splendor, majesty, and glory all things live, laugh, leap, and dance so sweetly, so prettily, so powerfully, and so comfortingly that no man on earth can describe it.

Interposed question: Who has seen it?

"Indeed," you say, "who has seen it and has been in heaven and come back down to us and testifies to these things? Or who has died and come back to life so that he can bear witness to it?"

Answer: Christ has seen it and knows about it.

Rev. 1:18

Answer: Listen, dear friend! The name is given in Scripture of one who has been in hell as well as in heaven, experienced all things, and emerged again from the dead and revealed it richly to us, even Jesus Christ, the Son of God and Mary. "I was dead," He says to the apostle on the island of Patmos, "and, behold, I live from everlasting to everlasting, and I have the keys of hell and death."

What the Son of God tells us about the condition of the elect soul.

John 5:21, 24, 29; Luke 13; 16:22; Rev. 6:11; Matt. 8:11; Rev. 7:17; Luke 16:25

Now, this man, in whose mouth no deceit was found, informs us that a believing Christian passes through death into eternal life and, as I just said, proceeds to God in His paradise as soon as he dies and is brought by the holy angels. And he is dressed in a white robe, sits at table with Abraham, Isaac, and Jacob, suffers no hunger or thirst nor is oppressed by the heat of any sun, but is led to the fountain of waters and sweetly refreshed. And lest any should doubt this, He relates the account of Lazarus, who died a blessed death and after dying was carried by the holy angels into Abraham's bosom, further indicating that he is comforted for his great poverty, misery, and grief which he suffered and bore here on earth.

St. Paul also was in the third heaven.

2 Cor. 12:1–5; Rom. 7:24; Phil. 1:23; 2 Cor. 5:8; Phil. 3:13–14

The holy apostle Paul also, as he himself testifies, was once taken up into the third heaven, that is, into paradise, and there heard unspeakable words which no man can utter. And although he was forbidden to boast of it, and he himself does not know whether he was in the body or out of the body, nevertheless it may be sufficiently deduced from his wish and yearning which he had for heaven, and now and then hinted at in words, how pleasing it was to him there. "Wretched man that I am," he says. "Who will deliver me from the body of this death?" "I have a desire to depart and to be with Christ." "We desire far more to walk apart from the body and to be at home with the Lord." "Forgetting what is behind and striving for what is ahead, I pursue the set goal for the prize which the heavenly calling of God presents in Christ Jesus."

Why St. Paul longs so heartily for eternal life.

1 Cor. 7:29–30

Behold, behold, how the apostle acts here! How he rushes, hastens, and cries out, that he may be soon delivered from his mortal body and be with Christ! Is it then not good to dwell on earth, where there is so much worldly passion, pomp, joy, and delight? Answer: St. Paul was in the third heaven and there drank of the rich goods of the house of God and experienced how the noble life of paradise is not to be bought with or compared to all the pomp, honor, riches, glory, and pleasure of the world. This is why he has such a thirst for heaven and would like all men to have such as well and to see this temporal life only with the left eye, and the eternal with the right, even as he writes, admonishing especially all godly Christians who have wives that they should be as if they had none, that those who weep as if they did not weep, those who rejoice as if they did not rejoice, and those who buy as if they did not possess, etc. We heard about this in the first part of this *Joy of Eternal Life*.[116]

Plato's address and confession of the soul's immortality.

The pagan Plato also, on his deathbed, said to his children, "Dear children, do not weep when I leave you, as if I am perishing like a beast. For while I was with you, you never saw the spirit that governs this body, but only knew it by its working. I depart from hence as from an inn, not as from a residence. For nature has given us here on earth a lodging, not to remain forever but to journey. Oh, blessed day when my spirit will join the fellowship of the heavenly spirits and the divine counsel! And if God granted me to be young again, I would not do it, for what else does this life have but toil and labor?"

Where Plato learned such words.

The pagan says this and seems as though he heard something of this noble mystery in Egypt from extant teachings of the ancient patriarchs and saw it as if from afar. How much more should we Christians retain this comfort and not let it wither since we have been given the clear Word of God as a strong and sure foundation on which we can build our faith and safely rely? If Socrates and Plato had had such a foundation, they would have defied death otherwise indeed and found much higher joy, protection, and deliverance from all manner of temptations.

The blessedness and blessed condition of the elect souls is concealed to reason.

Yet I gladly confess that this glory cannot be grasped or understood by our flesh and blood. For when a Christian dies, it seems to our physical eyes the same as when a pagan dies—indeed, as when a senseless animal dies. For who can see with his physical eyes the exiting soul or the exiting spirit of the man? Who sees the holy angels and hosts of God Almighty, how they encircle the dying Christian like fiery chariots and horses and attend his soul with great gladness? Who sees the present Savior, Jesus Christ, with the entire Holy Trinity? Who hears also the heavenly cry of jubilation and rejoicing which the holy angels raise? We see with our physical eyes nothing but the dead body; the rest is all deeply concealed from our senses.

Reason must not be consulted in this mystery. God and the holy angels as well as the elect souls see one another.

But here we must dismiss the judgment of our senses and give heed to the Word of God only, which declares the truth to us and does not lie. In addition, you

116 See above, p. 107.

should know, dear brother, that God's being, as well as the natures of angels and the spirits of men (although invisible to our physical eyes), nevertheless are truly able to see and hear one another. For I ask you, is God Himself not present with His angels? But who sees these present spirits? Who sees God Almighty? Who sees the holy angels? No man on earth sees them with the eyes of the flesh. And yet it is certain and not to be denied that, though we do not see them, they still see one another, even as Christ explicitly says that the angels (which are around little children and attend them) always see the face of God in heaven. So also I say of the souls of deceased godly Christians: while we do not see them with our physical eyes, yet they see and know one another quite well and are indeed in the realm of sight. They see God the Father, God the Son, and God the Holy Spirit, likewise also the holy angels and all the elect patriarchs, prophets, and apostles—with all of whom they hold a seeing communion.

The life of paradise enjoyed by elect souls consists of three glories.

Now, as regards this noble life of paradise enjoyed by the elect souls, it has been revealed to us in God's Word, we should note, that it consists chiefly of three glories, which I will relate in order for the blessed comfort of all afflicted Christians whose friends have died and fallen asleep in the Lord and for the relieving of their sorrow.

(1) The first glory of elect souls is their communion with the holy angels.

Ps. 91:11–12; 34:7; Heb. 1:14

First, the holy angels, as heavenly princes and servants of God Almighty, are appointed to dying Christians to take up their souls (as soon as they depart from the world) with great joy and rejoicing and to bear them as it were on their hands. As it is written: "The Lord has given His angels charge over you to keep you in all your ways, that they should bear you up in their hands, lest you dash your foot against a stone." Likewise: "The angel of the Lord encamps round about those who fear Him and saves them." And to the Hebrews the apostle writes, "Are not the angels all ministering spirits, sent out for the service of those who are to inherit blessedness?"

Evidence that holy angels receive our souls after death.

Luke 16:22

Now, lest anyone think this should be understood as concerning only the protection and presence of the holy angels toward Christians in this life, the account of Lazarus explicitly testifies that it is to be applied to dying Christians also. For who can give us better information about this than our Redeemer and Savior, Jesus Christ? "The poor man died," He says, "and was carried by the angels into Abraham's bosom."

God's hosts, the holy angels, receive with great joy the elect souls going to heaven.

Luther, tom. 2, Witt. Germ., fol. 431.[117]

This much, then, is certain, and we have nothing to doubt in it: as soon as an orthodox Christian falls asleep in the Lord and the soul leaves him, God's hosts, even the holy, heavenly spirits of the Lord, are immediately present around the bed, and with a friendly, gracious look they welcome the departing soul and receive it with joy. Therefore, Luther says rightly, as his words read which were quoted above: "When a man leaves this life and dies to sin and the world, then God opens both of His eyes and all the angels must be present and attend to him, under and over and all around him, provided he is clothed with the Baptism of Christ and with faith and God's Word, that he may be numbered with those who are called the saints of God."

Contemplation of this glory.

But who can sufficiently extol this majestic splendor and heavenly glory—that God Almighty, the Maker of heaven and earth, causes His children to be welcomed and so grandly escorted by His angels?

Comparison with a king who has a beggar escorted by dignified princes and taken to him.

Imagine a little, dear Christian, if the Roman emperor or the mighty king of Persia caused a poor beggar lying captive in a deep dungeon to be offered royal adoption and the kingdom for his inheritance and thereupon sent a stately legation, several princes, counts, and prestigious nobles with magnificent carriages, riders, and horses to the prison to receive the prisoner (as soon as he should be released) and to bring him to himself; and when all this was done with rejoicing, the stately and mighty princes, counts, barons, and potentates with their processional garments encircled the prison, the poor prisoner emerged from the deep, muddy dungeon, and they received him with great shouts of triumph and gladness, seated him in a carriage of gold, and brought him with heartfelt joy to their king—what higher, nobler, and more magnificent thing might or could a man encounter in all the wide world?

All worldly pomp and earthly exaltation is rubbish next to the honor that the Christian soul has in being received and escorted from the world by the angels of God.

Eccl. 1:2; Matt. 18:10

However, this is all child's play, puppetry, patchwork, rubbish, and (as Solomon says) "vanity of vanities" compared to the heavenly honor and glory wherein the great King of all creation, the Son of God and Mary, has prepared for us His holy, heavenly watchers, thrones, and hosts, the dear angels (which always behold the face of the Father Almighty) to attend the exiting souls as soon as they depart from the world and to surround them like a precious treasure in their midst, that

117 From *Two Sermons at the Funeral of Elector Duke John* (1532): cf. AE 51:247 (= WA 36:260).

in the midst of the angels they might appear before God and with gladness gain sight of His most beloved being.

The holy angels are like the bridal escorts of God when they carry the elect souls to the bosom of Christ.

Ps. 45:10–15

Here the dear angels are like bright-shining morning stars and like exceedingly joyful bridal escorts. But the soul released from the jail and tent of its body is like a triumphant bride clothed in the snow-white righteousness of her heavenly Bridegroom, Jesus Christ, and made bright and beautiful with His crimson-red blood. Here without doubt the holy angels address her and say, "Hearken, O daughter, and consider, and incline your ears. Forget also your own people and your father's house (the world in which you have dwelt until now). So shall the King take pleasure in your beauty, for He is your Lord, and you shall worship Him. Then"—as David says—"she shall be brought to the King in raiment of needlework. With joy and gladness shall she be brought and shall enter the King's palace."

Sweet and splendid is the blessed ascension of the believing soul into heaven.

Oh, the blessed journey home, the great joy and bliss, and the comforting glory, where the soul is separated from its mortal body and thus welcomed and surrounded in a stately manner with heavenly splendor! Oh, the wonderful honor, where it is welcomed not by earthly kings, princes, counts, and nobles, but by the heavenly kingdom's most glorious and mighty princes and the servants of the living God; nor carried in banner-draped carriages, couches, or litters, but borne on the hands of the angels! Oh, the wondrously lovely radiance shining on every side, above and below and around it! How the heart must take hold of nothing but joy and bliss! How it must wonder at the wondrously pleasant, wondrously friendly, and wondrously comforting face of the wondrously beautiful Champion of God!

The brightness and glory of eternal life is not far removed from dying Christians.

Neither may we suppose that this heavenly radiance, gladness, and bliss is far removed from Christians by several thousand miles and beyond all the visible heavens, as the enthusiastic spirits and Calvinist speculators fancy, but a godly man has eternal life in actuality forever, here in this world in faith, and immediately when he dies, the soul has it before it in sight—just as a child in the womb has his natural life and is already in the world, only this life is enclosed and concealed and cannot see the fair world. But as soon as he puts off his old skin, the *secundina*, and by natural birth leaves the matrix, he sees before him the worldly existence, is amazed at the light that shines in his eyes, and hears the friendly, gracious voice of his mother and other relations, who hold him, kiss him, embrace him, carry him, rock him, and smile at him warmly.

Application of the comparison.

It is no different with the elect souls. In this world, the heavenly life and salvation of the soul, as Paul says, "lie hidden in God," since God's Word is its womb and spiritual lodging. In addition, it also deals with the old Adam and mortal body as with an old skin, so that it cannot see the heavenly blessedness, but walks merely in faith and not in sight. But as soon as by temporal death it puts off the tent of its body, it is born from the realm of faith into the realm of sight and sees manifestly the glory of God, holds converse with the holy angels, has heavenly gladness in actuality before its eyes, and cannot marvel at it enough.

Comparison with a blind and deaf man who, though being and living in the world, does not see or hear that life until his eyes and ears are opened.

Indeed, the eternal life of a godly Christian, as soon as he has fallen asleep in the Lord, is truly like an opening of the eyes and unclosing of the ears, so that the soul sees as if it were hitherto blind and hears as if it were hitherto deaf. For if the bright, glorious sun surrounds a deaf and blind man with its radiance and light and likewise all manner of strings, cymbals, and harps, organ and suchlike sound in his ears with all of their might, nevertheless the poor man can see and hear none of it on account of his blindness and deafness, even though he lives in the midst of the glorious sunlight and surrounded by the sweet sounds of music. Now, if a good eye surgeon and physician should come and pierce his cataracts and tear the thick, obstructive skin from the blind man and open his ears, so that he could suddenly see the light and suddenly hear the pleasant sound, what do you suppose he would think, especially when he saw the clear day, the dear sun, and the fair world and heard the tuneful cymbals and trumpets, pipes and similar instruments around him? He would surely confess and say that the rest of his life had been a half-death and not until now had he learned what life was.

The nature of our heavenly life is explained by the previous comparison.

In this way you are able to imagine well the different nature of our heavenly life. For an orthodox Christian in this world is already blessed and has in actuality the almighty Lord of Sabaoth, God the Father, Son, and Holy Spirit, along with His heavenly angels, as a heavenly hedge of fire around him, and there is no doubt that the dear angels which surround him continually worship their Maker and sing to Him without ceasing: "Holy, Holy, Holy Lord God of Sabaoth." A Christian in this world is simply unable to see or hear this heavenly radiance, majesty, and glory of God and His elect angels, since he walks in faith and not in sight and is, in addition, as Scripture says, oppressed by the mortal body as with an earthly tent. Thus it remains for him only to put off the old Adam completely and by temporal death at last to be delivered from his sinful body; then he will have the heavenly glory in sight in an instant and dwell in unspeakable joy in the midst of the angels of God.

How a Christian can take comfort in the different condition of his heavenly life.

I do not doubt that, were a Christian in the world to grasp this rightly, he would always heartily rejoice in the imminent presence of God and His dear angels and think: "I am blessed already, and my walk is already in heaven, since I cling to God's Word and am carried within it like a child enclosed in the womb, and God very kindly surrounds and enfolds me on every side with His angels. And although I do not see the glory with my physical eyes nor hear the angelic voices with my physical ears, but only walk in faith, which things must continue till death, yet after death the revelation will begin, and my soul, delivered and summoned from this body, will at once have eternal life in sight and hear God Almighty and His holy angels themselves.

Demonstration of the cited explanation from the example of the Lord Christ.

John 3:13; Matt. 4:11; Mark 1:13; Matt. 17:2–4, 9; Mark 9:2–3; Luke 9:29–31

That this is the case with our blessedness and that the heavenly joy and the glory of angels is not far removed from us but close in front of us and only lies in the distinction of faith and of sight, we see first in our only Redeemer and Savior, Jesus Christ, who, when He walked visibly on earth, was at the same time in heaven as the Son of Man; as He says: "The Son of Man which is in heaven." And the holy angels were around and about Him and ministered to Him, as the evangelists Matthew and Mark plainly testify. Now, no heavenly majesty or glory was seen in Christ, nor was it seen how the heavenly hosts and holy angels attended Him as the mighty Champion of God. It was not seen with physical eyes since His heavenly life and glory lay covered and hidden under the cross and state of humiliation. Yet this heavenly glory was not removed or separated from Him by several thousand miles, nor a distance beyond all the firmament, but was close in front of Him and nothing was lacking except only the revelation, that He did not wish to uncover it, which He could have done if He wished. For when He was on the high mountain with His three disciples and wished to show Himself to them somewhat as He already was in heaven, behold, His face shone as the sun and His clothes became white as a light, and Moses and Isaiah appeared with Him and spoke to Him concerning what He must suffer in Jerusalem.

Demonstration from the example of the prophet Elisha.

2 Kings 6:15–17

Next, we have a remarkable example in the prophet Elisha, who also found hope in this heavenly glory and the holy angels' dwelling with him and did not doubt it, even though he did not see it with his physical eyes. For when he was besieged by the Syrians in the village of Dothan and his servant was so greatly troubled because of the siege that he cried out and said, "Alas, my master, what shall we do?" Elisha comforted him and said, "Fear not, for there are more of those who are with us than those who are with them." Further, Elisha prayed and says, "Open his eyes, O Lord, that he may see." Then the Lord opened the eyes of the young man, and he saw: and behold, the mountain was full of fiery horses and chariots round about Elisha.

Every orthodox Christian has the kingdom of God in actuality within and around himself, in faith here and in sight immediately after death.

Here you see how the existence of the heavenly glory and the holy angels as fiery chariots and horses constantly surround a godly man on earth and are not far from him, but close at hand. Therefore, every orthodox Christian, as long as he is living on earth, has the kingdom of God within him, above him, and around him and lacks nothing more but to see manifestly. And this he encounters as soon as he has overcome death and laid aside the mortal tent of his body. Then he sees at once the heavenly hosts and solemn servants of the eternal God Almighty before him and marvels at the clear new light of the great glory and eternal brightness, just as a young child, being born from the womb into the world, opens his little eyes and looks at the daylight with wonder and the radiant light of the sun that shines and enlightens all things.

As soon as the soul of the elect leaves the body, it has heavenly joy in actuality.

In this way, the elect soul, after its blessed departure from the mortal body, has all heavenly joy in actuality, God is present with it, the holy angels are present with it, and the great, unspeakable glory is present with it. It has everything actually in sight, even though the people who stand by the bed do not see the angels present nor hear with their physical ears their rejoicing with which they welcome the exiting soul and take it into their charge. This is covered and hidden to the eyes and ears of their flesh since they are still mortal and dwell in the body. But the soul of the deceased sees the dear angels manifestly and hears their voice, what they say explicitly and personally, and it sees and hears these things without hindrance since it no longer lives as a pilgrim in the body but is wholly released and gone forth and delivered from all its sins.

Joy of the holy angels at the arrival of the soul from this world into eternal life.

Luke 15:10

How wondrously sweet and wondrously joyful it is when the heavenly spirits of the Lord welcome the elect soul into their midst and bear it up in their hands. For then they rejoice that a man has repented and as a penitent taken his leave of the world. At this they are glad and rejoice far more and with far greater glory than at heaven and earth and themselves and all who have no need to repent.

Comparison with a noble child's birth.

We see in kings' palaces and the courts of great nobles, when a young lord is born to the world, what great joy is raised there. Then the tender babe is wrapped in splendid swaddling cloths and carried with gladness. The closest relations take him up in their arms, embrace him and kiss him, and smile at him tenderly, and the harder the birth has been, the more it was feared the child would be stillborn (which God graciously prevent!), the greater the mother's joy that follows thereafter. In the same way the holy angels rejoice and shout for great joy that the soul of a man has overcome harsh, bitter death in faith by the blood of the Lamb and the comforting words of the Gospel and has passed into the paradise of eternal joy—at this they rejoice and are glad for the blessed soul, which they bear in their hands, embrace it and kiss it, and address it with wonderful kindness, and look at it with utterly friendly faces, as though a tender newborn infant.

The elect soul in heaven is treated gently when it is carried by the holy angels and in the hand of God.

No young infant on earth can be so comforted by his soft swaddling cloths and warm blankets in which he is wrapped, nor indeed by his mother's lap, as the triumphant soul is comforted at heart by the angelic rejoicing and glory of eternal life. For on every side it has, in the midst of the hosts of God, or in the midst of the stately, mighty princes of heaven, nothing but joy and bliss. And the comforting hand of God the Father Almighty and the sun-bright hands of the holy angels are like a gentle swaddling cloth and bundle in which it is swaddled and is carried and rocked like a newborn infant.

The soul is with God as if it were swaddled in a swaddling cloth and bundle.

1 Sam. 25:29

To King David the wise woman Abigail preaches about this wondrously comforting swaddling cloth and bundle of the elect soul and thereby strengthens him against his persecutors, saying, "When a man shall exalt himself to persecute you, then shall the soul of my lord be bound in the bundle of the living with the Lord your God."

For the elect soul in heaven, the face of the holy angels is not terrible but pleasant to see.

Now just as the face of gracious parents and of dear brothers and sisters is not terrifying to the newborn infant, but pleasant and comforting to look at, especially when the father, mother, brother, sister, and other relations smile at him sweetly and speak to him kindly, so also the face of God and the holy angels in the heavenly paradise to the elect souls are not like angry masks or terrifying specters, but only wondrously lovely, wondrously comforting, and wondrously friendly images which speak in wondrously pleasant ways with the soul, gladden them in a wondrously comforting manner, and surround them with a friendly look on every side. For the angels love the Lord our God with their whole heart and love blessed men as themselves, and because this love, which is the fulfilling of the Law, has its course and activity with God Almighty in His life and kingdom of sight, what terrifying and abhorrent thing can appear in the holy angels from which the human soul should recoil?

Why a man in this world cannot endure the face of God and of His holy angels.

It is true that a man in this world cannot view and endure any angel's countenance, much less the face of God, with his physical eyes, as we see in the prophet Isaiah, Daniel, Manoah,[118] and St. John on the island of Patmos, how sorely they are troubled and their countenance falls when God and His angels reveal themselves to some extent visibly. Yet such fear and anguish comes from the fact that they were still trapped in the sinful skin of the old Adam and because their rebirth was not yet completed. Therefore, just as it would be wholly dangerous and certainly deadly for a premature infant to see the world and men in this world before his birth, so we in the mortal tents of our body cannot with the eyes of our flesh see or endure the face of God and His holy angels without peril to life and limb until we go home from this valley of sorrow and our soul is fully delivered from the realm of faith into the realm of sight.

The blame for this weakness should be ascribed not to the nature of God or the holy angels, but to that of our sinful Adam.

Therefore, the blame for this anguish, terror, and danger should be ascribed not to God and His angels, as if they by nature were kindled with a fiery and consuming hatred of mankind, which is hardly the case, but to our carnal weakness, sin, and frailty. For God is Love Himself, and that we might be able to bear His powerful love, He formed and bore us in this world by His Word unto the eternal life of eternal love. Likewise, whenever the holy angels have appeared to godly people in this valley of sorrow and noted in men their carnal fear, anguish, and trembling, it was always their highest intent to see that that fear and anguish were taken away and removed from the people in need.

The holy angels, when they appear, are always inclined to comfort godly Christians.

Luke 2:10; Isa. 6:6–7; Dan. 10:18–19

We find beautiful and notable examples of this in Scripture. The shepherds in the field at the time of the birth of Christ were very afraid of the angel of the Lord who by night shone around them with heavenly glory. But then he comforted them and said, "Fear not. Behold, I declare to you a great joy which shall come upon all people." Also when at the face of an angel the prophet Daniel was utterly shocked, his joints shook, and he sank to the earth from great weariness, the angel with gracious quickening power took care to console and strengthen the terrified prophet and therefore touched him and said, "O dear Daniel, fear not. O Daniel, fear not, dear man, peace be with you, and take heart, take heart."

In this world we cannot see the angels of God with physical eyes.

Behold, so sweet and gracious are the holy angels with words, gestures, and thoughts. It is only the fault of our great weakness that, just as an immature infant in the womb cannot come out before his birth to see the world or look at

118 The father of Samson. See Judg. 13:1–23 and 14:2–4.

the face of his parents, brothers, and sisters without danger to life and limb, so in this world we cannot (as just stated) see the face of God and His angels with our physical eyes without harm to our life, as God Himself tells Moses, saying, "No man who sees Me shall live."

In that world, or the heavenly paradise, the soul is delivered from all sins and therefore can certainly endure the face of the angels and God.

But in that life and with God in His heavenly paradise, the elect soul has attained to its blessed rebirth and passed through temporal death and the putting off of the sinful body, out of the realm of faith into the realm sight. Therefore, it there beholds the face of God and the wondrously beautiful form of the holy angels with gladness and is sweetly revived and strengthened by it so that it is in no way troubled nor knows of any fear, anguish, timidity, or sadness, but has unspeakable desire, joy, and bliss in this viewing. And if anyone interrogated it concerning this state of its life, it would doubtless confess that it would not exchange this glory for heaven or earth, the whole world, or all the riches, splendor, honor, and joy that are in it.

Contemplation of the glory that many angels accompany the soul.

Luke 15:10; 16:22

In addition, this glory is also great and prestigious in that not only one but many angels are appointed for every soul, as Scripture openly tells us that "there is joy in the presence of the angels of God over one sinner who repents"; likewise, the poor man died and was carried by the angels to Abraham's bosom. "Why," says Chrysostom, "does it say here, 'He was carried by the angels'? Was not one angel able to do it or strong enough to bear up and carry poor Lazarus? Yes, indeed, one angel would certainly have been enough for this task. But many join in the work to show that they take great joy in the salvation of men. For every angel takes pleasure and joy in doing this service, and every angel gladly accepts this task of bringing men into the kingdom of heaven."[119]

Differing appearances of a dead body and the triumphing soul.

Behold, then, what different sights and contrasting processions occur: the dead body of the deceased Christian lies there like a block and stone, knows nothing, is wrapped in a cloth, laid in a coffin, borne on a bier to the house, and afterward taken away to the churchyard and buried under the earth. The next of kin, neighbors, and relatives follow the body in black mourning-garments with heartfelt sighing, crying, and weeping according to the greatness of their love for

119 Pseudo-Chrysostom, *Homilia de Divite,* evid.; see Aquinas, *Catena Aurea,* Luke 16:22–26. Nicolai's wording comes from Basilius Faber, *Tractetlein von den Seelen der verstorbenen, und allem ihrem zustand und gelegenheit* (Leipzig: E. Vögelin, 1569), which Nicolai references at the end of this book.

the deceased. The mourning songs also are sung: "Shall we receive good,"[120] "In the very midst of life,"[121] "From depths of woe I cry to Thee,"[122] and the like. Or else tyrants and bloodthirsty men in their hostility cause the body of a Christian to be pierced, beheaded, hanged, tortured, and then the dead body burned to ashes, torn in pieces, or cast before wild beasts, all for the sake of the truth he confessed—which is all awful to behold and abhorrent to attend such a spectacle.

The soul lives with God and moves in joy.

But meanwhile the unbound soul travels not among mortal men on earth but among the angels of God in the height of heaven, released from all sorrow, distress, temptations, worry, and heartache. It knows no longer of anguish or mourning, but is jubilant, sings, exclaims for joy, and triumphs in its deliverance. And its blessed journey of gladness among the princely hosts and bright-shining chariots and horses of the everlasting, almighty God is many hundred thousand times grander, more magnificent, more joyous, more powerful, and more glorious than if you had risen to high estate here on earth, been seated in a carriage of gold, and escorted by every emperor, king, prince, and noble of all the wide world in great pomp, solemnity, and joy, with many thousand covered carriages and well-adorned horses, as well as merry horn players, trumpeters, tympani, pipes, cymbals, and organs, and were conducted into the fairest and mightiest palace that could ever exist in Europe, Asia, and Africa to take and possess it.

The holy angels that escort and guide the elect soul are like chariots of fire and horses of fire.

Ps. 68:17; 2 Kings 2:11; Song 8:6

The thoughts of men on earth cannot fathom this heavenly joy and glory, much less can we describe it with our tongue. In it there are many thousand times thousands of the chariots of God, and as attested by the ascension of the prophet Elijah, they are chariots of fire and horses of fire—not that they injure, ignite, singe, burn, or consume anyone with material or earthly fire on his heavenly journey, but they are the dear angels of God, which travel and move as with fire on account of their great glory, heavenly joy, and unspeakably great love in which they well up and burn sweetly for the souls committed and entrusted to them by God, whom they guide and escort. For according to the chief royal decree of the Law, they love God their Lord without any doubting, with all their heart, with all their soul, and with all their strength, and their neighbor as themselves. But this perfect love is like a fiery coal, as Solomon writes, and like a flame of the Lord. Therefore, because the dear angels in heaven gloriously encircle and comfortingly enclose each blessed, triumphant Christian with fervent love like a fire, they glow

120 A traditional funeral responsory from Job 2.

121 "Mitten wir im Leben sind" (Luther, 1524) (*LSB* 755).

122 "Aus tiefer Not schrei ich zu dir" (Luther, 1524) (*LSB* 607).

and shine forth with the radiance of love and flames of love as if they were really chariots of fire and horses of fire.

The journey of the soul and its residence among the holy angels is an eternal triumph.

But especially here we should take note and know that this journey of joy and glory is truly a triumph of the soul, in that it is carried by the angels of God and sets forth as a mighty champion who by the blood of Christ in faith has overcome not the Tatar, the Turk, and the Muscovite, but all the devils of hell, death, the streams of Belial, and the whole world. Therefore, it rejoices and is triumphant precisely as if a brave hero had put his enemies to flight and won the battle and then came home with gladness, seated in his sumptuous carriage of gold, and then was received by kings and was escorted in all magnificence by a great procession of notable princes, counts, and knights and nobility.

The triumphal procession of Emperor Titus after subduing the Jews.

Josephus, Jewish War, bk. 3, ch. 2[123]

How splendid it was when Titus, having subjugated the Jews and gained the victory, came home by sea from Judea to Italy! He was met with great rejoicing by the Roman citizens in a countless throng outside of the city. But he, Emperor Titus, and his father, Vespasian, marched along, their heads adorned with wreaths of gold-wrought laurel and robed in garments of Roman purple. In this triumphal procession was seen all kinds of things made of gold, silver, and ivory, following one after another in orderly manner, as if it were not being carried but actually flowing, curious garments of purple and hangings embroidered and dyed with Babylonian artistry and many sparkling gems in crowns of gold and set in other pieces of jewelry. The honorable orators stood then in silken garments and crowned with wreaths of laurel and praised the valiant deeds of their conquering prince. The whole people rejoiced, and all of Rome was glad.

Heavenly triumphal procession of the believing soul.

Rev. 2:10; 3:5

But what is this brief, ephemeral pomp and joy compared to the everlasting triumphal procession and eternal joy of a soul that ascends on high among the holy angels and rejoices in God its Savior, that it has conquered in Christ and overcome the whole world along with its prince, the despicable devil? Therefore, it is also very splendidly crowned in heaven by our Savior, Jesus Christ, and extolled before God the Father and His angels forever. "Be faithful until death," says the Son of God, "and I will give you the crown of life." And again: "He who overcomes shall be robed with white garments, and I will not blot out his name from the Book of Life, and I will confess his name before My Father and His angels."

123 Josephus, *Bellum Judaicum* 7.5.4–5.

The heavenly triumph of the soul begins right after death.

Now if poor Lazarus, when he died, was immediately taken by the holy angels and carried to eternal joy, and if the converted thief on the cross right after his death was in the heavenly paradise with Christ, and if it is certain that a godly Christian passes quickly through death to life (as God's Word expressly attests, and we may not doubt it at all), then truly this triumph must happen at once, and it must be seen that the noble soul of a deceased Christian will shout for joy and rejoice in the heavenly paradise immediately after death and with unspeakable honor be instantly welcomed and lauded and crowned by its Bridegroom and Savior, Christ Jesus, and by all the angels be hailed as blessed.

The great glory where Christ lauds and extols a triumphant soul before His holy angels is not to be fathomed.

Matt. 10:32–33; Rev. 2:13; Ps. 36:8

Now in all of Europe, all Asia, all Africa, in the beautiful kingdom of China, in all the lands of the Orient, in the newly discovered islands, there has never been seen or heard such exceedingly splendid pomp and glory as this is and must be; a high pomp of gladness and joyful glory, where the great King of heaven and earth, Jesus Christ, receives the elect souls and extols them before His holy angels, where they stand before Him thousands upon thousands, and He says to them, "Behold, O angels and archangels, cherubim and seraphim, heavenly thrones, dominions, principalities, and powers! This is the prophet Isaiah, this is My disciple Peter, this is the doctor Augustine, this is so and so, etc., who was not ashamed of Me and did not deny My Word, but until death openly confessed it before all the world and honored Me in faith and true confidence with prayer, thanksgiving, hearing, and careful meditation of My saving doctrine. Behold, O angels, this is the blessed man, the elect soul, the dear child, My dear sheep, My treasure and dearly bought good. Let him sit with you at table, and make merry with him, and let him drink among you of the rich goods of My house and be given to drink of the utter heavenly pleasure as with a river."

History of the eastern emperor Michael.

See Leunclavius's Annals of the Turks, p. 407[124]

How gently must it affect the noble soul when it is so highly honored by the Lord Jesus above all holy angels! We read of the Roman emperor in Constantinople, named Michael; when he sensed great fidelity in his servant by the name of Basil Macedo and by his diligence was saved from his enemy by the name of Bardas, he boasted of him before the whole kingdom and had it publicly declared: "By craft did Bardas seek my life and would have slain me, had not my faithful servant Basil prevented the calamity. Therefore, I desire that this Basil should be

124 Johannes Leunclavius (d. 1594), *Annales Sultanorum Othmanidarum* (Frankfurt am Main: Marne & Aubry, 1588).

my partner in government and be proclaimed co-emperor with me." Then Basil began to weep and fell at the emperor's feet, but the emperor had him crowned and publicly proclaimed co-ruler in the imperial government.

Christ causes the triumphing soul of a Christian to reign and rule with Him.

Rev. 3:21; Ps. 126:1–2

So it is in heaven, and yet many thousand times sweeter, more glorious, and more powerful, when our Immanuel boasts before His holy angels that the blessed soul was thus faithful to Him until death and furthermore crowns it so that it may reign and rule with Him; as He says, "He who overcomes, to him will I grant to sit with Me on My throne, as I have overcome and sat down with My Father on His throne." Surely the elect souls may weep for joy then, so that it seems to be mourning, and what is said, sung, and joyfully proclaimed with laughing mouth is all as though it were happening in a dream. As David prophesies of this, saying, "When the Lord shall redeem the captives of Zion, we will be like those who are dreaming. Then our mouth shall be filled with laughter and our tongue with boasting."

The glory that the angels in heaven speak comfortingly to a soul is indescribable.

Likewise, it is not an earthly, princely, and kingly pomp, majesty, honor, and glory, but super-princely, super-kingly, and above all that of the world when the princes of heaven, Gabriel, Raphael, cherubim, seraphim, with all the angelic thrones and dominions, encircle the elect soul, highly extol and exalt it, and speak comfortingly to it of pure indescribable joy and bliss.

History of the great triumph and great boast of the widow Judith.

Judith 15:9–10

When the pious and godly matron and widow Judith obtained from God the victory for her people against the Assyrians, all the Jews praised her and said, "'You are the crown of Jerusalem, you are the bliss of Israel, you are a glory of the whole people, because you have done such pleasant deeds and have shown such great goodness to Israel that God in turn has delivered it. Blessed be you with God forevermore.' And all the people said, 'Amen, Amen.'" And yet this earthly glory is jesting and child's play compared to the great heavenly glory where the royal and princely hosts of the eternal and immortal God take between them the blessed Christian (who has departed this miserable valley of sorrows) and boast of his steadfast faith by which he swallowed up death and overcame all his enemies.

How the holy angels praise as blessed the elect soul in heaven.

Luke 1:28, 45; 1 Tim. 4:7–8; Rev. 7:14; Ps. [122]; Heb. 12:22–23; Ps. 118:17

Oh, how sweet it must sound when they intone, sing, play, shout, and call out with great joy in good Angelic: "Oh, how blessed are you, elect soul, blessed are you who have believed. For to you now there shall be a performance of those things which were told you from the Lord. You have fought the good fight, you have finished your course in the world, you have kept the faith. You have come out of the great tribulation; you have washed your garments and made your garments bright in the blood of the Lamb. We bless you who are from the house of the Lord. Behold, you have come to the heavenly Jerusalem and to the multitude of many thousands of angels and to the congregation of the firstborn, who are written in heaven. You have not died, but you live and are now to proclaim the work of the Lord.

The excellent boast and comfort which the elect soul receives from the angels of God.

Dan. 10:9; Ps. 91:12; Heb. 1:14; Ps. 34:7; 2 Kings 6:17; Luke 16:22; 1 Pet. 1:12; Rev. 19:10

"Therefore, fear not, dear child! Peace be to you and be of good cheer. Take courage, and fear not, dear soul, blessed Christian, dear child. Behold, we bear you up upon our hands and are sent forth from the great King of heaven and earth as ministering spirits for your service. We encamped round about you when you were still in the flesh and you feared the Lord our God. And although you did not see us with your physical eyes, yet we surrounded you like chariots of fire and horses of fire and took heartfelt joy in your repentance, when you departed from sin and devoted yourself to the Lord Christ and His preached Gospel, into which things we desired to look. Therefore, behold, dear brother, we are your fellow servants and of your brethren who have the testimony of Jesus."

The elect soul and holy angels praise God with one accord and love one another.

This angelic glory the elect soul sees and hears and rejoices in the royal honor, the sweet happiness, and the blessed fellowship that it has with cherubim and seraphim, with the most serene hosts of God, and with all heavenly thrones, principalities, and dominions. With one accord they praise and glorify the everlasting and almighty God and love Him with all their heart, with all their soul, and with all their strength, and they love one another—the angels the men and the men the dear angels—as themselves. This is their *commercium*, communion, bond, and eternal union, full of great gladness, full of great honor, full of great pleasure, majesty, and glory.

The joy and bliss of souls at the fellowship they have with the angels of God in heaven.

Oh, how this joy and bliss must affect the heart of a soul! Oh, how much it must marvel at the powerful honor and glory that it finds there! How it must frolic and sing for eternal gladness! How comforted it feels when it recalls how it went around in great affliction, sorrow, anguish, and misery on earth and suffered poverty, persecution, contempt, scorn, and mockery because of the Gospel and was made out to be a fool, a curse, and an offering to the ungodly villains, but now lives and moves among the holy angels in eternal joy and bliss. Then it spurns and despises the proud pomp of the puffed-up world and thinks: "Fie upon the stinking arrogance of earth, where one exalts himself above another, parades around in silk and satin, builds stately mansions, seeks only honor and ways to insinuate himself into kings' palaces or princes' courts and rule over others! But what is the world, emperors, kings, princes, and potentates compared to the holy angels? And what is all the world's pomp compared to the angels' glory? Here God inclines to me the whole of heaven with all holy angels, and I lead such a life of gladness among them that I would not exchange it for a hundred thousand worlds or ten times a hundred thousand earthly kingdoms."

The elect souls in heaven do not desire this earthly life again.

Behold, dear Christians, this is the first glory of the elect soul of which it becomes partaker as soon as it is loosed from the mortal tent of its body and in which it rejoices unspeakable joy and bliss. And just as a man in this world thinks his natural life and conversation here on earth is different, better, and more perfect than when he was enclosed in his mother's womb and led a confined life, so that he does not desire that confined and concealed life again, even if he could return to it, so the reborn soul in heaven leads a truly pleasurable life of paradise among the holy angels, compared to which this world in which it dwelt for a season seems far more cramped and narrow than a womb, and it does not desire to reenter it, even if it were permitted and given leave to do so.

(2) The second glory of the elect soul in heaven is communion with God.

Ps. 36:9; 17:15; Luke 23; 2 Cor. 12:4; Rev. 7:15–16; Wisdom 3:1–9, 14

Its second glory is the blessed communion that it has with its betrothed Redeemer and Bridegroom, Jesus Christ, whom it there sees in plain sight, as well as God the Father and God the Holy Spirit, and it is with the entire Holy Trinity in heavenly paradise and in that place hears unspeakable words which no man can utter and feels no hunger or thirst and is disturbed by no pain, nor assailed by any sun nor by any heat at all, but serves God Almighty day and night in His temple and is led by its Immanuel to the fountain of living water and is heartily comforted from all contempt, scorn, mockery, persecution, and misery that it had to bear in the world for His sake.

Testimony of Scripture regarding our communion with Christ after this life.

John 12:26; 17:24; Luke 23:43

"Where I am," He says, "there shall My servants also be. And he who shall serve Me, him will My Father honor." Likewise: "Father, I will that those whom You have given Me may be with Me where I am, that they may behold My glory, which You have given Me." These are wonderful and wondrously comforting promises which apply to all orthodox Christians and explicitly say that they will be with their heavenly Savior and Redeemer and see His eternal glory. And that no one may suppose that this revelation of glory will not begin until the Last Day and that the souls of the deceased Christians meanwhile do not see or know of it at all, our Immanuel clearly bears witness to the contrary when He explicitly says to the converted thief, "Truly, truly, I say to you, today you will be with Me in paradise."

As soon as a blessed child of the light dies, he is with Christ in paradise.

Consider carefully, you who are simple, these words which I have also exhorted above, and think what they entail and comprehend. The thief dies on the cross and his soul departs from him, but where does it go? Answer: it belongs to Christ and comes to Him and remains with Him. Where? Answer: not in hell nor in the wilderness nor in a deep, stinking dungeon, nor in some dark forest where there are bloodthirsty highwaymen, murderers, vipers, dragons, wolves, and lions, but it goes to Him in paradise. So also each believing soul, as soon as it has entirely died to the old Adam and the tent of its body, comes to Christ in paradise and dwells in paradise and its whole life that it leads with its Bridegroom, Jesus Christ, is nothing but a joyful life of paradise.

An elect soul, after departing the world, comes to Christ in paradise, just as a bride is conducted to her bridegroom in grand and solemn manner.

Here the dear angels are like an escort for the royal bride. The elect soul is the royal bride and Jesus Christ is the royal Bridegroom and heavenly Adam. After her blessed departure from this world, she is brought to Him quickly by the heavenly hosts, that she may be with Him. And just as it is seems very magnificent, joyful, and prestigious when a stately bride is conducted with great, joyful solemnity to her bridegroom in an exceedingly beautiful pleasure garden in the beautiful, pleasant season of spring, when the noble nightingale is heard everywhere—so, when a child of the light falls blessedly asleep in the Lord, his life of paradise begins immediately after death, in that the noble soul, just as in a royal pleasure garden, escorted by many hundred thousands of angels, comes to its most beautiful Bridegroom, the Lord Christ, with whom it finds sheer joy of paradise, life of paradise, pleasure of paradise, and glory of paradise and is refreshed with His fervent love.

The soul grows light in the heavenly paradise and rises like a moon.

Song 6:10; 7:6; Ps. 126:2

Here straightaway and in its full vigor commences that blessed joy and heavenly pleasure spoken of with pregnant words in Solomon's Song of Songs. There the soul comes out of the realm of faith and into the realm of sight, and there its confidence which in this world it set on its heavenly Bridegroom, along with its blessed hope, becomes a noble light and radiance so that it there rises as the dawn and as the beautiful moon in the midst of the holy angels and looks with opened eyes upon its dear Beloved and Redeemer, of whom it has heard so much on earth and whom it so often extolled, confessed, praised, honored, and glorified with its lips. There its mouth is filled with laughter, its tongue with boasting, its heart with gladness, and its soul with delight.

Christ the Lord receives the elect soul in paradise as a bridegroom his bride.

Song 3:6; Wisdom 2:2–3; 1 Cor. 15:32

Its Bridegroom and most beloved Jesus Christ receives it also with gladness and appears in great majesty and glory. "Who is this," says He, "that rises from the wilderness like a straight pillar of smoke, like a fragrance of myrrh, incense, and all powders of the apothecary?" It is as if He would say, "The world is a true wilderness, desert, and wasteland, in which the scoffing Epicureans neither care about nor believe in eternal life, but think that the soul disappears and dissolves like a smoke and a vapor. The breath in our nostrils, they say, is like smoke, and our utterance is a spark that is stirred up from our heart. When it is extinguished, the body goes away like ashes, and our spirit dissolves like empty air. Therefore, let us eat and drink, for tomorrow we die. This is the motto of the children of the world. But who is this noble soul which I see coming yonder from the desolate world, not as a passing vapor and smoke, but as a straight, piercing smoke which passes through death to Me in this paradise and smokes pleasantly with heartfelt confidence and fervent love for Me, like a fragrance of myrrh, incense, and all powders of the apothecary?"

The elect souls complain to their Bridegroom in heaven how for His name they had to suffer all kinds of grief and persecution in the world.

Rev. 6:10

Now, just as a bride who for her bridegroom was made to suffer much scoffing, great calumny, and all kinds of persecution from her enemies and adversaries, as soon as she sees her darling bridegroom, weeps for joy and tells him the great anguish and danger which she bore and endured for his sake—so, too, do the elect souls, who in this world are readily expelled by burnings, persecuted, ridiculed, tormented with scorn and mockery, and pitifully slain by the devil and his fellows because of their Savior and Bridegroom, Jesus Christ, and because of His Word and because of the witness which they bore, who cried with a loud voice and said, "O Lord, holy and true, how long do You not judge and avenge our blood on those who dwell on the earth?"

The lament of the elect does not arise from carnal affects.

These words spring and arise not from carnal hostility, spite, and desire for vengeance, but rather from a great love for Christ and from a yearning desire that He would defend and preserve His honor against the devil and all stubborn enemies, persecutors, and tyrants.

The elect soul in heaven is like a bride that burns with great love.

Song 5:1; Rev. 22:17; Ps. 118:1–18; Jer. 20; Matt. 10; 1 Cor. 4:9–13

And thus the soul of a persecuted Christian before God in that life (for which the Lord Christ has separated it from this world) is like a zealous bride, who out of burning love cries and weeps for great joy, and tells its heavenly Bridegroom all that it suffered for His name from Satan and the wicked, execrable world: "Oh, if I see You but once," it might say. "O great King of Glory, my most dearly beloved Head and my only Comfort, my sincere joy and bliss—oh, then You must be highly glorified, praised, and honored, O Root of Jesse, O bright Morning Star, and King of eternal life! Hosanna, Son of David! How the ungodly on earth pained, tortured, and afflicted me with such hostility for Your name's sake! I have confessed Your Word, I have borne witness to Your truth, and in Your name I have rebuked false teaching, idolatry, error, vice, and iniquity in the erring spirits and wicked villains. For Your sake I have been made a fool, a curse, a purge offering, and a spectacle; I have been despised, spit upon, mocked, chastised, slandered, and finally executed and put to death. O Jesus, how long will You let Your honor be put to shame? How long do You not judge and avenge the blood that was shed for Your sake?"

Christ comforts the elect soul.

Song 4:8

Thereupon Jesus comforts it and gives it a white garment (as St. John reports), which here signifies the new light, glory, and heavenly gladness with which it is girded. And just as if it had been a hind wretchedly hunted by lions and leopards over mountain, hill, and dale and had been persecuted and had therefore become weary and tired, so its Bridegroom laments it and calls it tenderly to Himself and says, "Come, my bride, with Me from Lebanon, go in, approach from the height of Amana, from the height of Senir and Hermon, from the lions' dens and from the mountains of the leopards."

The friendly voice of the Lord Christ in heaven to the elect soul.

Song 2:10–14

He also comforts it with the heavenly gladness, pleasure, and refreshment which it is to find and possess with Him forever in the wondrously beautiful paradise of eternal life, with the declaration that all its grief, tribulation, and misery, like a rough winter and like a tumultuous rain, have now passed. From henceforth it will therefore lead a true life of paradise in the land of the living and in this heavenly pleasure garden will know no more of any winter or tempest of sorrow, but it will experience only gladness and bliss. "Arise," He says to it, "My love, My beauty, and come. For behold, the winter is past, the rain is finished and gone. The flowers have sprung up in the land, the spring has come, and the turtledove is heard in our land. The fig tree has budded; the vines have blossomed and give forth their fragrance. Arise, O My love, and come, O My beauty, come, O My dove, in the holes of the rock, in the crevices of the cliff. Show Me your countenance; let Me hear your voice."

The elect Christian's death is counted precious in the sight of God.

Ps. 116:15; 56:13; Rev. 7:14

In summary, the death of His saints is counted precious in His sight, even as He has plucked their souls from death and their eyes from tears and their feet from slipping, that they might walk before Him in the most beautiful, most delightful, and most precious paradise or land of the living. "They have come," says Scripture, "out of the great tribulation and have washed their garments and made their garments bright in the blood of the Lamb. Therefore, they are before the throne of God and serve Him day and night in His temple."

Likeness describing how the elect soul feels in heaven.

And this seems to it precisely as if it had been in a cold, dark, northern land in this world, where it is always freezing, hailing, snowing, and only blustery winds are heard, which on every side push frost and snow into the eyes so that nothing is seen but thick darkness, snow, frozen waters, snowy peaks, blocks of ice, icicles, and barren trees, and where on every side one must fear ravenous wolves, bears, and similar wild beasts, raging, roaring, and growling for the prey and tearing to pieces whatever they meet with. But now by death it is, as it were, suddenly transferred and transported in the blink of an eye from this frosty, wretched, barren, gloomy, and wholly dangerous land of winter into a heavenly summer-land, where winter is past, the rains are finished and gone, where the spring is always flourishing, the sun never goes down, the Holy Spirit, as the true heavenly turtledove, sends forth His friendly voice, and the holy angels like nightingales, parrots, skylarks, and handsome woodland birds with joyful mouth sing to the Almighty King of glory their "Holy, Holy, Holy Lord God of Sabaoth."

The soul's food and drink in the heavenly paradise.

Rev. 7:16–17; Ps. 36:8; Luke 16:25; Heb. 11:37–38; Isa. 59; 65

Further, Scripture informs us that the elect souls neither hunger nor thirst there, and that the sun does not strike them, nor any heat. For the Lamb of God in the midst of the throne of eternal glory and honor feeds them and guides them to the living fountains of water, that they may have drink of the rich goods of His house and be given to drink with pleasure as with a river. If poor Lazarus on earth received evil things, now his soul is comforted in heaven, and if the elect children of light wander about in this world in furs and goatskins, being destitute, afflicted, and tormented in deserts, in mountains, and in the dens and caves of the earth, now their souls are full of delight so that they eat, drink, rejoice, and make merry with good cheer.

The joy and glory of the heavenly banquet.

John 6:47–58; Matt. 26:26–29; 1 Cor. 13:12; Ps. 34:8; 36:8; Song 5:1

While on earth we eat the body of our Lord Christ and drink His blood both spiritually in faith and sacramentally with the external mouth in the most worthy Supper, yet hereafter in the heavenly paradise the elect soul no longer sees and tastes in faith nor through a glass darkly, but manifestly, how pleasant and kind its Bridegroom is. It eats of the tree of life which is in the paradise of God and hears the pleasant, gracious voice of its King to all the elect: "Eat, O My beloved ones, and drink My joy and be drunk."

King Ahasuerus's banquet.

Esth. 1:4–8

And this is a true banquet that lasts forever and surpasses all royal splendor and glory that is seen here on earth. When King Ahasuerus caused the mighty men of Persia and Media, the stewards of the land, and the chiefs of his 127 territories to see the glorious riches of his kingdom and the great splendor of his majesty and at his command a magnificent feast was prepared for all the people in the royal garden of Shushan the palace, there were white, red, and yellow hangings of linen fastened with scarlet cords to silver rings and pillars of marble. The couches were of gold and silver, fashioned upon pavement of green, white, yellow, and black marble. And the drinks were carried in vessels of gold and ever diverse vessels and a vast quantity of the royal wine, as the king was able to provide. And no limits were set on what anyone might drink. For the king had commanded all those who presided over his house that everyone should do as he pleased.

The heavenly banquet and feast of the elect souls is given not in an earthly but in a heavenly manner and way.

Now God Almighty in His heavenly paradise before His angels and chosen people uses no such earthly and lovely pomp with couches, benches, dishes, cups of gold and silver, wrought hangings and tapestries, satin and silk, etc., but in an undiscoverable and heavenly manner and way which no man on earth understands and no tongue can tell. Yet the high, unspeakable magnificence and splendor of the everlasting heavenly wedding is indicated by earthly images in Solomon's Song of Songs, as well as here and there in other parts of Scripture, and as it were explained from afar, that in this world we might begin to outline and spell out for young children something of this noble, joyous mystery until one day our soul is summoned from this valley of sorrow in faith and taken up into the paradise of heavenly joy and blessedness, where it sees for itself all things present.

The glory of the heavenly table: It is unspeakable.

But we can truly declare and regard it as undeniable that that nuptial joy and glory in the kingdom of God will appear many hundred thousand times more excellent, stately, lovely, and joyful than if all emperors, kings, princes, and lords from the whole earth brought all their goods, power, pomp, and glory together and spent it all on one banquet.

How Christ comforts the elect soul in paradise after the griefs that it often endured.

Rev. 7:17; Matt. 5:3–12; Luke 16:25

In addition, it is lovely and comforting beyond measure to hear what the Holy Spirit further indicates concerning the elect souls in heaven, namely, that God washes away every tear from their eyes; that is, He comforts them heartily, as a mother comforts her child, and, according as the souls were on earth in anguish and distress, He embraces and kisses them and says to them, "Oh, blessed are you, My love, My bride, My dove, that on earth you were poor in spirit. Behold, now the kingdom of heaven is yours. Oh, how blessed are you, that you have wept and endured suffering. For behold, now you shall laugh and be comforted forever. You were hungry and thirsty for righteousness; now therefore you shall be satisfied. You were persecuted for righteousness's sake; but behold, heaven is yours. Men hated you and shunned you and cursed you and rejected your name as that of a wicked man for My sake, but now rejoice and leap for joy, for behold, great is your reward in heaven."

The soul hears Christ speaking personally in heaven.

Ps. 45:2; Song 5:13; Ps. 19:10

This and similar words of comfort the precious soul hears there, spoken no longer in a glass darkly (as here on earth before) but personally by the only-begotten Son of God, its Bridegroom, and it is heartily glad at this. "Oh, how comforting and gracious are Your lips!" it says. "They are like roses that drip with flowing myrrh, and Your words are sweeter to me than honey and the honeycomb."

The elect soul sees the Lord Christ in His paradise face-to-face.

Ps. 45:2; Rev. 1:14; John 17:24; 1:14; Eph. 1:20; Ps. 8:6; Dan. 7:9; Eph. 4:10; Heb. 1:2–4

There it sees its most dearly beloved, the Lord Jesus, as the fairest of the children of men. It sees His head and His beard white as white wool and white as snow. It sees His eyes as it were flames of fire. It sees His glory which God, His heavenly Father, gave Him, the glory as of the only-begotten Son of God. It sees the two natures, the divine and the human, personally united. It beholds Him exalted to the right hand of God the Father Almighty and seated above all principalities, powers, virtues, dominions, and all that may be named not only in this world but also in the one to come. It beholds all things put under His feet and beholds His filling all things and how the holy angels serve Him and how all creatures are subject to Him.

In Christ it sees the Father manifestly.

Col. 2:9; 1:19; John 14:9–11; Heb. 1:3; 1 John 3:2

In Christ it sees the whole fullness of the Godhead. It sees Him as the exact image of the invisible God. It sees and beholds in Him the face of the almighty, everlasting Father. It sees the Father manifestly in His Son as in a bright gleam and mirror of His glory and in the true reflection of His being. It sees in Christ the Father as He is, and through Christ the Father reveals His fatherly countenance and looks upon the soul as His dear child chosen in Christ. The soul rejoices and is glad forever with Him because of this wondrously lovely, wondrously tender, and wondrously comforting vision of the Father. It sees the Father in the Son and the Son in the Father. It sees the two persons in one indivisible being. It sees both with sweet amazement and can never have enough or grow weary of this seeing and beholding.

In Christ and in the Father it sees the Holy Spirit.

John 16:7; Col. 2:9; John 2:19; Revelation 14; John 3:34; Col. 2:3; Rev. 21:23

It also sees the almighty, everlasting Comforter, God the Holy Spirit. It sees Him in the Father and in the Son. It sees the entire Holy Trinity in distinct Persons and in one eternal, indivisible substance. It sees the Son in the Father, the Father in the Son, and the eternal Holy Spirit in them both. It sees the whole fullness of the Godhead. It sees also the temple of this fullness, the Seed of the woman, and the Son of the noble Virgin. It sees the Spirit given to Him not according to measure. It sees lying hidden in Him all the treasures of wisdom and knowledge. It sees that the blessed Lamb is the lamp of the glory of God.

It sees that God is Love itself, and all things in God are full of fervent love.

1 John [4]:8; Ps. 2:7; John 16:15; Rev. 1:5–6; John 3:16; John 1; 2 Cor. 5; Titus 3:4–7

And how wondrously lovely, wondrously comforting, and wondrously pleasant beyond measure it is that it sees that God is Love itself and that His being is a fire and the coal of love! It sees that in this essential Love the Father begets the Son from love, as the Son dwells in the bosom of the Father, and both the Father and the Son have one Spirit, who is the bond of their love. It also sees and understands that God the Father, out of fervent love, created all things through His Son for the sake of man and man for His own sake and in His own image. It sees the Father's heart—that out of great love He gave the world His Son. It sees that God's Son, out of great love, was made man and appeased the wrath of the Father and redeemed us from death, from the devil, and from hell and obtained for us the Holy Spirit. It sees that the Holy Spirit, out of fervent love, comes from the Father and from the Son and makes us temples of God and children of the eternal light.

The soul in heaven rejoices in the unspeakable love and kindness of God.

Song 1:2, 13–14; 2:5

Its heart is filled with joy when it sees these things, and with joy it marvels at the great, unspeakable honor that our flesh and blood in Christ are so highly exalted and have attained to personal union with the Son of God, and hence the fullness of the Godhead and the fullness of love and kindness gazes out and breaks forth from the same temple. There all things burn and glow with pure heavenly love, joy of love, honor of love, and glory of love. There the Lord Christ kisses the elect soul as His love, His bride, and His sister, with the kiss of His mouth, and to her it is as a bundle of myrrh that hangs between her breasts and as a cluster of camphor in the vineyards of Engedi. He refreshes her with flowers and feeds her with apples from the tree of life. He lays His left hand under her head and His right hand embraces her.

It is restored with the love of God.

It finds in Christ all that its heart desires and would not exchange this life of paradise for heaven and earth. It is restored with the great love with which it is loved by God the Father, God the Son, and God the Holy Spirit. The entire Holy Trinity loves it as God's temple, God's bride, and God's possession. Of this it speaks, of this it sings, on this it ponders forever.

It burns with fervent counter-love for Christ.

There it also burns with perfect counter-love for its most beautiful and most gracious Immanuel. It beholds Him with fervent eyes, as if He were an army set in array, and embraces Him with true, burning love as with a necklace of gold. It devises and reveals to Him its loving heart, as if reaching its breasts to him, and blesses, praises, honors, and exalts Him with choice words as if sheer milk and honey were under its tongue and its lips flowed from a dripping honeycomb. All its actions are indications of the holy, perfect counter-love and its whole heavenly life is like a fragrance of love which surpasses all spices, for it is anointed and filled with the Holy Spirit, who thoroughly possesses, cleanses, and illuminates it so that it looks wondrously beautiful and is pleasing to its Bridegroom. It takes His heart and closes it in its heart and therein lets it well up eternally as a living water, and what it does with it in its heart, it expresses publicly before all angels by means of various heavenly hymns, precious psalms, and sweet songs of praise, precisely as if it were a closed spring and a fenced garden of all pleasant fruits and of the best spices.

The heavenly Bridegroom, Jesus Christ, blesses the heartfelt love of His entrusted souls.

Song 6:4–5; 4:9–15

Its Bridegroom blesses this fidelity and love toward Him and extols it before God His Father and before the whole host of heaven. "You are beautiful, O My love," He says, "as Tirzah, as comely as Jerusalem, terrible as an army set in array. Turn away your eyes from Me, for they make Me to burn. You have taken My heart, my sister, dear bride, with one of your eyes and with one chain of your neck. How beautiful is your love, My sister, dear bride! Your love is finer than wine, and the fragrance of your soul surpasses all spices. Your lips, O My bride, are like dripping honeycomb: honey and milk are under your tongue, and the smell of your garments is like the fragrance of Lebanon. My sister, dear bride, you are like a garden enclosed, a spring shut up, a fountain sealed. Your plants are like an orchard of pomegranates, with pleasant fruit; camphor, with spikenard, spikenard with saffron; calamus and cinnamon, with all the trees of frankincense; myrrh and aloes, with the best spices: like the fount of a garden, like a well of living waters flowing from Lebanon."

Testimony of St. Augustine to the blessedness of the soul, Meditations, ch. 23[125]

St. Augustine uses many similar words from Solomon's Song of Songs and applies them to the elect soul and its blessed condition in eternal life. "Blessed," he says, "is the soul released from the earthly body, which ascends free and unhindered into heaven, is safe and at peace, and fears neither foe nor death. For it has always before it and sees the most immaculate Lord, whom it has served, whom it has loved, and to whom it has come with joy and rejoicing. This glory and honor of this blessedness endures eternally, and no ungodly man can diminish or take it away.

All children of light in the heavenly paradise honor the elect soul ascending from the world into heaven. Christ addresses the soul most tenderly.

Song 6:8; 8:5; 6:9; 2:11–14; Matt. 25:21; John 16:22

"When the daughters of Zion saw it,[126] they proclaimed it blessed: the queens and the concubines praised it, saying, 'Who is that who comes up from the wilderness, moving in delight, leaning upon its beloved?' Who is that arising as the dawn, fair as the moon, elect as the sun, terrible as the army set in array? How joyful it goes forth! How it hastens, and how it runs, when it hears with astonishment its Beloved saying to it, 'Arise, My love, My fair one, and come! For lo, the winter is past, the rain has over and gone! The flowers have appeared on the earth, the spring has come, and the turtledove is heard in our land. The fig tree has put forth green figs, and the vines have budded and given their fragrance. Arise, My love, and come, My fair one. Come, My dove, into the holes of the rock, into the clefts of stone. Show Me your face; let Me hear your voice; for your voice is sweet and your face is comely. Come, My elect, My fair one, My dove, My pure one, My bride. Come, and I will set you upon My throne, that I may see your face.

125 Author uncertain, *Meditationes* 23 (PL 40:918).

126 That is, the soul. "It, its" here for "her," etc., since English does not use the grammatical gender which rhetorically connects the Latin *anima* (f.) with the bride in Song of Songs.

Come, that you may rejoice in My presence with My angels, whose fellowship I have promised you. Come, after you have suffered and endured so many and various perils, griefs, distresses, and labors, come, and enter into the joy of your Lord, which no man shall take from you.'" Thus far Augustine.

The elect soul sits with Christ upon His throne.

Rev. 3:21; 2:26–28

Relevant here is the fact that the elect soul dwells with Christ, its royal Bridegroom, in an undivided life and on the same throne on which He sits, that it may reign and govern. For His promise reads: "He who overcomes, to him will I grant to sit with Me upon My throne, even as I have overcome, and am seated with My Father upon His throne. And he who overcomes and keeps My works unto the end, to him will I give power over the nations, and he shall rule them with a rod of iron, and as the vessels of a potter shall he break them; even as I have received power from My Father. And I will give him the morning star."

What the elect souls do in heaven with Christ. Answer: they rule with Him.

In these precious, comforting promises we find a thorough answer to the question, what kind of works the souls of the elect are able to do with Christ in His heavenly paradise before the Last Day, especially the souls of the apostles, the dear holy fathers Athanasius, Augustine, Ignatius, Polycarp, etc., and all faithful teachers, martyrs, preachers, church ministers, and confessors of the noble truth, who have borne witness to the Gospel, rebuked false teaching, idolatry, vice, hypocrisy, shame, and iniquity in every age of the world and by the stirring of the Holy Spirit carried out these works unto death? Here I can answer and say: They sit with Christ upon His throne and reign with Him over the nations and with a rod of iron break them as the vessels of a potter.

The glory of the soul's ruling with Christ is unfathomable.

Rev. 14:13–15

In this life, however, we are unable to learn in the least how this may properly come to pass. I can only say in truth that it is a great heavenly glory to sit with Christ upon His throne and with Him to rule, govern, and subdue the opposing enemies, and that these works of heavenly governance begin in the elect Christians immediately after their death, as it is written: "Blessed are the dead who die in the Lord from henceforth. Yes, says the Spirit, that they may rest from their labor. For their works follow them." Here, you hear that godly Christians and faithful servants of the Word have great toil and labor on earth, namely, with upright teaching, confession of the truth, and opposition to idolatry, sects, and factious spirits. There they are ridiculed, persecuted, and executed, and so their labors must continue till death. Now when they have died, this wearisome labor is ended, but their works follow them, and then at last they reign and judge the world with Christ and break the nations and with great astonishment see how all those threats are fulfilled, effected, and brought to completion with which they threatened the contemptuous world according to the Word of God and rebuked it relentlessly with zealous sermons of repentance.

Example of the shared governance.

Rev. 18:20

We have a glorious example of this in the holy prophets and apostles, who foretold the coming, tyranny, and downfall of the pope. And although they have long since died and are not now living in this age, when the Roman Antichrist's kingdom, the whore of Babylon, has been discovered, revealed, and cast down by the pure doctrine of the Gospel, nevertheless the Holy Spirit bids them rejoice and shows that God has performed their judgment on the whore: "Rejoice over her, O heavens," He says, "and you holy apostles and prophets. For God has executed your judgment against her." I can say the same about Luther, that dear man of God. Although he died fifty years ago[127] and is no longer writing against the papacy and factious spirits, nevertheless he sits this day with Christ upon His throne and breaks His enemies as the vessels of a potter and mightily fulfills his saying:

> Pope, I will be your plague; your death I will be after dying.[128]

Ps. 149:4–6

Likewise, all godly teachers govern and rule with Christ this day—John Hus, Jerome, Bugenhagen, Brenz, Urbanus Rhegius, etc.[129]—who gave God the glory, publicly testified to the evangelical truth, and in the Church of God laid bare papistic idolatry, as well as the errors of the Sacramentarians, Anabaptists, Schwenkfelders, and factious spirits of their ilk, and forcefully refuted them with the Word of God. They rule and govern with Christ, although we do not see or

127 Luther died in 1546, thus 53 years previously.

128 See *Table Talk* no. 3543a–b, WA TR 3:390, 392; cf. Johann Bugenhagen, *A Christian Sermon for the Funeral and Burial of the Reverend Dr. Martin Luther* (1546), AE Bio:35 (= *Eine Christliche Predigt/ über der Leich und begrebnis/ des Ehrwirdigen D. Martini Luthers* [Wittenberg: Georg Rhau, 1546]).

129 John Hus (1369–1415), Jerome of Prague (ca. 1379–1416), and Girolamo (Jerome) Savonarola (1452–98) taught against the practices of the Roman Church of their day, especially the practice of Communion in one kind for the laity, indulgences, and the immorality of the clergy. Hus and Jerome were condemned as heretics by the Council of Constance and burned at the stake. Savonarola also was charged with heresy and executed in Florence. Johann Bugenhagen (1485–1558), Johann Brenz (1499–1570), and Urbanus Rhegius (1489–1541) were contemporaries of and fellow reformers with Martin Luther. Bugenhagen served as pastor of St. Mary's in Wittenberg and also traveled extensively to help establish Evangelical teaching throughout Germany and in Denmark. Brenz especially advanced Lutheran reform in southwest Germany. Rhegius was the leading reformer of Augsburg and published frequently in support of Lutheran teaching.

know what it is like and how this governance is done. "Let the saints rejoice," says David, "and glorify and boast upon their beds. Let their mouth exalt God and sharp swords be in their hands, that they may exercise vengeance among the nations, punishment among the Gentiles, to bind their kings with chains and their nobles with bands of iron, that they may treat them justly, for it is written, such honor shall all His saints possess."

With what the godly teachers fought in this world, and how they now rule with Christ after death.

Heb. 4:12; 1 Cor. 6:2–3; Ps. 4:3

The Word of God was their weapon and two-edged sword in this world, with which they fought the devil and his fellows, and therefore were made to suffer all manner of danger, derision, mockery, and persecution. Of this they now speak with Christ personally and tell Him it, and He comforts them and causes them to sit with Him upon His throne and shows them the power of His Word, how He wondrously protects and sustains His Church and the precious truth against the devil's cunning and violence. Here the blessed teachers in Christ shout for joy in their almighty Prince of victory who trampled the serpent and see the whole governance of heaven and earth, the rule of His kingdom, how wondrously He leads His saints in the world through the cross, and they themselves help to judge the world and have the desire and joy of their heart in seeing how, presently, before the Last Day, the Gospel is spread throughout Europe, Asia, Africa, America, and every land, and the devil's kingdom is mightily destroyed.

Example of the glory of the temporal government.

You would count it a great glory if you were able to be the sultan of Constantinople, to sit there on the imperial throne, and to reign over many important islands of the Mediterranean Sea, and to learn every day and every hour what was happening in every land, in every city, fortress, village, and town. But what is this passing glory and majesty compared to that of an elect soul in the paradise of eternal life? There as a royal bride the soul sits with Christ, its Bridegroom, upon His throne and sees not only how He mightily governs the great edifice of heaven and earth and calls, gathers, enlightens, and sanctifies His Church throughout the whole wide world, but also itself helps to judge the world, to sentence the enemies, and to break them as the vessels of a potter.

Even in this world a Christian rules over death, devil, and hell, but here it is a hidden rule concealed beneath the cross.

John 16:33; 1 John 5:4; Eph. 6:12; Heb. 4; 2 Cor. 10:8; Rom. 8:17; Rev. 3:21; 2:26

But an elect soul, who has overcome the last hurdle of death and in saving faith bidden farewell to the world, dwells in the paradise of God and rules with its Bridegroom, Jesus Christ, no longer through a glass darkly, but manifestly, as a serene queen, in great majesty, power, and glory. And it does not possess this power of itself, but receives it from its Brother, Jesus Christ, just as He received authority from His heavenly Father. Therefore, He says explicitly that he who overcomes, to him will He grant to sit with Him upon His throne, just as He overcame and sat down with His Father upon His throne, and that He will also give him authority over the nations, just as He received it from His Father.

The soul's communion with Christ in His heavenly paradise is a superior glory.

Oh, the superior honor of the great splendor and the mighty glory, that the soul of a godly Christian who has fallen blessedly asleep in the Lord has a portion and part not only with the holy angels and archangels, cherubim and seraphim, and all the heavenly thrones, principalities, and dominions, but also with Jesus Christ, the great King of heaven and earth, its wondrously sweet and wondrously comforting and wondrously beautiful Bridegroom, and sits with Him upon His throne, that it may reign and govern with Him over death, devil, and hell and the whole wide world! Oh, the blessed gladness and bliss, that in Christ, as in a bright mirror and reflection of the divine radiance, it sees the wondrously tender face of the everlasting, almighty Father and at the same time sees in the Father and in the Son the true Paraclete, the heavenly Comforter and Gladdener, God the Holy Spirit! Oh, the noble wedding banquet and the royal joy of paradise with which it is forever crowned and encircled!

The second glory is far higher and greater than the first, although both go together.

Truly, this second glory spreads its wings on high and rises above all the world's splendor, majesty, power, honor, and glory. It is also many thousand times higher, nobler, and grander than the first—as much higher as God is than His angels and as much as our fellowship with God surpasses the fellowship that we have with the holy angels. Yet they both are appropriated in that world so that the elect souls simultaneously have a blessed fellowship with God and with His holy, heavenly spirits and rejoice over both. They rejoice forever with God the Father, rejoice forever with God the Son, rejoice forever with God the Holy Spirit, and rejoice forever with all the holy angels.

(3) The third glory of the elect souls in heaven is their blessed fellowship which they have with the patriarchs, prophets, apostles, and all godly men.

The third glory of the elect soul in the fatherland of eternal life is its blessed and joyful communion which it has with all the elect patriarchs, prophets, apostles, and other triumphant Christians who died entirely to the world and this perishable life and have passed into eternal life.

Gen. 15:15; 25:8; 35:28–29; 49:33

For the soul of a true Christian, as soon as he has fallen asleep in the Lord, ascends from the mouth up to heaven and there arrives at a great people and multitude of the children of God who have gone before us and await our arrival in the heavenly paradise on high. "You shall go," says the Lord to Abraham, "to your fathers with peace." And afterward, Scripture says, "Abraham died in peaceful old age, when he was old and satisfied of life, and was gathered to his people." So also of Isaac: "Isaac decreased and died, and was gathered to his people, old and satisfied of life." Likewise: "Jacob put his feet together on the bed, and departed, and was gathered to his people."

Testimony of Luther, tom. 10, Wit. Germ., fols. 587, 597[130]

On this verse, Luther writes, "This is a beautiful and glorious comfort, namely, the most lovely description of death, which he does not call death, but speaks pleasantly and sweetly of it thus: 'You shall go to your fathers, and rest with Noah and other mighty men.'" Likewise in another place: "These words of the Holy Spirit are not in vain, nor are they addressed to senseless beasts, but to men, and they testify powerfully that after this life there is another and better, in that also before the advent and incarnation of Christ there was a people which dwelt in the land of the living and to which the faithful were gathered from this life." And immediately thereafter: "The words in both texts are set down precisely and plainly: 'You will be gathered to the other saints who died before you.' Therefore, the fathers live and are people, which is not said of the ungodly, but is only said of the holy and righteous."

Example of the heavenly gathering.

Luke 16:22; Matt. 17:3; 2 Sam. 12:23

We find reliable examples also by which this gathering and fellowship of the saints in the heavenly paradise is confirmed. For Lazarus lived many hundred years after the time of Abraham, yet as soon as he died, he was promptly carried by the angels to Abraham's bosom. Likewise, Elijah lived several hundred years after Moses, but when he ascended into heaven, he came to Moses, for which reason they were together on the holy mountain at the time of Christ's transfiguration, both conversing with Christ. In addition, David says of his dead infant that the infant will not come to him, but he, the father, will go to the infant, which later occurred when he fell asleep and was gathered to his people.

The elect soul is gathered to its people after death.

Come, then! We have a strong and sure basis that, when a Christian dies blessedly in the Lord and his soul departs from hence, it is then received and escorted in grand fashion by the holy angels, comes into paradise to its most beloved Bridegroom, Jesus Christ, and there finds with Him a great people and number of many elect souls. Indeed, you hear that it goes to its fathers and is gathered to its people. By this it is clearly shown that an orthodox Christian's soul comes to its kinsmen, father, mother, brothers, sisters, relatives, and acquaintances who, in

130 From *Lectures on Genesis* (1535–45): cf. AE 3:39; 4:310 (= WA 42:576.19–21; 43:358.24–28, 29–32).

faith and blessed confidence in the blood of Christ, departed before and passed through death into the heavenly fatherland. Then a dying brother or a dying sister comes out of this valley of sorrow to them and is gathered to them as soon as death is past and has eternal fellowship with them.

Whether the elect souls in heaven also see one another.

Luke 16:23

Neither may we doubt that this fellowship is visible, although the substance of the soul, as also the substance of the angels, is not to be seen in this world with the physical eyes. For, as I have also said above, just as the angels of God are invisible spirits to our physical eyes and cannot be seen in this world with carnal eyes, yet they are certainly able to see one another. In the same way, the souls of men also are invisible spirits, which are not seen with carnal eyes in this world, but, when they are released from the mortal tents of their bodies and are separated and cut off from the world by temporal death, they can certainly see one another, as the account of the rich man and poor Lazarus attests, about which the Lord Christ states that the rich man, after his death, when he had been buried and lay in hell, lifted up his eyes and saw from afar Lazarus in Abraham's bosom.

The elect, godly souls in the heavenly paradise see one another face-to-face.

Matt. 17:3; Deut. 34:5; Jude 9

Likewise, Moses and Elijah saw each other on the holy mountain at the time of our Lord Jesus Christ's transfiguration. And it is well to note that Scripture expressly states that Moses died in the land of the Moabites and was buried in the valley of the same land by the house of Peor and that the archangel Michael disputed with the devil about the body of Moses. I interpret these words simply as they sound, by which it is shown that Moses truly died and his body was truly buried. Nevertheless, he appears with Elijah on the holy mountain, conversing with the Lord Christ. From this it irrefutably follows and is clearly to be concluded that not only Enoch and Elijah, who were taken up body and soul into heaven, but also the souls of deceased godly Christians, with great clarity and glory see one another face-to-face in the heavenly paradise of eternal life, though our flesh and blood do not yet comprehend how this may be.

The elect souls in heaven recognize one another.

Luke 16:23; 23:43

However, they not only see one another, but in their seeing one another, they also recognize one another; for the rich man recognizes Lazarus from afar despite the fact that he is lying in hell. And how should an elect soul know that it has been gathered to its people if it does not recognize its people in that world? Furthermore, if that life of the children of light in heaven is a life of paradise, as the Lord says to the thief ("Today you will be with Me in paradise")—if, I say, it is a life of paradise, it follows that just as Adam and Eve in the earthly paradise, before sin and death entered the world, knew each other and loved each other from their heart, so also triumphant Christians in the heavenly paradise of eternal life, after they have overcome sin and death by faith in Christ, embrace and recognize one another with pure, untainted love.

Adam and Eve recognized each other in the earthly paradise.

Gen. 2:23

It was a true life of paradise on earth when Adam was without sin and recognized his wife, Eve, when she was first brought to him immediately after his slumber. He did not ask, "What kind of creature are you? Where do you come from? What do you seek?" but said at once, "This is bone of my bone and flesh of my flesh. She shall be called woman because she was taken from man." Likewise, the woman at once recognizes her husband from whose rib she was formed and does not ask at length who and from whence he might be, but joins and clings to him as her own flesh and blood and truly familiar friend. Behold, such was the pleasant existence and familiarity among men in the earthly paradise before anything was known of sin and the power of death!

The children of light recognize their friends and relatives in heaven as soon as they have passed from this world through temporal death into eternal life.

In the same way, it may also be said of the heavenly paradise, which is free from the wrath of God, sin, and all tribulations of death and is swept clean, that the souls of the elect know one another there as Adam and Eve did before the fall. And when someone there sees his brother, sister, father, mother, etc., departing from the world and the noble soul putting off the mortal body and coming in the company of holy angels, he knows it at once and does not ask long who he or she is, but says without hesitation, "Behold, there comes my dear father! Behold, there ascends my dear mother! Behold, that is my brother, my sister, my cousin, my aunt, my kinsman, etc., who is coming, and ascending from the world's deep valley of sorrow up to us in this paradise! Oh, welcome in the name of the Lord, my dear father, my dear mother, my dear husband, my dear wife, my dear brother, my dear sister, my dear kinsman! O God be praised forever that I should see you come and be gathered to this our people! Oh, joy of joys, that you also have swallowed up death in the victory of our Savior, Jesus Christ, and by faith have passed into eternal life and to us!"

A godly soul that departs this world into the heavenly fatherland immediately recognizes there its friends who died and left this world before it.

Likewise, as Eve immediately recognized her Adam as soon as she saw him in the earthly paradise, so the elect soul of a godly Christian, as soon as it has put off the tent of its body and passed through death into life, immediately recognizes all its friends who died and were gathered together in the heavenly paradise long before it. And it does not ask at length, "Who are you? What is your name?" but says at once, "O dear father, O dear mother, O dear husband, O dear wife, O dear child, O dear brother, O dear sister, O dear kinsmen, do I find you all rejoicing in this precious paradise and land of the living? Then thanks and praise, honor and worship be to the Lord Jesus, our Redeemer and omnipotent King of glory, with God the Father and God the Holy Spirit forever and ever! Alleluia! Oh, then let us rejoice, shout for joy, and be glad, and joyfully await the Last Day and the blessed resurrection of our body!"

The elect souls know one another better in heaven than they did on earth.

In addition, I hold without doubt that the elect souls of the deceased friends and family, such as father, mother, husband, wife, children, brother, sister, neighbors, relations, etc., know one another many thousand times better in that life than they did in this world. For in this world bitterness, anger, and strife at times interrupted it. But there they are in a state of perfection, delivered and purified from all sins, so that they love God with all their heart, with all their soul, and with all their mind, and they love one another as themselves. Now, therefore, if love toward God and toward neighbor is, as it ought to be, entire and perfect, then so must knowledge, which is a good portion of love, be free from deficiency. It must be just as perfect and precisely as strong as love.

They rejoice in the blessed friendship that they have with the patriarchs, prophets, and apostles.

Matt. 8:11

But especially they rejoice at the glorious friendship which they fully enjoy with the holy patriarchs, prophets, and apostles, of whom they heard and read a great deal in this world. But there they converse with them personally and hear them speak for themselves, and so they fulfill the prophecy of the Lord Christ, when He says that many shall come from the east and the west and sit at table with Abraham, Isaac, and Jacob in the kingdom of God. The more zealous, therefore, a Christian has been in this life for the pure doctrine of the Gospel and the greater eagerness he had for the godly patriarchs, prophets, and apostles, the more intensely and more highly will he be extolled and honored by them.

Example: Dr. Luther has blessed fellowship today in that life with all the elect saints.

Dr. Bugenhagen, in his funeral sermon[131] for the blessed Dr. Luther, sets that man before us as an example of this when he writes, "We should rejoice with Dr. Luther in the wholly joyful, blessed, eternal fellowship that he now enjoys with God and the Son of God, our Lord Jesus Christ, and with the holy fathers,

131 Nicolai misidentifies the source of this material. It is from Philipp Melanchthon, *Oration at the Funeral of Dr. Martin Luther* (1546): cf. AE Bio:48–49 (= *Oratio in Funere Reverendi Viri D. Martini Lutheri* [Leipzig: Valentin Babst, 1546]; cf. CR 11:726–34).

prophets, and apostles—that place, which, during his life, in faith and confidence in the Son of God, he always most highly desired and awaited with great longing, where he now not only hears that his difficult labor and faithful care that he took to plant and spread the pure doctrine of the Gospel are lauded and honored by God and the whole heavenly blessed Church in eternal life, but also he himself, being released from this mortal body as from a prison and coming to a different and far higher and more glorious school of divinity, now sees and discerns in plain sight the high, unfathomable, eternal essence of the divine Majesty and the two natures, divine and human, united in the single person of the Son of God, and the entire, lofty, marvelous divine counsel by which He created and redeemed His Church in mankind. And, because he pondered by faith this immeasurably lofty and incomprehensible matter here enveloped and covered in the Word and brief sayings of divine Scripture, he now has the unspeakable joy to behold these things manifestly before his eyes and gives thanks to God without ceasing for this highest of all benefits."

Dr. Luther had great longing to see the blessed fathers and has now come to them.

Likewise:[132] "Many of us also still remember how eagerly and with what great pleasure he used to speak of the holy prophets' governance among the people of God and of their doctrine and good counsel and of their struggle, peril, and persecution which they suffered and how God delivered them wondrously and how with great understanding and high wisdom Luther compared the whole age of the Church of God in the world, that he might sufficiently show how great a longing he had to be with those lofty people. Now he has joined them and rejoices to hear their living voice and to talk with them. And they in turn are heartily glad in this their schoolfellow and fellow servant, they have received and saluted him kindly, and so both he and they give endless thanks to God, who out of boundless grace and goodness has gathered and preserved His Church in mankind." Thus far Dr. Bugenhagen.

What the elect souls discuss.

Luke 16:25; Gen. 4:10; Rev. 6:10

The souls also discuss their grief, cross, persecution, and misery, which each was made to endure and allow to pass over him in the vile, obnoxious world, as may be deduced from the fact that Abraham the patriarch says of Lazarus that his life on earth was evil, and now he is comforted; likewise, from the fact that the souls of the slain Christians cry out and lament over their persecutors.

132 Nicolai misidentifies the source of this material. It is from Philipp Melanchthon, *Oration at the Funeral of Dr. Martin Luther* (1546): cf. AE Bio:50 (= *Oratio in Funere Reverendi Viri D. Martini Lutheri* [Leipzig: Valentin Babst, 1546]; cf. CR 11:726–34).

The elect souls in heaven speak of the sorrows and afflictions which they endured in this world. Example of St. Paul.

2 Cor. 11:23–30; 2 Cor. 4:17; Phil. 1:21

But they speak of the anguish and molten misery which they bore, not that they still feel some of these sorrows and afflictions, but rather they extol the exceeding high comfort that they richly and superabundantly received from God Almighty. Of this we may take an example from the apostle Paul, who now and then laments in his epistles the persecution with which the devil assailed him. But he takes comfort in the coming glory that he knows is prepared for him after death. Now there is no doubt that, just as he wrote of these things, he would also speak of them orally with the elect of God in the heavenly paradise and say, "I was often captured, often in the throes of death, I was in danger by water, in danger among robbers, in danger among the Gentiles, in danger in the cities, in danger in the wilderness, in danger at sea, in danger among false brethren; in toil and labor, in much keeping vigil, in hunger and thirst, in much fasting, in frost and nakedness, but now I see that my temporal sufferings were not worthy to be compared with the glory that is now revealed to me. I see now that my temporal and easy afflictions produced for me an eternal and immeasurably weighty glory. On earth, Christ was my life, but now I see how dying has become my gain, and I have thereby multiplied life much more."

Sweet conversation of godly parents, children, husband, wife, brothers, sisters, etc., in that life.

Likewise, all godly Christians, and especially familiar kinsmen (whom death here on earth has separated), come joyfully together in that heavenly paradise so that one says to another, "O dear father, mother, brother, sister, etc., how often we suffered many kinds of danger, anguish, and misery in the world! And how often one of us had to lament his distress to another! How troubled, despondent, wretched, and forsaken I was when you died and left me behind as a widow, an orphan, or a poor child! How many tears I shed for you and nearly wept my eyes dry! Now, behold, our grief, tribulation, and misery has come to a blessed end, and although our bodies now are dead and rest in the earth, yet our souls are alive and free from all lamentation, and here we appear together again in great, unspeakable joy."

Glorious joy and bliss of the elect soul.

John 16:21–22

Then their heart is filled with joy and bliss, and as a wife, when she has given birth, no longer remembers her anguish for joy that a man has been born into the world, so also is their joy in heaven many thousand times greater than their sorrow and heaviness was with which they were pained and tormented in the world.

Their heart is full of joy, and with gladness they praise and glorify in unison God the Father, God the Son, and God the Holy Spirit and are also eternal consorts and fellows of the holy angels in eternal joy and in eternal heavenly glory and await us with heartfelt joy and hope, that we, after the completion of our temporal life in this world, also may come to their joy and the place of their glad assembly.

Comparison to the kingdom of China located in the east. (Here refer to the books of Johannes Mondria Hispanus.) Glory of the fields as well as the cottages and pleasure gardens in China. Customs and usages of the Chinese.

People have written of the mighty and far-flung kingdom of China in the furthest Orient beyond India and of its fifteen provinces, its exceedingly great and many cities, its surpassingly great riches in pearls, precious stones, gold, silver, and all metals, and of its wise governance and political order, the likes of which have never been found in any chronicle of the Medes, the Persians, Assyrians, Indians, Greeks, Romans, or any other nation in the wide world. The cities are all surrounded by big, strong walls of hewn stones: the walls are high, white, and strong, so that they can scarcely be pierced by a pickax, and augmented from place to place with pinnacles and towers and with very beautiful castles outwardly and furnished with pleasure paths and gardens. The streets in the country are made with great care, and the streets in the cities are paved in the most beautiful way and so broad that fifteen men on horseback can ride abreast. The streets are also furnished with many triumphal arches in equal distance from one another and of good worked stones, engraved and prepared with very numerous and various beautiful and amusing engravings, like the ancient works of Rome, from which they are as fair to look upon as ever might be. The houses on the inside are white like milk and the walls as if they were covered with polished paper, the beams made of precious wood and spread with gold paint so that they gleam brightly. In addition, all the houses have courtyards and gardens full of flowers and plants, and there is none that lacks a fishpond, no matter how small it may be. The fields of that country are not only fertile, but also utterly pleasant to look upon and exude a lovely fragrance, for they bear many and various sweet-smelling flowers of countless varieties, along with the fact that the hedges beside the streams and brooks which run through them make the country very attractive. There is a great number of beautiful gardens and cottages much employed by the people for leisure and refreshment. They converse with one another amiably, with propriety and honor, and have a great many happy assemblies where they not only eat and drink but also enjoy pleasant diversions with fiddles, harps, lutes, cornetts, clavichords, lyres, flutes, and other instruments. In short, the kingdom of China is described and extolled in such a way that it might well be called a paradise on earth.

If our deceased kinsmen had gone to the kingdom of China and there become rich lords, we would rejoice. Much more should we rejoice and count it a great glory that they are in heaven.

Here when I am in mourning at the mortal departure of my godly kinsmen, I take thought and say to my soul, "Why are you downcast, and why so disquieted within me for the death of my relatives? They have fallen blessedly asleep in the Lord and now dwell in the heavenly paradise of eternal life. If they had gone to China, and someone brought the trustworthy report that there in the most beautiful cities, in the beautiful cottages and pleasure gardens, they had all been welcomed, honored, and entertained in the most glorious manner as if they were kings, princes, and mighty potentates and knew of no anguish, of no tribulation or misery any longer, but were all happy and in good spirits without ceasing and were awaiting your arrival with gladness, that you might come to them as soon as possible and partake of their royal glory, splendor, and prosperity, truly, you would rejoice at these tidings and would feel just as the godly patriarch Jacob must have felt when he thought his son Joseph had died and then learned after a few years that he was still alive and was the royal steward of all Egypt."

All the world's kingdoms with their splendor cannot compare to the glory of the heavenly paradise.

But what is the kingdom of China and what is Egypt compared to the heavenly paradise of eternal joy and glory? If the elect souls are together in the heavenly Canaan and in the city of the living God above (which thing no Christian man should doubt) and lead a nuptial life with the only-begotten Son of God, their fairest Bridegroom, they are many hundred thousand times better thus and in greater joy, glory, and prosperity than if they sat at table with the splendid king of China and took a stroll there in the most sumptuous salon, of which people write that it is covered with nothing but carbuncles and other stones in such a grand and sumptuous manner that the salon thereby shines as brightly and clearly in the gloomiest night as if it contained burning candles.

Glory of the heavenly dwelling, the heavenly joy, the heavenly fellowship.

The heavenly dwelling, as well as the heavenly glory, splendor, joy, and pleasure, of the blessed elect souls is exceedingly higher, nobler, and more prestigious, and their assembly, society, and fellowship with God and His holy angels surpasses any fellowship that a man on earth may enjoy with earthly kings, princes, and lords because God loves them and is in turn loved by them with all their heart, with all their soul, and with all their mind. And from this love and counter-love they shine brighter than the glorious sun, just as their fellowship which they have with one another is nothing else than fervent love, full of heavenly radiance and glory.

The souls of the elect in the heavenly paradise also remember their kinsmen left below.

Besides all this, I will not deny that the souls, although they live and move in unviewable joy and bliss, nevertheless remember their father, mother, brothers, sisters, husband, wife, children, etc., which they left below. For in hell, the rich man remembers his five brothers with the sincere wish that they might be warned against this torment and pain. If the damned man does so, how much more do the elect also remember their kinsmen? In addition, pure, perfect love prevents one from forgetting one's neighbor since it loves him as itself. And the souls in heaven are angelically pure and without sin and exist completely in love, in that they love God above all things and their neighbor as themselves. And if they love their neighbors as themselves and remember them, then surely they must not forget those of their familiar society which has been left behind.

Explanation of Isaiah's saying, "Abraham does not know us," etc.

Isa. 63:16. Rev. 2:23; 19:10

Now, therefore, when the prophet Isaiah says, "You are our Father, for Abraham does not know of us, and Israel does not acknowledge us," it is to be understood as referring to the searching and examination of our heart with respect to the troubles that weigh upon us, our depressing thoughts, and our various heavy tribulations, as well as the hearing of our groanings and prayer, which indeed neither can nor may be addressed to any other person either in heaven or on earth but the eternal, omnipotent God and Jesus Christ, His only-begotten Son, who alone with the Father and the Holy Spirit desires to be prayed to and called upon and who alone knows and understands our thoughts, as His words declare, where He says, "All the churches shall acknowledge that I am He who searches the heart and the reins." Therefore, this work may not be appropriated to any angel, much less to any man, as though they should search the reins and the heart, discern the thoughts, and answer the prayer. We see this also in the holy angel on whom St. John wished to call in his Revelation, when he refuses this honor and says, "See that you do it not. I am the fellow servant of yours and of your brothers and of those who hold the testimony. Worship God."

Although the holy angels and elect souls in heaven are not searchers of hearts and hearers of our prayers, nevertheless they remember us.

But despite the fact that the dear angels do not search the reins and the heart and do not hear our prayer, which honor is to be ascribed only to the Most High, nevertheless they are constantly around us and with us, remember us, and rejoice in us when they see that we repent and cling diligently to the Gospel, into which they delight to look with us. Likewise, I can say of the patriarch Abraham that, although he is in heaven and does not know our thoughts on earth and does not know the troubles and anguish which weigh upon us, nor our groanings and prayers, as Isaiah testifies, nevertheless he certainly knows of the rich man's five brothers which he left behind, as seen in the evangelist Luke, that they have Moses and the prophets, and wishes that they may hear them and obey them.

Elijah the prophet in heaven remembers his disciple Elisha.

2 Kings 2:9–10. Luther.

In the same way, the prophet Elijah promises to intercede with God on behalf of his disciple Elisha and to assure him that, when he should be taken from him alive up to heaven, a double portion of his spirit would be with him. Likewise, the blessed man of God and the third Elijah, Dr. Luther, writes in his letter to the provost of Bremen shortly before his death:[133] "As little as I doubt that your prayer for me is efficacious, so little should you doubt that mine avails for you. Even if I go before you (which I hope), yet I will draw you after me. But if you go before me, you will draw me after you. For we confess one God and with all the saints await our Savior."

Our deceased kinsmen in heaven remember us.

Now as there is no doubt that the prophet Elijah, when he came to heaven, did not forget his disciple Elisha, but by holy intercession procured for him from God the double power and operation of the Holy Spirit, and just as Luther promised that he would remember the godly provost and, with Christian intercession, draw him after him to eternal life if he should be the first to die and depart the world to God, so I have no doubt that godly parents in heaven remember their children left behind on earth and that godly children who are with God in paradise remember their dear parents, brothers, sisters, and good kinsmen who are still on earth.

The thoughts of the elect souls in heaven are not carnal but spiritual.

And these thoughts of theirs without a doubt conform to the standard of perfect Christian love so that an elect soul in heaven is no longer carnally minded, but only spiritually, and says, "I am, God be praised, in this precious, beautiful paradise! My parents, my husband or wife, my children, my brothers, my sisters, etc., are still on earth, and my heart's desire is that they may all believe the Gospel and be saved. Now, then, they have Moses and the prophets, and in addition the writings of the evangelists and apostles. O Lord, my God, grant that they may listen to them. If they do so, they will also pass through death into this paradise and be my dear parents, my husband, my wife, my children, my brothers, my sisters and remain so forever. If not, You, O Lord, are just to punish and condemn them, and I will no longer acknowledge or think of them as my parents, children, brothers, sisters, etc. For although they are dear to me, yet You, O Lord my God, are many hundred thousand times and immeasurably dearer, and I love You so

133 From Luther's letter to Jacob Probst, January 17 1546: cf. WA Br 11:263.

heartily that all those things which, according to Your righteousness, You hate, curse, and condemn, I also hate, curse, and condemn, no matter if they be called father, mother, husband, wife, children, brothers, or sisters."

Intercession of the godly parents in heaven on behalf of their children left behind.

These are the thoughts of the patriarch Abraham in heaven, as may be deduced from his words, which may also rightly be ascribed to every elect soul there, and it may certainly be the case that, when the godly parents die and their children follow soon after, or whenever anyone else falls asleep in the Lord and his trusty kinsmen shortly thereafter also takes his blessed Christian departure, that the deceased godly parents and kinsmen who went before secured this from God with their intercession, in consideration that the world is ungodly and desperately wicked, and young children, as well as other pious hearts, may soon be deceived and be tragically deprived of their blessedness. Therefore, when a godly mother dies and the child follows shortly thereafter, I am pleased to hear it said, "Oh, his mother prayed for him. There is not much good to meet with in the world. Therefore, God heard the parents' prayer and could do no better for the child than to take him away from here."

Blessedness of the godly children who die in infancy.

Wisdom 4:10–16

"He pleases God," says Scripture, "and is beloved of Him and is taken away from life among sinners and is set apart, lest wickedness pervert his understanding or false teaching beguile his soul. For the evil examples deceive and corrupt the good to one, and the jesting passion perverts innocent hearts. He was made perfect in a short time and fulfilled many years. For his soul pleases God; therefore, He brings him out of this life hastily. But the people who see it do not regard it or take it to heart, namely, that the saints of God are in grace and mercy and that He has respect unto His chosen. For the righteous who is dead condemns the ungodly who is living; and a youth who is soon perfected, the long life of the unrighteous."

Consideration of this fifth benefit of God conceived in three glories.

This, therefore, is the threefold glory which all godly, elect souls in the heavenly paradise encounter and of which they are certainly partakers even before the Last Day in the present state of their salvation, namely, the joyous fellowship which they have, first, with the holy angels; second, with the Lord Jesus Christ and the entire Holy Trinity, and, finally, with all patriarchs, prophets, apostles, and elect children of light who have died blessedly before this and by death have passed into life.

Why the fellowship of the elect souls with the holy angels is set first.

Among these glories, I have set the heavenly fellowship which they have with the angels of God first because the Lord Christ, in the account of poor Lazarus, mentions them first and makes the angels the heavenly bridal escorts, who immediately take the souls of the godly, when they have been released from their bodies, between them and bring them to the everlasting, almighty Bridegroom.

Comparison to a king surrounded by stately servants.

For just as a great king and monarch in the world is surrounded by stately servants, such as a princes, counts, barons, knights, and noble persons, and when he wishes to have some member of his poor subjects honored and brought before his presence, then, at his royal behest, the subject is first welcomed by the stately servants and then brought to him—so, too, God has His heavenly hosts, principalities, thrones, and dominions, namely, the holy angels, which at all times stand at His bidding and fulfill His will by receiving the godly souls from this valley of sorrow, whom they bear with gladness—not that this happens in an earthly manner with earthly splendor, since God is not a finite being that may be circumscribed with spatial locations and with angels, as a king on earth is spatially encircled and circumscribed with servants and vassals; but rather, this happens in a heavenly and hidden manner, of which no man on earth knows, until, after the conquest of temporal death, he sees this glory before him and experiences it in reality.

Ambrose, in The Good of Death, *ch. 11., gives seven orders of heavenly gladness*[134]

St. Ambrose also writes not unfittingly of the orders of heavenly gladness with the following words: "The gladness of the righteous souls is apportioned in certain orders [4 Esdras 7:49ff.]: The first joy is that they have overcome the flesh and are not deceived by its enticing passions. The second is that they lived, for the sake of their flesh, in God's calling and innocently toward others; they were peaceable and were not, like the souls of the ungodly, enveloped in error and tribulation, nor tormented with the remembrance of their vices, nor afflicted with many cares. The third is that, by faith, they fulfilled the Law of God, relied on God's testimony, and do not fear what will happen to them at the Last Day or how they will depart. The fourth joy is that they begin to understand their rest and foresee their future glory, by which they comfort and refresh themselves, and there is peace in their dwellings with highest security, and they are surrounded by the protection and hedge of the holy angels. The fifth gladness, or the fifth order of their gladness, is the all-surpassing sweetness and loveliness that they have come out of the prison of the perishable body to light and freedom and possess the promised inheritance. . . . The sixth joy is that it is demonstrated in them that their faces are beginning to shine like the sun and to give light like the stars in the

134 Ambrose of Milan, *De bono mortis* 11.48 (PL 14:561C–562B).

heaven, the radiance of which shall never pass away. The seventh joy is that they have sure confidence and comfort and rejoice without terror, hastening to see the face of Him whom they served, and they await the perfect reward for the little toil and labor which they had; beginning to receive which, they recognize what is said in Romans 8:18: 'We hold therefore that this time of suffering is not worthy of the glory that is to be revealed to us.'" Thus far St. Ambrose.

Another question interposed.

But someone might ask: How can you speak at such length of it, when Scripture here and there speaks reservedly with brief sayings and nowhere preaches about it in such a form with many words?

How the blessedness of the elect Christians in the heavenly paradise may be spoken of at length.

Answer: No matter how brief that may be which God's Word reveals and implies concerning the blessed condition, gladness, and glory of the elect souls in the heavenly paradise, every Christian may certainly expand, enlarge, extend it with many words for his own comfort and the strengthening of his faith. And as many upright, godly hearts who mourn the mortal departure of their deceased kinsmen with hot tears and are themselves not a little alarmed at death often wish and desire that they might be well-informed concerning the eternal life of deceased Christians, they can obtain such information from the cited testimonies of Scripture, if they only take care to remember and to learn to understand them richly, as I have herein given brief guidance for doing so.

Why Holy Scripture uses few words to describe the blessed condition of the elect souls.

Isa. 8:19–20

But the reason why Scripture touches on this glory of the elect souls with few words and does not speak at such great length of the realm of sight as of the realm of faith is, first, that we living Christians possess the same blessedness simultaneously with those who have fallen blessedly asleep in the Lord, and the only distinction is that we have it in faith while the souls of the righteous which have fallen asleep have it in sight. Second, God wishes hereby to curb human curiosity so that the revealed Gospel in the prophetic and apostolic Scriptures is not despised and set aside, nor assistance sought from the dead in good pagan and papistic fashion, which, without a doubt, would happen if He were to lay bare to us the whole process, namely, how the apostles and martyrs together with the rest of the elect sit with His Son upon His throne, how they reign with Him over the nations, and how they are lords over death, the devil, and hell, etc. Then our reason would instantly fly up, erect them as patrons, worship them, and ask them for help, as has happened and still happens in the papacy. But God forbids this and therefore speaks little of the soul's glory in His paradise, that He may preclude such idolatry. "Should they inquire of the dead on behalf of the living?" He says. "Yea, according to the Law and testimony—if they shall not speak this, then shall they not have the dawn."

How a Christian is to prepare and ready himself for eternal life.

As long as a Christian lives on earth, he is to concern himself only with the realm of faith, adhere to the revealed Word of God, hear diligently the preaching of the Gospel, go to the Supper, make confession, believe, pray, conduct himself as a Christian—this is what he is to carry on until death and then not doubt that the soul will depart this life and the realm of faith into the realm of sight, and what he has often heard and believed about his blessedness here from the preached Gospel, he will see there in plain sight, and there will have visible fellowship with the entire Holy Trinity, with all holy angels, and with all godly men, patriarchs, prophets, apostles, parents, brothers, sisters, and many thousand saints who died and passed through death into life before him.

The elect souls in the heavenly paradise desire the just beginning of the heavenly joy. A parable.

Neither should any Christian doubt this, but rely confidently on it, as well as on the fact that, as soon as he falls blessedly asleep in the Lord, be it today or tomorrow, his soul will immediately be in the midst of the holy, jubilant angels, will see God face-to-face, and will be gathered to its people. This heavenly fellowship and gathering is the true beginning of the great, unspeakable joy, honor, and glory that will last forever. Just as where the attendants of a wedding gather one after the other with the bride and groom in their beautifully built house and are received with a joyful welcome, an honorable drink, and dainty confections and such things, and they enjoy pleasant and gracious conversation until all the guests are together, whereupon the bride and groom are married with nuptial solemnity, and only then is their joy perfect and complete—so also do the souls of the elect in the heavenly paradise gather and with their Bridegroom, Jesus Christ, enter upon the beginning of their nuptial joy and glory until the Last Day dawns, when they will receive their bodies again from the earth and in their flesh shall see God, and only then will the glory and gladness proceed in fullest measure.

In heaven the elect know no great length of time.

2 Pet. 3:8

In the meantime, however, they know of absolutely no time or great length of years so that because of the unspeakable, great joy, a thousand years seems to them as a day, as St. Paul reports, from which it may be deduced that, if I were to ask the holy apostles in that world, who died fifteen hundred years ago, concerning their condition, "Dear Thomas, dear John, dear Paul, how long have you been in this high, heavenly joy, or how long does it seem to you that this life of paradise has lasted for you?" they would answer, "Ah, do you ask how long? In this joy and glory, we know of no worldly time! Our life is such a life that it feels as if it has hardly lasted a day and a half." Likewise, when you come to your blessed parents, husband, wife, children, brothers, sisters, etc., if they have already been dead twenty years, yet they will confess and declare to you that this life in heaven hardly seems to have lasted a quarter of an hour.

Comparison.

And consider yourself, if you went to a distant land or a newly discovered island and there beheld what your heart desired—beautiful order in the Christian church, beautiful rule of law, and utterly peaceful household management—and perceived with what gladness the people clung to the pure doctrine of the divine Word, what worthy and blameless lives they led, and how they received you with sincere gladness and delight and treated you with all kindness, you would doubtless have a desire to dwell there and would not weary of it because of this friendly fellowship, especially if you found your brothers, sisters, husband, wife, children, and other kinsmen there, whom you thought had died many years ago. But this is all child's play compared to the blessedness of the elect souls in the heavenly paradise, where in the blessed gathering of all the elect, even today before the Last Day, this gladness, pleasure, and glory are enjoyed so that all time is forgotten and no passing of years or months, days or hours is known.

Profit and use of this fifth benefit of God's.

Therefore, this fifth benefit of God's was so made that a godly Christian who will simply contemplate it with diligence can, at the hour of his death, commend himself much more willingly to the fatherly will of God, learn to prepare himself and make himself ready for it, take his leave of this world with gladness, and think of it precisely as if he is departing from the land of winter to a land of summer and from the valley of sorrow to the fair paradise of life everlasting.

The Sixth Benefit of God: The Future Resurrection of Our Flesh unto Eternal Life

Description of the sixth benefit of God.

Job 19:25–27; 1 Thess. 4:13–17

The sixth and final benefit will be the resurrection of our flesh at the Last Day unto eternal life, according as Scripture in many places testifies to this. "I know," says Job, "that my Redeemer lives, and afterward He will raise me from the earth, and afterward I will be enveloped by this my flesh, and in my flesh I shall see God. Him shall I see for myself, and my own eyes shall look upon Him, and not another's." Likewise, St. Paul: "We would not have you to be ignorant, dear brethren, concerning those who are asleep, that you may not mourn as others who have no hope. For if we believe that Jesus Christ died and rose again, even so those also who have fallen asleep will God bring with Him through Jesus. For this we say to you as a word of the Lord, that we who are alive will not precede those who are asleep. For He Himself, the Lord, shall descend from heaven with the shout of battle, and the voice of the archangel, and with the trumpet of God, and the dead in Christ shall rise first; then we who are alive and remain shall be caught up together with them in the clouds to meet the Lord in the air: and so shall we always be with the Lord."

How godly theologians in our time have explained this article.

Of such testimonies the Holy Scriptures of the Old and New Testament are full, and in our times Luther, Mathesius,[135] Basilius Faber,[136] and other godly teachers have made very fine expositions of it, on which I do not know how to improve. Therefore, I will only speak of it using their words and from their writings and only say what pertains to this.

The resurrection of our flesh explained by comparison to a seed that falls into the ground and springs forth again[137]

1 Cor. 15:37, 42–45

First, "What you sow," says St. Paul, "is not the body that will be, but a mere kernel, namely, of wheat or another kind. But God gives it a body as He will, and to each seed its own body." What he means is, a man's body, when he is dead and buried, is not the body that will be. In the resurrection, it will assume a different form far more beautiful and glorious than it is at present, just as the kernel, after it decomposes, grows up far more beautiful. While it retains its substance and nature, it takes on a different form; it is not a dry, wrinkled kernel when it grows out of the ground, but a green, fresh, living kernel. So will it also be with the human body. When it has decomposed, it will rise far more beautiful and glorious. It will remain the very same body of a man as it was created, but it will be a different form and usage of that body: it will not eat, drink, digest, beget children, manage a household, etc. Rather, it will have no need of anything that pertains to this perishable life and support of the body. This same body and soul which everyone

135 Johann Mathesius (1504–65) was Luther's student in 1529 and then again from 1540 to 1542. He served as a teacher and, after his final two years in Wittenberg, as pastor for the mining town of Joachimsthal. His series of biographical sermons on Luther delivered in the 1560s remained in print for nearly two hundred years (see "History," in *Sixteenth-Century Biographies of Martin Luther*, Luther's Works Companion Volume [St. Louis: Concordia, 2018]). He also published numerous collections of sermons.

136 Basilius Faber (ca. 1520–76) was rector of the school in Nordhausen and helped to produce a portion of Luther's commentary on Genesis published in 1557, in addition to his textbooks for the classroom.

137 The first section is from Martin Luther, *Sermon on the Resurrection of the Dead* [1 Cor. 15:39–44] (1544): cf. AE 58:123–24 (= WA 49:429–30).

has will continue in its nature according to every member, but it will not retain the form which it now has except as pertains to its substance. Neither will there be the same use of the body as it is at present.

Distinction of male and female will remain.

Gen. 1:11

"Yet the distinction of male and female will remain, even as God has created each. As the kernel retains its nature and kind—from a kernel of wheat there grows nothing other than a stalk of wheat, from a kernel of barley nothing other than a stalk of barley, and so on—so all continues in its nature and substance. The kernel brings forth the same kind. The kernel of barley does not turn into a stalk of wheat, nor the kernel of wheat into a stalk of barley. As a thing's nature was created and remains according to the Word, that everything should bring forth fruit according to its kind and have its own seed in itself, each according to its kind, so also in the resurrection, God will give to each his own body. What was created a human being shall remain a human being, male or female—God will not alter His creation or creature. As each one has been sown, so will he rise again as the very same kind and nature, and yet will be far more beautiful and glorious than he was sown. He will have keen eyes able to see through a mountain and keen ears able to hear from one end of the world to the other."

All the godly have believed this article and longed for the day of the resurrection.[138]

"All the God-fearing have believed this article and hoped and waited with longing and comfort for this glad day, the day of the restoration of all things, when everything will be restored to us. And they have taken comfort in this day whenever they thought of the day of the blessed hope and of our redemption and reviving; they have also gladly remembered the restitution, that is, the fact that they will return to what is theirs, just as Job the wretched also, in his greatest troubles, heartily took comfort in the fact that in the end he would be raised from death and would truly see His Savior and Redeemer with human flesh in the fullness of time, clothed with seeing eyes in his brand-new flesh, and would live with Him forever and ever.

Confession of godly Job concerning this precious article.

Job 19:25–27

"'I believe,' says our Job, 'that my Redeemer lives and reigns, who from my father-in-law's nephew will take on human flesh and in it die for our sins, and rise again from the dead with His incorruptible flesh, and as the firstfruits among those who are asleep rise with all flesh in its order, and all my bones will be renewed and blossom again like the green grass, and I will see my Lord, Redeemer,

138 The following section is from Johann Mathesius, *Ein Trostpredigt daß die im Herrn entschlafen mit Freuden wieder zusammenkommen* (Nürnberg: Neuber, 1567).

and Savior, even with my own eyes, which at that time shall be renewed and made clear. And as I shall see my Lord in His flesh, so will I also see again all my kinsmen who awaited the promised Seed of the woman and in eternal gladness eat and drink with them without end and for all eternity. Amen.'

Confession and comfort of the prophet David.

2 Sam. 12:22–23 [; Luke 7:11–17; John 11]

"So was King David also comforted in his sorrow when his dear little child departed, for he says in 2 Samuel 12: 'I cannot bring my dear child back to me in this misery, but I know that afterward I must go to him. For when I go the way of all the world, I will come again to him, when the Savior of the whole world, after the resurrection, will restore and deliver him to me again.' Here the prophet David also believes and confesses our article that he will come again to his infant son when the Son of God will restore him to him, even as here in this life, after a short time, He delivered to the mother of Nain her son and to the enlightened leader of the synagogue[139] his young daughter and to the sisters of Bethany their dear brother.[140]

Comfort for all Christians who shed fervent tears as they attend the funeral of their kinsmen who have fallen blessedly asleep.

"This, therefore, is a blessed comfort for all who bury their loved ones, that they may be assured that as truly as God and Christ, the Son of God, and His Word is the very truth and as certainly as Christ will be the Judge of the living and the dead and all flesh must appear in the air before His judgment throne, so truly also shall all who are related to one another in the Christian faith, as on the true Church Day, appear before the face of Jesus Christ and every believer will be presented to his own loved ones again, just as here the Son of God delivers to the poor mother her little son. David was able to forget his circumcised [sic[141]] child in the firm hope that the child would come to him again because he had departed in his innocence upon the future blood of the promised Seed. But Absalom, his own flesh and blood, he could not forget because he would never see him in glory and bliss.

We will go to our kinsmen.

"Therefore, when our God summons from Christian parents their baptized [sic[142]] and believing infants, or calls out of this misery a God-fearing husband's dearest treasure in the true knowledge and invocation of Christ and tears out a

139 I.e., Jairus.

140 I.e., Lazarus.

141 Uncircumcised. David's son died on the seventh day (2 Sam. 12:18), thus his comfort comes "because he departed in his innocence upon the future blood of the promised seed." This fits the context of the present paragraph. It should be noted that all the editions have *beschnittenen* ("circumcised") here. The next paragraph follows in the same error, where the comfort offered is to those who have lost an unbaptized child, akin to David's loss.—Editor

142 Unbaptized. See previous note..

piece of his heart, or else good friends forged and sustained in honorable friendship must part with sorrow, they should take comfort in the Word: 'I know he will not return to me, but I will go to him and will see him again and remain with him in undivided togetherness. This return causes me not to esteem so highly this temporal separation. Come, Lord Jesus Christ, and bring me and my dearest loved ones together again soon through Your coming, and give me my loved ones again, as on this day You gave this widow her dear son again in this temporary life!'"

The transfiguration of the whole substance of the man.[143]

Second, we are also to take comfort and rejoice in the fact that "the renewal and transfiguration of Christians, in which they are to be with the Lord Christ in eternal life, will affect the whole substance of a man, that is, body and soul and all their members. In such a transfigured and glorious body will the eternal life of blessed Christians be—in such a body, I say, which is completely freed from all fragility, frailty, deficiency, and uncleanness with which it is polluted in this life through sin, but there it will be clothed and adorned with a wonderful perfection in all its members inside and out. For the soul will be freed from its uncleanness and from every burden that it had to bear before in the mortal body, and it will be clothed and adorned with the most wonderful, purest, and mightiest abilities, as it would have been in Adam before the fall, such as the fact that the man is gifted and graced with perfect and highest wisdom and knowledge of God. And with his whole being and will, the Christian will receive with highest inclination and fearlessness and with sheer pleasure and highest delight will attend to and accomplish all that God will desire; out of utter love toward God and all good instigations and thoughts, commensurate with the will of God, he will burn and understand the wondrous counsel of the divine Majesty concerning the work of the creation and redemption of mankind, together with the reasons for all wondrous works of God which have occurred and been performed for all time since the beginning of the world.

Perfection of the soul.

2 Pet. 1:4

"This perfection of the soul will then also be followed by the whole body with all its members, which will all become as perfect, powerful, and ready as possible. For Paul says that we will not retain our previous sluggish, foul, disease-ridden, and powerless bodies, but rather we will receive heavenly bodies, which are as healthy, radiant, quick, and light as the holy angels, indeed, as the Son of God Himself, even as we have now been made partakers of the divine nature, as Peter says in his Second Epistle, chapter 1, and shine far more beautifully than the stars

143 The following section is ultimately from Basilius Faber, *Allerley Christliche, nötige und nützliche unterrichtungen von den letzten Hendeln* . . . (Eisleben: U. Gaubisch, 1564) fols. [L5v]–[M6r].

and the dear sun, which are as quick as the thoughts with which a man can be heard in this life over many thousand miles, whenever he will.

Perfection and transfiguration of the bodies.

Rom. 8:29

"For after we have then been conformed to the likeness of the Lord Christ's transfigured body, as Paul says in Romans 8, then we will also have the properties of Christ's body. That is, just as He walks through closed doors, ascends into the clouds, and is instantly wherever He wishes in heaven or on earth, so will it also be with our bodies, which will be as swift as our thoughts in this life. They will see through every wall and mountain and fly up in the air and be wherever we wish in heaven or on earth far quicker and sooner than we may now imagine, like God Himself, like the dear angels, holy, righteous, blameless, and full of the peace and joy of the Holy Spirit forever, so that all angels and created things will marvel at our beautiful bodies and God Himself will have delight and pleasure in them.

Power and strength of the elect in the resurrection.

"Every blessed Christian in particular will be so full of strength and power that He will be able to manage a great burden with one finger and remove a large and towering mountain whenever he might wish. For a man will then be filled with utter power so that nothing will be impossible for a righteous and blessed man. He might well strike down many hundred thousand men by himself, as we read in the Bible of the strength of the angels. Our eyes and ears will become so keen that we will see and hear to the ends of the whole world.

The bodies of the elect in the resurrection will be conformed to the likeness of Christ.

Phil. 3:20–21; 1 John 3:2

"This is because our bodies will then become spiritual and will no longer be heavy, sleepy, rusty, filthy, and slow bodies, but will possess utter life and power and senses vigilant and quick, and strength in them. We will be able to demonstrate this with the testimonies of Scripture. For St. Paul says, 'Our conversation is in heaven, from whence we also await the Savior, Jesus Christ, who will transform our vile body, that it may be conformed to the likeness of His glorified body, according to the working with which He is able to make all things subject to Himself.' And in his First Epistle, chapter 3, John says, 'We will be like God, and see Him as He is'; that is, we will be like God Himself—righteous, holy, and undying—and will move and walk everywhere in heaven and on earth as He does. We will see Him not as the holy patriarchs saw Him in His alien form, as Augustine says, but as He is, in His divine and almighty life and essence, which we cannot do in this mortal and sinful life because our eyes, senses, and reason are far too frail and weak and cannot tolerate or endure this radiance of the glory of God, just as we cannot look at the sun, though its brightness is nothing compared to that of the heavenly glory with which we are all to be clothed like God Himself.

We will become partakers of the divine nature.

2 Pet. 1:4; Matt. 13:43; 22:30; Rom. 14:17

"In 2 Peter 1, it says, 'We will become partakers of the divine nature, if we flee from the perishing lusts of the world'; that is, in eternal life we will become like God, Christ, and the holy angels if in this life we cling to Christ with true faith and do not put our trust in temporal things, but rather take comfort and rejoice in, long for, and desire the Gospel. And in Matthew 13, Christ says, 'Then' (after the resurrection of the eternal life) 'the righteous will shine like the bright sun,' and so heaven and earth will be made completely new and will be more than many thousand times more beautiful and brighter than they are now. 'Indeed, a little star,' says Dr. Luther, 'will be far more beautiful than the whole world.' In Matthew 22, Christ says further, "We will be like the angels.' Likewise: 'In the resurrection, we will neither marry nor be given in marriage'; that is, in that life the estate of marriage will cease, and all misfortune and reluctance, all cares involving one's wife, children, and livelihood which we used to have, will cease, and we will live forever without any care or fear, as bright, righteous, nimble, and strong as the dear angels. In Romans 14, St. Paul also says, 'The kingdom of God is not eating and drinking, but righteousness, peace, and joy in the Holy Spirit,' that is, such abundant, incomprehensible joy that no eye has ever seen it, no ear has ever heard it, and it has never entered into the heart of any man, as we heard above from St. Paul. Indeed, it is the joy in which God Himself lived with all angels from eternity and will live henceforth in the same with all His elect from everlasting to everlasting, without end, without time—the joy that the Holy Spirit, as true God (by whom we shall be filled), shall work in us, to strengthen, quicken, enliven, heal, gladden, and cheer us to such an extent that we will never remember any eating or drinking, but that every elect Christian will say, 'If I had the smallest speck of this heavenly gladness, I would not exchange it for all the glorious confections and sumptuous foods of all emperors, lords, and princes that have ever been made since the beginning of the world—indeed, for all the glory of the whole world.' For then God will completely end the eating and drinking and similar physical and natural things with which we are burdened and afflicted here in this life and will feed us with the food from which He and the dear angels have lived from eternity and from which we will have been made a hundred thousand times more alert, stronger, fairer, gladder, and more brilliant than we were by the most noble, best, and most glorious foods and drinks here in this world.

We will always be with God.

1 Thess. 4:17

"St. Paul further says in 1 Thessalonians 4: 'We will always be with God'; that is, we will be in all places, wherever we wish, as God Himself is, before we even imagine it, we will already be where we wish, in heaven above or here on earth. For God will be all in all, that is, we will have in God all that we wish, desire, or imagine.

We will have all things in God.

"All that we now seek and have in creation we will have there in God richly and to overflowing, in body and soul, so that no food, no drink, no malmsey is so delicious nor so able to satisfy as God Himself will do with His look, so that you will always be strong and alert, healthy and glad, and brighter and more beautiful than the sun and moon, so that all garments and pieces of gold which a king or emperor wears will be sheer dung compared to when we are illuminated only by a divine look. Neither will we have any need of a protector, nor any authority, money, or property, hearth or home, nor other goods, but will have all sufficiency in Him alone. Thus we will have all spiritual goods, eternal righteousness, comfort, and joy of conscience so that no one will terrify, deceive, or disquiet us any longer. In short, whatever we, in this age, have had to take piecemeal and in part here and there from all created things (although it still all comes from and is given by Him), we will instead have from Him immediately, without any deficiency or interruption.

God will Himself satisfy and fill body and soul.

"Then we will have no regard for bread or wine, nor need nor desire any apostle or physician, but will have abundance only in the look and beholding of God, who will make the whole body so beautiful, alert, and healthy, indeed, so light and nimble, that we will go along like a spark, indeed, as the sun runs in the sky, so that in the blink of an eye we will be here below on earth or above in heaven. I believe that all things will be far more beautiful there—water, trees, and grass—and that there will be an entirely new earth, as St. Paul says, so that it will be a delight to look at it. But it will be for God Himself to sustain soul and body since He alone shall be all in all, and His look shall give more life, joy, and delight than all created things have power to give. And you will have to say, 'I would not exchange one glance in heaven for all the property and joy of the world, even if it were to last a thousand years, and yet another thousand.'

The preaching office will cease.

"Thus preaching or the pastoral office also will cease, as I have said, as will princes or worldly dominions and government. And in short, there will be no offices or estates any more. The persons, as men and women, shall abide, and the entirety of mankind as it was created, but none of the necessities pertaining to this life, but every person shall be a perfect being and have for himself all things in God so that he will have no need of any father, mother, master, servant, food, clothing, house, etc.

We will have all that we are simply able to desire.

"Now consider yourself in your heart what you would be eager or wish to have. If you would like to have money or property, food and drink aplenty, a long life, a healthy body, beautiful clothes, a fine dwelling, everlasting joy and delight, as well as perfect wisdom and understanding of all things, dominion and glory, then only look here. You will get everything abundantly. He will clothe you finer than any emperor may be clothed, indeed, more beautiful than the sun and all precious stones. If you wish to be a lord, He will give you more than you can desire. If you wish to have sharp vision and hear through walls and bulwarks and be so swift that you can be wherever you wish in the blink of an eye, either here on earth or above in the clouds, it will all be so, and whatever else you can imagine, whatever you might desire in body and soul, in which your heart will seek pleasure and joy—you will have it richly if you have Him. For wherever God is, there must all goods, joy, and pleasure be at the same time. And as He, when He looks at creation, takes pleasure, joy, and delight in it, so will we, too, who no longer need anything but to find joy in it, as it were in some culinary dish meant for show, and we will look upon the beautiful new heaven and earth and praise and love God for it, but in Him we will have all that we need and full abundance.

"Behold, this is the comfort that we have in the next life, that God Himself will be ours and all in Him. For however you regard yourself, you will find nothing better or dearer to wish for than to have God Himself, who is the life and inexhaustible depth of all good and eternal gladness. Now there is no nobler thing on earth than life, and all the world fears nothing more than death and desires nothing higher than life—and we will have that treasure in Him without any limitation and without ceasing. Then will heaven (if you wish) rain utter Joachim's thalers[144] and gold, the Elbe flow full of nothing but pearls and precious stones, the earth fulfill any kind of pleasure, so that if you said to a tree that it must bear silver leaves and golden apples and pears, and grass and flowers should shine upon the field like sheer emeralds and all kinds of precious stones, and, briefly put, whatever your heart desires and delights in will be there in abundance. For it says that God Himself will be all in all, and wherever God is, there must be with Him every good for which anyone can ever wish.

The whole Godhead will be manifested.

"Another aspect of this surpassing glory of eternal life is the fact that the entire Godhead will reveal and discover Himself, and we will see God as He is, as John says, namely, in His divine majesty and omnipotence, which the ungodly

144 The silver coins minted in Joachimsthal were called "Joachimstaler," or "Thaler" for short.

will never have the opportunity to see for eternity, so that we will behold Him and therein have all our delight and joy, as stated, and in His knowledge continually increase, in which all blessedness and eternal life will consist, as Christ says (John 6). Likewise, that we will live with our Redeemer, the Lord Christ, be everywhere around Him, hold conversation with Him, and hear Him teach and instruct us concerning the highest, heavenly, and divine things, concerning the causes of all God's works. But what sort of glory that will be can be imagined by no heart or mind of man in this life, but we must wait until we discover and experience it in operation and truth.

Fellowship with the dear angels.

"And what further glorious delight and gladness will there be? The sweetest fellowship that we will have with the dear angels, over whom we will have power, who will serve us and attend to us, and with us will help to praise and glorify God, as the fathers have said concerning them; likewise, the fellowship of the holy prophets, patriarchs, apostles, with all our ancestors and descendants, and, briefly, all Christians and saints who ever lived on earth with whom we have dealings, and they with us will talk to them most amiably about the things of God. We will marvel with one another because of the unspeakable love, grace, and goodness of God which He showed in the redemption of mankind, and with one another will praise and glorify Him forever. Then those words will resound: 'Praise our God, all you His servants, and you who fear Him, both small and great!' And then the loud voices of the great throng will follow, saying, 'Alleluia! For God Almighty has come into His kingdom. Let us rejoice and be glad and give Him the glory!' as written in Revelation 9:6–7.

"Oh, it would be no surprise at all if a man, after simply considering a little these lofty, comforting things, did nothing else in his whole life but call upon God continually to deliver him at once from this sinful and miserable life, forgive him his sins for Christ's sake, and take him up to that great glory in His eternal kingdom!"

Recognition of friends and family.[145]

Third and last, we must also particularly note and retain the fact that "Christ will restore to each person what is his," and "we will assuredly see one another before the judgment seat of the Lord and recognize one another. For it is not the least aspect of eternal life, when sin and death are entirely removed from us and we have attained to life and righteousness, that there will also be a complete knowledge of God and of ourselves and of all creation.

145 The following and final section, quoted at length by Johann Mathesius, *Eine Trostpredigt . . .* (Nuremberg, 1565), is ultimately from Basilius Faber, *Allerley Christliche, nötige und nützliche unterrichtungen von den letzten Hendeln . . .* (Eisleben: U. Gaubisch, 1564).

"Before the fall, when Adam had not yet forfeited the eternal and spiritual life, he recognized his Eve—that she was formed from his flesh and bone which he had never yet seen. So also the three apostles in the transfiguration of the corporeal Son of God on the holy mountain recognized Moses and Elijah who appeared with Christ and comforted Him.

"In the same way, Mary Magdalene recognized the risen Christ in His words, although at that time He had hidden Himself in the form of a gardener, as also St. Stephen saw the Lord Christ in His glory standing at the right hand of His Father and recognized Him. Likewise, the faithful recognized the saints who rose with Christ and appeared to many of them.

"Then those who are asleep will rise and retain their flesh and blood that they had before, although it will be renewed, being transformed into a spiritual and incorruptible body.

"Now, if a mortal man with his natural eyes sees and recognizes those who are risen in their spiritual bodies, shall not those who are raised in their new life and full powers recognize their friends and family in eternal life?

"Moses will make excuse for and bear witness to his Jews before the presence of God, and the Corinthians will be St. Paul's wreath of honor at the Last Day, as all the godly will boast of and honor him by whom they came to the faith and knowledge of Christ and to the blessed life. Therefore, the recognition of our neighbors and relatives cannot be denied. The Holy Spirit does not remove the natural powers and imprinted affect and sensory faculty from our mortal body, but rather He purifies them. Thus although God will be all in all His people and those who are raised will receive the tithe and fullness of the Spirit of God and be thoroughly, perfectly pure and new in body and soul and spirit, yet they will not be without thought, sight, and knowledge. What sort of eternal life would that be if one did not recognize his dearest ones? Behold and acknowledge the true rich devourer, who lay in the infernal torment, Abraham, and the poor Lazarus in his bosom, although a great chasm was between them? From this the learned wish to conclude that the blessed also know the damned in their torment and ascribe proper justice to God's judgment.

"Although it gives the dying David occasion for thought that he must see his flesh and blood condemned eternally in the disobedient and ungodly Absalom, yet the recognition of the righteousness of God and all-natural love and longing outweigh it, even as in the world the greater affects outweigh the lesser.

"So does the fact that the unblessed also recognize the blessed in their gladness, by which their own torment and agony become all the greater, when they see in bliss and gladness those whom they trod underfoot and regarded as the *shabab* and tormenting spirits of the world. Job is supremely comforted by the fact that, in the resurrection, he will see his Lord and Savior with a new body and spiritual eyes and will speak and interact with Him and that, in his rejuvenated flesh, he will behold the transfigured and corporeal Son of God.

"Therefore, those who believe in Christ should not doubt the article at all. As truly as we shall arise in this our flesh or body in the same transfiguration and glory as the body of Christ, to the likeness of which we shall be conformed; and as truly as we will come to Him, see Him, and recognize Him and glorify Him as the highest Person of mankind, so truly will all believers in Christ also come together and recognize one another again.

"This, then, is a sweet comfort for those who are separated from their loved ones for a time. Here on this earth, no one returns, nor do we see one another here again, though devils may take on human form in their demonic enterprise and appear in the form of a ghost resembling Samuel or Scipio. Yet it is not correct to say, 'Today you will see me for the last time and never again.' For this is how the pagans and unbelievers talk. But we say in the throes of death: 'God bless you, my dearly beloved. We will see one another here no longer, but hereafter we will, God willing, be reunited in glory and joy and dwell together inseparably and indivisibly forever and ever, when the Son of God shall wake us and bring us together.'

"In truth, dear friends, whoever ponders these thoughts and establishes them on the basis of God's Word can be comforted and at peace and await this joyous day in strength and assurance and be and abide with one another in love and tender affection. For, concerning this third part, you are to know that in gladness and eternal life we will not only come together with God and before His presence and know and converse with one another, but that also the old Christian friendship which you forged here in the knowledge of Christ and kept until the end and carried with you to the grave will rise again with us and will be new, entire, and perfect and remain so forever and ever.

"The highest and most blessed friendship will be perfected hereafter, when we shall stand with God the Father, His Son, and the Holy Spirit, and all the angels of God in love, favor, and friendship and will feel His fatherly love and fidelity forever as the dear adopted children of His Child. Then it will be discovered what a Father God is and how His fatherly love and fidelity surpass whatever may and can be called a father or fatherhood or fatherly love and fidelity.

"For now, no ear has yet heard nor eye seen, nor has it entered into the heart of any man, how sincerely and how like a mother our dear Father loves us because of and in His beloved Son. Only then will the brotherly fidelity of our Lord and Brother Jesus Christ allow itself to be appropriated and the reason why He shed His blood for us and carried us in His womb be perceived. Only then will we gaze upon the essential flame of the Holy Spirit and be perfectly inspirited in our heart and enkindled and inflamed with pure and divine love and burning ardor.

"Now, therefore, as this love of the Father, Son, and Holy Spirit which we have only tasted a little in faith shall only become perfectly perceptible in us in the next life, so the bond of love with which God binds together man and wife, parents and children, brothers and sisters, and other relations of blood and marriage by their nature will become perfect, when sin and death, all disorder and unkindness, suspicion and mistrust, which vile Satan craftily sows in us, are purged in the new and holy life, and the incipient kinship shall be wholly renewed and strengthened.

"Love and friendship are not the basest part of our rational and immortal soul which Christ purchased and saved. As the soul, then, is delivered and will live forever, so also will all that is implanted or formed in the soul avoid corruption and cessation. Therefore, since love and friendship, along with all faculties of desire, belong to the essence of the immortal soul, it is certain and incontrovertible that everyone who here on earth is bound in the knowledge of Jesus Christ with desiring thoughts of love toward another and has found joy and refreshment in honest and genuine friendship here—they will still abide forever in eternal life in constant and heavenly love and heartfelt friendship with and among one another before God and with their eternal, sweet, and amiable coexistence will compensate for every grief which loved ones felt in the valley of sorrow, both in their frequent anguish and distress and finally in their mournful separation. For here on earth that saying is true: 'That which is dear may dampen our cheer.' Godly parents and children, husband and wife, and good friends do not have unmingled joy in one another's misery. Often a great deal of sadness breaks in when one is deeply afflicted by the other's adversity and misfortune, and one's joy in true friendships is often overly salted with calamity. But in the resurrection of the righteous, love and gladness will be eternal and perfect. Then we will have joy and bliss, honor and kinship in one another.

"But we must not understand this new, heavenly friendship and eternal familiarity as the Sadducees in the time of Christ, when they inquired concerning a woman who had had seven husbands in succession whose wife she would be in the resurrection—nor as the scandalous Turk think and speak of it today, who know of no other joy than to boast and swagger and have many wives at once and to manage this sinful and corrupt flesh only with delights. Such people our Lord Christ calls ungodly fools, mockers, and despisers of God and His Word, who do not understand the Scriptures and power of God and entertain only carnal, Epicurean thoughts.

"They are exactly like that pig whom the beasts told of a splendid banquet at which they had been guests with the people and had a splendid, magnificent time; and the filthy pig asked if they had had bran and husks as well. Those desperate mockers and Epicureans are similar. They discount the blood and death of Christ and dishonor and slander His Word, so the foul, unclean spirit blinds and enchants them with the result that they do not think or speak of God and the life to come but as conceived in their Epicurean and filthy hearts. However, we know (thanks and praise be to God!) from the true Word and report of Christ that the blessedness to come, for which we hope, is an angelic, heavenly, and spiritual life in an undying, spiritual, and incorruptible body, where we will need no marriage nor any created thing, but God will be and remain all things in all the blessed, as Christ says to the scoffing Sadducees: 'The children of this world marry and are given in marriage. But those who are worthy to obtain that world and the resurrection of the dead will neither marry nor be given in marriage, for they cannot die anymore, and will be like the angels of God in heaven.'

"For as Moses writes and as St. Paul expounds the words of Moses, God created us men for two lives: first, for the natural life; second, for the spiritual. In this natural life, God has instituted and ordained the marriage estate, where by God's Word two are joined together in one indissoluble bond so that they grow in the flesh according to God's ordinance and are to multiply, that the earth may be filled and the kingdom of heaven built up. From this human race God, by the eternal intercession and merit of His Son, gathers for Himself an eternal Church and heavenly congregation through the Word and the Sacraments and replenishes the number of the fallen angels. But when the number of the elect is fulfilled and Christ the Judge of all flesh shall appear with His joyous advent in the clouds and all the living in the last fire shall change in the blink of an eye and all the dead shall be raised up by the last trumpet, the teaching office, political rule, and marriage estate with the whole domestic order shall be abolished, and a new heavenly, spiritual, and angelic life will commence. Then we will be with God forever and see His face in perfect gladness, and we will rejoin our dearest ones and in eternal joy and true divine love live together with one another unceasingly in the new heaven and earth. And if, according to God's gracious pleasure, many a poor widower or widow has had two or three successive wives or husbands in this life, it will be nothing in the life to come, just as that sensible wife said that the living one was dearest to her. Hereafter there will be no distinction, no envy or jealousy. He will see and know them all again, and all will be sincerely dear to him (yet in the angelic life), because their hearts are bound together by God's Word, and in their chaste marriage bed they knew the Lord Christ and called steadfastly upon Him in faith.

"It will also be a beautiful instance of thanksgiving and gladness when the second or third wife has had sincere respect for the ancestors of her husband and children and has faithfully raised them in the fear of God, in discipline, and in virtue, for then will that verse be fulfilled:

> True love increases in true godliness and faith,
> And godliness is the nerve of friendship true."

Part Three
Hymns

A SPIRITUAL WEDDING HYMN

OF THE BELIEVING SOUL CONCERNING JESUS CHRIST, ITS HEAVENLY BRIDEGROOM, BASED ON THE 45TH PSALM OF THE PROPHET DAVID BY DR. PHILIPP NICOLAI

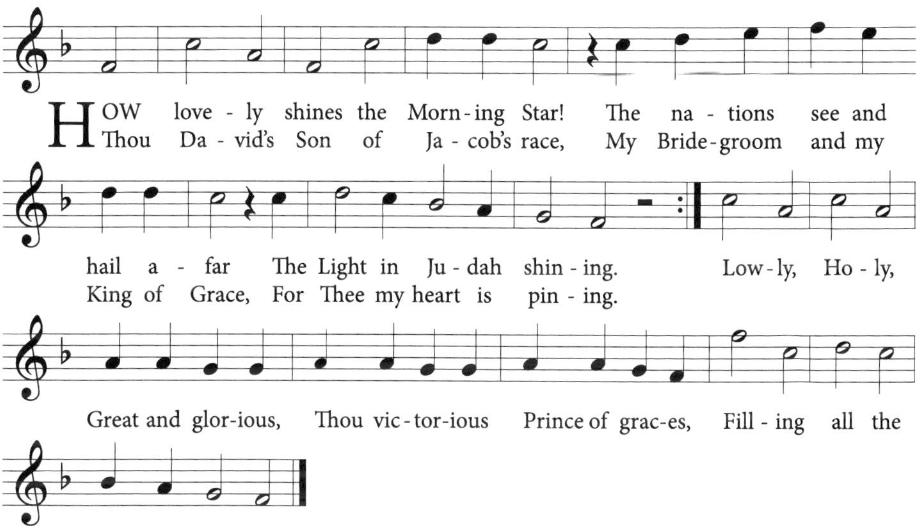

[How beautifully shines the Morning Star, full of grace and truth from the Lord, the sweet root of Jesse! O Son of David from Jacob's tribe, my King and my Bridegroom, You have possessed my heart, and sweetly, tenderly, beautifully and gloriously, greatly and honorably, rich with gifts, You have highly and very splendidly exalted it.]

II

O highest joy by mortals won,
True Son of God and Mary's Son,
Thou highborn King of ages!
Thou art my heart's most beauteous Flow'r
And Thy blest Gospel's saving pow'r
My raptured soul engages.
Thou mine, I Thine;
Sing hosanna! / Heav'nly manna
Tasting, eating,
Whilst Thy love in songs repeating.

[Ah, my Pearl, precious Crown, true Son of God and Mary, highborn King, my heart calls You a lily! Your sweet Gospel is sheer milk and honey. Oh, my Floweret, Hosanna!—heavenly Manna which we eat, I cannot forget You.]

III

Now richly to my waiting heart,
O Thou, my God, deign to impart
The grace of love undying.
In Thy blest body let me be,
E'en as the branch is in the tree,
Thy life my life supplying.
Sighing, Crying,
For the savor / Of Thy favor;
Resting never
Till I rest in Thee forever.

[Pour the flame of Your love very deep in my heart, bright Jasper and Ruby, and make me glad, that I may remain a living rib in the body of Your elect. O gracious Rose of heaven, for You I am sick with love, and my heart, wounded by love, smolders.]

IV

A pledge of peace from God I see
When Thy pure eyes are turned to me
To show me Thy good pleasure.
Jesus, Thy Spirit and Thy Word,
Thy body and Thy blood, afford
My soul its dearest treasure.
Keep me Kindly
In Thy favor, O my Savior!

Thou wilt cheer me;
Thy Word calls me to draw near Thee.

[A ray of gladness comes to me from God when You look at me kindly with Your angels. O Lord Jesus, my beloved Good! Your Word, Your Spirit, Your body and blood renew my life inwardly. Receive me tenderly in Yours arms, that I may be warmed by grace. At Your Word I come, invited.]

V

Thou, mighty Father, in Thy Son
Didst love me ere Thou hadst begun
This ancient world's foundation.
Thy Son hath made a friend of me,
And when in spirit Him I see,
I joy in tribulation.
What bliss is this!
He that liveth To me giveth
Life forever;
Nothing me from Him can sever.

[Lord God, Father, my mighty Champion, in Your Son You loved me eternally from before the world. Your Son betrothed me to Himself. He is my treasure, I am His bride, most highly gladdened in Him. Oh, oh! He will give heavenly life to me above yonder. My heart will praise Him forever.]

VI

Lift up the voice and strike the string,
Let all glad sounds of music ring
In God's high praises blended.
Christ will be with me all the way,
Today, tomorrow, every day,
Till traveling days be ended.
Sing out, Ring out,
Triumph glorious, O victorious,
Chosen nation;
Praise the God of your salvation.

[Pluck the strings of the cithara and let the sweet music resound wholly joyful, that I should dwell with dear Jesus, my wondrously handsome Bridegroom, in constant love. Sing, leap, make merry, celebrate in triumph, thank the Lord. Great is the King of glory.]

VII

Oh, joy to know that Thou, my Friend,
Art Lord, Beginning without end,
The First and Last, eternal!
And Thou at length—O glorious grace!—
Wilt take me to that holy place,
The home of joys supernal.
Amen, Amen!
Come and meet me! Quickly greet me!
With deep yearning,
Lord, I look for Thy returning.

(Tr. composite, *TLH* 1941)

[How heartily happy I am that my treasure is the Alpha and Omega, the beginning and the end! He will receive me into paradise to His glory. I knock at His hands. Amen, amen! Come, beautiful crown of gladness, do not tarry long. I wait for You with yearning.]

HYMN OF THE VOICE AT MIDNIGHT

AND OF THE WISE VIRGINS, WHO GO TO MEET THEIR HEAVENLY BRIDEGROOM (MATTHEW 25) BY DR. PHILIPP NICOLAI

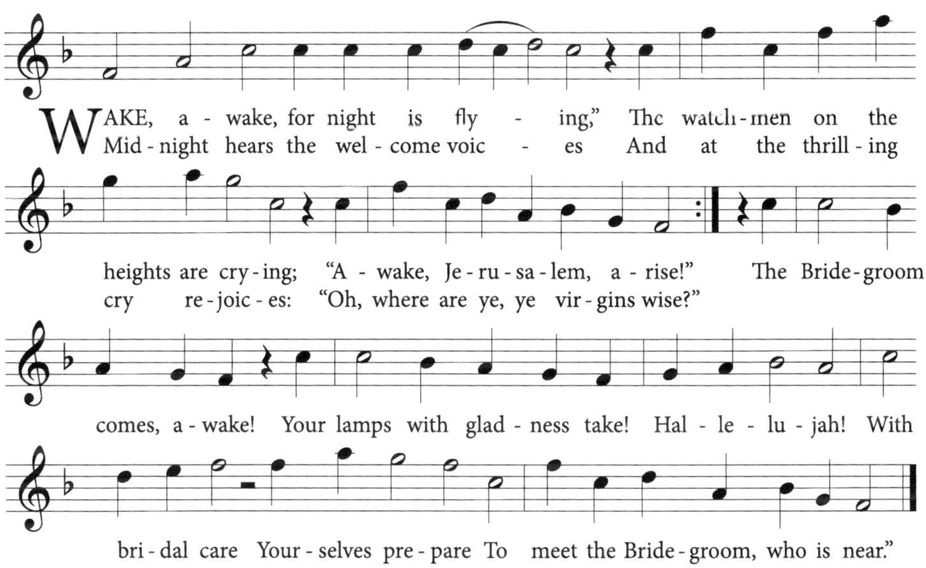

["Wake up," the voice calls us, the watchman very loudly upon the pinnacle. "Wake up, O city of Jerusalem. This hour is midnight." They call to us with clear mouth, "Where are you, you wise virgins? Up, the Bridegroom comes. Look up, take the lamps. Alleluia! Make yourselves ready for the wedding feast. You must go to meet Him."]

II

Zion hears the watchmen singing,
And all her heart with joy is springing;
She wakes, she rises from her gloom.
For her Lord comes down all-glorious,
The strong in grace, in truth victorious;
Her star is ris'n, her light is come.
Now come, Thou Blessed One,
Lord Jesus, God's own Son,
Hail! Hosanna!
We enter all / The wedding hall
To eat the Supper at Thy call.

[Zion hears the watchmen singing. Her heart leaps for gladness. She wakes and stands up in haste. Her Friend comes splendid from heaven, mighty with grace, powerful with truth. Her Light is made clear; her Star rises. Now come, O precious Crown, Lord Jesus, Son of God, Hosanna! We all follow to the hall of gladness and join in keeping the Supper.]

III

Now let all the heav'ns adore Thee,
Let saints and angels sing before Thee
With harp and cymbals' clearest tone.
Of one pearl each shining portal,
Where, joining with the choir immortal,
We gather round Thy radiant throne.
No eye has seen the light,
No ear has heard the might
Of Thy glory;
Therefore will we / Eternally
Sing hymns of praise and joy to Thee!

(Tr. C. Winkworth, 1863, alt.)

[Glory be sung to You with tongues of men and angels, with harps and cymbals fair! Of twelve pearls are the gates of Your city. We are fellows of the angels high around Your throne. No eye has ever sensed, no ear has heard more, such gladness of which we are happy, I-o, i-o, eternally *in dulci jubilo*, that is, in sweet rejoicing.]

FAREWELL TO THE WORLD

FROM A SOUL ATHIRST FOR HEAVEN BASED ON THE 42ND PSALM OF DAVID BY DR. PHILIPP NICOLAI TO THE TUNE "SO WÜNSCH ICH IHR EIN GUTE NACHT"[146]

[Thus I wish it good night—the world—and let it go, though it causes me much grief; God will preserve me. I thought the world was only gold. I find it now far different.]

II

Like as the hart by serpent stung
For water fresh goes panting,
So has the world dried up my tongue,
Deep thirst within me planting.
The ancient snake / Makes me to quake,
And Godward brings my crying.

146 The tune, originally omitted, has been inserted here from Zahn 3:63 (no. 4405a), the form closest to that intended by Nicolai. It had already been used by Remigius in 1587 for the hymn "Herr Jesu Christ, in Namen dein."

[A hart stung by serpents pants after fresh water, so also the accursed world has roused me to thirst, and the ancient serpent frightens me so that I must cry to God.]

III

When shall I see Thy paradise
Where sainted hosts are dwelling,
And praise Thee there before my eyes,
Robed with the sun excelling?
When wilt Thou bring / Me hence, O King,
To see Thy face in heaven?

[When will I come into Your paradise where many Christians dwell, and sing to You glory, honor, and praise, clothed with the sun? When will You take me into the kingdom of heaven, where I will see Your face?]

IV

My soul in need and anguish lies,
That I so long must tarry.
To this sad vale bound by life's ties,
As 'twere a cart I carry.
The lying horde / But scorn afford
And mock me in my trouble.

[My soul has distress and suffers torment, that I must wait so long, tied on the vale of tears as if I drew a heavy carriage. They purvey their mockery, the false horde, with me in my distresses.]

V

"Where is thy God," they always cry,
"That He may bring thee gladness?"
My heart is vexed by mockery
So that I weep for sadness.
Come soon, My Rock! / My Refuge true
And from the earth retrieve me!

[They ask, "Yea, where does your God abide—yea, that He may appear to you?" The mockery sickens my heart and blood so that I weep for sadness. Oh, come soon, my refuge, and retrieve me from the earth!]

VI

Oh, take me to the gladsome hall
Prepared by Thee in splendor,

Where patriarchs and prophets all
To Thee their praises render,
And hosts of bright / Angelic might
Around Thy throne are thronging!

[Oh, take me into the hall of gladness prepared by You above, where all the patriarchs with the prophets praise You, and where the host of the angels bright swarm around Your throne.]

VII

Why, O my soul, so sad and ill?
Be firm and do not waver!
God is my hope and comfort still—
Indeed, my mighty Savior.
Give thanks therefore, / A moment more,
And grief will yield to gladness!

[Why are you sick, my poor soul? Be still and do not waver. God is my fortress, my comfort and salvation, for which I will still thank Him. Restrain yourself and suffer a little while. After anguish comes joy and bliss.]

VIII

A precious herb must patience be,
Not in all gardens growing;
Oh, God, help me to wait for Thee,
A patient heart bestowing!
So let me not / Make worse my lot
On earth with fear and anguish.

[The plant patience does not grow in all gardens. Oh, God, always cause me to be able to wait for You, or I else I am very afflicted and heavy with anguish on this earth.]

IX

Thine anger like a flood I see
As on the land it seizes.
Its noises rumble terribly
Whene'er Thy wrath increases.
These billows high / That fill the sky—
By these I too am stricken.

[I see that Your anger, like a flood, encounters the whole land, and that it roars terribly when Your wrath rises. The waves I also experienced, together with Your billows of water.]

X

Therefore I weary of the world,
All night and day I'm weeping,
Nor cease till I shall see unfurled
Thy grace upon me leaping.
Haste to me here, / My Rock most dear,
And to Thy peace conduct me.

[Therefore, I am so weary of the world, all day and night I weep, and do not relent until Your goodness promised to me appears. Now hasten forth, my beloved Rock, and take me into peace.]

XI

How long shall I in sorrow go,
Where many a foe afflicts me?
My bones are filled with murd'rous woe;
Their mocking word constricts me:
"Say, where is Christ, / Thy Savior prized?
Yea, let Him come redeem thee!"

[How long shall I walk sorrowful here where enemies afflict me? There is murder in my bones so that they ask altogether mockingly, "Say, where is your Jesus Christ? Yes, that He may redeem you?"]

XII

Impatience here, sad soul, dispel—
Here patience oft is needed,
Till by thy dear Immanuel
Thou from vile earth art speeded
To paradise / Before His eyes,
Where we will ever thank Him.

(Tr. M. Carver, 2021)

[Patience, patience, sorrowful soul, patience is needed here, until dear Immanuel plucks us from this wicked clod to Himself in paradise, where we will give thanks to Him.]

HYMN ON ETERNAL LIFE

BY JEREMIAS NICOLAI
TO THE TUNE
"AUS MEINES HERTZEN GRUNDE"[147]

[Lord Christ, grant me Your Spirit, that I may sing. What heaven is and is called makes me heartily rejoice—a heavenly paradise in which the Lord will redeem me from all evil, I know is prepared for me.]

II

A Day has been appointed
By God the Lord on high;
My heart, by Him anointed,
His grace doth magnify
When I think on that Day—
The Last Day, when He'll wake me
And to all gladness take me,
And grant me good alway.

147 The tune, originally omitted, has been inserted here from Zahn 3:355 (no. 5269b).

[A day is appointed by the Lord my God, my heart exults greatly when I think of it. The Last Day, I mean, when the Lord shall wake me and joyfully quicken me with His pure bounties.]

III

Death, sin, distress, and sorrow,
Grief, sickness, misery—
All troubles on that morrow
In heav'n their end shall see.
Away, all sorrows, flee!,
In God my hope is founded,
Who hath a mansion
Built in eternity.

[Death, sin, distress, sickness, sorrows, anguish, grief, and misery, and whatever afflicts hearts, has an ending in heaven. Depart, all sorrow, my God, whom I trust, has built me a hall of joy in eternity.]

IV

With joy and consolation
He will my soul relieve;
He is my one salvation
My comfort when I grieve;
His Son will wipe away
All tears of grief and mourning,
Of those who feel the scorning
Of godless men today.

[He will joyfully embrace me and comfort my soul. For that I long, that is my comfort and salvation. Then His dear Son will wipe away all tears from those who weep here and endure scorn and mockery.]

V

My soul and body, changèd,
Will shine like sunlight there,
And all will be arrangèd
As my heart thinks most fair.
For in that realm above
We will not sinful tremble
But beauteously resemble
Thy hosts in grace and love.

[My body, my soul, glorified, shall shine as the sun, and what my heart desires will be its reward, for there in that kingdom, with respect to beauty and expressions, we will all be like Your dear angels.]

VI

There with all jubilation
Our Savior we shall see,
Who by His blood and Passion
Unbarred eternity.
There we before our eyes
Shall see the Father truly,
The Son and Spirit holy,
In joyous paradise.

[There with joy we will behold the Savior, who by His blood and Passion opened heaven. There before our eyes will become clear God the Father with the Son, and the third Person will be revealed to us.]

VII

Here we as children murmur,
And with frail accents sing;
In yonder endless summer
What bliss our God will bring
Whom we our Lord do call,
Our very Sun appearing,
All Christian spirits cheering!
He will be all in all.

[Here we must still lisp like little children, but there the Lord Himself will be all in all. In that summertime, with joy and bliss, God will appear as the sun of all Christians.]

VIII

There they are now united
Whom death here drew apart.
All those by Christ invited—
Who died with Him at heart;
There all men—man and wife,
And kinsmen of all stations,
All children, friends, relations—
God's love fills all their life.

[There are found together what here death tears apart. Those only who have fallen asleep in Christ's name are in God: The husband, his spouse, son, daughter, and acquaintances, kinsmen, siblings, and relatives—they all love.]

IX

There thousand dwell, now sainted,
Whom we have never met,
The patriarchs lamented,
The prophets small and great—
The apostolic band,
The martyrs crowned, victorious,
Men, women now made glorious,
Who served God as He planned.

[In addition, many thousands of men whom we never saw, the ancient patriarchs, prophets major and minor, the number of the twelve apostles, the martyrs with their crowns, many males and females who all served God.]

XI

They as our brethren, rushing,
Will welcome us within,
And we will not be blushing
To be the angels' kin.
The godly spirits will
With fond embrace draw near us,
And heartily will cheer us
Our hearts with gladness fill.

[They will receive us as their brothers, and we will not be ashamed to be with the angels. The godly spirits will with longing embrace us in an entirely brotherly manner and mingle among us.]

XII

We will not ask or question
Who anyone may be;
In part is now our vision,
Then all is clarity;
We'll know their every name;
So will we know each other
And love each as our brother
With love's unfading flame.

[Then we will not need to ask, Who is that, or that? Everything that our eyes will see they will recognize. Seeing in part will cease, we will know each other well, burn with true love which will never cease.]

XIII

Then will we hear resounding
The strains of heav'nly string
What joy in God abounding
The choir of heav'n will bring!
With gladness they will press
Around our Lord amazing—
Our Jesus, on them gazing
With eyes of tenderness.

[Then will be heard sounding the heavenly string music: The choir of heaven will bring much joy in God, will press the dear Jesus in the midst of us admirably, and gaze tenderly with His eyes.]

XIV

We'll sing with angels solely
In joyful praise of God
The "Holy, Holy, Holy,
Lord God of Sabaoth!"
Our new song then shall be:
"Praise, honor, adoration,
Pow'r, riches, and salvation
Are God's eternally!"

[With the angels we will sing to God most joyfully: Holy, Holy, Holy is the Lord of Sabaoth. A new song of joy: Honor, praise, blessing, and wisdom, power, riches, salvation, and glory be to God forever.]

XV

No ear hath heard the gladness,
No eye the joy hath seen,
That after present sadness
God grants His heirs in heav'n.
With this before my eyes,
My heart soars up in wonder,
From earth is set asunder;
The world I then despise!

[No ear has ever heard, no eye has seen the joy which has been granted those who are the heirs of God. When I consider this, my heart soars aloft and goes in full leap so that I despise the world.]

XVI

Let us in tribulations
Not feel despair therefore!
Although the worldly nations
Afflict us, yea, and more:
A little while and then
From heav'n will come the Savior,
To care for us forever:
Help is not far from men!

(Tr. M. Carver, 2021)

[Therefore let us not despair, who are in tribulation now, although the world afflicts, and is fiercely hostile to us. A little while and the Champion will soon come along and refresh us eternally. His help is certainly not far.]

THE END